Praise for *Governing*

A *Financial Times* Best

Shortlisted for the 2013 PEN Hessell-Tiltman Prize for History

"Impressive . . . A significant contribution to historical scholarship . . . Simply for giving us this lucid account, Mazower deserves our gratitude. But *Governing the World* is also an intriguing read because of the strong argument he places within it: that it may be that this grand idea, with all its variants, is coming to an end." —Paul Kennedy, *Financial Times*

"A topical and readable account." —*The Washington Post*

"Mazower is a fine intellectual historian. . . . Mazower's history illustrates how risk-averse we have become in facing up to transnational economic challenges and how ambitious global leaders used to be."
—Michael Ignatieff, *The New Republic*

"Fascinating . . . A well-articulated, meticulously supported study."
—*Kirkus Reviews*

"This is a book that needed to be written. . . . Truly illuminating . . . The story is a fascinating one, and Mazower tells it with authority and verve."
—*The Literary Review*

"[A] fluent, thought-provoking, and erudite history . . . Mazower has set the table for other historians." —*Humanity*

"Makes an otherwise familiar story new and exciting . . . A wonderful read." —*Democracy*

"[A] rewarding work of international history. Its ambitious sweep does justice to the variety of thinkers and actors who have contributed to generations of progress, at once arduous and inevitable, toward greater global cooperation." —*Current History*

"Mazower, with his original analysis, places himself in the company of other ambitious young historians of the postwar intellectual environment."
—*Columbia Magazine*

"Absorbing . . . For critical thinking about internationalist histories and futures, *Governing the World* is an invaluable place to start."
—*The Cleveland Plain Dealer*

"Thought-provoking history . . . A fascinating book that shows how the competing visions of advocates of liberal free trade, nationalists, and communists underpin contemporary society." —*The Global Dispatches*

"Mark Mazower has strengthened his claim to be the preeminent historian of a generation. . . . On rare occasions, a work of history emerges that not only fundamentally refashions our understanding of the past, it enables us to reassess the present and, with luck, influence our future. I advise everyone who is concerned about our precarious situation to learn from and absorb Mazower's remarkable achievement." —Misha Glenny

"A dramatic, novel account of ideas and institutions in collision with hard realities. Indispensable also for its full and subtle account of American policies since 1917, always with a fine touch for the hitherto neglected person or little noticed moment that illuminates historic processes. Profound, relevant, and morally instructive—and a pleasure to read." —Fritz Stern

"The idea of global government has entranced the world for centuries. Mark Mazower's brilliant book shows how much effort has gone into this idea—and how futile it has mostly been in an era of individualism and growing divisiveness."
—Alan Brinkley

"Governing Europe, and then the whole world, for the greater good of mankind, an idea spanning almost two centuries, at once noble and megalomaniacal, visionary and delusional, and ultimately doomed to failure: this idea has found its perfect chronicler in Mark Mazower, whose perceptions are cosmopolitan, humane, learned, and properly skeptical. What is more, his history is written in clear, elegant prose. Essential reading not just for historians, but anyone interested in the troubled world we live in."
—Ian Buruma

PENGUIN BOOKS

GOVERNING THE WORLD

Mark Mazower is the Ira D. Wallach Professor of History at Columbia University. He is the author of *Inside Hitler's Greece: The Experience of Occupation, 1941–44*; *Dark Continent: Europe's Twentieth Century*; *The Balkans: A Short History* (which won the Wolfson Prize for History); *Salonica: City of Ghosts* (which won both the Duff Cooper Prize and the Ruciman Award); and *Hitler's Empire: How the Nazis Ruled Europe*. He has also taught at Birkbeck College, University of London, Sussex University, and Princeton. He lives in New York.

Governing THE World

The History of an Idea, 1815 to the Present

MARK MAZOWER

PENGUIN BOOKS

PENGUIN BOOKS
Published by the Penguin Group
Penguin Group (USA), 375 Hudson Street,
New York, New York 10014, USA

USA | Canada | UK | Ireland | Australia | New Zealand | India | South Africa | China
Penguin Books Ltd, Registered Offices: 80 Strand, London WC2R 0RL, England
For more information about the Penguin Group visit penguin.com

First published in the United States of America by The Penguin Press,
a member of Penguin Group (USA) Inc., 2012
Published in Penguin Books 2013

Excerpt from "Is It the Dawn?" by James T. Shotwell. Published in *Think*, 11 (April 1945).

ISBN 978-1-59420-349-7 (hc.)
ISBN 978-0-14-312394-1 (pbk.)

Printed in the United States of America
10 9 8 7 6 5 4 3 2

DESIGNED BY MARYSARAH QUINN

To Selma, Jed, and Marwa

Contents

Introduction

The millenarian expectations aroused by the ending of the Cold War first surfaced in December 1988 when the Soviet Communist Party general secretary Mikhail Gorbachev addressed the United Nations General Assembly. Dramatically announcing deep unilateral cuts to troop numbers along the borders of the USSR, he called for a "new world order" in which ideological differences would melt away. As American intellectuals hailed the end of history, U.S. president George H. W. Bush offered his version of "the vision thing." Speaking to Congress shortly after Iraqi troops had invaded Kuwait, he pledged to get them out and predicted:

> Out of these troubled times . . . a new world order can emerge: a new era, freer from the threat of terror, stronger in the pursuit of justice, and more secure in the quest for peace. An era in which the nations of the world, East and West, North and South, can prosper and live in harmony. A hundred generations have searched for this elusive path to peace, while a thousand wars raged across the span of human endeavor. Today that new world is struggling to be born.[1]

For both Gorbachev and Bush waning superpower tensions presaged an era of international cooperation and a revitalization of the United Nations. But to others, this meant the onset of an unprecedented tyranny. In his 1991 bestseller *The New World Order,* televangelist Pat Robertson warned of the malign forces conspiring to take over the world in the name of virtue. A few years later, when an apocalyptic thriller of the coming End Times, the Reverend Tim LaHaye's *Left Behind,* hit the bookshops, the Antichrist featured prominently in the shape of a handsome, articulate, and charismatic young secretary-general of the United Nations: Nicolae Carpathia is a man of violence masquerading as an apostle of peace, a ruthless Romanian who intends to use the UN to establish a global totalitarian dictatorship.[2]

Some who particularly disliked the idea of a more powerful United Nations were reminded alarmingly of the prophecies of H. G. Wells. In his 1933 fantasy *The Shape of Things to Come,* Wells had foretold the eventual triumph of world government—he called it "manifestly the only possible solution of the human problem." The book had described a decade-long war in Europe, a devastating plague, and the near collapse of civilization—a lengthy descent into chaos halted only once an English-speaking Dictatorship of the Air smashed the world's organized religions and established an era of worldwide stability. A few years later, as the war he had anticipated erupted in Poland, the British novelist called on readers to fight for the better future a New World Order would usher in. "Countless people . . . will hate the New World Order . . . and will die protesting against it," Wells had written in the first months of the war. "We have to bear in mind the distress of a generation or so of malcontents." In the first U.S. presidential campaign of the new millennium, right-wing candidate Pat Buchanan recalled these words. "Well, Mr. Wells," declared Buchanan. "We are your malcontents." Buchanan's nationalism was extreme, as his 0.4 percent of the vote suggested. But even before the victory of George W. Bush there was no mistaking the slump in American public approval ratings for the United Nations nor the mauling international organizations got whenever their funding was debated in Congress. The new president too turned his back rather publicly on his father's multilateralism. "Thank God for the death of the UN," wrote a Bush adviser, the neoconservative Richard Perle, in March 2003, as the bombs rained down on Baghdad.[3]

More than the passing of time separates Wells's *The Shape of Things to Come* from the world of Tim LaHaye, Pat Buchanan, and George W. Bush. The technocratic assurance of British imperial modernism forms a striking contrast to the libertarian anxieties of the fin-de-siècle American heartland. If one exudes confidence in the capacity of government and institutions to define problems and find solutions, the other sees in Big Government at home and abroad the always-present threat of totalitarianism. To be sure, plenty of people in Wells's day thought his ideas far-fetched—every bit as far-fetched as most Americans find the talk of black helicopters and a New World Order engineered by a conspiratorial global elite. And of course, since the tragic fiasco of Iraq, U.S. foreign policy has returned to multilateralism, reluctantly during Bush's second term and more decisively under Barack Obama. Yet the basic trajectory is real enough. We have moved from an era that had faith in the idea of international institutions to one that has lost it.

But we have lost more than that. For the Wellsian idea of a rational supranational government for the world was just one species within a much larger genus of secular internationalist utopias that go back the best part of two centuries and span a vast ideological range. In contrast to the Wellsians, for instance, communists, free-market capitalists, and anarchists have all sought to get beyond the state completely and imagined a kind of postpolitical mingling of peoples. Somewhere in the middle, between world government and no government, lies a vision of organized cooperation among nations—in technical terms, intergovernmentalism rather than, or modified only weakly by, supranational institutions—of the kind that has inspired the United Nations, the European Union, and other such multilateral organizations. Embedded in a matrix of hopes, fantasies, and fears, what these all have in common is the vision of a better future for mankind, one that lies within our grasp and power and promises our collective emancipation. My aim in this book is not to peddle my own alternative to the many versions of this dream that have emerged nor to promote any one of these over the others. It is rather to explore their historical evolution, to show how some of them have shaped realities through the institutions that they have inspired, and to ask what is left of them today.

These ideas and institutions originated in Europe before spreading across the Atlantic and around the globe during the two centuries of Western world hegemony that are now drawing to a close. The story is thus in its essentials a Western one that begins in the early nineteenth century among the diplomats of the European restoration. In 1815 they created the very first model of international government—the conclave of Great Powers known as the Concert of Europe—to manage the continent after Napoleon's defeat. From 1815 onward, its statesmen met regularly to prevent any single power from ever again dominating and to stamp out revolutionary agitation before it could lead to war. But the logic of thesis and antithesis was soon at work. If the Concert was a response to Napoleon, internationalism as the nineteenth century understood the term was nothing if not a response to the Concert. Even the word "international"—which was coined at this time—carried a radical charge. Internationalists embraced nationalism, the age's most powerful transformative political creed, and assumed that nationalism and internationalism would go hand in hand to make the world a better and fairer place. Convinced that they held the keys to the future, they defined themselves against the conservative diplomats they despised, as well as against one another. Some like Karl Marx dreamed of workers banding together; Giuseppe Mazzini, who detested Marx, hoped republican patriots would forge a world of nations. Protestant evangelicals mobilized to hasten the brotherhood of man. Merchants and journalists called for free trade and the spread of industry. Scientists dreamed of new universal languages, spreading technical knowledge and carrying out great engineering projects that would unite humanity. Anarchists believed that states were the problem and formed a short-lived anarchist international. Lawyers believed politicians were the problem and urged states to give up war and to allow their differences to be settled by arbitration or through a world court. By the century's end, even Europe's secret policemen were holding international congresses to combat terrorism: the international had become the terrain upon which widely differing political groups and ideologies mapped their dreams and nightmares.

If the first chapters of this book explore these developments, the later ones trace what happened once internationalism was embraced by the architects of a new world order and ideas meshed with power politics in unpredictable ways. Large international organizations such as the League of Nations and the UN did not grow up gradually. On the contrary, sponsored by Great Powers, their births were abrupt, and war was their midwife. Interwar commentators, who believed strongly that political institutions should evolve organically, understood that this very artificiality and novelty imposed a challenge, and thought that if the League of Nations won over large sections of global opinion through the ideals it embodied, it would gain the time to evolve in men's hearts in the way that empires had done. Hard-wired, therefore, into the new international bodies from the start was an inevitable tension between the narrower national interests that the Great Powers sought to promote through them and the universal ideals and the rhetoric that emanated from them.

Most Great Powers in history have not, of course, felt the need for anything like the League or the Comintern or the UN. The Nazis, for example, dismissed the very idea of international organization. What really demands explanation is why first the British, at the height of their world power, and then the Americans should have invested time and political capital in building up international institutions at all. Historians whose writings celebrate internationalism as the gradual triumph of a virtuous sense of global community do not generally consider the question worth asking; neither conversely do those scholars who dismiss institutions as mere masks for Great Power wishes. Political scientists *have* addressed the question of the benefits of multilateralism, but mostly as part of an American conversation among scholars and policymakers about the character of U.S. foreign policy and the usefulness of the United Nations to the American national interest. Couched in the quasi-scientific language that this literature prizes, there is much talk about rationality and burden sharing, game theory, and the logic of risk. But because its chief function is to counsel those in power in Washington, it has rather little to say about the ideological goals behind liberal internationalism in its various incarnations.[4]

In fact, both Britain and the United States had good reasons of their own to accept the compromises inherent in an internationalist policy. If the British supported the League of Nations in 1918 as a way to ratify a new territorial dispensation in Europe and safeguard their empire, the Americans for their part engaged to build up its successor in order to preserve the Great Power understandings reached during the Second World War and to provide a framework for diplomacy that would make world leadership acceptable to an American public always suspicious of lasting entanglements beyond the nation's shores. It helped that Washington's participation in the world body turned out to carry only minor risks of constraint since the United States was able to combine universalism and exceptionalism to an unprecedented degree, writing the rules in a way that mostly served its core interests and generally exempting itself from those rules its legislators disliked. Since everyone else wanted the United States in on almost any terms, these double standards were tolerated.

The control of international organizations and the selection of their personnel necessarily therefore became and remains a vital interest for those powers centrally involved, from the choosing of a British secretary-general for the League of Nations at the end of the First World War down to our own day when the Japanese director-general designate for the International Atomic Energy Agency was described as confidentially reassuring a U.S. diplomat in 2009 that he "was solidly in the U.S. court on every key strategic decision."[5] Yet this is not a story that can satisfactorily be told solely as one of behind-the-scenes manipulation, and Washington policymakers should not be viewed as hypocrites, preaching universalism while remaining nationalists at heart. Sincerity was the essential lubricant of the entire mechanism, which could not have functioned without the widespread belief on the part of many of those most intimately concerned that the values of American liberalism were identical to the interests of the world writ large.

The results, especially after 1945, were impressive. Multilateral institutions are not easy to control by any single state, as their history demonstrates. In fact, their lack of obedience was always one of the most persuasive unilateralist objections to them, and the main reason for the American disengagement from the UN in the 1970s, and the subsequent turn to the more easily controlled World Bank, GATT, and IMF. But these complications, estrangements, and tensions do not alter the fact that the blisteringly fast emergence of American global power after 1945 is unimaginable without the assistance and cover of the panoply of international institutions and the vast and noble ambitions—to stabilize the world's money, eradicate its infectious diseases, spread democracy and growth—they incarnated.

Today there is more global policymaking, in more varied forms, than ever before, and the unwary student soon finds him- or herself stumbling through a landscape of obscure acronyms that stretch endlessly into the bureaucratic haze. There are military alliances, such as NATO and WEU; intergovernmental organizations in the classic mold, from the UN to specialist agencies such as the ILO, ICAO, ICC, WHO, and GATT; regional bodies, like the Council of Europe, the European Commission, and the Organizations of American and African states; postimperial clubs, like the Commonwealth and the Organisation internationale de la Francophonie; quasi-polities like the European Union; and regular summit conferences like the G-20. Nor should one ignore the vast number of NGOs of all kinds, many of which also now play a more or less formalized role in shaping global politics.

Navigating this crowded and ever-shifting terrain has never been straightforward and is about to become more difficult still. For if internationalism originated as an expression of Western political philosophies and Great Power needs, it is clearly now moving beyond that into something much more multicentered and fissiparous. It would be hard to overstate the significance of the threshold we are crossing as the West's share of world GDP drops below 50 percent for the first time in at least two centuries. As new states such as Brazil, India, Indonesia, and China acquire power and influence, the international system (a comforting phrase that obscures more than it reveals) will change radically. As a result, much more will certainly be written from the vantage point of what was once known as the Third World to reframe the version of the history told here. What this book does is to focus upon the European and American actors who were primarily responsible for the originating institutional and conceptual apparatus. At a time of immense confusion about the purpose and durability of our international institutions, a better understanding of how we came to this point may help us. Today our very vocabulary for understanding where we stand in the world is hostage to confused thought and poorly articulate premises. What is "governance"? Who speaks for "civil society"? Is there such a thing as an NGO? The history of the evolving idea of governing the world may not provide definitive answers to such questions, but it can offer signposts.

THIS BOOK is in many ways a product of Columbia University. Perhaps no university is better situated to reflect on the relationship between international institutions and national power, and I have benefited from a group of colleagues and students unmatched anywhere for their knowledge of this subject. My thanks in the first place to the following people who read much and in some cases all of the manuscript for their immensely generous help: Michele Alacevich, Matthew Connelly, Marwa Elshakry, Nicholas Guilhot, Daniel Immerwahr, Martti Koskenniemi, Thomas Meaney, Samuel Moyn, Anders Stephanson, and Stephen Wertheim. I have also learned an enormous amount from Alan Brinkley, Deborah Coen, Vicky de Grazia, Nick Dirks, Carol Gluck, Jean-Marie Guehenno, Ira Katznelson, Greg Mann, Andy Nathan, Susan Pedersen, Rhiannon Stephens, and Fritz Stern. Students to whom I am indebted for their own work in this area and for stimulating conversations include Dov Friedman, Aimee Genell, Mira Siegelberg, and Natasha Wheatley. I owe a special thanks to Stephen Wertheim not only for his rigorous criticism but also for conversations that started the day he came to the department to see if he liked it, and that I hope continue long after his own dissertation is complete. For their assistance with diverse aspects of this sprawling project, my thanks too to Nikos Alivizatos, Margaret Anstee, Elia Armstrong, Duncan Bell, Eyal Benveniste, Manu Bhagavan, Fergus Bremner, Christina Burnett, Bruce Burnside, Benjamin Coates, Saul Dubow, Michael Doyle, Jan Eckel, Edhem Eldem, François Furstenberg, Maurice Fraser, Paul Goodman, Michael Gordin, Greg Grandin, Cecilia Guevara, William Hagen, David Kennedy, Thomas Kelley, John Kelly, Daniel Laqua, Peter Mandler, Petros Mavroidis, Jeanne Morefield, José Moya, Timothy Nunan, Dan Plesch, Silvio Pons, Gwen Robinson, Carne Ross, Steve Shapin, Brendan Simms, Bradley Simpson, Fritz Stern, Gillian Tett, Nicholas Theocarakis, John Thompson, Yanis Varoufakis, Joseph Weiler, Carl Wennerlind, and John Witt. For giving me the opportunity to inflict arguments from this book on various audiences, I thank Helmut Berghoff, Halil Berktay, Jim Chandler, John Coatsworth, Jonathan Hall, Stefan-Ludwig Hoffmann, Claudia Koonz, Thomas Laqueur, Jim Lehning, John McGowan, Gyan Prakash and Brigitta van Rheinberg, David Priestland, Susan Sutton, and Adam Tooze.

With renewed appreciation of their brilliant blending of critique, patience, and encouragement, I thank my editors Scott Moyers and Simon Winder. And for his support, to the best of agents, Andrew Wylie. I was starting to write this book when my father died and it became a way of thinking about the achievements and outlook of his generation: I should like to acknowledge his influence and the constant encouragement of my mother. My greatest debt, infinite, is to Marwa Elshakry: I dedicate this book with much love to her and to our two children, Selma and Jed.

New York
May 2012

PART I

THE Era OF Internationalism

PROLOGUE

The Concert of Europe, 1815–1914

> A phenomenon without precedent in the history of the world.
>
> —Friedrich von Gentz, 1818[1]

BY 1953, the year of Stalin's death, the young Henry Kissinger had already completed his military service, sped through an undergraduate degree at Harvard, and was putting the finishing touches to his doctorate. His topic—of seemingly antiquarian interest—was how after Napoleon's defeat nearly a century and a half earlier, the Great Powers had managed the peace in Europe. The main protagonists were the victorious Big Four of the day—Austria, Russia, Britain, and Prussia—and their diplomats. They had continued to meet regularly long after Napoleon had been packed off into exile, allowed France itself to join them once the monarchy had been restored, and convened thereafter whenever a crisis threatened the stability of the continent. In the story of their meetings at places like Aix-la-Chapelle, Laibach, and Troppau (the very names conjured up a musty past), Kissinger saw a lesson of enduring value for his adoptive country. What long-dead European aristocrats like Metternich and Castlereagh could teach the United States was how to constrain a revolutionary superpower—for France read the USSR—and bind it into the rules of the international game.

Kissinger's focus upon the Concert of Europe, as the coalition was known, was understandable for another reason as well. Even at the time, its architects had been conscious of innovating in international affairs. "A phenomenon without precedent in the history of the world" was how Austrian chancellor Prince Metternich's right-hand man, Friedrich von Gentz, had described it. Before the French Revolution, there had been endless alliances of states and princes, constantly shifting in order to preserve or disrupt the prevailing balance of power. The war against France had started out in this way, as a traditional coalition, but it had ended, Gentz wrote in 1818, as something new—"a principle of general union, uniting all the states collectively with a federative bond, under the guidance of the five principal Powers."[2]

Although Napoleon provided the catalyst for this, his conception of how to govern Europe had been very different. Huddled in furs in his coach on the retreat from Moscow a few years earlier, he had attempted to persuade his outspoken foreign minister, the Marquis de Caulaincourt, that he had been fighting "in the interests of the older Europe and civilization." Caulaincourt did not mince words. "It is your Majesty they fear," he told the emperor. "The Governments are afraid of a universal monarchy." Aiming at continental domination, French rule had aroused strong popular reactions and made "the hatred of you into a national force." Where the French sought unity, the Concert prized plurality. While Napoleon sought to draw up a new, uniform system of law across much of Europe, his opponents insisted on preserving the constitutional, legal, and social differences that distinguished nations from one another. He dethroned rulers and crowned his own relatives and colleagues; they wished to protect and where necessary to restore legitimate rulers. Most importantly of all, of course, he aimed to give France power above all others, whereas they believed in the overall supremacy of no single nation.[3]

They did not, however, believe that all states were equal, which would have been a very different matter. They were conscious that Europe's fate lay in their hands and saw themselves as the principal guarantors of its stability. In March 1814, the four powers agreed that their alliance would last for at least twenty years, and after Waterloo they drew up plans for periodic discussions of their "common interests." France was accepted into the fold under the Bourbon king Louis XVIII. But Europe's minor royalty were emphatically marginalized, something they tolerated only for the sake of peace and because they had no alternative. In Gentz's words, "The states of the second, third and fourth rank submit tacitly, though nothing has ever been stipulated in this regard, to the decisions made in common by the great preponderant Powers."

The justification for this hierarchy—at least in the minds of the major powers—was that they articulated the collective interests of the continent. "And so Europe seems really to form a grand political family," wrote Gentz, "united under the auspices of a high tribunal of its own creation, whose members guarantee to themselves and to all parties concerned, the peaceful enjoyment of their respective rights." The victorious coalition against Napoleon thus became a political instrument that spoke of rights and law in the name of Europe just as much as Napoleon himself had done. But of course in Europe's name many different programs were possible, and the continent's small states were not the only ones to challenge the Concert and its claim to govern.

For the Concert itself had a deeply conservative sense of mission. Based on respect for kings and hierarchy, it prioritized order over equality, stability over justice. What had been unusual and disturbing about the Napoleonic Wars for Gentz and his superiors was not that they had been waged by France but that they had attempted to export revolution. Gentz himself was a former student of the philosopher Immanuel Kant, but he had been converted to Edmund Burke's view that the triumph of the French Revolution meant nothing less than the death of Europe. For the Anglo-Irish parliamentarian Burke, the Jacobin spirit and the desire to overthrow all inherited institutions placed the revolutionaries outside the pale of civilization so that a war against them could not be a limited conflict as in the past but must involve the total extirpation of their ideas and their power. Gentz agreed, but (unlike Burke) he believed that the restoration of the old order was impossible because too much had changed. What was needed to save what remained of the old was the creation of an entirely new set of arrangements among Europe's states. "Things must change in order to stay the same": no one understood better than Gentz and Metternich the wisdom articulated later in Giuseppe di Lampedusa's great novel of nineteenth-century political transformation, *The Leopard.*

Thus it was not surprising that the Concert of Europe started to claim the right to intervene across the continent in others' domestic affairs. Gentz hailed the Concert's achievement in rapidly stabilizing international relations, but he saw the possibility of revolution everywhere. "The interior of all European countries without exception," he wrote in 1818, "is wracked by a burning fever, companion or forerunner of the most violent convulsions the civilized world has known since the end of the Roman empire. It is struggle, it is war to the death between the old and new ways, between the old and the new social order."[4] Everywhere—including in Britain—the managers of the new peace did their best to snuff out the still-smoldering "revolutionary embers." In the German lands, where there were new restrictions on liberty of thought to ward off "revolutionary plots and demagogic associations," the press and post were tightly censored; universities were kept under surveillance and secret policemen eavesdropped on seditious gatherings in taverns and cafés. "There is only one serious matter in Europe," commented Metternich, "and that is revolution." The 1819 Peterloo Massacre, in which fifteen people were killed when cavalry charged a large Manchester crowd demanding parliamentary reform, showed that British elites were in no mood to compromise either: legislation was introduced threatening anyone organizing a meeting for reform with arrest for "an overt act of treasonable conspiracy."

The Concert thus became associated with the idea of a conservative restoration across the continent, a restoration that would spy on radicals and intervene by force if necessary to put down revolutionary insurrections whenever they challenged the principle of monarchy. One of the dominant figures within the victorious coalition, Russia's Tsar Alexander I, wanted much more even than this—he hoped to make the Concert a Holy Alliance of Christian powers. Having fallen for a time under the influence of a mystically minded Baltic German widow, the Baroness von Krudener, the tsar was convinced that Napoleon represented the Antichrist and the "Beast"; Europe's salvation therefore rested on fostering a new sense of supradenominational Christian solidarity (preferably under his own leadership). As Russian troops marched in triumph through the streets of Paris, he and the baroness drafted the outline of an alliance that would bring Europe's rulers together "in the name of one great Christian nation . . . for the protection of religion, peace, and justice."

The ostentatious piety and mysticism in all this were not attractive. But the idea of a peacetime commitment to rooting out subversives and radicals appealed strongly to Metternich in particular, and after a little creative rewriting, the Holy Alliance came into being as a subgroup of conservative powers within the Concert. Meeting at Troppau in Austrian Silesia, the Russian, Austrian, and Prussian monarchs insisted that they would regard states whose governments had come to power as a result of revolution as a threat to "legal order and stability" until they had proved their peaceful character. If others felt threatened by them, the three kings committed themselves "by peaceful means, or if need be, by arms, to bring back the guilty state into the bosom of the Great Alliance."

For the British, on the other hand, the alliance that defeated Napoleon had never been intended to be a "union for the government of the world or for the superintendence of the internal affairs of other States." Castlereagh's successor as foreign secretary, George Canning, opposed "the doctrine of a European police," arguing that it was only when the national interest was affected by developments in another country that it was right to intervene. Thus right at the start of the history of international institutions we find states and politicians arguing over the limits of "the government of the world": what in general terms was at stake in the dispute between the British and the central European empires was how far the creation of a set of arrangements among states might serve to legitimize military involvement in other people's affairs. If this resonates today it is because, with the contemporary UN doctrine of the "Responsibility to Protect," and the scale of U.S. military involvement in small wars around the globe, we find ourselves once more in a hierarchical world in which some states are more sovereign than others, and justify deep intrusions into the domestic affairs of others on the grounds that they collectively stand for the principle of "legal order."[5]

Interventionism and its limits were the grounds of the diplomatic rift between Europe and the Americas that took place in these years as a direct consequence of Concert policies. In 1823 France completed its swift rehabilitation as a conservative power when it invaded Spain, with the backing of Austria and Russia, and drove a revolutionary government out of Madrid. The return of absolutist monarchy there, with all its implications for the Spanish imperial domains in the Americas, had fundamental long-term consequences for world history. Confronted with the possibility of the Holy Alliance exporting counterrevolution across the Atlantic, U.S. president James Monroe warned the Europeans against intervening in the Western Hemisphere. This was scarcely a compelling threat at the time, given the size of the American navy. But it gained in force when backed by British foreign secretary George Canning, himself no lover of the Holy Alliance, who famously called on "the New World to redress the balance of the Old." Not only did the two men thus open up the possibility of a distinctively hemispheric American conception of liberal internationalism that would serve the interests of progress rather than reaction, but Canning in particular anticipated the fundamental development of the twentieth century—the rise of Anglo-American hegemony and through it the creation of distinctively new international organizations based upon a repudiation of the very idea of the Concert's European diplomacy.

Resistance to the Holy Alliance also saved the spirit of republicanism. By effectively declaring the postimperial republics of the Americas off-limits to the conservative monarchs of Europe, Monroe and Canning kept the principle of democratic nationalism alive at a time when it was being repressed in Europe itself. This was critical for the subsequent history of international thought: Jeremy Bentham's ideas, to take one example, were far more powerful in South America than they ever were north of the Gulf of Mexico. South Americans such as Chile's Carlos Calvo and Alejandro Alvarez were important pioneers of the new international law, and Pan-Americanism itself emerged as an alternative to the ossified hierarchies and rivalrous alliances of Europe. The South American contribution to the League and the United Nations, to postwar global debates about development and neoliberalism, begins here in a nineteenth-century hemispheric counterdiplomacy that unified North and South in a common if uneasy embrace against European diplomatic hegemony.[6]

In the short run, the Concert of Europe survived because too much was at stake for it not to. In the words of Britain's Prime Minister Castlereagh, "the Great Powers feel that they have not only a common interest but a common duty to attend to." Consultation checked their aggressive impulses, and even the Russians and the British hesitated before acting unilaterally in European affairs. Until the 1850s, in fact, the powers were united by much more than divided them: still sensitive to memories of the French Revolution, all the major powers talked about the sanctity of treaties and were suspicious of the growing agitation for parliamentary representation and workers' rights, not to mention national liberation and tariff reform. Even the British, who were the most inclined to support liberal causes, did not want to jeopardize the settlement of 1815. Continental émigrés fled to the safety of Dover and agitated on the streets of London for the cause of Poland, Hungary, or Italy, but they did not generally succeed in turning Whitehall's foreign policy in their direction. In 1848, Prime Minister Russell resisted calls to help the oppressed nationalities as they rose up against despotic rule across the continent, justifying his aloofness by arguing that it was for the sake of "the political independence and liberties of Europe." English interests, in short, were identified with the preservation of the Vienna order, and Europe was defined in terms of the liberties of its sovereigns, not of their subjects or the rights of nations. "Each nation has its own rights," was how the diplomats put it during the conference that created Belgium in 1831, "but Europe too has its right, given it by the order of society." "Society" for the diplomats still meant the society of states, not that far more dangerous new terrain of class war and clashing economic and cultural interests that awaited them at home.

Those social forces were, however, about to sweep away the Concert's Europe. The political order it existed to defend looked very different from today's. If a nation-state is defined as a state ruled in the name of an ethnic majority, there were no nation-states with the exception of France, and nothing that would approximate a modern understanding of a representative democracy. Neither Germany nor Italy yet existed. Instead there were some very large absolutist empires, a few constitutional monarchies, and a large number of tiny intermediary statelets with their own rulers, laws, and currencies. Poland had been partitioned in a land grab among the Great Powers that made perfect sense in terms of the logic of the Concert itself but seemed increasingly immoral as democratic sentiment spread. It was this political kaleidoscope that was swept away in the First World War, bringing into being a "New Europe" through the League of Nations that was in effect a dramatic and ambitious countermodel to the old and by now discredited arrangements established at Vienna a century earlier.

By then, the Concert system had been in decline for some time. The revolutions of 1848 might have seemed like a failure—Alexis de Tocqueville had discerned in 1852 "a reaction against democracy and even against liberty"—but they were in retrospect the beginning of the end.[7] Metternich himself had been forced into exile, spending his first winter out of power in the fashionable new English seaside resort of Hove. Going in the other direction was the first ever French president, Louis Napoleon, soon to declare himself emperor like his uncle. The Crimean War of 1853–56, which pitted the Concert's members against one another in battle, may be taken as the onset of the transition. But the Franco-Prussian War of 1870–71 was the real watershed—beginning a new, far more intense rivalry among the powers, fueled by nationalism and Germany's own ambitions, and made more menacing by the rise of large conscript armies, opposing alliance systems, and the deadly new technologies of machine warfare. By the time of the Balkan Wars of 1912–13, the old order really had broken down and the wishes of the Great Powers meeting in concert in London were blatantly ignored by Europe's newest powers in the Balkans. Yet vestiges of the old Concert habits survived even the First World War. Alongside the new League of Nations that was supposed to have put paid to such archaic practices, Great Power diplomacy still went on—brokering peace between Italy and Greece in 1923, and trying to with Hitler at Munich in 1938. But the failure of "Peace in Our Time" underscored that a century after the apogee of the Metternichian system, the Concert presupposed fundamental agreement on the rules of the game, and could not work in a world of ideological warfare.

OR COULD IT? The murderous turbulence of Europe's mid-twentieth century contrasted sharply with the stability of the Metternichian era, and Henry Kissinger was not alone in looking to the past to help guide the world toward a less chaotic future, nor in finding in the long peace of the nineteenth century a golden age of farsighted statecraft. Viewed from the era of the Korean War—where diplomacy seemed to be the only thing saving the world from conflagration—the architects of the Concert system seemed like visionaries. In the words of the leading American historian of the subject, Paul Schroeder, "Only the Vienna settlement got things right."

Yet what was odd about this positive verdict was that it diverged so sharply from what people had said about the Concert of Europe in its lifetime. For what looked like achievements when viewed from the bloody perspective of the twentieth century had struck pre-1914 observers and commentators much less favorably. A century of peace? But Europe after 1848 had certainly not been free of wars. Nationalists, especially in Germany and Italy, castigated the Concert's failure to appreciate the desire for liberty in European affairs or to understand how to accommodate it. Democrats excoriated its secrecy, elitism, and repressive instincts. Activists like Shelley and Byron were revolted by the scale of reaction from the very start and made no distinction between the despots of the Holy Alliance and British statesmen like Castlereagh. "Here lie the bones of Castlereagh," wrote Byron. "Stop, traveler, and piss."

For them and many others like them, the Concert of Europe had not mastered the new art of international government; it was, on the contrary, a symbol of the very problems—autocratic leadership, bellicosity, an incomprehension of the value of freedom and the power of social change—that a true internationalism was needed to solve.

CHAPTER 1

Under the Sign of the International

The great question of this era is the coexistence of many of the leading races or nations, united by the same international laws, religion, and civilization, and yet divided as nations.

—Francis Lieber, 1867[1]

COSMIC HARMONY has a long history. Isaiah tells us that God will wreak catastrophic destruction upon the nations of the world before creating "new heavens and a new earth" in which "the wolf and the lamb shall feed together."[2] The Roman imperium sought to embrace the entire civilized world under a single system of law, while Christianity and Islam both aspired to bring about the universal rule of God on earth. The medieval papacy and the Ottoman Empire legitimated themselves in similar terms. "The heavens themselves, the planets and this center," proclaims Ulysses in Shakespeare's *Troilus and Cressida,* "observe degree, priority, and place."[3]

But the emergence of the idea that the rulers of the world make up a kind of international society is more recent and emerged out of dissatisfaction with medieval notions of universal empire. "Most of us dread the name of World Empire," wrote Erasmus. "A unified empire would be best if we could have a sovereign made in the image of

God, but men being what they are, there is more safety in kingdoms of moderate power and united in a Christian league." Machiavelli argued that Europe's very multiplicity of states encouraged civic virtue. It is from such beginnings that we can discern the origins of a European exceptionalism that made a virtue out of the slow political disintegration of Christendom and laid the foundations for modern internationalism. Over the course of several centuries, people moved from thinking about the rules governing an international society of kings and princes to jettisoning the divine right of kings and imagining a world of different peoples, an international society of societies.

What, worried early modern political theorists, could unite the rulers of different states if not fear of God? The chief characteristic of international politics was and is anarchy—the absence of a single authority to compel members of the societies of nations to the sort of obedience they themselves expected from their subjects. Thomas Hobbes portrayed the absence of an overarching sovereign pessimistically as a source of endless strife, but others regarded it with greater equanimity. Did not nature, as Aristotle and Augustine had taught, have its own laws? In the sixteenth and seventeenth centuries, the idea of a law of nations that could be deduced from natural law emerged; by the eighteenth, theorists of peace were advancing confederative schemes based on respect for rights enshrined in treaties and equality of membership. Arguing as Machiavelli had done that Europe's heterogeneity was a strength not a weakness, Enlightenment intellectuals such as Montesquieu, Gibbon, and Hume contrasted the supposed stagnation of despotic Asian empires with the vitality of a continent whose multiple states traded goods and ideas with one another. Commerce brought peace, they said, and so did the balance of power created by the natural operation of rivalrous sovereigns. Whereas earlier authors had thought unity imperative to heal Christendom's divisions, the *philosophes* embraced the existence of political difference and the clash of competing self-interests: all would naturally work out through some cosmic harmony, and rivalry was beneficial because it promoted innovation, challenged the status quo, and led to progress.

If conflict was integral to the life of nations, most Enlightenment theorists did not regard this as a bad thing.[4]

Critics charged advocates of balance-of-power politics with rationalizing the status quo and underplaying the need for change. Rousseau despairingly thought only rigid confederation could guarantee the social contract and that since this was almost unimaginable on any scale larger than the Swiss republic, Europe must tend to disunity. Thomas Paine found the continent "too thickly populated with kingdoms to be long at peace," and offered an early argument for the difference of the Americas, seeing them as "an asylum for mankind" from tyranny and oppression. The French Revolution increased the intensity of these attacks. For revolutionary ideologues, the balance-of-power system of the ancien régime had already irrevocably broken down and Napoleon's France was in fact the "friend of mankind," setting Europe on a new path.[5] For the revolution's opponents, on the other hand, Napoleon threatened Europe with a new version of the old detested Universal Monarchy. A ferocious and multifaceted debate thus started that drew in some of the foremost intellectuals of the age: it was about Europe in the first place, but it was also about the nature of international politics in general. Through it we can trace not only the germination of the idea that the "international" constitutes a separate zone of political life with its own rules, norms, and institutions, but alongside it the idea that this zone of politics was in some sense *governable,* and governable not by God, nor through nature, but by men.

WELL BEFORE he published his classic essay on perpetual peace in 1795, the philosopher Immanuel Kant had already clashed with his sovereign, the Prussian king Friedrich Wilhelm II, over matters of religion, and indeed most of Kant's philosophical writings were not directly connected with politics. But then the French Revolution broke out, and shortly afterward, the Kingdom of Poland, once one of the largest states in Europe, was excised from the map of Europe, carved up by its neighbors. These shattering events suggested that the natural law theorists of the eighteenth century had been much too complacent about the pacific nature of European civilization. It was against this background that Kant produced his famous outline of the path to perpetual peace, a text that would intermittently influence generations of thinkers about world government down to our own day.

In the late twentieth century, Kant's arguments were reframed by American political theorists arguing for an activist foreign policy that would support and extend democracy around the world in the name of peace. But this new post–Cold War Kant looked rather different from the Enlightenment original who had not written in praise of *democracy* at all, did not believe that these things could be rushed by the policies of statesmen, and certainly did not divide the world into liberal and illiberal states. Kant's own view, steeped in the classical tradition, was that it is republics—not democracies—that lead to peace, since what really matters is the effective separation of powers. In fact, like many Enlightenment rationalists, he regarded democracies simply as states with majority rule, which without effective separation of powers may degenerate into despotisms. The reason, Kant says, that republics love peace is simple: they rely on their citizens, not mercenaries, to fight. A democracy that relied on a professional army would not have filled him with hope.

Equally jarring to our contemporary sensibilities is Kant's extreme hostility toward international lawyers, an attitude explained by his belief that they basically acted as apologists for power and hence did nothing to advance the cause of peace. In fact, he argues, they hinder it by acting as mere temporary restraints on violence:

> The only conceivable meaning of such a law of nations might be that it serves men right who are so inclined that they should destroy each other and thus find perpetual peace in the vast grave that swallows both the atrocities and their perpetrators. For states in their relation to each other, there cannot be any reasonable way out of the lawless

> condition which entails only war except that they, like individual men, should give up their savage [lawless] freedom, adjust themselves to the constraints of public law, and thus establish a continuously growing state consisting of various nations which will ultimately include all the nations of the world. But under the idea of the law of nations they do not wish this, and reject in practice what is correct in theory. If all is not to be lost, there can be, then, in place of the positive idea of the world republic, only the negative surrogate of an alliance which averts war, endures, spreads, and holds back the stream of those hostile passions which fear the law, although such an alliance is in constant peril of their breaking loose again.

Kant thus argues that states bound by rules designed merely to avert war are no substitute for an eventual cosmopolitan world order, something he imagines emerging gradually and inevitably, as states federate and attract others to join them. He specifies no mechanism through which this could come about; we are not yet in an age comfortable with theorizing the problem of *organization*. But it would certainly not be through commerce, as others believed it might, because Kant did not think that commerce civilized: he took a dim view of European traders and their impact on the rest of the world, and he criticized "the injustice which they show to lands and peoples they visit (which is equivalent to conquering them)." Basically, Kant believed that the movement toward "the world republic" would inevitably prosper and intensify principally because men everywhere are reasonable and will come over time to understand that it is in their interest. We thus find in his essay not the praise of a world of democratic peoples expressed by President Bush fils, nor the paean to free trade of devotees of globalization, but strong criticism of the European state system as it existed at the end of the eighteenth century combined with what would become a powerfully influential outline of an evolutionary path for mankind to tread that equated the cause of peace with that of freedom and reason. Idealist in the strict sense that progress along this path depended upon the spread of ideas,

Kant was also rationalist in his confidence that humanity not only possessed reason but would ultimately be guided by it.

These assumptions already seemed out of date to other thinkers of the Revolutionary era. To Kant's faith in universal reason, they counterposed the importance of sentiment and feeling; to his world consciousness, they preferred the idea of European unity and the tug of patriotism. Edmund Burke famously castigated the French Revolution for its "violent breach of the community of Europe," a community whose supposed foundations he identified not in reason but rather in the sentiments of reverence that the ancient institutions of monarchy and church elicited among their faithful subjects and believers. The revolution was, in his words, "a schism with the whole universe"; manners, habit, and sentiment—the essential building blocks of social life—were all threatened by this eruption of barbarous passion. In Burke's hands, therefore, criticism of the revolution conjured into being not the old Enlightenment picture of a system of self-interested rulers, of balance, poise and counterpoise, but rather a fictitious but compelling romanticized image of a community of Europeans united in feeling and outlook. The young German mystic Novalis took this idea even further, arguing in a text written in 1799 that Europe needed to recapture the ethos of a time long distant when it was "one peace-loving society," when "*one* common interest joined the most distant provinces of this vast spiritual empire." For Novalis, Europe needed to turn away from philosophy and Enlightenment and back to the Middle Ages, to poetry and the spirit and a "more exact knowledge of religion." In mystical, allusive language, he suggested that efforts to bring peace through intellect itself are doomed. "It is impossible that worldly powers come into equilibrium by themselves. All peace is only an illusion, only a temporary truce. From the standpoint of the cabinets, and of common opinion, no unity is conceivable." Indeed, for Novalis both the revolutionaries and their opponents "have great and necessary claims and must put them forward, driven by the spirit of the world and humanity." Only faith can reconcile them. "Where is that old, dear belief in the government of God on earth, which alone can bring redemption?"[6]

. . .

THE MAN who coined the term "international," English philosopher Jeremy Bentham, was unimpressed by this kind of backward-looking emphasis on faith, Christianity, and God. Not surprisingly for a man who had been made an honorary citizen by the French National Assembly on the eve of the Terror, Bentham was not in favor of Burkean conservatism or counterrevolutionary sentimentality, and he certainly did not boil the problems of the world down to the question of European unity. In the process of swinging from support for the revolution in its early years to vehement criticism of its excesses, he forged the philosophy of administrative rationalization—simultaneously radical and antirevolutionary—that was to achieve such extraordinary influence in the decades that followed.[7] Bentham sought to argue for the primacy of matter and reason, for the reduction of philosophy and metaphysics to matters of sensation and quantification. Above all, he sought to place law on a new and more powerful footing as the essential foundation of government.

When Bentham invented the term "international," he did so because of his discomfort with the ideas of one of his Oxford teachers, the formidable British jurist William Blackstone, whose *Commentaries on the Laws of England* became a standard work that gave the common law "at least a veneer of respectability."[8] Bentham had little time for the common law, which he regarded as an unsystematic mess. And in an unpublished manuscript that he wrote around 1775, he criticized Blackstone for talking too complacently about "the law of nations" as though it was obvious where this came from. Was it "our old friend, the Natural Law," which Bentham—like Kant—thought little better than no law at all? Or was it existing treaties and diplomatic agreements, which were often not laws either? Bentham's intellectual dissatisfaction prompted him to go on in his influential *Introduction to the Principles of Morals and Legislation* to introduce to readers the notion of the "international" for the first time.

Here law was conjoined with philosophy in a new theory of government. Believing that the rationalization of England's hopelessly disorganized administration must begin with the cleaning up of its laws, and that this necessitated setting law on strict and precise philosophical foundations, Bentham begins the *Introduction* with the famous utility principle. Mankind is governed by pain and pleasure, and utility consists in the maximization of the latter and minimization of the former. Both are quantifiable for the individual and—most importantly for the policymaker—for the collectivity as well. He then proceeds to classify the kinds of legislation that confront the policymaker, for there are for Bentham only two arts of government, administration and legislation, and of these the latter is the more important to the philosopher since it concerns matters of a permanent nature, whereas administration deals merely with the provisional.

It is in discussing the categories of law that Bentham introduces a novel distinction between "internal" and "international" jurisprudence. Immediately recognizing that some readers might be thrown off by the new word, he writes in a footnote:

> The word *international,* it must be acknowledged, is a new one: though it is hoped, sufficiently analogous and intelligible. It is calculated to express, in a more significant way, the branch of law which goes commonly under the name of the *law of nations;* an appellation so uncharacteristic that, were it not for the force of custom, it would seem rather to refer to internal jurisprudence.[9]

In its original context, Bentham seems simply to have wanted to clarify two technical matters that he felt the old "law of nations" muddled: the need for a sharp distinction between law within a state and law between states, and another distinction between legal disputes affecting individuals—say, disputes over contracts—and those affecting the sovereigns of states. He left open at this time the question of whether "mutual transactions between sovereigns, as such"—in other words, international law—could really be regarded as a form of law at all. His disciple John Austin was perhaps the most famous exponent of the idea that international law is nothing but pious intentions and words dressed up in its guise. Bentham himself disagreed and followed his utilitarian argument to its conclusion: "the end that a disinterested legislator upon international law would propose to himself would . . . be the greatest happiness of all nations taken together." A new body of law could thus indeed be drawn up by the right people for everyone in the world. "If a citizen of the world," he wrote, "had to prepare a universal international code, what would he propose to himself as his object? It would be the common and equal utility of all nations; this would be his inclination and his duty." The prerequisite was a kind of cosmic calculus that would, in principle, allow an internationally minded social scientist to do the necessary sums worldwide, taking cultural, geographic, meteorological, and other variations into account.

Such a system of law would not be the apologia for power that Kant despised but the necessary foundation of universal peace. Indeed, the idea of an international legal code led Bentham to posit the need for an international court able to adjudicate between disputing nations (the outline is in his own *Plan for an Universal and Perpetual Peace*). Always blending the frankly implausible and the practical, he saw codification (another successful new Bentham coinage) as a stepping-stone along the road to world peace through international law. The idea caught on, and perfecting the style of laws of all kinds would become as the century progressed one of the chief tendencies in internationalist thought.[10]

By the time Bentham published a new edition of his classic work, nearly forty years after its first appearance, he had the great satisfaction of seeing his neologism part of common speech. "As to the word *international,* from this work," he wrote in 1823, "it has taken root in the language. Witness reviews and newspapers." Benthamites were busy whipping up interest in the master's ideas: they were active with plans to modernize newly independent Greece and Egypt, and in some South American countries the fight between his supporters and opponents became the chief battleground for larger constitutional and educational arguments. By midcentury, "international" had already become an -ism, a radical project closely connected to the rise of professions and the bourgeoisie, manufacturing and commerce, and to their ideological expressions in the form of the powerful new social philosophies that emerged for the first time in the post-Napoleonic restoration.

The sign of the international thus existed in close but uneasy relationship to the phenomenon of widening political representation and its handmaiden, the growing force of public opinion. In the year that the Congress of Vienna met, an extraordinary political chameleon named the Abbé de Pradt disavowed his emperor as the man who had, in his words, covered Europe with "wrecks and monuments": he called on the victors to eradicate "the military spirit" and return Europe to its "civil state." He then went on to say that this would require them to recognize the "rise of a new power called opinion," and with it, civilization. It had been civilization—that "divinity," in de Pradt's words—that had emerged to delegitimize despots, given meaning to the idea of humanity, and thrown war into disrepute. But civilization was inseparable from the new politics: "Nationality, truth, publicity—behold the three flags under which the world for the future is to march. . . . The people have acquired a knowledge of their rights and dignity." The dictator overthrown by the sheer power of public opinion: it is the start of a trope with a very promising future.[11]

Dominique-Georges-Frédéric Dufour de Pradt—at one time or another a staunch monarchist in the Revolutionary Estates-General, bishop of Poitiers, Napoleon's go-between with the Vatican, and finally ambassador in Warsaw—might not have been best placed to preach this message. But he was nothing if not attuned to the European mood (his political career culminated in his election as a liberal deputy in Restoration France), and the idea of the power of public opinion gained ground as a critique not only of Napoleonic despotism but also of the Concert of Europe that had defeated him, and its ingrained conservatism. The powers might have tried to use their congresses to erect barriers against "the torrent of what are called 'new ideas'," wrote the *Literary Gazette* in 1823, but the greater power of public opinion offered the best guarantee of their failure. The principle of "association" was hailed by political theorists as the motor of modernity, and the very conferences and congresses that the monarchs of Europe had turned into a mechanism for managing the continent's affairs were adapted by their opponents as a forum for open, democratic politics. Soon it seemed that the most unsuitable types were holding meetings and forming associations. By 1848, Europe's monarchs had ceded control of this mode of policymaking in the face of the threat posed by "the people." In the words of Frederick Augustus II of Saxony, writing to the king of Prussia, "There has long since been great prejudice against congresses of princes. People could easily decry such a gathering as a conspiracy."[12] Metternich's conspiracy theories had thus been turned on their head: now it was kings who feared being denounced, and an uncontrollable press that had the power to shape politics. Internationalism, in its modern sense as a movement of cooperation among nations and their peoples, was moving from the realm of marginal ideas into the mainstream, while monarchy was obliged to accommodate itself to the era of large electorates and parliamentary power.

A REMARKABLE NOVEL PUBLISHED in Paris two years after Bentham's death (and just after the first steamship crossing of the Atlantic) demonstrated internationalism's (and Bentham's) growing hold on the European imagination. Felix Bodin's 1834 *Le roman de l'avenir* (*The Novel of the Future*) marked a new departure for what was already an incredibly popular genre.[13] The action takes place at some unspecified point in the twentieth century and shifts between North Africa—the French annexed Algeria the year the book came out—and the city of Centropolis in the Central American republic of Benthamia where the annual debate of the world's Universal Congress is taking place. This constantly moving world parliament (it meets some years in midair, at others at sea) unites all kinds of nations and states and brings together "the greatest and most illustrious intellectuals, industrialists and politicians in the world."

Bodin filled his work with the flourishes of the futurist genre: flying machines feature prominently, and there are provocative predictions of a greater role for women in politics, the fall of the Russian and Ottoman empires, the emergence of a new Babylonian empire, and a Kingdom of the Jews. But his real innovation lies in his attempt to sketch out a certain vision of the triumph of representative government at the global level. In this sense Bodin is a true follower of Bentham and attempts—as the author states explicitly—to use narrative in order to work on the imagination and hasten "the progress of humanity" far more effectively than "the finest displays of theoretical systems."

How far intellectual life had traveled since the Enlightenment is evident if we compare this work with an earlier utopian classic, *L'an 2440* by the French dramatist Louis-Sebastien Mercier, that had been published in 1771. In Mercier's dream-fable, peace is achieved by the abolition of armies, slavery, priests, and taxes, but the setting is Paris and the framework is basically that of enlightened monarchy and the idealized city-state. The political problem—and dream—of internationalism as such does not exist for Mercier as it does for Bodin. Sometime between the 1770s and the 1830s, in other words, it became possible, against the backdrop of the French Revolution and the Concert of Europe, to imagine an alternative international politics, one that acknowledged the diversity of peoples, beliefs, and forms of government and showed their reconciliation under the banner of civilization.[14] This was new. And it was connected with something broader, for Bodin's work suggests that we should see internationalism in the context of a fast-changing society's ravenous appetite for ideas about the future in general.

"Let us reckon upon the future!" urged the French scientist François Arago in 1839, barely a decade before he took a leading part in the revolutionary government of 1848. Historians of overseas European settlement have recently begun to argue that what was once written off as the boom/bust mentality of the colonial frontier needs to be taken more seriously as a kind of bet on the future that emerged quite suddenly in the nineteenth century in response to the shrinkage of time and space, a moment when the pace of change seemed to be accelerating. This "future thinking" drove both capitalism and colonialism. It expressed itself in speculative fevers and land grabs, survived the inevitable crashes, failures, and disappointments, and found confirmation in rapidly growing cities, new transcontinental communications infrastructures, and a succession of technological marvels. Such dreams of the future brought hundreds of thousands of Europeans to Texas and California, as well as to the farming uplands of southern Africa, Australia, and the Upper Chaco.[15]

This era of accelerated migration forged a culture increasingly attentive to the idea of the world as a unity, and created a public with a vast and growing appetite for learning about transcontinental travel. It was at just this time that geography emerged, lavishly funded by the state, as a Janus-faced science indispensable for military conquests and intelligence, on the one hand, and given to visions of universal harmony on the other. This was the age of the great universal geographies, bestselling illustrated periodicals such as the French *Le tour du monde,* and associations like the National Geographic Society. The International Geodesic Association was founded to help map the world accurately, and its scientific missions—like innumerable other expeditions public and private—transformed people's consciousness of the planet. Scholarly geography boasted world thinkers from Halford Mackinder, founder of the twentieth-century discipline of geopolitics, and the German Friedrich Ratzel with his beautifully illustrated three-volume *History of Mankind,* to the great anarchist universalists like Elisée Reclus and Piotr Kropotkin, men of the left for whom nationalism was a geographical error and geography was a way of showing humanity's diverse tribes what they shared. Maps stuck on school walls, miniature globes in middle-class homes, newspapers reporting on the fate of missionaries or officers in the heart of Africa all contributed to a late-nineteenth-century willingness to frame a politics of the future in global terms. Against the backdrop of the Scramble for Africa journalists penned blueprints for a Greater Britain that would meld the empire into a single polity, and drafted plans of universal federation to extend the process of political unification further still.[16]

Science was a powerful driver of these developments.[17] Speaking to the new Institute of Electrical Engineers in 1889, the British prime minister Lord Salisbury hailed the telegraph because it had, in his words, "assembled all mankind upon one great plane, where they can see everything that is done and hear everything that is said, and judge of every policy that is pursued at the very moment these events take place."[18] This consciousness of the world as an interconnected whole cannot be separated from the impact of steamships, rail, the telegraph, and airpower and the sense of living through an epoch of unprecedented technological advance. Jules Verne was to become the master of the "*voyage fantastique*" in which machine-powered travel—whether by submarine or by balloon (far and away the favorite traveling apparatus of these authors)—annihilated distance and marked out the potential for science to transform civilization and change perspectives. As Verne's works suggested, science allied to storytelling provided an immensely popular vehicle for articulating internationalist visions of the unification of mankind.

Futurist novels were therefore much more than mere cultural froth cresting the deeper socioeconomic surge. On the contrary, as H. G. Wells said, complaining of critics' tendency to carp at his writings as "pseudo-scientific fantasies," what they incarnated as well if not better than any other genre was "a new system of ideas." Foremost among these was the belief that a sufficiently focused and expert attentiveness to the future might allow man to throw off the shackles of received thinking and the shibboleths of the past. "Let us die calmly in the communion of mankind and the religion of the future," French philosopher Ernest Renan wrote in 1890. A few years later, French sociologist Gabriel Tarde proposed a reverse determinism that saw events caused by the future rather than the past and scripted his own projected world confederacy in his 1896 *Fragment d'histoire future.*[19]

By the end of the century, a kaleidoscope of wildly divergent internationalist forecasts emanated from a now vast and ever-growing futurist literature, much of it dedicated to imagining impending war in Europe and the world that might follow. As the Concert fragmented into competing alliance systems, and governments raised taxes to pay for large conscript armies armed with ever more destructive technology, fiction kept pace, and a future international politics was articulated in much greater detail than ever before.

One of the best examples was provided by the English journalist George Griffith, an influence on the young H. G. Wells, and a popular journalist of socialist inclinations. Demonstrating the close connection between fiction and technology, his son Alan would become an engineer and the inventor of the Rolls-Royce Avon axial flow jet engine. Griffith himself not only shattered the record for round-the-world travel but penned *Angel of the Revolution,* a sensational yarn written in 1892 at the height of the world's obsession with anarchist terror. In this tale, the Brotherhood of Freedom is a terrorist group headed by an elderly Russian Jew and his beautiful daughter, Natasha. When the European states tear themselves apart in a war between the two major alliances, the terrorists take over. Their power comes from possessing state-of-the-art aerial technology (its young inventor falls in love with Natasha), and, helped by a massive popular uprising in America, which brings to power a sympathetic government in Washington, they end up conquering the world with airships of devastating destructive power, having already persuaded the British to come in alongside the Americans. Airships, anarchists, Americans, and the beneficent British: it is the classic synthesis of the main elements of the internationalist imaginary as seen from the fin-de-siècle London suburbs.

What was left of the Concert of Europe in such a worldview is revealed in the novel's fantastic climax, a description of a diplomatic conference run by anarchists that is called in London to forestall what would be a war of annihilation. As the revolutionary hero Tremayne outlines the Brotherhood's terms to Europe's defeated and humiliated monarchs—universal disarmament, land redistribution, an international police force—the German kaiser rises in protest:

> "From what we have heard it would seem that the Federation of the Anglo-Saxon peoples considers itself as having conquered the world, and as being, therefore, in a position to dictate terms to all the peoples of the earth. Am I correct in this supposition?"
>
> Tremayne bowed in silence, and he continued—
>
> "But this amounts to the destruction of the liberties of all peoples who are not of the Anglo-Saxon race. It seems impossible to me to believe that free-born men who have won their liberty upon the battlefield will ever consent to submit to a despotism such as this. What if they refuse to do so?"
>
> Tremayne was on his feet in an instant. He turned half round and faced the Kaiser, with a frown on his brow and an ominous gleam in his eyes—
>
> "Your Majesty of Germany may call it a despotism if you choose, but remember that it is a despotism of peace and not of war, and that it affects only those who would be peace-breakers and drawers of the sword upon their fellow-creatures. . . .
>
> "You deplore the loss of the right and the power to draw the sword one upon another. Well, now, take that right back again for the last time! Say here, and now, that you will not acknowledge the supremacy of the Council of the Federation, and take the consequences! . . .
>
> The pregnant and pitiless words brought the Kaiser to his senses in an instant. He remembered that his army was destroyed, his strongest fortresses dismantled, his treasury empty, and the manhood of his country decimated. He turned white to the lips and sank back into his chair, covered his face with his hands, and sobbed aloud. And so ended the last and only protest made by the spirit of militarism against the new despotism of peace.[20]

Griffith's dream of a world forced into peace by revolutionaries was what gave others nightmares. After all, it conjured up the ultimate defeat of the European order inaugurated by the Concert and the Holy Alliance. In it emperors were deposed, and anarchists, terrorists, and Jews triumphed. To conservatives, Griffith's "despotism of peace" looked not like utopia but rather a new kind of international dictatorship of unprecedented severity and scope.

Appropriately, given the imperial Russian role as archvillains of Griffith's yarn, it was from the innermost recesses of the tsarist secret police that the most telling counterfiction emerged. It is not often that we are privy to the fantasies of counterrevolutionary policemen, but this is what the *Protocols of the Elders of Zion* give us. Composed within a few years of Griffith's *Angel of Destruction* at a time when the Okhrana were deeply enmeshed in a dirty struggle with anarchist terror across Europe, the Elders of Zion are depicted imagining a day when non-Jews "will be compelled to offer us international power of a nature that by its position will enable us without any violence gradually to absorb all the State forces of the world and to form a Super-Government. In place of the rulers of today we shall set up a bogey which will be called the Super-Government Administration. Its hands will reach out in all directions like claws and its organization will be of such colossal dimensions that it cannot fail to subdue all the nations of the world." This Super-Government will rule, the *Protocols* tell us, by persuading people that it protects and looks after them; preplanned acts of terrorism (fiction was here mirroring reality: the Okhrana itself set off explosions to scare public opinion) will give its rulers the chance to intervene to demonstrate their power to preserve order; economists will explain why their rule is necessary. The only chance of opposition comes from the remnants of loyal monarchists and the blind passions of the national mob, but the danger is that both will be neutralized.[21]

It is an extraordinary document, in which every development that nineteenth-century liberals hailed as signs of progress—from constitutionalism, the press, and the widening suffrage to the development of international arbitration—is revealed as part of a demonic plot whose outcome is the establishment through a coup d'état of a world dictatorship with "one king over the entire earth who will unite us and annihilate the causes of our discords—frontiers, nationalities, religions, State debts." Here is the triumph of internationalism—its political program elaborated in some detail—but presented not as utopia but endless tyranny. It is the ultimate act of intellectual homage: by the end of the nineteenth century, even the opponents of radical internationalism had come to think naturally under the sign of the international.

CHAPTER 2

Brotherhood

> I see the frontiers and boundaries of the old aristocracies broken,
> I see the landmarks of European kings removed.
> I see this day the People beginning their landmarks (all others give way;)
>
> ....
>
> Are all nations communing? Is there going to be but one heart to the globe?
> Is humanity forming en-masse? for lo, tyrants tremble, crowns grow dim,
> The earth, restive, confronts a new era.
>
> —Walt Whitman, "Years of the Modern"

THE PEACE MOVEMENT

In the first half of the nineteenth century, there were no more ardent internationalists to be found anywhere than among evangelical Christians. "Is it possible," wrote one peace activist, "that any Christian, of whatever sect, who believes the New Testament to be anything better than a fable, can doubt for a moment that the time will come when all the kingdoms of the earth shall be at peace?"[1] Napoleon's defeat coincided with a resurgence of evangelical expectation, and Christian groups on both sides of the Atlantic read the dramatic social and technological changes taking place around them as signs that the millennium was imminent. Taking advantage of growing European power overseas to propagate their own version of the civilizing mission, they opened schools, printed and distributed Bibles, and campaigned against the evils of drink and slavery, notching up an early success when they managed to get the slave trade condemned in the Treaty of Paris in 1815.[2]

But their abiding cause was the battle for peace. Appalled at the toll of intercontinental warfare and domestic repression over the previous two decades, British dissenters and evangelicals started a Society for the Promotion of Permanent and Universal Peace in 1816 that announced it was "principled against war, upon any pretense." The American Peace Society was founded about the same time, and beneath these national bodies an extraordinary network of small local peace societies sprang up across the United Kingdom and the United States. Whether they aimed to criticize the privileged or to join them, the pacifists constituted a distinctive new voice in politics. They were one of the earliest instances of what contemporaries termed "association mania"—that spirit that Tocqueville had found in America and attributed to the nature of democratic society—and they brought with them an acute appreciation of the new power of public opinion, "which in the long run, governs the world." Their presses printed dozens of tracts each year, and thousands of copies were distributed in the first year alone of the London Peace Society's existence. Fervent and passionate, they dreamed of "pictures of thrones and glories, triumphs and felicities, to be won by the church, when her now invisible Lord shall descend in person to lead her armies." Peace became the creed of activists, who were critical of those "who idly sit, and wait the time of God." They believed that they had already wrought great changes "in the minds of multitudes," that "the spirit of war is chased away."[3]

It took time for these activists to organize international meetings, but when they did they were pioneering and quickly emulated. The Anti-Slavery Convention that met in London in 1840 was the first of no fewer than ten international conferences that took place in that decade. Three years later, the General Peace Convention that met above the Freemasons Arms in London in 1843 had a significant American presence, an expression of the increasingly close ties linking American and British pacifists. The organizers declared that Anglo-American cooperation was mandated by God "to do his great work of love to the human family in spreading the light of civilization and Christianity over all the habitations of men."[4] In venue, style and temperament, their activities could scarcely have been more different from those of the statesmen of the Concert, and they were in fact deeply ambivalent in their attitude toward worldly authority in general. Their "Address to the Civilised Governments of the World" urged Europe's rulers to renounce war on principle. Suspicious of political elites, even as they sought to influence them, they proposed to set up "a central committee of Vigilance for the peace of all nations" that would deploy public opinion against any statesmen who threatened recourse to war.[5]

The "learned blacksmith" Elihu Burritt, a self-taught Massachusetts journalist who implausibly claimed to understand fifty languages, was one of the movement's leaders. An advocate of what he called "people-diplomacy" in contradistinction to the aristocratic elitism of the diplomats, he publicized the idea of a League of Universal Brotherhood at the World Temperance Convention in August 1846 and used his newspaper, the *Christian Citizen,* to preach the cause of popular pacifism. Metternich's interventions across Europe were grist to his mill, and Burritt quickly found allies among Quakers and free marketeers alike. Within a year he had thirty thousand signatories and dreamed of seeing the movement spread to Europe and the United States. For Burritt, it was up to workingmen to band together, because if they refused to fight one another, the warmaking classes would be hindered. Marx of course would take this idea and incorporate its assumptions within his critique of capital and industrialization.

As the movement extended its support into middle-class circles, it moved closer to respectability. The late 1840s were its heyday, as the erosion of the Metternichian order in continental Europe offered hope to its activists, and a peace congress in Brussels in 1848 (displaced from Paris by the revolution there) gave them publicity. They were further encouraged when at the start of 1849 France's new president, Louis Napoleon, made the most significant disarmament proposal of any major power, offering to limit naval armaments to any level provided the British followed suit. He intended this as a means of improving ties with England, and the idea probably owed little to any lobbying by the peace movement. But it suggested that their ideas were not unrealistic, and even the British rejection did not dampen their spirits, especially as Louis Napoleon went on to make unilateral reductions in French arms spending later that year. As one historian notes, "Formal diplomacy and peace agitation, hitherto separate streams, here intermingle for the first time."[6]

Under Louis Napoleon, republican France was eager to claim leadership of the forces for change that the European revolutions of 1848 had brought to the surface, and a major international peace conference was hosted in Paris in August 1849. This time the participants included such renowned luminaries as Alexis de Tocqueville, the minister of foreign affairs, who welcomed the delegates at the Quai d'Orsay, novelist Victor Hugo, and English free trade hero Richard Cobden, attending in a show of support. But among those also present, figures of a very different station in life testified to the peace movement's humbler origins, and one of the delegates of the American Peace Society, William Wells Brown, had actually been born into slavery in Kentucky. In the very city where in 1815 Great Power rule had been restored by Metternich, Castlereagh, Talleyrand, and the Russian tsar, the presence of a former slave as international peace delegate marked the emergence of a dramatically new mode of global politics.

An abolitionist and an accomplished writer, and often hailed as the author of the first novel to be published by an African American, Brown records in his journal the unprecedented scene in the Saint Cecilia Hall as the conference started—the curious French spectators who swarmed in, the balcony with sofas reserved for distinguished delegates, the platform crowded with nationals from half a dozen European countries, and the grand entry of the Congress's officers, led by Victor Hugo, who delivered "one of the most impressive and eloquent appeals in favor of peace that could possibly be imagined." Looking forward to the day when the nations of Europe would merge in a single European brotherhood, lay down their weapons, and "the only fields of battle" would be "markets opening up to trade and minds opening up to ideas," Hugo hailed the nineteenth century as "a prodigious and admirable epoch" in which international enmity was subsiding and "everything is moving at once—political economy, science, industry, philosophy, legislation—and converging upon the same end, the creation of well-being and benevolence." Brown noted the terrific enthusiasm that greeted the speech: "An English gentleman near me said to his friend, 'I can't understand a word of it but is it not good?'"[7]

Even at a peace congress, however, not everyone was happy about Brown's presence. "That nigger had better be on his master's farm," muttered one compatriot. "What could the American Peace Society be thinking about, to send a black man as a delegate to Paris?" remarked another. But European liberals were welcoming, Madame de Tocqueville was gracious, and Brown himself offers us a brilliant view of the proceedings whose political ambiguities he was more aware of than most.

He was especially critical of the conference's decision not to permit any discussion of contemporary events. The organizers might hail the march of progress—"the boon of Providence"—and be eloquent in defense of their "holy cause . . . the advocacy of the principles of peace," but they were nervous about displeasing their official French hosts, anxious about the fragility of their movement's own unity, and keen to increase their influence and respectability. One reason for caution was that only a couple of months before, French troops had been sent in to Italy to restore papal rule and to oust the republicans led by Garibaldi and Mazzini in Rome; on this controversial development the organizing committee had ordered silence. "They put padlocks upon their own mouths," noted Brown, "and handed the keys to the government." A new spirit of pragmatism colored the closing resolutions too. Gone was the old blanket condemnation of war and in its place a more practical agenda of compulsory arbitration, reduced spending on armaments, and "the formation of a Congress of Nations, to revise the existing International Law, and to constitute a High Tribunal for the decision of controversies among nations." It was almost as though the leaders of the meeting foresaw that other conference that would take place at Versailles seventy years later to set up an organization remarkably similar to the one they were calling for.

The uprisings of the time were thus as much a challenge for the peace movement's organizers as an opportunity: were they to be against war even when this allowed a noble cause to go down in defeat, as happened in Poland in 1846 and again in many European capitals two years later? In 1849 the Hungarian politician Lajos Kossuth was greeted by enormous crowds when he arrived in London later that year, whipping up anti-Russian feeling in his Shakespearean English, annoying Queen Victoria, and even splitting the British government by his presence. Pacifists started to argue over the question of whether or not to support oppressed nationalities like the Hungarians and the Poles. Brown had already noted their abject silence when the Italians Garibaldi and Mazzini, two other lions of liberal London, had come under attack. And the drums of war were beating closer to home too as Louis Napoleon's coup d'état in France scared the English and led to calls for a new anti-Napoleonic campaign: his support for the peace movement now looked merely like another insincere example of his revisionist realpolitik.

The peace movement was running out of steam. The most exciting feature of their gathering at Frankfurt was the appearance of a Native American chieftain who had taken the name Reverend Copway; he presented a peace pipe to the delegates in the name of the "Great Spirit." Things improved a bit in 1851, the year of the Great Exhibition at the Crystal Palace, when four thousand people crowded into London's Exeter Hall and for the first time their meeting attracted a large amount of international attention. Even so, for insiders like Brown, the movement's star was already fading, and he found the meeting less memorable than the exhibition or indeed Elihu Burritt's Brotherhood Bazaar, an abolitionist rally featuring "American Fugitive Slaves" and the "largest gathering of Teetotalers ever assembled in London," who marched in an orderly procession some fifteen to twenty thousand strong to picnic at the exhibition.[8]

Among the other American visitors to London's 1851 Peace Congress was Horace Greeley, perhaps the most distinguished American newspaperman of the era. Greeley was struck by the meeting's strongly democratic character—the absence of the "Lords, Dukes, Generals, Princes" whose names adorned the supporters of other kinds of movements. He was impressed too by the way the peace movement had come to embody the organizational energies of Christians much more than any strictly religious body for spreading the word of Christ. But above all, like Brown, he was struck by the quietist political implications of Christian pacifism—the extent to which the movement implicitly accepted the status quo in Europe and tolerated "Despots" and their abuse of "downtrodden nations." Alongside its denunciation of colonialism and demands for disarmament, the congress had concluded by taking a strongly anti-interventionist stance, describing intervention as "a frequent cause of bitter and desolating wars."[9] But the public in whom it reposed such trust was not persuaded and the outbreak of the Crimean War in 1853 revived the always latent belligerence of the British against the Russians and sounded the peace movement's death knell. In 1857 the Peace Congress Committee was disbanded, while the American Civil War saw most former American peace activists commit themselves in support of the Northern side.

The Crimean War showed that the spirit of war had certainly not been abolished, as evangelical activists mistakenly believed. On the contrary, it tore apart the European Concert—by pitting Russia against France and Britain—and it prompted a war fever that sustained a bloody three-year conflict that extended from the Baltic to the Caucasus and raised the specter of an even larger "war of nationalities" that could have dragged in the Poles and the Circassians. A peace conference at Paris patched things up and ended the fighting, but the exhaustion was only temporary. The Russians invaded the Caucasus a few years later and expelled hundreds of thousands of the inhabitants into Ottoman lands, paving the way for a new cycle of violence in the Balkans and Anatolia; in 1870, the Franco-Prussian War broke out, bringing conflict back to western Europe as well.[10] In mid-Victorian Britain, a new cult of Christian manliness emerged, and churches resounded to the strains of "Onward, Christian soldiers, marching as to war." One of the results was the emergence of a more chastened internationalism, often still professing Christian principles but pursuing other, more indirect paths to peace. The new internationalists relied less on public opinion and God, and more on the building of new institutions. And as they learned to pay greater attentiveness to the bounds of the politically possible, they had near at hand one great model of success, closely linked ideologically to their own: the movement for tariff repeal and free trade.

FREE TRADE

In the summer of 1847, the Radical member of Parliament Richard Cobden, a well-known advocate of free trade, was invited to dine in Vienna with the aging Prince Metternich. Covered in glory, Cobden was touring Europe on a mission. He had just led Parliament's repeal of the Corn Laws, the barrier to imported grain that had been voted in at the end of the Napoleonic Wars for the sake of the landed interest. Repeal of the Corn Laws had galvanized a coalition of merchants, manufacturers, workingmen, and journalists agitating for free trade: the newly established *Economist* was the movement's mouthpiece. Cobden himself was widely credited as the prime mover in a political earthquake that showed better than any other how fast power was moving in the United Kingdom into the hands of the rising classes of the Industrial Revolution. With their ascent they brought the most important and durable variant of utopian internationalism to emerge in the mainstream of Victorian politics.

Free trade might strike us now as an argument for self-interest—a battering ram for whichever states enjoys competitive advantage internationally to open up foreign markets—but although it is couched in terms of tariffs, relative costs, and other economic technicalities, it has always stood for much more noble ideals than that in the eyes of its devotees. From Cobden in the 1840s to the "Tennessee Cobden" (as Roosevelt's secretary of state Cordell Hull was known a century later), and down to the globalization ideologues of our own times, free trade has often been depicted in almost cosmic terms as a means of facilitating communication among men and bringing peace to the world. Its supporters regard tariffs as a step toward isolation and belligerence, open economies as the prerequisite for both prosperity and global harmony, trade as the means of reconciling self-interest and the general welfare. "Commerce," advised Sir Robert Peel, who presided over the repeal of the Corn Laws, was "the happy instrument of promoting civilization, of abating national jealousies and prejudices, and of encouraging the maintenance of general peace."[11]

Cobden's tour of Europe in 1847 marked out his larger ambitions and suggested interconnections between the causes of international cooperation and domestic reform. In his eyes, now that Britain had led the way, it remained to enlighten other nations and get them to follow suit. He had toured North America in the past and had been heartened by reports that the United States had responded to news of the repeal of the Corn Laws by spontaneously relaxing their own tariffs. This was important, because there was no greater advocate of the virtues of protectionism (nor any greater advertisement of its benefits) than the rapidly industrializing United States. But the decisive scene of battle was Europe, and Vienna was its heartland. Cobden's dinner with Metternich thus marked the symbolic confrontation between the old and new visions of international order.

Seventy-four years old, Metternich was now both foreign minister and chancellor and as energetic as ever in repressing any sparks of those "revolutionary embers" that flared up from time to time. The year before, while Britain repealed the Corn Laws, Austrian troops suppressed an uprising in the Polish city of Cracow, annexing it and thereby extinguishing the last scrap of independent Poland. Even as he and Cobden sat down to dinner, Habsburg soldiers were occupying the Italian city of Ferrara. Metternich could scarcely have guessed the scale of the revolutionary fervor that was to erupt less than a year later, as Europe was shaken by a series of insurrections and revolts that nearly toppled the Austrian monarchy and caused Metternich himself to flee. But Cobden would have been less surprised. Even that brief meeting with the principal architect of the Vienna system left him feeling sure that the aging statesmen of the Concert were out of touch with the rapid socioeconomic changes transforming the continent. He wrote after their encounter that

> [Metternich] is probably the last of those State physicians who, looking only to the symptoms of a nation, content themselves with superficial remedies from day to day, and never attempt to probe beneath the surface to discover the source of the evils which afflict the social system. This order of statesmen will pass away with him, because too much light has been shed upon the laboratory of Governments, to allow him to impose upon mankind with the old formulas.[12]

The "laboratory of Governments"—the very phrase suggests that government is not a matter of ruling in the name of the past, of legitimacy and the rights of the sovereign, but is instead a science, a matter for experts who understand the laws of nature and man. If Margaret Thatcher understood economic liberalism to imply, in her famous phrase, that "there is no such thing as society," Cobden's view was the exact opposite: underlying any system of government were social forces upon which the successful management of international affairs depended. This is the deeper meaning of Cobden's charge that the Concert of Europe, conceived in an antirevolutionary spirit, and seeing territories and populations as the property of their rulers, was incapable of dealing with the impact of the dramatic changes sweeping the continent. Its outlook, by denying the existence of a society in flux, was simply blind to the real forces at work. Repression might work for a time against nationalist uprisings. But it was not only nationalism whose power was now emerging for the first time. Steam and the railways were bringing about the most revolutionary modernization of communications and transportation since Roman times. Manufacturing was being transformed and entire regions were being turned into its agents, altering the nature of work and time for those caught up in it. Literacy rates were starting to rise fast—a further challenge to the Metternichian surveillance and censorship system—and with them the size of the reading public and the market for ideas.

And because the architects of repression saw their task as interconnected, and came where necessary to one another's aid—this was, after all, how the Concert of Europe was supposed to function—Radicals such as Cobden, and domestic reformers in general, were driven for this reason too to pursue strategies of international cooperation. They naturally connected the cause of domestic constitutional reform with a larger assault on Europe's governing class and its assumptions. They talked of Christian fellowship, but in democratic not paternalist terms. They talked not of stability but of peace—a peace that could come only when the old habits of secret courtly diplomacy and high taxation for war were replaced by a world in which war itself would cease to seem a natural recourse for settling grievances. And this world, so the most common argument went, required something very simple but very radical—a shift to some form of democracy, since people left to themselves were naturally peace-loving, and only driven to war by the selfish ambitions of their old masters. Cobden himself looked forward to the day when nations were united by "race, religion, language . . . not by the parchment title deeds of sovereigns." The spread of democracy and trade went hand in hand.[13]

The cause of free trade itself had a pedigree that stretched back to before the French Revolution. Kant might have dismissed the supposed civilizing virtues of commerce, but throughout the eighteenth century critics of absolutism had praised them, contrasting land-based centralized despotisms in Europe and Asia with the benign providential work of maritime powers like Britain with its self-governing colonies. Napoleon himself had posited an alternative view—that Britain through its leading commercial position was exploiting the rest of Europe: right to the end of his reign, Britain was the great enemy and the blockade system was extolled as a trade barrier in the interests of the continent, an early harbinger of the argument that other continental powers would make in the next two centuries and that generated competing visions of European integration—European Free Trade Area versus Common Market—deep into the Cold War. But Napoleon's defeat encouraged an ever more sweeping defense of commercial society by the Anglophiles. Trade was not only more civilized, more efficient, freer, and more prosperous than its rivals; it was also more peace-loving. The Abbé de Pradt had contrasted the martial and the trading spirit, and looked forward to the triumph of the latter. Benjamin Constant's 1814 *De l'esprit de conquête et de l'usurpation* presented Europe under Napoleon as "merely a vast prison" and England as "generous asylum of free thought and illustrious refuge of the dignity of mankind." His essay was a call to France to repudiate militarism and to join the "commercial nations of modern Europe, industrious, civilized."[14]

Cobden's free trade movement was the leading and unquestionably most successful version of radical internationalism to emerge in the first half of the nineteenth century. But this success was a mixed blessing. It was the fate of radical visions of international harmony when they failed (as the peace movement did) to be forgotten. But when they triumphed, it was because they were taken up by politicians and turned to ends their original architects had never envisaged. Something of this kind happened to free trade in the hands of Whitehall civil servants. What had started out as a peace movement of its own was quickly used to underwrite another kind of imperial policy, and the door into other people's economies was soon being forced open by British diplomats, backed by gunboats, everywhere from West Africa to Istanbul and Peking.

The irony is that Cobden himself was a consistent anti-imperialist, and no one outlined the global benefits of the spread of commercial capitalism better. As he had put it in a speech for the Anti–Corn Law League in 1843:

> Free Trade, what is it? . . . Why breaking down the barriers that separate nations; those barriers behind which nestle the feelings of pride, revenge, hatred and jealousy, which every now and then break their bonds and deluge whole countries with their blood.[15]

Liberal political economy—which provided the new doctrine's theoreticians—had these assumptions embedded within it, and even the least effusive of the classical theorists, David Ricardo, could not resist pointing out the wondrous linkage free trade made between individual self-interest and universal well-being:

> The pursuit of individual advantage is admirably connected with the universal good of the whole. By stimulating industry, by rewarding ingenuity, and by using most efficaciously the peculiar powers bestowed by nature, it distributes labor most effectively and most economically; while by increasing the general mass of productions, it diffuses general benefits, and binds together by one common tie of interest and intercourse, the universal society of nations throughout the civilized world.[16]

The era's characteristic blend of economics and fervor was evident at the international congress of economists held in Brussels at the end of 1847. "We come for the first time," declared the Belgian president of the association for free trade, "to examine the question of the brotherhood among all men . . . to put into practice the words of God: 'Love one another.'" The *Economist,* just beginning its long career as a mouthpiece for free-market capitalism, applauded the promotion of commercial liberalism through the enlightenment of public opinion, and with it the promotion of something it called "internationalism."[17]

In London, the Great Exhibition of 1851—Cobden was among

the principal organizers—constituted a kind of architectural manifesto for this creed, its magnificent prefabricated iron and soaring glass building a marvel of modern technology: open, democratic, and global. "We are living at a period of most wonderful transition which tends rapidly to accomplish that great end toward which, indeed, all history points—*the realization of the unity of mankind,*" stated Prince Albert, its patron, underscoring the millenarian fervor that the organizers shared with so many other Victorian progressives.

It is no coincidence that the distinctive ethos of internationalism emerged at this time. Bilateral commercial treaties seemed to offer a new model for regulating affairs among states, more practical, more democratic, and less hidebound than the Concert model of Great Power consultation. And more global too: the commercial treaties the British and French signed with the Ottomans and the Chinese might have been unwanted by the latter, but to the European mind they signaled the spread of civilization itself. Within Europe, the 1860 commercial treaty between Britain and France was a watershed, and another sixty such treaties followed, turning western Europe into a closer approximation to a single market than anything before the end of the twentieth century. Contemporaries talked about the "Commonwealth of Europe," and saw trade as the motor of an internationalism that now rivaled the fading mechanisms of the Concert. By the mid-1860s, it was commonplace to see internationalism as the great modern contribution of the "discoverers of the laws of political economy," and to describe "the mercantile classes" as driven by the desire for "intercommunion and international cooperation."[18]

As for Cobden, he was hailed as "the international man" par excellence. "It is strange but true," noted an obituarist on his death in 1867, "that there had been no international men of any note before his time." It had fallen, he went on, to Cobden to make people aware that new political institutions could reduce suspicion among nations and to use free trade as an instrument to show that war was not an inevitable part of the natural order but a form of "anarchy" that men could tame should they choose, to demonstrate above all that nationalism, rightly understood, was not a bar to internationalism but the path to it. The spread of democracy and representative government and world peace all grew out of this commitment to tariff reform: "Inasmuch as the time was not ripe for that full development of internationalism which consists in some form of political union, he saw that the work cut out for him in life was to prepare the way for it by habituating so far as might be possible the public mind to the idea, by removing obstacles to its progress and by advocating and pushing forward every measure of legislation or policy which could tend to its realization. Foremost among such measures was the liberation of commerce."[19]

It was, as the lines above suggest, in the awakening of the "public mind" that the free traders believed lay the best means to ensure the triumph of their creed. Their basic assumption, which they shared with evangelical thought, was that humanity's fraternal impulses would make themselves felt through the democratic power of opinion. The implication, so powerfully transmitted to several generations of liberals and thence to the architects of the League of Nations, was that humanity is peace-loving when left alone by governments. It is politicians who entangle men in wars, and special interests that corrupt man's innate selflessness: allow the free association of men and ideas and one constructs a force for peace. Free trade was thus an ideology of internationalism that required no special international organization beyond machinery to reduce tariffs, a world with at most some version of the World Trade Organization but none of the numerous other agencies that populate international politics today. It offered a fundamentally antipolitical conception of international solidarity, hostile to the still largely aristocratic elites who ran things, which would eventually translate into Woodrow Wilson's call after the First World War for a new kind of world order with international public opinion as its principal sanction. But by then Wilson himself sounded rather like a throwback to the assumptions of a previous century, and one of the reasons he was greeted by liberals in Europe with such euphoria in 1919 is that they could scarcely believe that the most powerful man in the world was speaking the language of their spiritual forefathers. For the problems with this argument had become visible generations earlier, and indeed had emerged with stark force to confront Cobden himself in his final years.

The thrust of Cobden's argument with the old diplomacy was essentially that it served a particular class interest—that of the militaristic aristocracy. In measures like the Corn Laws, he alleged, politicians interfered with the natural operation of trade for their own purposes. They went on and on about the balance of power in order to rationalize the need for high taxes and unnecessary spending on armaments; then they went in search of conflicts to justify this spending. Low taxation was thus a peace policy, while the balance of power was "not a fallacy, a mistake, an imposture, it is an undescribed, indescribable, incomprehensible nothing." He therefore wanted Britain to keep out of all foreign entanglements: it had no business supporting Turkey, for example, or going to war with Russia. It would be much better for the Englishman "to give up the fruitless attempt to promote the good of his neighbours, and the peace and happiness of the world by dint of the cudgel: that he may remain quietly at home; gradually get his house into repair; cultivate his rich estate according to his fancy."[20]

Yet the Crimean War brought Cobden and many of his followers face to face with the "war spirit" that was pushing politicians to war. It came as a severe shock that the press and the public opinion they had been accustomed to appealing to could turn to aggression so easily: "Are we, after all, rational and progressive creatures?" Cobden asked himself. His advice to the peace activists was to lie low until the war itself proved its own irrationality. For his part, he retained his confidence that analysis of the economic facts offered the best ground for educating the masses. But increasingly political analysts questioned whether the masses were really driven by reason at all. Reflecting the new conservative drift of Victorian liberalism, John Stuart Mill modified the doctrine of utilitarianism to take account of the fact that the educated classes were simply more rational and farsighted than the masses. When Benjamin Disraeli published his novel of the 1850s, *Endymion,* it offered a scathing critique of Cobden's radical rationalism. "They have got a new name for this hybrid sentiment," declares an ambassador. "They call it public opinion." "How very absurd!" says Zenobia ("the queen of London, of fashion, and of the Tory party"), "a mere nickname. As if there could be any opinion but that of the Sovereign and the two Houses of Parliament." As for the press, shrill headlines and campaigning front pages made it hard to present it as the voice of reason. Even at the time of Crimea, the prime minister, Lord Aberdeen, complained that "an English Prime Minister must please the newspapers . . . and the newspapers are always bawling for interference. *They* are bullies and they make the Government bully." Print and the rise of the public mind could, on this evidence, push statesmen into wars, not away from them.[21]

Cobden's free trade ideas did not disappear on his death. But the unrealized vision of a European tariff congress in 1875 was perhaps Cobdenism's last gasp. By then, the first "international man" was increasingly unheeded, especially on the European continent, and "national economics" was on the rise. The rise of powerful rival alliance systems after Germany's emergence in 1871 and the frenzied land grab in Africa and Asia after 1882 shattered free trade's universal pretensions. Nations were becoming more, not less militaristic as they became more national. Protectionism spread across the world. Banded together in the increasingly beleaguered Cobden Club, the great man's disciples faced a wholesale "retreat from free trade." Ironically, the British Empire, which Cobden had reviled, was now seen in Britain itself as a bastion of free trade in a world of rival trading blocs, but that simply made tariff reform look to everyone else like a self-serving doctrine tailored to Britain's temporary economic advantage. In short, like the peace movement with which it was so closely associated, free trade flowered in the internationalist moment of the 1840s and 1850s before withering again. It would have to wait another century, until after the Great Depression and the Second World War, before being taken up by a new world power—the United

States—and thanks to this support projected to global dominance in the 1980s.

NATIONALITY AS INTERNATIONALISM

The third novel element of mid-Victorian internationalism was what was known at the time as the principle of nationality. Today we tend to assume that national pride and the promotion of international harmony and world peace are contradictory impulses. But this assumption is a relatively recent one, and attitudes toward nationalism have changed enormously since its emergence as a political force in continental Europe. In 1919 President Woodrow Wilson traveled through Italy before arriving in Paris to help lay the foundations of the League of Nations. In Genoa amid pouring rain he spoke in front of a monument to one of the city's most illustrious native sons. "It is delightful for me," said the president, "to feel that I am taking some part in accomplishing the realization of the ideals to which his life and thought were devoted." The statue that looked down at him was that of Giuseppe Mazzini (1805–1872)—one of the architects of Italian unification, a revolutionary agitator against the Metternich system, and the "sacred apostle" of the cause of the Nation.

Mazzini turns out to be one of those rare figures one really should term seminal: his vision of a world that is at peace because it has been transformed into an international society of democratic nation-states proved long after his death to be enormously influential. It was, as Woodrow Wilson appreciated, this idea of an association of national states that won out over ideas of unitary world government in the making of the League of Nations, and later the UN. In short, Mazzini was among the first and most important figures to think seriously about international cooperation in terms of the politics of nationalism.

Mazzini's original enemies were the Habsburgs and behind them the Holy Alliance. It was their tyranny that led to his being imprisoned for membership in the secret revolutionary society, the Carbonari, before going into exile. The result was an antimonarchist credo: "We will not attempt any alliances with kings," he wrote in 1832, shortly after forming "Young Italy," his movement for independence and Italian unification. "We will not delude ourselves that we can remain free by relying on international treaties and diplomatic tricks. We will not beg for our well-being via the protocols of conferences or the promises of monarchic cabinet ministers. . . . Therefore listen Italian People: we will deal only with other peoples, never with kings."[22]

Disliking monarchs, Mazzini also had little time for the Enlightenment cosmopolitanism espoused by an earlier generation of Italian exiles. He sympathized with their idea that there was a higher obligation than obedience to kings and sovereigns, but he felt they exaggerated the importance of reason and the rights of the individual and failed to understand that the cause of humanity was best served by fighting collectively for the Nation. The Nation, for Mazzini, imposed a sense of obligation and duty. Its cause was altruistic and therefore ethical. Old-fashioned cosmopolitanism, on the other hand, idealized the self-centered individual and was thus egotistical. Mazzini despised Bentham and the utilitarians for this as well as for their materialism. Nationalism was for him above all about the spiritual elevation achieved through mutual aid and collective action, and as such it rose above individual self-interest. Just as the family as a unit existed above the interests of any one of its members, so did the Nation—and beyond the Nation, Europe itself, embracing all its constituent peoples. Mazzini was thus the proselyte of a continent of democratically organized national states, a Holy Alliance of Peoples. Three years after the founding of Young Italy, he and a small group of refugees in Berne founded Young Europe, to coordinate the national revolutions that would bring down the Holy Alliance.

There is something a little hard to swallow today about this grandiose high-mindedness, the endless exhortations of "the soul of Italy," attempting one insurrection after another, to little avail, and at the cost of many lives. Nevertheless, Mazzini's activism, his extraordinarily prolific letter writing (the Italian edition of his correspondence extends to ninety-four volumes), and his reputation all allowed him to grapple much more seriously than any contemporary peace activist with the practical difficulties of political mobilization. A "Holy Alliance of the Peoples" needed its own Tsar Alexander, and Mazzini was more than willing to take on the role of director of a transnational organization of European revolutionaries. Common sense suggested that coordinating national uprisings and insurrections carried a much greater chance of bringing down the autocrats of the real Holy Alliance than sporadic and disconnected unilateral initiatives. "What we need," he wrote, "[is] . . . a single union of all the European peoples who are striving toward the same goal. . . . When we will rise up simultaneously in every country where our movement is currently active, we will win. Foreign intervention [by the despots] will then become impossible."

Deeply critical of Cobden's isolationism, he called the policy "abject and cowardly, . . . atheism transplanted into international life, the deification of self-interest." Living for much of his life in exile in London, the center of political agitation against continental autocracy, he strove to convert the British themselves from pacifism and nonintervention to what we would now call humanitarian intervention and democracy-building. Even if he never achieved the coordinated approach to insurrection he dreamed of, his intellectual influence was pervasive. Through his friendship with Carlyle, Mill, and other prominent writers, and his frequent articles in the press, Mazzinianism circulated widely in Britain and thence across the continent and the Atlantic.[23]

The question of intervention troubled liberal opinion in mid-Victorian Britain, and Mazzini was one of the main troublemakers. Keen to get Europe's most powerful nation to weigh in on the side of the Italians and other oppressed nationalities such as the Hungarians and the Poles, he pushed the humanitarian case for international solidarity in terms that resonate today:

> People begin to feel that . . . there are bonds of international duty binding all the nations of this earth together. Hence, the conviction is gaining ground that if there is any spot of the world, even within the limits of an independent nation, some glaring wrong has been done . . .—if, for example, there should be, as there has been in our time, a massacre of Christians within the dominions of the Turks—then other nations are not absolved from all concern in the matter simply because of the large distance between them and the scene of the wrong.[24]

For an Italian, it was regrettable that the British should have intervened to help the Greeks win their freedom—as they had done in 1827 at the Battle of Navarino—but then failed to move against Austrian absolutism on the Italian peninsula. It was an argument that helped shift William Gladstone and important sections of British liberal opinion away from the Cobdenite stance of opposing all foreign entanglements. Indeed, even Cobden himself showed signs of being persuaded. This did not mean, of course, that oppressed European nations should not fight for their *own* liberty—Mazzini both wrote in favor of this and took a direct part in the uprisings of 1848. Once free he believed they should assume the burdens of civilization and acquire colonies of their own. Italy, for Mazzini, was destined to participate in "the great civilizing mission suggested by our times," and he recommended that it "invade and colonize the Tunisian lands when the opportunity presents itself." Liberal nationalism thus appeared to be both internationalist (when turned toward Europe) and imperial (at the expense of non-Europeans) at the same time, and here too Mazzini's thought in all its Eurocentric ambiguity would be deeply influential on international institutions in the twentieth century.[25]

THE MAZZINIAN NATIONAL PROGRAM stressed self-help, mutual aid, and the acquisition of learning—Mazzini himself supported a school for the children of poor Italian workers in central London. But his doctrine had no place for class struggle or anything that threatened to undermine the holy grail of national unity. As a result, the Italian was outspoken on the dangers posed by the new creeds of socialism and communism. In 1842, he wrote of the need to reach out to workers who had been "lost behind the error of Communism." And when, eight years later, he approved the idea of establishing a European Central Democratic Committee in London—intended as a kind of guiding council for his Young Europe grouping of democrats—he talked about the need to save "democratic nationalities" from "the anarchy of communist sects."[26]

New terms like socialism and communism—their meanings still fluid and ill-defined—were starting to circulate in the early 1840s. Then in 1846 there was an uprising in the semi-free Polish city of Cracow, quickly followed by an Austrian crackdown, and once more the Polish cause hit the headlines, threatening to split the radical movement in two. In London, Chartist leaders and journalists clustered around a radical grouping known as the Fraternal Democrats collected money for the Poles and sought to mobilize the revolutionary emigrants of other nationalities.[27] Yet Mazzini shunned the Fraternal Democrats because he feared their socialist sympathies. Instead he supported the creation of a rival and more respectable lobbying group—the People's International League—to push the Foreign Office in a pro-democratic direction. Over the next two years, the British radical press hosted an acrimonious give-and-take between partisans of the rival bodies. Among those who took part in these arguments were two German radicals, Karl Marx and Friedrich Engels, at this time representatives of the German Democratic Communists in Brussels.

The fascinating if indirect argument between Marx and Mazzini, so important for understanding international affairs right through the Cold War, begins here in the vigorous intellectual jousting of Victorian radical politics. In their arguments, one sees the outlines of two visions of internationalism, the one based on the principle of national emancipation within a capitalist system, the other on communist internationalism: each would find superpower backing in the twentieth century. Quickly taking up a position of mutual antagonism, in fact they shared a great deal, not least a fundamental realization that nations remained the essential building blocks of any international order.

It began when Marx and Engels wrote an article on the implications of Chartism in 1846. "The working class of England know very well," they stated, "that now the great struggle of capital and labor, of *bourgeois* and *proletarians* must come to a decision." This kind of language was anathema to Mazzini. His People's International League was fighting not for *workers'* rights but for "the Rights of Nationality and to promote a cordial understanding between the Peoples of all countries." The following April, Mazzini penned a bitterly fierce critique of communism in an English newspaper. In his "Thoughts upon Democracy," Mazzini argued that communism represented a denial of liberty, progress, and the moral development of humanity. It was inescapably tyrannical and threatened even to abolish the family.[28]

Mazzini did not at this stage have Marx and Engels particularly in mind. Indeed his primary target was not yet the radical left but that vein of materialism that for him originated with Jeremy Bentham. Nevertheless, many socialists were outraged and said so. At the end of 1847, Karl Marx came to London and made a speech to the Fraternal Democrats that was unmistakably directed against Mazzini and his version of internationalism. "Union and brotherhood of nations is an empty phrase which today is on the lips of all bourgeois parties," Marx declared. "The victory of the proletariat over the bourgeoisie is at the same time the victory over national and industrial conflicts which today create hostility among different peoples. The victory of the proletariat over the bourgeoisie is at the same time the sign of the liberation of all oppressed nations." Immediately afterward, back in Brussels, he and Engels penned the *Communist Manifesto* for a groupuscule of German radical workers who had recently changed the name of their organization from the League of the Just to the

Communist League. "A specter is haunting Europe—the specter of communism," is its famous opening. "All the Powers of old Europe have entered into a holy alliance to exorcise this specter: Pope and Czar, Metternich and Guizot, French radicals and German police-spies." The fact that it went on instantly to identify the cleavage between bourgeoisie and proletariat as the central fact of the age was sufficient to indicate Marx's opposition to the Mazzinian program.

The struggle between Mazzini and the socialists continued in the coming years. Following the failures of 1848, Marx himself settled in London and spent the next years working on his own research. But he knew how to hold a grudge. Privately settling scores—not so much with Mazzini as with the German émigrés who clustered around him—his satirical essay "The Great Men of the Exile" (unpublished until the twentieth century) skewered Mazzini too, dismissing his global pretensions as a sham. In Marx's words:

> The great drama of the democratic emigration of 1849 to 1852 had been preceded by a prelude eighteen years previously: the emigration of demagogues in 1830 and 1831. Even though with the passage of time most of the emigrants of this first wave had been ousted from the stage, there still remained a few worthy remnants who, stoically indifferent to the course of history and the effect of their action, continued to work as agitators, devised global plans, formed provisional governments and hurled proclamations into the world in every direction. It is obvious that the business experience of these seasoned swindlers greatly surpassed that of the younger generation. It was this very acumen acquired through eighteen years practice in conspiring, scheming, intriguing, proclaiming, duping, showing off and pushing oneself to the fore that gave Mr. Mazzini . . . the audacity and the assurance to install himself as the Central Committee of European Democracy.[29]

There was much truth in what Marx said. But could Marx himself do any better?

COMMUNISM

For much of the twentieth century the term "internationalism" was more or less synonymous with organized socialism, and above all with the rise of the Soviet Union to world power. After 1945, it was invariably deployed in relation to that sequence of Internationals that started with the 1864 First International (in which Marx had played an important role) and culminated in the Third—better known as the 1919 Communist International, an instrument established by Lenin for the greater coordination of communist parties worldwide—and Trotsky's rather less successful Fourth. But all this put the cart before the horse. The more accurate way to see Marxian internationalism was as one variant of the profusion of mid-nineteenth-century visions of world order, one that cannot be understood except in its Victorian context. The fundamental enemy was, as always, the conservative restoration of 1815. But by the 1840s, the Concert's prestige was waning, and as much if not more of Marx's fire was directed against those visions of international order that rivaled and threatened to undermine his own.

Free trade—then in its heyday—was one of these, and at Brussels and afterward Marx sought to turn the internationalist logic of classical political economy against itself: capitalism in spreading over the globe would in fact prepare the terrain for the eventual worldwide triumph of the working classes. As he wrote in a speech that he prepared for the Brussels free trade congress, "We are for Free Trade, because by Free Trade all economical laws, with their most astounding contradictions, will act upon a larger scale, upon a larger extent of territory, upon the territory of the whole earth; and because from the uniting of all these contradictions into a single group, where they stand face to face, will result the struggle which will itself eventuate in the emancipation of the proletariat."[30] In his journalism, Marx devoted considerable attention to the free trade movement, and to Cobden in particular, and he was attentive both to its political force and to its travails. As he discerned in 1857, after Cobden was humiliatingly defeated in his Manchester constituency, the forces of jingoism and adventurism abroad were far stronger than Cobden had anticipated, and the impact of public opinion, upon which he had placed such faith, far less certain. Of the idea of public opinion, Marx wrote scornfully that "it has been justly said that Palmerston manufactures one half of it, and laughs at the other half."[31]

More worrying for Marx than free trade—which after all he saw as serving history's purpose—was the distraction posed by Mazzini. Nowhere was this clearer, or more alarming to him, than inside the International Working Men's Association—as the First International was known at the time—which came to occupy so much of his time from 1864 and which eventually made his name a household word. What in fact the association stood for had not initially been very clear. Founded by British union organizers, its ideological position took time to emerge. When, two days before the inaugural meeting, a friend of Marx's, a tailor named Johannes Eccarius, had inquired what the program was, he had been bewildered by the vagueness of the reply, complaining to Marx that "I am supposed to speak in a public meeting about a program whose contents I do not know, whose language I do not understand."[32] Things were little better on the evening itself. The main speaker, a leading London labor unionist named George Odger, flew in generalities over the plight of Poland, the need for cooperation between English and French workmen, and above all the need to counter the "meetings and feasts" of "kings and emperors" with an effective "fraternity of peoples" that would cooperate for "the good of mankind" and "the cause of labor."[33]

Such lofty sentiments in fact echoed the language of Mazzini himself, at that time one of the best known of all the European exiles in London and a man Odger much admired. It was thus not surprising that when the new association began seriously to work on a platform of principles, its leading members turned to Mazzini for inspiration. It was Mazzini's man on the committee who read out the rules of the (Mazzinian) Italian Workingmen's Association—meeting just then in Naples. His proposal that they be adopted by the London general committee of the IWMA met with general consent.[34]

But not of course with that of Marx, who was already heavily involved in helping run the new organization. He was aghast. What they had come up with was, he informed Engels, "an appallingly wordy, badly written and utterly undigested preamble, pretending to be a declaration of principles, in which Mazzini could be detected everywhere." Moving rapidly, Marx managed to get this edited out of existence and replaced with a text of his own composition—the so-called Inaugural Address to the Working Classes. "I edited the whole preamble, threw out the declaration of principles and finally replaced the forty rules with ten. Insofar as international politics come into the address, I speak of countries not nationalities. . . . I was obliged to insert two phrases about 'duty' and 'right' into the preamble to the statutes"—this was his genuflection to Mazzinian theory—"ditto 'truth, morality and justice,' but these are placed in such a way that they can do no harm."[35]

Mazzini's influence has not much preoccupied historians of the International Working Men's Association, which they generally present as the genesis of communism's triumph—as if its foundation led inexorably to the revolutionary Moscow of Lenin's Third International. They talk easily of the First International as the pioneering venture that would help make Marx a household word. Yet Marx himself could scarcely claim the credit for the idea of setting up the association. The two principal organizers, George Odger and William Cremer, had won valuable organizational experience in the London labor movement. Abroad, Italian unification and the American Civil War were exciting radical sympathies. In March 1863, there had been a large public meeting in favor of the Northern side in the war at which Cremer had been among the speakers: Marx had attended, and the workers, he reported to Engels, "spoke excellently, with a complete absence of bourgeois rhetoric and without in the least concealing their opposition to the capitalists." Then came the uprising against Russian rule in Poland the same year. A deputation of union men called on the prime minister to demand that war with Russia not be ruled out. The final incentive to the new labor internationalism was French. In 1862 Emperor Napoleon III rashly helped some workers attend the London Exhibition, where over tea with their English counterparts they planned the creation of a corresponding committee in London to exchange ideas. It is not surprising that Marx should have discerned in that first meeting of the association, as he wrote to Engels, that "real powers" were involved.

The workers were on the move, in the heartland of the Industrial Revolution. But what remained uncertain was which direction the International Working Men's Association would take them: would it, as it were, choose Mazzini and his nationalist republicanism, or the more radical socialism of Marx? The Mazzinian spirit in which it started out was welcomed by the association's first official newspaper, the *Beehive,* which noted that the rights of labor were "to be advanced without unduly interfering with the legitimate rights of capital." Marx would not have been impressed, but from his position inside the association as secretary he proceeded more cautiously than anyone familiar with his earlier writings might have guessed. "It will take time before the reawakened movement allows the old boldness of speech," he confided to Engels. His Inaugural Address drew heavily in its analysis on his detailed work for *Capital,* and the rousing rhetoric of the *Communist Manifesto* was toned down. Like Mazzini, Marx understood the need for the intertwining of national and international action, but in his case this was filtered through the lens of labor activism—the rise of "cooperative labor . . . developed to national dimensions" facilitating the creation of "a bond of brotherhood . . . between the workers of different countries."[36]

Even though such formulations suggested that the two men shared a good deal, Marx fumed about Mazzini's continuing appeal for the English.[37] He was angry when the paternity of the International's foundational documents was attributed to the Italian and not to him. And he insisted that Mazzini's version of republicanism, by denying the existence of class struggle, would, as he told a journalist, lead only to "another form of bourgeois despotism." Still, Marx felt confident that the Italian was on the losing side of history. In September 1867, he wrote Engels with glee that numerous European workers' groups were flocking to the banner of the International: "And when the new revolution comes, and that will perhaps be sooner than might appear, *we* (ie you and I) will have this mighty ENGINE *at our disposal.* COMPARE WITH THIS THE RESULTS OF MAZZINIS ETC. OPERATIONS SINCE 30 YEARS! And with no money to boot . . . We can be well satisfied!"[38]

A real exchange of opinions between the two men finally emerged following the bloody suppression of the Paris Commune in May 1871. At the time of the actual fighting in the French capital between forces loyal to the Commune and the army of the new Third Republic, Marx had had little to say, but his subsequent pamphlet eulogizing the Commune was very widely read. Having followed the conflict chiefly through the press, he published *The Civil War in France: An Address of the General Council of the International Working-Men's Association* only a fortnight after the "Bloody Week" in which government troops shot more than twenty thousand suspected Communards. Marx himself had come to the conclusion that the Commune's failure illustrated the dangers of premature revolution. But the finer details of his analysis escaped the new French minister of foreign affairs, Jules Favre, who immediately gave Marx and the International itself valuable publicity by calling on his colleagues around Europe to help stamp it out as "a society breeding war and hatred." As a result, Marx enjoyed greater renown than ever before, and his revolutionary proletarian internationalism was now in the spotlight, even though it had had nothing really to do with the Commune and certainly did not propose to emulate its example. Interviews and profiles followed and even the first histories of the International itself. "I have the honor to be at this moment the best calumniated and most menaced man in London," he wrote. "This really does one good after a tedious twenty years' idyll in my den."[39]

Mazzini saw the Paris Commune more gloomily—as an anti-national and fragmentary autonomist movement that would lead to moral catastrophe. As he put it, "The sacred word Fatherland [will be] canceled out by the miserable cult of local material interests."[40] The civil war between the French horrified him. In his old age his whole world seemed to be crumbling as Rome was conquered by the Piedmontese monarchy, while in France republicanism tore itself apart. Marx and the International, he agreed with Favre, were part of the problem. Marx was a "German, a little Proudhon, fractious, angry, speaking only of class warfare." In 1872 the Italian's anger and concern that workingmen were being seduced by "principles of materialism and anarchy" spilled over into a public denunciation in the *Contemporary Review*. "The moving spirit [of the International]" he wrote, "is a German named Karl Marx—a man of domineering disposition; jealous of the influence of others; governed by no earnest, philosophical or religious belief; having, I fear, more elements of anger . . . than of love in his nature; and the character of whose intellect—acute, but dissolvent, resembles that of Proudhon." Mazzini went on to argue that "the only rational method of organization among the working classes of Europe would be one which would recognize the sacredness of Nationality," and claimed he had refused to join the International because it violated this principle.[41] Not surprisingly, Marx laughed when a visiting American journalist suggested that Mazzini was an influence, saying he "represented nothing better than the old idea of a middle-class republic." In 1875, after the Italian's death, he referred to him as "the most irreconcilable enemy of the International."

THE STRUGGLE OF IDEAS between Mazzini and Marx is important because the principles they stood for—nationality on the one hand, and communist internationalism on the other—shaped the rivalry that began in 1917 between Woodrow Wilson and Lenin for leadership of a postimperial world. But history rarely proceeds in straight lines, and in fact both creeds lost popularity after their midcentury heyday. We have already seen how the episode of the Paris Commune disheartened the elderly Mazzini: indeed, as early as 1861 he was writing that "we changed the sacred principle of Nationality into a mean *nationalism*." In Italy itself, his popularity dwindled after his death; ironically, when Woodrow Wilson paid his respects in Genoa, it was in a country that attached much less importance to Mazzini than he did.[42]

One reason for this was that Mazzini's appeal had been badly tarnished by his rift with the socialists. Another was that in the decades that led up to the First World War, it had become ever harder to argue for the benign, pacifying power of nationalism. In Germany it had produced a threatening new power in the shape of the Bismarckian Reich, locked in bitter struggle with France. An escalating arms race strained the budgets of all the major powers. Mazzini had also been astonishingly vague about how his ideas could be applied to the ethnically heterogeneous regions of eastern Europe. Sometimes he talked airily about "a Slav-Roumanian-Hellenic confederation on the ruins of the Turkish Empire," as if national independence was only for Hungarians and Poles.[43] In southeastern Europe, he wanted Serbs and Hungarians to rise up, and in this way detonate "the insurrection of a dozen nations" against the despotisms of Austria and Turkey. Yet by the 1880s at the latest, as independent states emerged, it was perfectly clear that in the region now becoming known as the Balkans, these new nations were very likely to go to war with one another.

And then there was the economic problem: in the cases of Italy and Germany, the nationalist program brought unification and amalgamation—the creation of larger states and larger markets from smaller ones; in eastern Europe, the effect was the reverse: to fragment markets and multiply borders and create other obstacles to communications. By the end of the nineteenth century, the argument *against* nationality, originally made with great force by the English historian Lord Acton in a famous 1862 essay on the subject, was widely echoed. Acton defended *empire*—as the defender of civil society against the despotism of majority rule, as polities that "include various nationalities without oppressing them"—and insisted that "the theory of nationality . . . is a retrograde step in history." More and more liberals agreed, questioning whether in central and eastern Europe one should not discriminate between greater and lesser nations, between "historic" nations like Poland and Hungary and unhistoric nations like the Slovaks, Serbs, and Ruthenians.[44]

But Marxist internationalism did not fare any better. Centralized revolutionary socialism of the kind Marx espoused was overshadowed in the 1880s and 1890s by the anarchist, highly decentralized vision of worker power advocated by the Russian Mikhail Bakunin. Before his death, Marx himself effectively scuttled the International by moving it to New York to prevent it being taken over by supporters of Bakunin. Among workers across southern Europe and in the Americas, anarchist ideas flourished. In Russia too, Marxist theory was overshadowed by the turn to anarchist terror in the 1880s that then spread across Europe, helped on its way by agents provocateurs of several imperial police forces. Anarchists were nothing if not internationalists, but incapable for the best of ideological reasons of organizing themselves with any permanence. The 1907 International Anarchist Congress in Amsterdam spent hours arguing whether it was a respectable anarchist position to organize at all, and when an international bureau was established it lasted even less time than Marx's International had done. After a series of assassinations and bombings by groups deeply penetrated and sometimes formed by the secret police—the subject of G. K. Chesterton's brilliant 1908 *The Man Who Was Thursday*—anarchism too was discredited, and by 1900 its brand of revolutionary socialism found itself on the defensive. Meanwhile, social democratic parties in the kaiser's Germany and Austria-Hungary accommodated themselves to parliamentarism much as the Labour Party was doing in the United Kingdom. The best commentator on the international left at this time, journalist John Rae, noted in 1901, "Revolutionary socialism, growing more opportunist of late years, seems losing much of its old phrenzy, and getting domesticated into a shifty State socialism, fighting a parliamentary battle for minor, though still probably mischievous, changes within the lines of existing society, instead of the old war *à l'outrance* against existing society in whatever shape or form."[45]

Marx turned into Marxism, a rich but malleable body of thought interpreted by powerful social democratic parties such as the German and the Austrian as a means to analyze contemporary capitalism rather than a guide to revolutionary action. As socialist parties gained a foothold in parliaments, the prospect of revolution faded. Their internationalism confined itself to a pacifist stance in foreign policy. Marx himself, critical of the old peace movements, had once argued that "the International Working Men's [Association] was in itself a peace congress, as the union of the working classes of the different countries must ultimately make international wars impossible." Yet the outbreak of war in 1914 showed the limitations of socialist internationalism.[46]

IN FACT all three of the major strands of radical internationalism of the mid-nineteenth century followed a similar trajectory: great initial optimism was followed after some public success by challenges they were unable to surmount and then stalemate if not stagnation. What had sustained and galvanized all three was antipathy toward the restorationist program of the Concert of Europe, and the belief that there must be a better way to manage the continent's affairs, one that heeded the expansion of political consciousness and the global interconnectedness produced by trade and communications. But all three shared a common failing, a tendency to assume away the political obstacles they would face, an excessive confidence that the forces of change were moving in their direction. They all underestimated the political challenges posed by the power of the modern state, the tenacity of diplomacy, and the belligerence of nationalism. Free traders and the peace movement were shocked by the militarism of public opinion and the return to protectionism at the end of the century;

Mazzini assumed that nationalists would share his belief in the common cause of humanity, but Bismarck or Cavour had little time for such sentiment. Marx and his followers regarded the ballot box as a distraction, and class solidarity as more powerful than ethnic or national loyalty, yet Europe's workers wanted the vote and went off to fight.

CHAPTER 3

The Empire of Law

Inventors of dubious social sciences, why do you sham at working for the good of the Human Race? Do you think that six hundred million Barbarians and Savages are outside the human race? And yet they suffer. Since you would possess the art of making us happy, do you think you will be carrying out God's plan when you try to limit that happiness to the Civilized peoples, who occupy only the tiniest part of the Globe? For God, the whole human race is one family. . . . It is His will that the entire race of men be happy, or that happiness should be enjoyed by none.

—Charles Fourier, *Théorie des quatres mouvements et des destinées générales* (1808)

The half-century beginning with the Declaration of Paris in 1856 and ending with the London Conference in 1909 has seen greater progress in the direction of internationalism and more successful attempts to improve and codify international law than any other in history, and perhaps more than all previous half-centuries combined.

—Amos Hershey, 1912[1]

As nationalism consolidated itself in Europe, and states gained internally in power rather than withering away, there emerged a new vein of internationalist thought and action, more practical and less revolutionary. It acknowledged the persistence of conflict and sought ways to ameliorate this and guide it into new more peaceable channels; it offered a more systematic philosophy of government itself and stressed the importance of founding durable international institutions, however modest. In short, while the forms of internationalism described earlier would be of enormous influence ideologically in the future, the movement toward international government itself would really take off only in the late nineteenth century from sources that were willing to compromise with power rather than seeking to do away with it entirely. Key among these were law and lawyers.

The 1851 Universal Peace Congress in London had called on "all the friends of Peace to prepare public opinion . . . with a view to the formation of an authoritative Code of International Law." Unlike pacifism itself, this appeal to law continued to resonate strongly. Over the following decades a new transnational elite emerged that shared the pacifists' view that the salvation of the world depended on transforming the conservative order created at the Congress of Vienna and challenging the authority of diplomats. But this elite's goal was codification and the professionalization of international legal practice, and their instrument was not mass mobilization but the formation of a new discipline with its own institutions, worldview, and sense of history. What they founded remains with us today in the form of international law, although it is now a mere shadow of what they hoped it might become, which was a complete alternative mode of conducting relations between states. For at that time many of them actually believed, in the words of an eminent British jurist, that what was at stake was whether "the legal school of International Jurists [will] prevail over the diplomatic school."[2]

For their part, those diplomats entrusted with the foreign policy of Europe's Great Powers realized that international law could actually in some circumstances make their work easier and more palatable to public opinion. As the "gentle civilizer of nations," it offered a means of regularizing relations among the increasingly bellicose and nervous governments of Europe; in an age of frenetic colonial expansion, it could provide an ethical rationalization of their will to global power. At the major diplomatic conferences of the late nineteenth century, therefore, even the most skeptical Great Powers brought legal advisers onto their negotiating teams. By the start of the twentieth, international law was the preeminent example of a once utopian internationalist creed harnessed and tamed by states themselves.[3]

THE MEN OF 1873 AND THE RULES OF WAR

In the midst of the American Civil War, President Abraham Lincoln asked a German-American professor of politics at Columbia University, Francis Lieber, to instruct Union soldiers on the proper treatment of civilians and prisoners of war. Lieber was neither a lawyer nor a pacifist: his youthful passion for German nationalism and for the cause of Greek independence help explain his disagreements with American pacifists and their grand schemes. On the other hand, as a liberal he strongly believed in the civilizing power of the law itself. Honored initially in the breach, his instructions were an unsystematic mélange of observations, recommendations, and prohibitions. But they were received with interest abroad, and before the 1860s were out he was in contact with European jurists exploring the idea of codifying international law as a means of encouraging better relations among nations. His faith in the power of internationalism grew as a result. "Internationalism," he wrote shortly before his death, "is part of a white man's religion, for it is the application of the Gospels to the intercourse of nations."[4]

The year of the Lieber Code (1863) saw another effort to humanize war that was a first step toward the internationalization of the laws of war: the founding of the Red Cross in Geneva. After seeing tens of thousands of badly wounded and dying men in 1859 on the battlefield of Solferino—where French and Habsburg troops had clashed over the fate of Italy—a young Swiss businessman named Henri Dunant had called for a neutral organization to care for wounded soldiers. Coming shortly after Florence Nightingale's campaign for army health reforms and professional nursing in the Crimean War, Dunant's appeal evoked a swift response. A Genevan lawyer, Gustave Moynier, took up the idea, and the committee that he and Dunant convened in 1863 is now regarded as the start of the International Red Cross Committee. The following year, the Swiss parliament organized a conference that led to twelve states signing an international convention for the care of the wounded in battle.

That first Geneva Convention was important for two reasons. Firstly, it took place entirely outside the Concert system—bringing together a number of small states, and leaving outside several major powers that only joined later. And second, it signaled a turn away from the older peace movement's effort to stamp out war entirely and toward the legal challenge of humanizing the way it was conducted. Yet then came the Franco-Prussian War of 1870–71 which shocked Europe with its summary executions, mass reprisals, and bloody denouement in the rubble of Paris. It was in the aftermath of these events, amid dismay that the combatants had failed to take notice of the new Geneva Convention, that a group of reform-minded young lawyers got together. The Red Cross's Moynier had been struck by the "savagery unworthy of civilized nations" in the recent war, something he attributed to the legal uncertainty that surrounded the laws of war. Others agreed, notably a Belgian lawyer, Gustave Rolin-Jaequemyns, who had begun publishing the world's first international law journal a few years before. In 1873 he brought in more colleagues and founded a new Institute of International Law in Ghent. What they aimed for was not a large political movement akin to the older peace lobby but rather a forum where a select group of professional scholars could meet and shape a discipline. "The men of 1873," as their historian has termed them, saw themselves simultaneously as impartial jurists, wedded to the scientific study of the law, and high-minded liberal guardians of the "legal conscience of the civilized world." They included the leading Swiss jurist Johann Kaspar Bluntschli, the American arch-codifier David Dudley Field (whose brother Cyrus was famous for laying the Atlantic telegraph cable between the United States and Britain), Gustave Moynier, and the inevitable smattering of figures from the Low Countries. The institute took over Rolin-Jaequemyns's journal, the new *Revue de droit internationale et de législation comparée,* which quickly won recognition and provided a mouthpiece for their creed.[5]

What it preached was the need to move beyond the dominance of diplomacy. Everyone is a statesman of a sort, Gustave Rolin-Jaequemyns had declared in its opening issue: international affairs were too important to be left to the diplomats alone. The point was that law was made not by kings nor even by parliaments but by deeper trends in society: the lawyer's task was to interpret and speak for these. Yet this potentially radical definition of the lawyer's task was tempered by Rolin's desire to do what he could to enhance the prestige of the institute and their profession. Hence Rolin urged both keeping aloof from "the virtuous utopians that wanted the immediate abolition of war" and avoiding the "timid spirits" who thought nothing could be changed in international affairs. He wanted to avoid pronouncing on European political matters and to concentrate on codification and tackling safer matters of private international law.[6]

The services of the institute and its members were soon being called upon by statesmen and proving their usefulness. At the initiative of Tsar Alexander II, a conference was called in Brussels in 1874 to which fifteen states sent delegates to make a first, halting effort to codify the laws of war. The meeting did not produce a convention, since few states were yet willing to bind themselves to one, but it did indicate the growing reach of the lawyers. Indeed, the new institute itself kept the codification effort going through the 1870s by examining the Brussels proposals further, and then at a meeting in Oxford in 1880 publishing its own manual on the laws of war.

But the conference's preeminent legal mind indicated the growing appeal of international law in another quarter as well. Fedor Martens, a law professor at Saint Petersburg University and the author of the basic text considered at the conference, was a jurist enjoying very close relations to the tsar. He was also a staunch defender of the idea that Great Powers stood to benefit from promoting international law. Unlike the British, whose global power meant that they were not especially interested in binding legal commitments, and the Germans, whose generals resisted legal constraints as disadvantaging them strategically, the Russians were keen to identify themselves with the idea of transforming warfare through legal means. "Whichever state claims the cause of the [1874] Brussels Conference," claimed Martens, "will claim first place among those states which understand the true goals of modern civilization and which respect the lawful aspirations of civilized peoples." Claiming the mantle of "modern civilization" itself mattered a great deal to the Russians, because they were so often accused of primitivism, and in the late nineteenth century that was not a charge any European power could accept with indifference.[7]

THE STANDARD OF CIVILIZATION

Despite the new profession's proud boast of its impartiality and its scientific approach to legal and social problems, late Victorian international lawyers rooted their discipline in the regnant ideological assumptions of the age. Preeminent among these was the belief in the superiority of European civilization. "I was convinced that international law existed in a relationship of reciprocal influence with the growth of civilization," wrote Bluntschli, "and that every major advance in human progress meant also progress for international law."[8] During the Napoleonic Wars, the French utopian Charles Fourier had repeatedly denounced civilization as a self-serving myth and called for philosophers to treat all mankind equally. But once the war ended this kind of critical romanticism retreated; indeed, civilization assumed a new and more popular meaning, especially once Benjamin Constant popularized the contrast between the militarism of the Napoleonic empire and the civilizing effects of the commercial British.[9] The term soon facilitated a kind of cultural mapping of the world, one with Europe at its center: civilization was regarded by men such as French historian-politician François Guizot both as what the various European states shared and as what demarcated the boundary between Europe and the rest of the world. John Stuart Mill, in his 1836 essay on the subject, argued that European civilization represented that superior stage of modernity enjoyed by peoples with urban societies under the rule of law that enjoyed internal stability and freedom of association. States like the Ottoman Empire, in contrast, were examples of civilizational failure, ruling over "populations now wholly barbaric, which have made some progress in state organization but which manifest incapacity to solve the problem of political civilization with any degree of completeness." Through such conceptions of civilization, Europe asserted its right to lead the world on the basis of a set of supposedly universal rules. In the grandiloquent words of the Mazzinian Italian lawyer Pasquale Fiore, "The unity of the human species conduces to the recognition that the empire of legal rules that are applicable to all forms of human activity in the *Magna civitas* must be universal."[10]

Granted the existence of very different cultures and societies around the world, what the lawyers did was to show how the idea of a standard of civilization could provide a criterion for determining global rank and appropriate diplomatic practice. At the top were assumed to stand the civilized—Europeans, or former European settler colonies. Below them stood "barbaric" powers like the Ottomans and the Chinese that had an institutional history and some state capacity. At the bottom were the "savage" peoples of Africa and the Pacific. This tripartite schema became more rigid over time, and indeed was eventually itself codified in the law textbooks. In 1840 it was still possible for the powers to extend an invitation to the Egyptian ruler Mehmet Ali to join the "Public System of Europe," and in

1856 a similar gesture was made to the Ottoman sultan at the end of the Crimean War. By the time of the next great Near Eastern crisis in 1876, such offers were no longer put on the table. The Ottoman and Egyptian polities had in fact modernized rather quickly, but European attitudes toward them had hardened faster still.[11]

Another of the founding members of the Institute of International Law, Edinburgh professor James Lorimer, taught that to the three levels of civilized society there were three corresponding kinds of state recognition—what he called plenary political, partial political, and finally natural, or merely human. That savages did not deserve full international recognition met with near universal agreement, but other lawyers disputed whether barbaric states like the Ottomans or the Chinese might be allowed a foot in the door. Although the new international law, wrote John Westlake, "was a product of the special civilization of modern Europe," nevertheless, "our international society exercises the right of admitting outside states to part of its international law without necessarily admitting them to the whole of it." Others disagreed: entry into the "circle of law-governed countries" was an all-or-nothing matter and "full recognition" for most non-Europeans all but impossible. Either way, they were definitely inferior—at least until they defeated European powers in battle, as the Japanese famously did in the 1905 war with Russia, an earthquake in world history precisely because it threatened to overturn the whole hierarchy posited by the standard-of-civilization idea. In the ironic words of a Japanese diplomat, "We show ourselves at least your equals in scientific butchery and at once are admitted to your council tables as civilized men."[12]

The potentially horrible consequences of these legal formulations emerged at the Berlin colonial conference of 1884–85. This was basically an attempt to manage European rivalries in Africa, but it was filled with talk of the civilizing mission as a rationale for legitimating control over Africans. The concluding act talked of the need to "initiate the indigenous populations into the advantages of civilization," and the lawyers discussed new constitutional arrangements such as protectorates "in which the touch of civilization is cautiously applied to matters barbaric." King Leopold of Belgium employed a prominent English lawyer, Sir Travers Twiss (another member of the institute), to act as his legal publicist and was awarded the Congo Free State on these high-minded grounds. Twiss himself was invited at the conference not only to draft the new constitution, which unsurprisingly gave sweeping powers to Leopold himself, but chaired the commission tasked with drawing up the legal rules that were to govern colonial occupations in general. The lawyers thus created a new language for European states to use to assess each other's claims to colonial territory. As a means of rescuing the mission of empire from its darker, dirtier side, this language of responsibilities, care, and duties survives with surprisingly few alterations into our own times as the vocabulary with which a postcolonial "international community" now validates rule by its own executive organs, in the shape of the United Nations.[13]

At Berlin, fellow institute members cheered from the sidelines. According to leading Dutch international lawyer Tobias Asser, the Congo Free State was founded "not with the usual narrow-minded intent to which European statecraft has accustomed us, but to ensure civilization and wealth in general." The founder of the Institute of International Law, Gustave Rolin-Jaequemyns, greeted the award with similar enthusiasm and regarded the entire Berlin conference as one in which the international lawyers had proved their usefulness in helping articulate clear standards for state behavior. Rolin-Jaequemyns, advocate of the "spirit of internationalism" (*l'esprit d'internationalité*), kept quiet as news of the horrors of Belgian rule in the Congo leaked out. His Belgian colleague, Ernest Nys, the first professional historian of international law, saw the 1885 Berlin Act as revealing the European powers' determination to look after Africans and help them along the path to civilization; attacks on Leopold he wrote off as motivated by British commercial rivalry.[14]

In an era of accelerated colonialism, therefore, lawyers were helpful, arguing that it was obviously "in the interest of the world's civilization that law and order and the true liberty consistent therewith shall reign everywhere upon the globe." Only Professor Lorimer was an exception to the general high-mindedness, cutting through the wishful thinking by reminding his students that all talk of law was really another means of claiming power:

> The moment that the power to help a retrograde race forward toward the goal of human life consciously exists in a civilized nation, that civilized nation is bound to exert its power; and in the exercise of its power, it is entitled to assume an attitude of guardianship, and put wholly aside the proximate will of the retrograde race. Its own civilization, having resulted from the exercise of a will which it regards as rational, real and ultimate, at least when contrasted with the irrational, phenomenal and proximate will of the inferior race, it is entitled to assume that it vindicates the ultimate will of the inferior race—the will, that is to say, at which the inferior race must arrive when it reaches the stage of civilization to which the higher race has attained.

In less academic language, what Lorimer was conveying was simply that the stronger knows best: we are already close to the idea that an international society of nations is obliged to care for its weakest members, whether they wish it or not, an idea that would produce the League mandates, the UN trusteeships of the twentieth century, and the quasi-protectorates of the twenty-first.

But nineteenth-century international law was double-faced; at the same time that lawyers justified the extension of colonial rule overseas, they defended its value for the emergent society of sovereign national states in Europe (and when they remembered, the Americas). In an 1868 essay on nationalism and internationalism, Francis Lieber stressed the compatibility of the two: "The civilized nations have come to constitute a community, and are daily forming more and more a commonwealth of nations, under the restraint and protection of the law of nations."[15] In this sense, law helped to formalize the Mazzinian vision for a Europe of nations.

The bifurcating impact of this new approach—humanizing relations between civilized states while simultaneously removing many of the impediments and inhibitions that older generations of legal theorists had built up to preserve civility in relations with less powerful peoples outside Europe—was nowhere more evident than in the lawyers' proudest achievement—the Hague conferences' codification of the laws of war. By 1898, when Tsar Nicholas II proposed a large international peace conference, the European arms race was under way and politicians were increasingly troubled by the costs of rearmament.[16] Yet once they all met at The Hague, the acute differences of approach among the participants nearly brought proceedings to a halt. In particular, the conference witnessed bitter arguments between the Germans, on the one hand, and the Belgians and Dutch, on the other, over the rules of military occupation. The Germans, with their experiences in France in 1870–71 fresh in their minds, wanted unconditional obedience from occupied populations; the others—equally mindful of the same events—wanted civilians to face no obligations but proposed stringent checks on the occupying power. Fortunately Fedor Martens devised a fudge, and the eventual preamble to the Hague regulations concerning the laws and customs of war simply noted with studied vagueness that "populations and belligerents remain under the protection and empire of the principles of international law, as they result from the usages established between civilized nations, from the laws of humanity, and from the requirements of the public conscience."

The legal doctrine of military occupation itself was intended to regulate a provisional state of affairs in which one sovereign's forces ran the territory of another without prejudicing the latter's claims to ultimate control. The very notion of occupation had only made its appearance since the defeat of Napoleon. Previously states had acquired title to the territories of other states simply by defeating them in war. But the Concert system challenged this because it was based on an assumption of tolerance for the claims of all member sovereigns. If sovereigns coexisted and the Concert had any meaning, then the unilateral right to take territory through war vanished, to be replaced by negotiation, consideration of how other powers might be affected, and eventual recognition through treaty. Thus formal military occupation as a provisional state—between actual fighting and the peace settlement—was first discussed only as late as 1844.[17]

But this approach, designed to smooth relations among European powers, did not apply to "savage peoples," since they lacked a recognized sovereign. The lands of "barbarians"—in North Africa, say, or the Middle East—could be "occupied"; but in practice, such occupations often became permanent, as happened after the Russian army invaded Ottoman Bulgaria and Habsburg troops took Bosnia during the Near Eastern crisis of 1875–78. Bulgaria became first autonomous and then independent, while Bosnia ended up inside the Austro-Hungarian Empire. Far from leaving existing Ottoman institutions intact, the occupiers introduced sweeping reforms: the Habsburgs had their own civilizing mission in Bosnia after 1878, as did the Russians in Bulgaria and the English in Egypt. A legal theorist writing after the American occupation of Iraq in 2003 called this "transformative occupation": it certainly bore no resemblance to anything agreed to at The Hague as between civilized states.

The 1899 discussions did produce some notable results in the realm of warfare. They outlawed bombing from the air, chemical weapons, and hollow bullets, and they succeeded in confirming that military occupation was a temporary, provisional state of affairs among two sovereign states. But the peace activists who followed the discussions were disappointed. Disarmament was never seriously discussed, and it became obvious that many powers had sent delegates to attend chiefly for fear of criticism if they did not; once at The Hague they did only as much as was necessary to placate criticism at home. The German foreign minister, for instance, instructed his delegation that "we must be able to demonstrate to German public opinion that we attempted to devote our best efforts to the humanitarian work of the conference, at the same time that we avoided unpractical and dangerous alternatives." And where military matters were concerned, the voice of the generals naturally remained far more powerful than the lawyers. The former were not apologetic about their profession—the post-Napoleonic antiwar mood had vanished long before: Field Marshal von Moltke reminded Heidelberg law professor Bluntschli in December 1880, for instance, that "perpetual peace is a dream and not even a beautiful dream. War is an element of the divine order of the world."[18]

In reflecting the standard-of-civilization approach, then, the Hague rules only aspired to regulate conflicts between two "civilized" powers.[19] But in this way, the spread of international legal arguments in diplomacy helped to remove the protection of the law from everyone else. One of the disturbing implications of being written off as uncivilized was that if Africans or Asians sought to resist European incursions they could be treated as if they lay outside the law. For legal discourse now started to shape the behavior of colonial troops. The 1914 British manual of military law noted that "the rules of international law apply only to warfare between civilised nations, where both parties undertake them and are prepared to carry them out. They do not apply in wars with uncivilised States and tribes, where their place is taken by the discretion of the commander and such rules of justice and humanity as recommend themselves in the particular circumstances of the case."

Reciprocity was the fundamental condition for inclusion within the "empire of law," and in its absence, some argued that anything was permitted that was necessary to compel obedience from an enemy too maddened or ignorant to converse with. This was a trope with a long life ahead of it, especially once airpower became an acknowledged instrument of colonial control. Long before "Shock and Awe" in Iraq, and half a century before CIA officer William Colby pioneered a highly controversial "hearts and minds" program to pacify Vietcong sympathizers, his father, the American counterinsurgency specialist Eldridge Colby, had penned a lucid and revealing essay on "How to Fight Savage Tribes" that summed up this approach. According to Colby, primitive peoples incapable of rational negotiation needed to be tackled differently from others:

> It is good to observe the decencies of international law. But it is a fact that against uncivilized people who do not know international law, and do not observe it, and would take advantage of one who did, there must be something else. The "something else" should not be a relaxation of all bonds of restraint. . . . But . . . this is a different kind of war. To a Frenchman, a shell striking Rheims Cathedral . . . is a lawless act of the enemy which infuriates the temperamental soul and arouses wrath. . . . To a fanatical savage, a bomb dropped out of the sky on the sacred temple of his omnipotent God is a sign and a symbol that God has withdrawn his favor. A shell smashing into a putative inaccessible village stronghold is an indication of the relentless energy and superior skill of the well-equipped civilized foe. Instead of merely rousing his wrath, these acts are much more likely to make him raise his hands in surrender. If a few "non-combatants" are killed, the loss of life is probably far less than might have been sustained in prolonged operations of a more polite character. The inhumane act thus becomes actually humane.[20]

Legal theory thus translated into the massacres, aerial bombings, and systematic detentions that characterized European imperialism and that pointed to the extreme brutality of conflicts deemed to be beyond law's sway. Even before Belgian rule in the Congo became a byword for savagery, a critical book by the young Winston Churchill had revealed how an Anglo-Egyptian force equipped with modern rifles and artillery under Sir Herbert Kitchener had killed ten thousand members of the Mahdi army in the Sudan for the loss of forty-eight of their own soldiers at the battle of Omdurman. The Hague Conventions did little to change this; if anything, they now allowed the case for brutality to be presented in a legalistic guise. Dropping bombs from balloons had been expressly prohibited in the 1899 Hague Convention—but only between signatories. From its first use by the Italians in Libya in 1911, through the campaigns waged in Afghanistan and Iraq by the Royal Air Force after the First World War, bombing from the air offered colonial powers a low-cost method of suppressing native discontent. Was there not some mysterious alchemy at work in a set of arguments that turned the civilized soldier into a substitute for God—yoking together omnipotence and virtue, and sowing death from the heavens—and all this in the name of progress and international law?

The British journalist W. T. Stead, writing shortly after the first Hague peace conference, was struck by the contrast between two contrasting forms of internationalism that were operative at the start of a new century. Inside Europe, civilization meant peace; outside it, violence. In Paris, visitors to the Exposition Universelle were reclining in deck chairs in the shadow of the Eiffel Tower watching the world spin by on an enormous *Globe Céleste*, and gawping at marvels like the first talking pictures and escalators. Yet at that very moment, what he termed the "new internationalism" of a rampaging expeditionary force was erupting in China—an international policing power, composed of "a motley host . . . men of all continents, of all religions and of all races." This made it all the more urgent, he went on, to take advantage of the possibility laid down in the Hague Convention to appoint an international committee of investigation to find out the facts. The question he raised was whether the true internationalism that the world so urgently needed could survive the crusading spirit of the international policing expedition and "the forces of grab and greed and insatiable aggression."[21]

Whatever the facts that had led to the uprising, the behavior of the expedition that was mounted to suppress the Chinese nationalist uprising known as the Boxer Rebellion could not have demonstrated more forcibly what was at stake in the Hague discussions. The Russians sent their men to China with orders to operate within the parameters of international law as they understood them, and they instructed their soldiers to show restraint, avoid "unnecessary bloodshed," and to pay for goods they confiscated. The German military took a harsher line. It was not just that the Chinese fell outside the law; they were presented as a legitimate object of vengeance. Kaiser Wilhelm made himself notorious by sending off his men with a bloodcurdling speech whose invocation of the Huns worried the diplomats so much that they issued an edited version and added a completely spurious exhortation to "open the way to civilization once and for all."[22]

Creating a sharp dichotomy between the civilized and the barbarian thus had disturbing implications; but the Hague rules themselves were not the solution to all problems either, not least because they left so much to the interpretation of individual parties. In Belgium in 1914—the test case for the British and Americans that proved the Germans really were Huns—the German army was in fact largely following their own understanding of what the new rules of war permitted. Much like the British in Egypt, who were unilaterally rewriting the rules of their occupation there at the same time, they took the view that a "transfer of authority" from the Belgian king to the occupying forces eliminated the king's claims to sovereign competence. The Germans claimed the right to legislate and issue decrees, to replace local officials, and to take over the economy for the war effort. In Serbia, the Habsburg army was similarly dictatorial, at once aiming to punish any signs of resistance with exemplary severity and keen to preserve its standing as a stern but fair dispenser of justice. The truth was that the Hague provisions covering the transfer of power from former sovereign to new occupation force were inherently ambiguous, as such ambiguity had been the price paid for getting international agreement in the first place.[23]

It is thus not surprising that by the turn of the century international lawyers had come to seem to radical critics—as they had earlier for Immanuel Kant—as much part of the problem as the solution. It was not just that so many of the men of 1873 had become more conservative and more nationalistic as they became more respectable and renowned—by the century's end, they were denouncing socialism and anarchism, drafting extradition treaties for political crimes, and sounding increasingly antidemocratic. It was rather that law itself looked like a rationalization of plunder, a world made free for the mighty to rob while claiming that justice was on their side. Indeed, some critical voices from within the international law profession started to wonder about whether the new doctrines in threatening non-Europeans with unrestrained violence did not in fact jeopardize European liberties as well. "The pretended right to spread civilization," wrote the French lawyer Frantz Despargnet, had been deployed "to despoil savage peoples of their sovereignty." Charles Salomon went one stage further: "Beware! The pretended right of civilization could serve to legitimize the gravest attacks, even in Europe. . . . Is there not a German civilization, a Slavic civilization, a Latin civilization? Have we not often supported the incontestable superiority of one over the other?" With the massive aerial bombing of European cities in the Second World War, Europeans would treat each other with the methods they had once reserved for "savages." That conflict marked the effective demise of the Victorian idea of the supremacy of European civilization itself and the onset of a crisis in the self-confidence and standing of international law from which it has never fully recovered.[24]

CREMER'S CAUSE

The follow-up to the 1899 Hague peace conference took place in 1907. More countries took part and there was a much greater participation of nations from outside Europe, especially from the Americas. The American lawyer representing imperial China, John Foster, attended with his grandson, a nineteen-year-old sophomore at Princeton University named John Foster Dulles, who was getting his first taste of diplomacy. For his grandfather, a highly experienced American diplomat, the 1907 conference was "in some respects the most important event in the history of the human race. It was the first time that the political representatives of all the nations of the earth had met together."[25]

The Peace Palace, which was constructed at The Hague shortly afterward, was an impressive testimony to the new forces that were transforming the conduct of international relations, still rooted in the European model of civilization but gesturing toward something more encompassing. Authority and hope were conveyed in the Renaissance aspirations of the gargantuan palazzo that emerged, its campanile soaring above the Dutch plains. Its paneled rooms were lit with electric candelabras, yellow copper chandeliers, and neomedieval stained glass and filled with gifts from nations that attended in 1907—Arabescato marble from Italy, Japanese silk wall hangings, a Swiss clock, rugs from Persia, a statue of Christ from Argentina, and an extraordinary 3.2-ton jasper and gilt vase from Russia. That the palace existed at all was equally instructive: it had grown out of conversations that took place at The Hague between two of the world's leading professor-diplomats, the Russian Fedor Martens and the American Andrew Dickson White, and it had been funded thanks to the latter's contacts with the phenomenally wealthy American-Scottish steel magnate Andrew Carnegie, a notorious union-buster who was also the world's most generous supporter of pacifist causes in the decade before the First World War.

Marking the first significant influence of private philanthropic wealth on the emergent institutions of the new internationalism, the palace testified in the most concrete terms to how much had changed in the world of diplomacy since Metternich's day. The United States itself was a new presence at the highest levels of international diplomacy, and the palace symbolized this. Carnegie, the emblematic self-made man whose career had begun as a humble telegraph operator, was a fervent supporter of internationalist pacifist causes, and of arbitration in particular, and he responded favorably when Dickson White broached the idea of a Palace of Peace.

Yet in terms of real political achievements, the palace was not much more than an act of faith in the future. The second Hague conference itself had been set back a year by the Russo-Japanese War, and when it did eventually meet, the public reaction in pacifist circles was again one of enormous disappointment. There was no initiative to rein in the arms race already under way between the major powers and no real support for the idea of creating an international police force to compel the results of international arbitration to be accepted by disputant states. In international law, there was little advance on the achievements of the first conference, and most of the lawyers looked ahead to a third meeting for any chance of progress.

The one area where some progress was made, however, was on the question of a new machinery of interstate arbitration. As a result, when the seventy-eight-year-old Carnegie visited the palace in 1913 to celebrate its opening, he unveiled the bust of a contemporary who was almost as remarkable as he was—the British peace activist Sir Randal Cremer, who had died five years earlier. Although today almost no one remembers the name of this former union organizer, he was a man known to and respected both by Carnegie (perhaps the age's greatest capitalist) and by Karl Marx (capitalism's greatest critic). It is not easy to find the stone stele that marks Cremer's final resting place in Hampstead Cemetery in London—far less signposted or visited than Marx's massive bust only a mile or so away. Yet Marx owed his invitation to join the International Working Men's Association in the far-off days of 1864 to none other than Cremer, and in the decades that followed William Randal Cremer came a long way. From a background that would have disqualified him from playing any role in the old diplomacy—his father was a coachman who had run away shortly after his birth—he became an MP after years spent fighting for workers' rights and electoral reform, and saw his career crowned by becoming the first Briton to be awarded the Nobel Peace Prize. He was well known as the founder of the Inter-Parliamentary Union, but his passion in foreign affairs and the basis for his receiving the Peace Prize was something else—the arbitration movement. Carved on his gravestone, a sword rests against an olive branch next to an open book engraved with the words "Arbitration Treaty." Through his life and work we can see the rise of what was by the outbreak of the Great War in 1914 probably the single most influential strand of internationalism—the campaign for international arbitration—a movement whose success in the years before the war was matched only by the marginalization that greeted it in the decades after it.

"THE FRIENDS AND ADVOCATES of peace are getting into very respectable society," noted Cremer's journal the *Arbitrator* in 1887, and it was indeed true that the arbitration movement by its nature required compromising with the existing system of diplomacy. It implied an adjustment, a revision of how politics were conducted between states rather than a wholesale change. As far back as the 1830s, American pacifists had argued for replacing Europe's old diplomacy with arbitration treaties, but it was the Crimean War, and what was widely regarded as the breakdown of the Concert diplomatic system, that spurred the search for new ways of improving international relations. The Treaty of Paris, which settled the peace in 1856, actually provided for mediation between any of the signatories in the event of friction. But how could this be enforced? Some argued that if states did not police themselves, the whole arrangement was moot anyway. The radical laissez-faire economist Gustave de Molinari argued that since Europe had actually been ruled by five Great Powers since 1815, the logical thing to do would be to ratify the existence of this *concert universel* and safeguard it by creating a small international police force able to enforce the settlement of disputes among its members. John Stuart Mill suggested making rules for the duration of treaties and laying down what should be done when they were superseded. He hoped that "the nations of the civilized world might concur in the framing of such a code."

Richard Cobden was a staunch supporter of the idea of arbitration, a cause he pleaded at length in the House of Commons, singling it out for its practicality as a plan "that does not embrace the scheme of a congress of nations, or imply the belief in the millennium, or demand your homage to the principles of non-resistance." From the heart of the peace movement, the longtime British activist and MP Henry Richard worked alongside Cobden in the campaign. In 1849

Richard participated with him at the peace congress in Paris; when he finally stepped down as secretary of the London Peace Society in May 1885, after thirty-seven years in the post, the "Apostle of Peace" argued that "the charges now being brought against us, of being missionaries and preachers of impractical Utopias," were simply wrong. With its support for international arbitration the peace movement asserted its realism. This was a constant motif, asserted ever more emphatically (and plausibly) over time: describing the men who participated in the 1907 Hague conference, one of the leading American figures in the arbitration movement praised them as "neither dreamers nor theorists but men of eminently practical experience in government, diplomacy and war."[26]

Randal Cremer himself entered Parliament for an East London constituency in 1885, the year of Richard's death, and he brought with him not only the concerns of labor but also the internationalist goals of the old midcentury peace activists. In the Cobdenite tradition, Cremer believed fervently that arbitration treaties could serve as a practical and effective means of guaranteeing peace among nations. As early as 1868, in his first unsuccessful run for Parliament, he had declared his support for setting up "international Boards of Arbitration to settle disputes among nations" and thereby usher in "an era of peace."[27] When he ran next, in 1874, he added to his program the idea of codifying international law and "the establishment of an international tribunal for the peaceful settlement of disputes among nations."[28] His Workingmen's Peace Committee advocated arbitration "as a substitute for war," and turned into the International Arbitration League, with its own newspaper and a publishing business that produced pamphlets attacking the British intervention in Egypt and imperialism in general.

What Cremer and the arbitrationists articulated was a further strand of nineteenth-century internationalism, quite distinct both from Mazzini's advocacy of a divinely inspired harmony among nations hastened through liberation struggles and revolution, and Marx's scientistic stress on a future proletarian nirvana. It mapped out the path to peace more gradually, explicitly, and deliberately than either of these—via the impartiality of parliamentarians and international jurors, guided by a consensual body of law and above all by the reason and trust implicit in the arbitration process itself. It is a strand that has remained in the shadows, however, perhaps because unlike the other two, it failed for most of the twentieth century to acquire serious Great Power sponsorship.

As two generations of pacifists had done before him, Cremer saw in the United States the best means of converting the Old World to a new mode of diplomacy, and as an MP he cultivated contacts in Washington. The Anglo-American connection was critical for the arbitrationists because the relationship was still rocky enough to be disturbed by major disagreements, yet close enough to make war seem irrational. But it was just in these years and through this movement that the foundations were laid for the later "special relationship." In 1872, the famous *Alabama* case over damages caused by British-built Confederate warships in the Civil War was settled through arbitration (thereby heading off an American threat to take over parts of Canada), and this gave the movement a valuable boost. It made the headlines again in 1895 in another, more serious Anglo-American crisis, when a disputed boundary between Venezuela and British Guiana turned into a major diplomatic argument that was again headed off by adjudication. Gladstone himself was only the best known of the many public figures in London, Cremer among them, who called for a permanent system of arbitration between the two great English-speaking countries. "Always Arbitrate before you Fight" urged the journalist W. T. Stead in a pamphlet of the time.[29]

There was idealism in this but politics and strategy too. British Liberals were well aware that the Venezuela crisis had only arisen because the United States had taken upon itself to interpret the Monroe Doctrine in a fashion that inaugurated a more possessive attitude toward Central and South America. But they did not mind, because they thought the growth of American power in the hemisphere and in the world was in Britain's interest, and they welcomed arbitration because it offered a way to cement an Anglo-American alliance. Cremer, who tirelessly promoted the idea of a general arbitration treaty between the United States and Great Britain, was thus in tune with the times, a policymaker whose ideals were turning out to be practical alternatives to the old diplomacy.

He was helped by his careful choice of allies. Increasingly assertive abroad, U.S. administrations at the turn of the new century adopted the arbitration cause for the same reason that the Russian tsar took on the cause of international law—as a means of eradicating threats while consolidating their reputation in the eyes of the world. Promoted at the 1890 International American Congress in Washington, which approved a motion to "adopt arbitration as a principle of American international law" throughout the hemisphere, the movement came for a brief moment to enjoy some success as a distinctively American contribution to world peace. Known for his gung-ho foreign policy toward lesser breeds, President Theodore Roosevelt supported the idea of arbitration as helpful in pacifying relations between Great Powers, and in 1902 he breathed life into the Permanent Court of Arbitration established three years before. When European peace activists complained to him that the new court was being sidelined and in danger of fading into irrelevance for lack of work, Roosevelt dusted off an old dispute with Mexico that both sides agreed to send to The Hague. It was also Roosevelt who suggested there should be a second international conference at The Hague to continue the work of the 1899 meeting, and when the Russo-Japanese War interrupted the preparations, he acted as mediator between the two sides in their peace negotiations, earning himself the Nobel Peace Prize in 1906. As the Norwegian statesman who presented the prize noted:

> Twelve or fifteen years ago . . . the cause of peace presented a very different aspect from the one it presents today. The cause was then regarded as a utopian idea and its advocates as well-meaning but overly enthusiastic idealists who had no place in practical politics, being out of touch with the realities of life. The situation has altered

> radically since then, for in recent years leading statesmen, even heads of state, have espoused the cause, which has now acquired a totally different image in public opinion.[30]

Cremer must have been deeply satisfied. Roosevelt's initiative to revive the Hague peace process had in fact been prompted by a call from another Cremer creation—the Inter-Parliamentary Union—which had held its congress in St. Louis in 1904. Cremer had been instrumental in setting up the IPU in 1889 and was its vice president and head of the British section. It grew very rapidly indeed in the last decade of the century (it is still in existence, a shadow of its former self), and it offered Cremer a platform to propagandize for the creation of an international arbitration tribunal. The Russian tsar and an American president might have been the figures publically credited for the two Hague conferences, but without Cremer neither would have happened. It was in recognition of all this that in 1903, three years before President Roosevelt, he was awarded the Nobel Peace Prize. That the coachman's son from Portsmouth could have risen to such prominence was an indication of the revolutionary changes coming over the conduct of international affairs.

In his acceptance speech, the elderly Cremer meditated on his long journey. Summing up the passage from the utopian preaching of activists in his youth to practical politics, he recollected how "pilgrims of peace" like himself had long been written off as dreamers. Now, though, the usefulness of arbitration had been amply demonstrated, and he cited in his support very recent events in the North Sea that had nearly led to war between Britain and Russia:

> Thirty-four years ago, when the organization of which I am secretary formulated a plan for the establishment of a "High Court of Nations," we were laughed to scorn as mere theorists and utopians, the scoffers emphatically declaring that no two countries in the world would ever agree to take part in the establishment of such a court.

> Today we proudly point to the fact that the Hague Tribunal *has* been established; and notwithstanding the unfortunate blow it received in the early stages of its existence by the Boer War and the attempt on the part of some nations to boycott it, there is now a general consensus of opinion that it has come to stay—and thanks to the munificence of Mr. Carnegie, this high court of nations will be provided with a permanent home in a Palace of Peace. If evidence had been wanting as to the desirability and usefulness of such a tribunal, the recent "Dogger Bank" incident supplied it. Had there been no tribunal in existence, Russia and Great Britain would probably have taken months to consider whether the so-called outrage was a fit subject to be referred to arbitration, and that delay would have been used by the crimson press to lash the public mind into a state of frenzy and to render a pacific solution impossible. But the very fact that the peaceful machinery was at hand, ready to be set in motion, suggested its employment, and notwithstanding the frantic efforts of some British journals to provoke a conflict, the two governments in a few days agreed to resort to the friendly offices of the Hague Tribunal.

In making this transition to practical politics, enlisting the support of the U.S. government had been vital, he continued. Arbitration agreements had proliferated, and their practical benefits showed it had been right to make them, not disarmament, the immediate priority. But for all his praise for the high and mighty who had supported him, Cremer was at pains to remind his audience that this achievement was first and foremost a "people's victory." Although it was a result of the success of the Inter-Parliamentary Union, its roots lay much further back in the past. Linking it to the radical labor activists of the middle of the nineteenth century with whom he had started out, he cast his mind back to when, many decades earlier, "British and French workmen inaugurated a series of conferences and meetings and the circulation of mutual addresses to their countrymen in favor of a better understanding between the peoples."[31]

Yet as none knew better than Cremer himself, the arbitration movement flourished only because it managed to enlist the support of some powerful figures in government. Cremer's most important partner in the IPU, for instance, was the French pacifist Frédéric Passy, a former minister. Another supporter was William Jennings Bryan, a leading prewar figure in the Democratic Party and Woodrow Wilson's first secretary of state: Cremer credited him with winning the IPU over to the arbitration cause. Preeminent among the Republicans was Elihu Root, secretary of state under Theodore Roosevelt, who believed in arbitration as a means of developing the Great Power status of the United States, sponsored the creation of a court to settle hemispheric disputes, and negotiated numerous arbitration treaties.[32]

By 1902 supporters of arbitration and international law in general were hailing half a century of progress in which "the awakened conscience of the world" had redefined the very notion of a concert of nations and transformed "the rules and regulation of international relations." Of course, they were constantly faced with the objection that arbitration provided no guarantee of peace. The left charged that there would be wars so long as capitalism existed. The right wanted to protect the nation's prerogatives and accused the peace movement, even in this most respectable of incarnations, of being led astray by high-mindedness.[33]

Yet the mainstream of the arbitration movement was made up of pragmatists who praised the relative modesty of their procedures and goals compared with the grander idea of international government. John Westlake, a British member of The Hague's Permanent Court of Arbitration, argued that it offered, in an age of growing attachment to the idea of national independence, a practical route to pacifying the behavior of states. It was in keeping, he wrote, with the evolution of human affairs—an important consideration in the Darwinian fin-de-siècle—and it would be most effective when least likely to raise nationalist hackles; in other words, by refraining from "trying to convert international arbitration into international judicature." There was, suggested Westlake, general agreement that there should be limits to international arbitration, and these limits were basically reached once questions ceased to be of a legal character but were essentially political. Arbitration was not the answer to all disputes, but that certainly did not mean it was worthless.[34]

When the American Elihu Root was awarded the Nobel Peace Prize in 1912, he too hailed the pioneers of the arbitration movement and the enormous practical change they had wrought in international affairs in only a few years. It was, he argued, no easy thing to reverse the impact of centuries of Darwinian struggle upon mankind—breeding for war could not be reversed overnight. Echoing Westlake, he felt that the idea of setting up "a parliament of man with authority to control the conduct of nations by legislation or an international police force" was wholly implausible; people had too fierce a sense of their own national pride. "Practical idealism" was establishing a "new standard of international conduct"—as some 113 treaties since 1906 testified. International law was also being placed on a firmer and more scientific footing. With proper education, it would be strengthened further. Worldwide public opinion was learning to "think internationally," and this was a new constraint on belligerence—"the general judgment of mankind" was "a great new force" at work in international affairs. As "civilised man" became "less cruel" and more conscious of the horrors of war and the need for "national self-restraint," there were grounds for "cheerful hope."

Root, however, like other leading international lawyers did not believe that arbitration itself was enough. In Europe, several of them called for the creation of an international court and in the United States, they sought to do precisely what Westlake warned against—moving beyond arbitration into "international judicature." Not only was the Permanent Court set up at The Hague a very weak and still marginal institution, but at a more fundamental level, the very idea of arbitration in their view revolved very problematically around the desirability of compromise between interests rather than fidelity to the law. The new Hague court, wrote a distinguished Greek international lawyer in terms Root would have entirely accepted, was not "a true international tribunal" but "an adjunct to the chancelleries." Root himself believed that impartial lawyers were better placed than necessarily partial diplomats for settling international disputes. The fear was that a series of arbitration treaties and decisions would by itself be insufficient to bring into being a body of consistent international law.

Thus early in the new century the legal professionals began to emphasize their differences with the arbitrationists. Growing out of the American arbitration movement, and moving away from it, leading U.S. international lawyers banded together in 1905 to form a new American Society of International Law that was directed "exclusively to the interests of international law as distinct from international arbitration." Supported once more from the ample pockets of Andrew Carnegie, they sought international backing for their own dream of law's apotheosis—the creation of a world court that would create a body of case law—and Root himself proposed this at the 1907 follow-up conference at The Hague, ushering in several decades of American commitment to the world court idea.[35]

A century later, when the American Society of International Law celebrated its centennial in the dark days that followed the invasion of Iraq, its members turned back to Elihu Root and invoked his memory to set America straight. They appealed to his faith in law and his belief in the superiority of democracies. But turning Root into an inspiration for American global leadership in the twenty-first century meant overlooking a lot that was central to his worldview and that of his generation. Root's democratic commitment was real but thin, for his was an elitist vision, which talked a lot about public opinion but regarded it as something to be educated, and believed power should be put in the hands of a small group of scientifically trained legal experts. It was a conservative vision in that it sought to defuse political, social, and economic conflicts by reducing clashes of interest and equity to matters of legal principle. And it was also of course for all its purported universal applicability a very American vision—often explicitly modeled on the functioning of the Supreme Court—that captured the imagination of the generation of lawyer/policymakers who dominated American foreign policy in the era in which the United States emerged as a Great Power.[36]

Root was a leading member of the American Society of International Law, but he was not alone: incredibly, between 1897 and 1920 every secretary of state except one was a member. Yet the society's reach was in fact quite limited. There was no equivalent to its dominance in any other major power, and outside the United States, enthusiasm for handing the destiny of the world over to a cadre of unelected jurists was very limited. Legalism had its sympathizers in France, Russia, and Britain, but its heartland was in America. Even there it faced great opposition, above all in the Senate, to any limit or constraint upon American sovereignty. So long as the project of international law was presented as requiring full American participation, its advocates would time and again run into this roadblock, and indeed the Senate voted down or circumscribed many of the diplomatic initiatives that Root, Bryan, and others advanced before the war, just as it would vote down the League of Nations after it. Only once the United States had risen to global hegemony after 1945 would it be possible to reconcile American universalism and American exceptionalism. But by that time, international law as a credo was a shadow of its former self, and hardly anyone believed that in an era of total war and nuclear power international arbitration could solve the world's problems.

CHAPTER 4

Science the Unifier

> **The co-operation of different nations in the joint investigation of the constitution of the terrestrial globe, of the phenomena which take place at its surface and of the celestial bodies which shine equally upon all, directs attention to our common interests and exposes the artificial nature of political boundaries. The meetings in common discussion of earnest workers in the fields of knowledge tend to obliterate the superficial distinctions of manner and outward bearing which so often get exaggerated until they are mistaken for deep-seated national characteristics. . . . I do not wish to exaggerate the civilizing value of scientific investigation, but the great problems of creation link all humanity together, and it may yet come to pass that when diplomacy fails—and it often comes perilously near failure—it will fall to the men of science and learning to preserve the peace of the world.**
>
> **—Arthur Schuster, "International Science" (1906)[1]**

THE CONCERT OF EUROPE had no bureaucracy of its own, no headquarters, and no secretariat. As for its radical critics, they generally thought little about creating permanent institutions either, since they saw the passage to universal peace in such spontaneous forces as the unfolding of human reason or of God's will, in tendencies within capitalism or through the emergence of public opinion. All of them were better at sketching out the contours of the coming utopia than at specifying the agencies through which it would be brought into being. If the story of international cooperation were confined to the Concert and its initial opponents, therefore, there would be next to no international *organizations* to talk about at all.

To understand how the latter emerged and then became an established feature of the modern political landscape, we have to look elsewhere—to the authority of mid-nineteenth-century science and technology and scientific visions of an internationally organized world. Across a range of new professions—statistics, engineering, geography, bibliography, public health—men emerged who did not want to do away with the state but to take it over, to replace aristocracy with a professionalized meritocracy, to push aside the well-connected amateurs and bring in new cadres of educated and rational elites. In their minds the fundamental unity of the world was a scientific fact. What was needed to improve the condition of humanity was to unite Christian compassion with education, the pursuit of truth, and the systematic organization of professional life. From this perspective, the international lawyers were a special instance of a larger phenomenon.

That society itself was an organic entity organized on the basis of natural laws was fundamental to their view of government. A leading Victorian statistician, speaking to the 1860 International Statistical Congress in London, reminded his audience of "the necessity under which all Governments are rapidly finding themselves placed, of understanding as clearly and fully as possible the composition of the social forces which, so far, Governments have been assumed to control but which now, most men, agree really control Governments."[2] Social science was *the* critical new instrument for doing this, and it was supposed to promote international cooperation too since this new professional class generally assumed that reason and science would show men what they shared and help to set aside prejudices. What internationalism offered in particular was the possibility of carving out a politics-free zone where men of science could meet, setting aside the factionalism of nations and treating the world and its peoples as the whole they really were.

Europe's pioneer theorist of the scientific organization of society was the restless French aristocrat the Comte de Saint-Simon (1760–1825), who fought on the American side with George Washington against the British, proposed constructing a canal at Panama when he was scarcely twenty, and combined fervor for the French Revolution with prophetic zeal for the coming age of industry. Never short of self-belief—he once tried to woo Madame de Staël by describing himself as "the most extraordinary man in Europe"—Saint-Simon was a thinker on the grand scale, and it is in his work that for the first time the idea of *organization* is elevated into a principle of international government.

In 1814—the year that the Concert of Europe emerged—he proposed a radical alternative to the work of the diplomats: the federation of the entire continent, with a single monarch and single parliament to bind "all the European peoples into a single political organization." European federation was not, he believed, immediately practicable, and it certainly would not come about through the usual diplomatic procedures. But the key was to create the appropriate organization:[3]

> Assemble congress after congress, multiply treaties, conventions, arrangements and all that you will do will still end only in war. . . . In all reunions of peoples, you must have common institutions, an organization.[4]

In the twentieth century, many political theorists saw Saint-Simon as the man who had anticipated the birth of the League of Nations and later the UN. Although this stretches things, he certainly did popularize the need for supranational organization very effectively. One reason he could do so was that in the early nineteenth century the idea of organization had a far more vibrant and energizing meaning than it does today. We have to think ourselves back past the Cold

War, before classics like *The Organization Man* turned the term into a synonym for 1950s conformity. For social theorists in the era of early Romanticism, it was a positive concept drawn from the study of living organisms and from biology in particular. Societies, they believed, were organisms much like plants that grew metabolically and in systems of increasing complexity and range. Machines formed part of this animate world as well and reflected the same life forces. Long before the age of robots armed with ethical cognitive capabilities, they even regarded automata as elements of the natural world. Saint-Simon's gaze was firmly fixed on the goal of peace and the fostering of brotherly love, but industry and mechanization provided the means to get there.[5]

After his death, his disciples propagated his ideas around the world. The ultimate goal, according to an exposition of his work that appeared in 1828, was radically internationalist: "*universal association*, which is to say, the association of all men on the entire surface of the globe in all spheres of their relationships . . . *universal association* can be understood only through the combination of all human forces into a peaceful direction." Saint-Simonians valued the coming together of men in "associations" as the best way of overcoming the enmities of the past; moreover, they imagined this process occurring not merely within streets, villages, or towns, but in a series of concentric circles the largest of which would ultimately envelope the globe and encompass all mankind.[6] Eventually one would see "unity of doctrine and action" in "the entire world":

> Until the day when this great concept . . . can become the direct object of the endeavors of the human spirit, all previous social progress must be considered as preparatory, all attempts at organization as partial and successive initiations to the cult of unity and to the reign of order over the entire globe, the territorial possession of the great human family.[7]

This fantastic blend of reveries of cosmic harmony, praise for the virtues of manual labor, and hard-nosed appreciation of the importance of capitalism's new technologies was promoted by the eccentric figure who led Saint-Simon's disciples in the 1830s, Père L'Enfantin. The self-proclaimed "High Priest" of what amounted to a new religion, L'Enfantin preached free love and the unity of East and West, and after a brief stint in a French jail on account of his scandalous ideas about sexual equality, his desire to help consummate this marriage of the world's two halves took him and some other Saint-Simonians to Egypt. In the era of the French conquest of Algeria, they were ardent believers in bringing together the peoples of the Mediterranean, and more broadly still of global reconciliation. They dreamed of turning Paris into "the new Mecca," drew up maps of a Europe covered with railway lines, and had a network of devotees that extended from the Levant to South America. In France their ranks included influential bankers, engineers, and scholars, men who were instrumental in persuading the erstwhile revolutionary Louis Napoleon to turn the 1850s and 1860s into an epoch of reform of both government and capitalism. Michel Chevalier, who had been jailed alongside L'Enfantin, was better known to history as the French senator who in respectable old age arranged perhaps the single most important free trade agreement of the century with Britain's Richard Cobden in 1860. The engineer Ferdinand de Lesseps, a former North Africa hand, achieved glory as the constructor of the Suez Canal, a typical Saint-Simonian project that encapsulated their blend of engineering and world harmony.[8]

For all the sectlike oddities of Saint-Simonianism, the creed articulated ideas that would become commonplace by the end of the century. One was the concept of the engineer as laborer for mankind, the technician as harmonizer of peoples. Another was the quasi-evolutionary rationale for the principle of international organization, connecting life's origins in small, simple biological microorganisms along a great chain of being to its ultimate flowering in complex social international structures. An early form of technocracy, this idea of an engineered world society prided itself on its rationalism while simultaneously resting on a deep, almost mystical faith in the perfectibility of man. The idea that nature itself was moving inevitably toward world harmony was taken up by many prominent internationalists, especially after Darwin. South African statesman Jan Smuts, a key figure in the founding of the British Commonwealth and the League of Nations, was a serious botanist and a philosopher whose personal doctrine of "holism" provided an evolutionary argument for international association very similar to Saint-Simon's. Woodrow Wilson too justified the need for a League of Nations on the grounds that it represented the culmination of nature's love of association. Men like Smuts and Wilson were politicians and administrators, not revolutionaries. They believed in reform, and in scientific and technical expertise being brought to bear on society by the emergence of a new leadership class. Nothing could be done without institutions, but they had to be placed in the right hands.

The elitism implicit in this approach was beautifully articulated in the work of Darwin's cousin Francis Galton. Traveling in Egypt, he met some of the Saint-Simonians and was impressed by their fervor. Having lost faith in the Church of England, he was already dreaming of becoming the citizen "of some state, modeled after Plato's scheme." For Galton, there was no social issue that could not be definitively resolved through the application of the scientific method; in a famous article, he even deployed statistics in order to estimate "the efficacy of prayer." And he founded his own very successful social science—eugenics—through which he hoped for the "establishment of a sort of scientific priesthood throughout the kingdom" to oversee health and social progress. (Later on, men such as British biologist Julian Huxley would attempt to internationalize the Galtonian vision through the United Nations.)

But the real Plato of this vision of disinterested social rule led by elites of the mind was Saint-Simon's former secretary and disciple, Auguste Comte. Peace and prosperity would be assured, Comte wrote in his 1822 *Plan of Scientific Studies Necessary for the Reorganization of Society,* through the systematic application of a scientific approach to matters of public administration. The world was entering what Comte saw as the last of three stages—the Scientific—after the passing of the Theological and the Metaphysical, and his new science of society, better known as "sociology," was designed to provide the toolkit for rational social management. For Comte this was primarily a national project, but he would scarcely have been true to his Saint-Simonian origins had he not been aware of the international implications. Comte believed—writing before the Scramble for Africa—that the age of colonialism was over and with it the cause of wars. Since militarism was on the wane, no political move toward confederation was necessary. Rather, all nationalities should meet "under the direction of a homogeneous speculative class," a supranational "spiritual power" rather than a "sterile cosmopolitanism." This spiritual power was, of course, Science, and more particularly the study of the laws that guided men in the aggregate.[9]

Such reasoning made statistics the key to good government, as they had been for Bentham earlier, because it was only through quantifiable data and statistical research that one could uncover the laws of progress, in society as well as in nature. As one popular scientist put it, "Man is seen to be an enigma only as an individual; in mass, he is a mathematical problem." If numbers cannot lie, how can policy do without them? Statisticians are thus more than the marshallers of facts. Knowing how to categorize them allows them to tell governments when their legislation would be effective, and to counsel them on the forces affecting policy outcomes. Indeed, according to the father of modern social scientific statistics, Lambert-Adolphe-Jacques Quetelet, that society was governed by statistical laws necessarily relegated politicians to a secondary role: the business of governing amounted to nothing more than adjusting policy to smooth the operation of these laws and to avoid disturbances. To do this, the politician obviously needed the statistician's guidance. Writing to his former pupil, Queen Victoria's consort, Prince Albert, in 1858, Quetelet described statistics as "that particularly governmental science."[10]

The prince consort himself did his best to publicize the statisticians' humanizing mission. In the last speech he made before his death, he congratulated the delegates to the 1860 International Statistical Congress on laboring for the universal happiness of mankind. At the time statistics as a discipline was still subject to "prejudice, reproach, and attack": Dickens, for instance, liked to parody the self-important claims of statisticians in the British Association for the Advancement of Science. But they soon shook off their early radical associations and demonstrated their utility—to insurers, doctors, and engineers among others. They held out the possibility of making generalizations about human affairs across national borders and between societies, and thus ultimately, in the Benthamite version, in legislating wisely for the world as a whole.

In order to do this effectively, it was not enough to gather data and statistics. One had to be sure that the accumulated information was categorized and made available in a standardized form, for without this, comparison and aggregation was impossible. Long before the era of global warming and the regulation of complex internationally traded financial instruments, comparison of data across countries and societies required prior agreement as to how data should be presented and how events and things were to be classified. It required, in short, an international effort at codification and standardization. Codification—the very term was another Bentham coinage—became the rallying cry of the professionals, and the mid-nineteenth century thus saw the inauguration of an intense effort to measure, collate, and categorize events, objects, and institutions.

If this effort helped to create new scientific communities across the world, generating new professional fora and bodies, it was chiefly around the task of developing generally agreed standards of measurement and value. In this era talk of standards came easily. The gold standard was an ideal of monetary internationalism, while the "standard of civilization," as we have seen, provided a template for mapping the world's peoples in terms of their fitness to be treated by international law. Most standards, though, were less glamorous and dirtier and more technological. Prince Albert's 1851 Great Exhibition had highlighted the development of precision engineering and led the British Association for the Encouragement of Arts, Commerce and Manufactures to propose the "adoption of a uniform system [of measurement] throughout the world." At the same time, statisticians tried to promote international agreement on medical nomenclature to facilitate the comparison of cross-country mortality data.[11]

The revolutionary social impact of standardization was nowhere more evident than in the case of the telegraph. The International Telegraph Union—the world's first public international union—was created very early, in 1865, in order to overcome the delays that had been caused by the need to print out telegraph messages on one side of the border and walk them across to the other side. The ITU got its members to accept all international messages, linked their systems into a single network, standardized rates for sending telegrams, and used the ITU as a clearinghouse for their accounts. As traffic soared and rates fell, the ITU was hailed as a model of international cooperation. No one could be made to join it. Yet the benefits of membership, or at least of behaving as though one were a member (as the British and Americans did), were self-evident. In similar fashion, the Universal Postal Union was formed in 1874, and within a decade commentators were presenting these institutions as the seeds of a future world government.[12]

There was at the same time a much more general drive to unify systems of weights and measures. In 1875 an international conference was held in Paris, and use of the French metric system spread rapidly. British engineers worried about the size of screws and bolts laid the foundations for the present-day International Standards Organization, perhaps *the* most influential private organization in the contemporary world, with a vast and largely invisible influence over most aspects of how we live, from the shape of our household appliances to the colors and smells that surround us. And the desire to standardize the measurement of time (facilitated by the emergence of radiotelegraphy) led eventually, over some four decades—there was a lot of inbuilt resistance among international meteorologists to this—to the establishment of a permanent International Time Bureau in Paris.

But confidence in the capacity of experts to harmonize across national borders was not confined to technical matters; it extended to questions of social and economic policy too. Penal policy—an area Bentham himself took a great interest in—was only one of the areas of social reform where the standardizers were also active; public health was another.[13]

The result was an explosion of meetings, conferences, and international networking. Saint-Simon's prophecy of the power of association through technology seemed to be coming true, and observers on the eve of the First World War discerned in such developments "an immense impetus" to "the organization of the world." In 1913 the first dissertation on internationalism was written: it talked about a "modern social phenomenon" of the preceding half century that had emerged, visible chiefly through "international diplomatic conferences, unofficial congresses, associations, bureaus and other organizations." While the number of states in the international system roughly doubled over the century after the Congress of Vienna, international governmental organizations shot up from single figures to about fifty, most of these founded after 1875. At least seventeen of these had permanent headquarters and an official staff.[14] They helped run rail and river networks, standardized property rights and units of measurement, and unified public health policies. Unofficial international bodies were even more numerous; a mere twenty-five in the early 1870s, they grew so fast that one specialist counted more than six hundred by the early twentieth century, half of them only a few years old.

The end of the nineteenth century thus saw the emergence of an entirely new kind of institutional presence in international life. Even Europe's monarchs patronized these organizations in order to associate themselves with their forward-looking spirit. Prince Albert and the Emperor Louis Napoleon were the earliest and most important of these, but other rulers followed their lead. The present-day Food and Agriculture Organization, for instance, would not exist without the king of Italy's sponsorship of its precursor, the International Institute of Agriculture—a body intended, in the words of Italian financial expert and politician Luigi Luzzatti, "to hasten the solution of problems which can be solved only through the association of scientific knowledge with legislative power." For Luzzatti, later prime minister of Italy, there was almost no limit to the good such an institute could do: it could improve conditions among the majority of the world's inhabitants who worked the land, thus warding off the spread of socialism, and it could protect those millions forced to emigrate around the world. Above all, it could encourage more new international bodies to be created. "On what a splendid network of new institutions the Twentieth Century might set her seal!" he exclaimed in excited anticipation.[15]

OTLET'S MUNDANEUM

Nowhere was such a prospect more fervently embraced than in King Leopold's Belgium, the center of fin-de-siècle internationalist life. Leopold's first venture into internationalism had been his horrible neofeudal experiment in the Congo Free State. By the time his egregious mismanagement and murderous treatment of the Congolese—millions are estimated to have died—forced the Belgian state to take it over from him in 1908, Leopold had already turned to other, worthier and less lucrative internationalist projects. In urgent need of positive publicity, he worked hard to turn Brussels into the world headquarters of the spirit of *internationalité*. By 1910 the Belgian capital had become the busiest host of international events anywhere, hosting more events than Paris and twice as many as London, with Berlin (the Prussians were deeply unenthusiastic internationalists) hosting barely a tenth the number.[16]

In 1907, a small group of Belgian internationalists sought Leopold's backing to set up a Central Office of International Institutions. Planned as a future organization of organizations, the new Central Office was intended to stand at the apex of the rapidly emerging worldwide system of formalized scientific and intergovernmental cooperation. The product of a desire to simultaneously collate data and promote world peace, it was the brainchild of one of the most remarkable figures in the story of fin-de-siècle internationalism—Paul Otlet, the founder of modern information science and bibliographer extraordinary, the forerunner of our contemporary Silicon Valley heroes of data collection.[17]

Born in Belgium in 1868, Otlet came from a prosperous family. His father had made his money selling trams around the world: Otlet was thus a scion of the new globalizing industrial bourgeoisie of the mid-nineteenth century. And of European diplomacy too. For there was a reason why tiny Belgium became such a hotbed of scientific internationalists besides Leopold's need for good public relations. A country split then and now between French and Flemish speakers, its very existence represented a triumph of optimism over the realities of European nationalism. Created in 1830 by the Concert of Europe, which had been typically sanguine about the dangers of linguistic separatism, its own internal unity could never be taken for granted. It was thus naturally an environment conducive to internationalist initiatives.

It was in this context that Otlet proposed a Central Office of International Institutions to coordinate and share information among the twenty or more bodies that had established permanent offices in the Belgian capital. Like many others, he had been disappointed by the outcome of the second Peace Conference that had met at The Hague earlier in 1907; in his view its noble aim of bringing peace to the world had been supplanted by the much more limited and questionable matter of how to make war bearable. He believed this was a defeat for the spirit of cooperation between nations, and that the reason for the defeat was that the forces of genuine internationalism—including pacifists, jurists, parliamentarians, socialists, and intellectuals—had been insufficiently coordinated. But Otlet was optimistic because he discerned a global trend to ever more intense internationalism that needed only to be made more effective in the face of resistance from traditional diplomats and the forces of militarism. Belgium in short was in his mind ideally positioned to lead the fight for humanity and world peace against the spirit of Vienna, the Concert, and its degenerate offspring, the European alliance system.

His primary weapon in this struggle was data, and it is not surprising therefore that the first task of his new Central Office of International Institutions was to compile an Annual of "International Life." Revamping an older and less ambitious series, the 1909 Annual weighed in at over fifteen hundred pages, and its editors and readers alike hailed the evidence of "the richness and fecundity of international life." But Otlet's idea of coordination went much further. The following year Brussels hosted not only the 1910 Universal Exposition but a World Congress of International Associations that discussed issues of legal status, and the standardization of scientific terms and weights and measures. One of its results was the emergence of a Union of International Associations, based in Brussels, at Otlet's Central Office.

"International congresses are the outcome of modern civilization," a Victorian geographer had noted approvingly in 1885. The next thirty years were perhaps the apogee of technical and scientific internationalism. An average of one or two international scientific conferences had taken place annually in the 1850s, but this had risen to twelve per year in the 1870s, and thirty in the last decade of the century.[18] Dozens of scientific associations banded together in their own professional bodies. Not far behind were hoteliers, architects, engineers, bankers, actuaries, and stenographers—all of whom began meeting internationally at the end of the nineteenth century. The growing authority of expert specialization spoke to an idealized vision of science and technical knowledge as a creed without borders. The scientific division of labor among the "best men" of different countries was not only the shortest route to truth but an example to the politicians of the payoff from international cooperation. Some participants of course devoted themselves to their work alone or defined their politics exclusively in national terms. But many others saw their scholarship and the needs of the human community as intimately connected, and tight networks of personal and professional connections bound them as scientists, activists, and public men.

Otlet himself worried, however, that specialization was driving men—and knowledge—apart instead of bringing them together. Facts were multiplying at dizzying speed with the progress of scientific inquiry, but mankind had failed to devise rational and efficient means of accessing them. The pros and cons of specialization itself were part of a fairly new debate—after all, the word "specialist" itself had only been around since the 1860s—but Otlet felt that coordination was essential if expert knowledge was to advance unimpeded without getting lost from sight or becoming useless. Aiming at the ultimate goal of producing a "Universal Book" in whose ever-revised pages all useful knowledge would be found, Otlet developed a conception of "documentation" that promised to systematize the extraction of facts from chunks of information. Long before the Internet, Otlet believed that getting knowledge to those who needed it meant turning old-fashioned libraries into information hubs. Like some Borgesian hero, he made a start by putting together a bibliographic database of information about sources of information, and his Universal Bibliographic Repertory, painstakingly transcribed onto individual cards, numbered some 400,000 entries in 1895, three million in 1903, and eleven million when the First World War broke out. This was a laborious enterprise but it was not an entirely quixotic one. In developing his own means of organizing this quantity of information, Otlet created the Universal Decimal Classification, a system still in use in many countries, and he also established an International Institute of Bibliography, which having gone through several face-lifts continues to function to this day.

But Otlet's vision went much further than bibliography. He wanted to turn Belgium into a kind of global data central: his Union of International Associations, with official Belgian backing, would become the coordinator of a new form of world organization, an agency that would exploit the increasing interdependence of material and moral life for "the general welfare of men." He dreamed of a World Palace—a Mundaneum—and used the UIA to set up an International Library, Museum, and University. These were to function as the organs of a new World City, of which the Mundaneum would be the brain. After the First World War, Le Corbusier was invited to submit proposals for the planning of such a city, part of a stream of suggestions to rationalize and consolidate the role of Brussels, alongside The Hague and Geneva, as cities devoted to world peace.[19]

Like many internationalists, Otlet regarded the outbreak of the First World War not so much as a refutation of his ideas but rather as confirmation of their necessity. To the national plight of Belgium was added personal tragedy when one of his sons died in combat in October 1914: Otlet himself is said to have searched the battlefield for his body. His means of coping was immediately to propagandize for a sweeping reorganization of international life after the war. Fertile in devising new institutions, he drew up plans for a Society of Nations that looked rather different from what was to emerge at Versailles. States in Otlet's highly centralized blueprint were to be brought together under a single sovereign supranational authority with its own parliament, judiciary, and executive—"an International Diplomatic Council authorized to direct and administer world interests"—backed by its own international army. This new body would "act throughout the whole world" in conformity with a founding World-Charter to be drawn up by a Congress of "all the Powers." It was a technocrat's dream.

Such an entity Otlet saw as the final stage in the political evolution of mankind. This had progressively governed itself in ever larger structures—the city, county, the duchy, and then the national state. Why, Otlet asked, should the state be considered as final? "On the contrary, the possibility of an organized community involving the higher national and human interests is now being explored by the best minds." A century after Saint-Simon, the idea that the evolution of nature would lead through nations to a world government was now a staple of internationalism. The business of peace was too important to be left to statesmen alone, Otlet concluded: "The spirit of diplomacy should not rule supreme. Politicians, jurists, scholars and businessmen must also introduce their points of view."[20]

Before 1914 such thoughts had been commonplace. After the war, however, the mood changed, and in Geneva there arose an actual League of Nations against which to compare these earlier dreams. Even at Versailles, Otlet's marginalization of national sovereignty and preference for rule through experts found little favor among the Great Powers, or indeed among the independent new states they helped set up in eastern Europe. Eventually, the Belgian government withdrew its funding for his work, and the Mundaneum closed its doors in 1934. Its contents were shunted from building to building, finding temporary lodgings in university offices. Otlet's calls for a transformation in world consciousness through a "rational and peaceful revolution" sounded increasingly plaintive, his demand for a World Police Force, a World Constitution, Government—and ultimately a World Plan to "prevent the nations exhausting themselves by pulling in different directions while thinking they are working toward the local good"—tired and out of touch. "What must be done, O World?" he asked in 1931 of behalf of "little Belgium." No one, it seemed, was listening: his was a voice from another era.[21] When Otlet's devoted biographer tracked down his papers after the Second World War (Otlet himself had died in the winter of 1944, shortly before the war's end), he found a scene of delapidation: piles of moldering papers, books, and files filled workrooms and stairwells. Many were housed in a former dissecting theater whose roof let in pigeons and rain. Faded wreaths garlanded Otlet's bust.

THE LIMITS OF INTERNATIONAL EXPERTISE

Why did Otlet's grandiose schemes wither away? After all, his scientific rationalism was widely shared before and even after the First World War, and H. G. Wells, another man with a strong interest in international documentation, was writing about the need for a

"World Brain" in the 1930s in terms that looked remarkably like Otlet's idea of a universally accessible storehouse of knowledge. The huge interwar market for works of scientific popularization showed that this idea had a wide appeal among readers. Yet by then some of the problems with his approach, and with the drive for scientific internationalism generally, had already emerged.

In the first place, scientific cooperation was often hostage to larger political considerations. It did not help that the French were especially ardent promoters of the standardization cause; old memories of Napoleonic efforts to codify Europe and suspicion of their motives were often enough to block their initiatives. The metric movement swept most of Europe by the 1880s, and looked poised for a moment to become the universal system many internationalists had called for, but then in Britain and the United States there was a backlash. "It is written in the stars that in the future this is to be an Anglo-American world," wrote Frederick Halsey, author of *The Metric Fallacy*. "Let us make it Anglo-American in its weights and measures." If the metric cause in both countries by 1950 was far weaker than it had been a century earlier, it is hard not to see political forces as responsible.[22]

Public health reform suffered for similar reasons even though there were increasingly obvious costs to failing to cooperate. After the Napoleonic Wars, the need to protect populations from contagious diseases brought in from abroad led most European governments to tighten up their quarantine regimes, and in 1851 the French foreign ministry held the first ever International Sanitary Conference, which produced an agreement designed to ensure that all signatories standardized their entry regulations. Yet such agreements meant little unless the signatories chose to implement and enforce them, as many international organizations would learn to their cost a century later. Little was done in this direction, even though cholera was a real threat for most of the century. In 1874, two years after some sixty thousand people had died in an outbreak, the French proposed setting up an international epidemics agency, but because the issue got bound up with rival imperial claims in the Levant and North

Africa this was not carried through either. There was still no agreement when over 100,000 people died in the great cholera epidemic of 1883—and at least as many in 1892. (Among the scientists arguing over the etiology of the disease was the French expert Adrien Proust, author of *La défense de l'Europe contre le cholera* and better known to posterity as the father of Marcel, who immortalized his father's concern with disease and cleanliness in his novels.) These endless conferences eventually gave birth to a bureaucratic mouse in the form of an International Office of Public Health, with its own small permanent secretariat, in Paris, that was staffed by health professionals from member states. Its chief role was informational not educative, it had little scope for active health promotion of its own, and it remained concerned with diseases emanating from the Levant. Then as now with global warming, the existence of a commonly acknowledged problem was not enough to generate an effective bureaucratic response.[23]

Historians have also now amply demonstrated that political differences often divided the scientists themselves, even when they considered themselves to be internationalists. The idea that science has no homeland certainly did not reflect the experience of nineteenth-century science, and it became even clearer after 1918 when German scientists were ostracized from many international fora. Otlet was characteristic of the older generation of scientific internationalists in simply ignoring all this. He was largely uninterested in problems of political implementation—the virtue and value of what he did was simply obvious to him. The idea that his ideas were in some way peculiarly Belgian—in that they spoke to that very unique country's predicament—he never bothered to address, perhaps because it would have been too damaging to his universalist posture.

Money tended increasingly to tie scientists to the state's apron strings. Much scientific research was not cheap, and the age of the independent man of science was passing rapidly. Otlet had money of his own—before it ran out—and could thus, at least before the First World War, conduct his own research on his own terms. But not even the private wealth accumulated by a successful Belgian industrialist like his father was enough for the grand schemes he dreamed of. It was all very well to stand at one remove from the state and politicians, but the result was constant shortage of funds. Many professional associations were therefore very constrained in what they could actually do, especially at the international level, and ended up serving as clearinghouses for information rather than as active educational agents in their own right. When the state did get behind science—as it did increasingly in the mid-twentieth century–scientists reaped the financial benefits but often faced an awkward choice between harnessing their energies to the national interest and remaining faithful to the older ecumenical vision. Science's militarization made this problem worse: the imposition of secrecy upon basic laboratory research in the era of chemical and nuclear weapons pushed scientists further and further away from the path of Otlet's internationalism.[24]

UNIVERSAL LANGUAGE

The most fundamental, though, of all the obstacles holding back the scientific universalists from carrying through their transformation of international life was the scientists' own frequent internal disunity. The unity of science was an inspiring rallying cry and a creed, but in reality science was a messy business. Establishing the truth of things was not quite as straightforward as Saint-Simon and Comte implied, and in the laboratory scientific discord was as important as scientific unanimity, and sometimes drowned it out. Thus scientists might share a pretension to universalism, but once one digs down into the professional pages of science journals themselves, one finds—as is to be expected—not only argumentativeness but often very divergent views about how to reach that goal.

One area where the experts' inability to agree seemed particularly revealing was in the search for a universal language, a search characteristic of late-nineteenth-century confidence in the potential of internationalism. While philosophers and linguistics sought to uncover the underlying structures and forms common to all languages—or all truth-bearing sentences—in mathematics or semiotic systems, others called for the creation of a single new language that would be available for world use. In 1870, a French botanist named Alphonse de Candolle (creator of the current international code of plant names) published an exposition of the "Advantage for Science of a Dominant Language," and looked forward to English serving this role in the coming century. Others felt that inventing an artificial language would be better. More than a dozen were devised in the run-up to the First World War but by far the best known of these was Esperanto.

Brainchild of a Russian Jewish linguist named Ludwig Zamenhof, a typically polyglot product of the tsarist Pale, Esperanto might be seen as an abstraction of the realities of life in the late-nineteenth-century east European imperial borderlands just as much as Otlet's projects reflected the situation of Belgium. In 1887, under the pseudonym Dr. Esperanto (Hopeful), the young Zamenhof published a guide to a universal language, a task that had obsessed him since high school. A decade earlier, he had celebrated his nineteenth birthday by singing a hymn to internationalism in his own new language:

Malamikete de las nacjes,
Cadó, cadó, jam temp' está;
La tot' homoze in familje
Konunigare so debá.

(Enmity of the nations,
Fall, fall, it is already time;
All mankind in [one] family
Must unite itself.)[25]

As this suggests, linguistics was for Zamenhof about more than simply communication: it was about fostering peace, a view that made eminent sense in an age of growing nationalism—above all for the Jews of eastern Europe. In 1905, the first international Esperanto congress took place at the French resort of Boulogne-sur-Mer, where delegates wearing the movement's symbol, the green five-pointed star, sang first the rather martial "Marseillaise" and then their own hymn ("on the foundation of a neutral language / people understanding each other / will agree to form one great family circle"). Zamenhof himself prayed for world peace and a new future. Unfortunately, despite attracting some eminent supporters, his movement quickly got bogged down in an unpleasant argument after some serious-minded Esperanto supporters broke away and developed their own supposedly improved alternative called Ido. Tempers quickly frayed in the Ido-Esperanto schism. In 1908, one of Zamenhof's men wrote a "Raporto de la Prezidanto de la Lingva Komitato al la Universala Kongreso de Esperanto" that gives a sense of the bitter passions this quixotic venture aroused and that makes it clear that even the search for a common tongue provoked bitter arguments within the ranks of its most ardent supporters.[26]

Within the ranks of the much more specialized research field of fin-de-siècle seismology, another disagreement raised what was in some ways the most fundamental question of all. The point at issue was whether data could be said to present themselves naturally from the observation of phenomena or required organizing in what were intrinsically arbitrary schemes of classification. In short, was the classification of data dictated by the very structure of the world or was it in fact a matter of pragmatic choices, dictated by the purposes for which data were collected and the kinds of models that were generated by scientists themselves? Earthquake science tended to internationalism because of the need to share and pool data. Yet Europe's leading experts in the subject simply could not agree over how best to collect and present the data that would allow them to clarify the pattern of earthquake activity across space and time. International comparisons of tremors over space seemed to require different kinds of information than historical comparisons in a single locale over time. Setting standards, seismology suggested, was becoming ubiquitous, but who set which standards was not always clear. As incompatible visions of what a particular science was for came into conflict, the world's silent drift toward standardization enveloped often acrimonious battles over which standards to adopt.[27]

For all these reasons and more there was to be no World City and the drive to universal standardization turned out to have limits. Even today, inches still contend with meters, and travelers pack a universal adapter—"one world, one plug"—to cope with the several electrical systems in use globally. But just because scientific internationalism did not sweep everything before it does not mean it was a failure; it simply means that the expectations of its most ardent followers were exaggerated. In fact, it turned out to be an extraordinarily potent institution-creating force in itself, and many of the specific international specialized agencies Otlet and others created survive into the present. The effort to coordinate food policy and production internationally led to the founding of the Food and Agriculture Organization by the United Nations. The drive to standardize time finally resulted in the International Meteorological Organization's designating Greenwich mean time as the universal standard in 1946; the same year saw the replacement of relatively small interwar bodies with very powerful successors like the World Health Organization. Because of its relative invisibility and supposedly noncontentious character, the nongovernmental International Standards Organization has been perhaps the most powerful of all. Such bodies still embody the old nineteenth-century idea—with all its inbuilt presuppositions and blind spots—that policy is best left to technical experts who know no nationality but that of humanity.

CHAPTER 5

The League of Nations

There is something intensely inspiring to Americans in the thought that when they surrender their isolation, they do it not to engage in diplomatic intrigue but to internationalize world politics.

—Walter Lippmann, *New Republic* (June 1916)[1]

The transformation which would be wrought in human affairs by an effective league for permanent peace would be greater than any that has taken place since the beginning of human history.

—George Burton Adams, *The British Empire and a League of Peace* (1919)[2]

THE INTERNATIONALIST ALTERNATIVES to traditional diplomacy set transparency above secrecy, and participation above exclusion. Internationalists believed in cooperation among nations driven by scientific and commercial progress, and they regarded militarism and alliance diplomacy as irrational and retrograde. Many of them were also, within the civilizational and racial limitations of the age, globalists. In contrast to the exclusive conclaves of the Great Powers, new technical bodies for the exchange of expert and specialist knowledge were opened to small and non-European states: Egypt was not even fully sovereign when it became a founding member of the International Postal Union. And their durability, despite their limited resources, was impressive.[3]

Yet the limits of nineteenth-century internationalism are as striking as the ambition. Internationalism suited small states like Belgium and Switzerland in particular, and they were among its principal sponsors. But the buy-in of the major powers was still very limited, as the paltry results of the Hague conferences demonstrated. No overarching organization like the United Nations existed; prewar American proposals for an international court fell on stony ground. The critical question for historians is why this changed—why, in other words, during the First World War, some of the most powerful states in the world threw their weight behind the construction of a permanent peacetime world security organization and built the League of Nations.

A negative answer would be that some of the principal promoters of the idea of a Concert of Europe in 1815 no longer existed or mattered in 1918. The Habsburg empire—in some ways the Concert's animating force—collapsed; Germany was defeated and prostrate. Tsarist Russia dissolved in civil war. In any case, even they had come around by 1914 to supporting the idea of arbitration and the spread of international law, and during the war German and Austrian leaders proclaimed their support for President Wilson's League of Nations too. Yet even taking into account this change of heart, we are still left with a puzzle. Why did Britain and, even more strikingly, the United States, emerge from the First World War convinced, not as many believed, that internationalism had failed, but that it must be given new prominence and political weight? Why above all did they come down in favor of a permanent world *organization*? Many British policymakers continued to believe in the idea of a revived Concert; and indeed it did not die. Enough powerful figures in both countries nevertheless supported the new internationalism strongly enough to insist that the peace conference at Versailles in 1919 should create a permanent League of Nations. Of these, it is fair to say that without one of them in particular, any eventual world body would certainly have looked very different from what actually emerged: that one was the U.S. president, Woodrow Wilson.

THE AMBIGUITIES OF WOODROW WILSON

Historians of international organizations are prone to hagiography. Figures such as Eleanor Roosevelt (though more rarely her husband) and Dag Hammarskjöld (though not his predecessor Trygve Lie) are often depicted as saviors of mankind. Raphael Lemkin, father of the genocide convention, has been proclaimed a prophet; Kofi Annan and René Cassin have their admirers. But no one received more adulation in his lifetime and after it than Woodrow Wilson. To the two million Parisians who turned out to watch his arrival at the end of 1918 he was "the God of Peace"; in Milan, "the savior of Humanity" and "the Moses from Across the Atlantic." To his supporters, he incarnated an America that cared for and about the world and refused to turn inward: his untimely death, following the failure to win Senate backing for the League, was portrayed as a kind of modern martyrdom. Decades after his death in 1924, he even became an -ism. Later still, George W. Bush, Dick Cheney, and Donald Rumsfeld did their part for the Wilson cult too: after the 2003 invasion of Iraq, many critics, deeply anxious about the American turn away from multilateral institutions, looked back to Wilson and sought in his example the inspiration for a new century.[4]

His role in founding the League was indeed absolutely critical. Without his support, the British cabinet would have not backed its own internationalists and the League would probably have remained a blueprint. But the real story of Woodrow Wilson is less one of virtue triumphing over vice than of a set of political choices that determined the character and powers of the new world body, choices that completely bypassed what had been until then the prevailing American mode of internationalist engagement. Unlike Elihu Root or even his own predecessor William Howard Taft, Wilson wanted to keep power with the politicians rather than give it to lawyers, and he made sure that his League would be a forum for quasi-parliamentary deliberation rather than a judicial court to deliver verdicts. Because he regarded institutions as organic and evolutionary manifestations of the collective will that evolved and proved themselves over time, the founder of the world's first collective security organization was surprisingly little interested in collective security, international law, or indeed in organization itself. He left the nuts and bolts of the League to the British to sort out, and its structure—part debating chamber and part bureaucracy—was mostly London's work. Behind the Wilson cult, in other words, lies a fusion of American missionary zeal and British imperial calculation, a combination of powers and perspectives that turned the League into a bridge between the world of nineteenth-century empire and the twentieth-century rise of the nation-state.

IT WOULD NOT HAVE BEEN SURPRISING if nineteenth-century America had simply kept aloof from Europe's internationalist initiatives. The federal structure of the United States, its own vast and highly protected internal market, its Anglo-Saxon legal system, and above all the always fraught relationship between Congress and the presidency all counted against extensive participation. And indeed in some areas of international cooperation, such as the international standards movement, the country was (and remains) surprisingly marginal. But none of these factors was decisive, and from the middle of the nineteenth century, as we have seen, American administrations identified themselves more and more closely with the cause of internationalism. It was a sign of the new role they sought in the world that in 1881 Washington, D.C., became the venue of the first major diplomatic conference ever to be held outside Europe; others followed.[5]

Woodrow Wilson's foreign policy grew out of this preexisting commitment to novel forms of mediation and peacemaking even as it departed sharply from its guiding legalist principles. American diplomacy's pre-1914 identification with the idea of arbitration in particular had garnered both the Republican secretary of state Elihu Root and President Theodore Roosevelt the Nobel Peace Prize. As for Wilson's predecessor, the lawyer President William Howard Taft, he was an even stronger advocate. With a Progressivist's faith in the "eternal principles of law and equity" and convinced of the need for a permanent "court of nations," Taft worked for full treaties of arbitration with Canada and Britain. Prefiguring the difficulties Wilson himself would face, however, Taft found it impossible to get these treaties—described unsparingly by their historian as "an outstanding example of slovenly drafting and bumbling political management"—ratified in the Senate. There was the determined opposition of Henry Cabot Lodge in the Senate on what we might call nationalist grounds, while Elihu Root regarded Taft's ideas as too sloppy and sweeping to do anything other than discredit the legalist cause. Taft's predecessor and still powerful political rival, Theodore Roosevelt, simply thought him unrealistic: arbitration treaties were useful between countries like the United States and Britain because they shared sufficient common interests; in more hostile or fraught relations they would not bear the burden Taft placed on them.[6]

This debate among the legalists went on long after Wilson had crushed the Republicans—split between the wrangling Taft and Roosevelt—in the 1912 elections, and it set the terms in which most Americans thought about a possible international government after the Great War. Shortly after it began, Roosevelt called for the establishment of a World League for the Peace of Righteousness to enforce the rule of law via the "international police power" he had urged in his 1910 Nobel Peace Prize address: the sanction of force was essential, in his view, if peace was to be enforced by more than vapid moral pronouncements. But the secret to making such a league effective was to be realistic about the issues it could tackle and not to try to do everything. It should use military force, but only to enforce commitments that had already been made between signatory states. Its success, and the modesty of its expectations, would encourage others to participate and slowly entrench international law and mediation as the instruments of global harmony. The vastly popular wartime lobbying group that was headed by Taft, the League to Enforce Peace, went much further: it wanted all "justiciable" disputes to be submitted to an international court by league members (and all other disputes to be submitted to a panel of arbitrators), who would sign up to fight any state that declared war before making such a submission. On the other hand, in Taft's system, states would not be obliged to accept the rulings of international adjudication.[7]

There were obvious problems with both these proposals. Roosevelt's was limited to a small number of states and exempted matters of "vital interest" and "national honor" from law's verdict. Taft and the League to Enforce Peace made the arbitration process both too automatic—forcing states to go to war over *any* refusal to submit a case to law—and too lax, since the court's judgments had no sanction behind them at all.[8] Woodrow Wilson's impatience with the entire legalist paradigm for achieving international peace was thus understandable. The lawyers and their supporters thought they could solve the world's problems, but while they fetishized law they could not explain how to enforce it properly.

For the president they were all on the wrong track. What really mattered were not institutions and legal codes but mental attitudes and values. The son of a Presbyterian minister, Wilson thought in biblical terms of covenants, not contracts, and he sought to build something that would grow organically over time to meet mankind's universal aspirations, not the interests of a few powers who could probably get along anyway. The idea that peace could be achieved so long as the lawyers got the details right struck him as absurd. Words functioned to inspire, not to delimit. Like Mazzini, Wilson saw democratic politics as "a sphere of moral action" (the phrase is from an 1885 essay of his on "the Modern Democratic State"). And because Wilson was both an elitist and an optimist about the progressive evolution of human society, he was happy to trust in the political instincts of the peoples of the world as expressed by their representatives. After all, if they could not be trusted, the best laws in the world would not stand against them.[9] Thus although he made occasional politic noises in support of the League to Enforce Peace, Wilson talked and thought in an entirely different language, one that was inspired by the Presbyterian covenant theology of his father and the Social Gospel movement. In May 1916 he told the League to Enforce Peace that he wanted "a universal association of nations" that could "prevent any war contrary to treaty covenants, guarantee territorial integrity and political independence"—something that was far beyond the league's idea of a limited grouping of like-minded states.[10]

More important an influence on Wilson than legalism was Americanism. Since the 1870s, a series of "inter-American conferences" had been taking place in the Western Hemisphere. They led to a Pan-American Union that was initially a U.S. initiative to expand trade but became an instrument for encouraging hemispheric cooperation, with its own office in Washington. There was no parallel, wrote an observer, for the sight "of twenty one nations, of different languages, building together a house for the common deliberations." Here was an early forerunner of Wilson's League, hailed by Argentinian politician Luis Drago as "a separate political factor, a new and vast theater for the development of the human race, which will serve as a counterpose to the great civilizations of the other hemisphere and so maintain the equilibrium of the world."

Nineteenth-century believers in hemispheric cooperation like U.S. secretary of state James Blaine had always argued that Pan-Americanism pointed the way to an alternative to older European models of diplomacy:

> Hearty cooperation, based on hearty confidence will save all American states from the burdens and evils which have long and cruelly

> afflicted the older nations of the world. . . . A spirit of justice, of common and equal interest between the American states, will leave no room for an artificial balance of power like unto which has led to wars abroad and drenched Europe in blood.[11]

Spurred by the revolution going on next door in Mexico, the State Department's wartime efforts to forge a multilateral American partnership for peace took place under this sense of expectation. Indeed, influential Americans believed that the Mexican crisis in particular provided a test for possible European solutions. Charles Eliot, the president of Harvard, urged the formation of an "American League" to restore order south of the border, claiming that this body would offer "a suggestive precedent for a European League to keep the peace of Europe." Wilson heard similar thinking from his closest adviser, the Texan "Colonel" House. In December 1914, House mused that an inter-American agreement might "serve as a model for the European nations when peace is at last brought about."[12] And when, after the failure of these efforts, the Brazilians proposed revisiting the idea of a Pan-American treaty in 1917, Wilson himself speculated that such a treaty "might serve in part to show the European peoples a way to secure peace when the war is over." The ordering of a continent of independent national states based on republican and democratic principles, committed to the benefits of trade and the protection of property rights, was something that could be applied to Europe as much as to the Americas. The Europeans could themselves learn the advantages of a system that guaranteed territorial integrity and did not regard invasions and land swaps as part of the natural order. When in the summer of 1918 the British received the very first indications from Wilson's adviser, Colonel House, of what the president was thinking, this emphasis on territorial integrity, drawn from earlier Pan-American Pact drafts, attracted their attention.[13]

Legal codification and arbitration might have formed part of the political culture of Pan-Americanism, but they were not for Wilson its primary attributes, as his "Peace without Victory" speech to the

Senate showed. Speaking in January 1917, he laid out the need for America to play an active role in securing the "international concert of peace" that would bring stability to Europe after the war, and he explicitly invoked the hemispheric model of the Monroe Doctrine:[14]

> I am proposing, as it were, that the nations should with one accord adopt the doctrine of President Monroe as the doctrine of the world: that no nation should seek to extend its polity over any other nation or people, but that every people should be left free to determine its own polity, its own way of development—unhindered, unthreatened, unafraid, the little along with the great and powerful.
>
> I am proposing that all nations henceforth avoid entangling alliances which would draw them into competitions of power, catch them in a net of intrigue and selfish rivalry, and disturb their own affairs with influences intruded from without. There is no entangling alliance in a concert of power. When all unite to act in the same sense and with the same purpose, all act in the common interest and are free to live their own lives under a common protection.

The implied contrast between this new "concert of power" and the old Concert of Europe became more explicit at the start of April in the speech to Congress with which Wilson announced the severing of relations with Germany and urged the entry of the United States into the war. What was actually at stake, Wilson stated, was "to vindicate the principles of peace and justice in the life of the world as against selfish and autocratic power and to set up among the really free and self-governed peoples of the world such a concert of purpose and of action as will henceforth ensure the observance of those principles." The problem with autocracies such as the Prussian monarchy was that their rulers did not heed the wishes of their people; indeed, Wilson explicitly declared that the United States had no quarrel with "the German people." They too were victims, since this "was a war determined upon as wars used to be determined upon in the old, unhappy days when peoples were nowhere consulted by their rulers and wars were provoked and waged in the interest of dynasties or of little groups of ambitious men who were accustomed to use their fellow men as pawns and tools." And he continued, "A steadfast concert for peace can never be maintained except by a partnership of democratic nations. No autocratic government could be trusted to keep faith within it or observe its covenants. It must be a league of honor, a partnership of opinion. . . . Only free peoples can hold their purpose and their honor steady to a common end and prefer the interests of mankind to any narrow interest of their own." The old republican and democratic critique of Metternich and the Vienna system was thus revived by the president to address the very different conditions of 1917.[15]

Much like the men of 1848, Wilson was drawn to the language of religious passion. The extraordinary Protestant theologian George Davis Herron, who shared Wilson's overheated blending of Protestant eschatology and Mazzinian nationalism, hailed the war as "between a white and a black governing principle, each striving for possession of the world." Having fled the United States (following a scandalous second marriage) for Genoa and then Geneva in order to be close to the spirits of his heroes Mazzini and Calvin, Herron, who was perhaps the most colorful in a long line of unconventional presidential confidants, described the European war as a struggle between the Christian ethic of love and satanic self-interest and competitiveness. Wilson, he wrote admiringly, sees "the law of love . . . as the only practicable social basis, the only national security, the only foundation for international peace. . . . He cunningly hopes, he divinely schemes, to bring it about that America, awake at last to her national selfhood and calling, shall become a colossal Christian apostle, shepherding the world into the kingdom of God." It was a portrayal that resonated with Wilson himself, and presented him as the culmination in a long line of American peace activists eager to spread the good word into a fallen Europe.[16]

Yet in the president himself theology was combined with a deep commitment to political pragmatism. There were good tactical domestic reasons for this, but there was also philosophical inclination: Wilson's ideal of politics as inherently deliberative underpinned his commitment—a deeply elitist commitment—to democracy and public opinion as the bedrock of any living political order. From the time the United States entered the war, Wilson preferred to avoid the war aims debate entirely. But that became harder when in late 1917 the Bolsheviks seized power in Russia, stepped up their antiwar propaganda, and called for a "democratic peace." Like Woodrow Wilson, they blamed secret diplomacy and the old elites for the war, but they went further than him in breaking with diplomatic protocol, denouncing past treaties, publishing secret documents, and giving accounts of Trotsky's negotiations with the Germans to reporters as they happened. The Soviets called for a general peace, and believing that all governments were under pressure to stop fighting, they addressed themselves to "all belligerent peoples" and only secondarily to their governments.[17]

Where the Bolsheviks led, the Americans and British followed. News that the new leaders of Russia were parleying with the Germans—Lenin and Trotsky's peace negotiations with the Central Powers went on through the winter of 1917–18—made it seem imperative to do whatever was possible to keep their country in the war. Wilson warned that "the voices of humanity that insist that the war shall not end in vindictive action of any kind" had been exploited by "the masters of German intrigue to lead the people of Russia astray." He was quickly followed by British prime minister Lloyd George, who spoke out against annexations and emphatically in favor of national self-determination.

This term, which was to become so associated with Wilson, had in fact been highlighted far more emphatically by Lenin, heir to a long tradition of rich Marxist debate on nationality that went back to the Habsburg debate of the early twentieth century and before. In his October 1917 "Decree on Peace," the Bolshevik leader had gone into some detail about the plight of small nations forced against their will inside the borders of larger and powerful states, and insisted they should have the right to determine their own fate. This was a clear reference to the nationalities of the Habsburg monarchy and an effort to destabilize the Central Powers. Neither Wilson nor Lloyd George, by contrast, were committed at this stage to breaking up the Austro-Hungarian Empire (read carefully, not even Lenin was actually saying that small nations *had* to be independent—an important proviso for later communist policy), but they did see themselves competing with the Bolsheviks for European public opinion.

However, Wilson himself had little knowledge of the details of European political ethnography, and he relied upon a secret team of experts, the so-called Inquiry, which collected basic data on nationalities in Europe in order to help him draw up his own peace program. Thanks to the Inquiry's experts, that program—better known as the Fourteen Points—went into some detail about specific European countries and nationalities. They were vague on some nationalities questions—hedging bets about the fate of the Habsburg empire, for instance—and surprisingly specific on others, such as the shape of a future Poland. But in keeping with the avowed pragmatism of the Inquiry's precocious young secretary, Walter Lippmann, there was no general commitment to the principle of national self-determination nor any precise outline of the shape of any postwar body. Instead Wilson talked about the need for "a general association of nations" that would guarantee the territorial integrity and independence of the members: this could have implied something as weak as the Pan-American Union, or indeed a continuation of wartime inter-Allied cooperation. There was only one fleeting mention of international law—in relation to restoring Belgian independence—and none of the need for a new world *organization*.

Wilson's partner, the British prime minister, David Lloyd George, had been a lot clearer than that when he spoke publicly only a few days before the Fourteen Points speech. Like Wilson, he stressed the fact that "the days of the Treaty of Vienna are long past" and insisted that settling territorial issues alone was not enough. But he then went on to highlight (in admittedly ambiguous terms) the "general principle of national self-determination," and insisted that "a great attempt must be made to establish by some international organization an alternative to war as a means of settling international disputes." The clarity was not accidental, since Lloyd George's speech was in part an effort to flush Wilson out on the matter (hence Wilson's reference, not altogether positive, in *his* speech, to the "admirable candor" of the British premier's words.) For unlike the Americans, whom Wilson had steered away from the subject, the British and their imperial cousins had been thinking seriously about the contours of this new international organization for nearly three years and they now wanted to know whether there was any support for their views in Washington.[18]

THE BRITISH EMPIRE AS A LEAGUE OF NATIONS

"I am for a league of nations," Lloyd George was to declare in September 1918. "In fact the league of nations has begun. The British empire is a league of nations."[19] This is, from our own perspective, a wonderfully counterintuitive view of what the League of Nations was about. But in fact by linking the rise of the League to ideas about empire it provides us with a way into the critical question: how was it that the British policy establishment, by tradition deeply cautious about the idea of permanent peacetime commitments beyond the Channel, should have come round to the idea of a League of Nations?

Preserving the Anglo-American alliance into the peace was vital for most British statesmen concerned with the preservation of the empire, a view shared by Wilson, who later spoke publicly in London of the need for a "single overwhelming powerful group of nations who shall be the trustee of the peace of the world." The president was sympathetic to the basic idea of Anglo-American solidarity, but it was clear that American public opinion demanded that this come through a larger and more universal grouping of states and not through any "selfish and entangling alliance," nor anything that hinted at the old racial narrow transatlantic Anglo-Saxonism.[20] Public opinion in Britain itself was pushing strongly for a League of Nations too. Cobden's heirs in bodies like the Union for Democratic Control demanded an end to secret diplomacy and a more democratic foreign policy; other groups, like the League of Nations Society, built on prewar internationalist arguments and called openly for some kind of organized peace. The Labour Party embraced the idea as well. In Whitehall itself, the policymaking elite was deeply split. While some thought all talk of an international organization preposterous, others believed it could not be ignored and might indeed be turned to the advantage of Britain and the empire. There were even a few, like the undersecretary of foreign affairs, Robert Cecil—son of the great skeptic Lord Salisbury—who actually believed in the idea, and it was ultimately to Cecil as much as to Wilson that the League owed its birth.

When thinking about the form of a postwar organization, the British were less drawn to legalist ideas than the Americans—as the world's most powerful state, Britain was never inclined to repose too much faith in law and its potential constraints; thinking in practical terms about functions and bureaucratic form, on the other hand, was much more focused. Leonard Woolf, a former colonial civil servant, wrote a report on international government during the war for the socialist Fabian Society that was striking in the level of administrative detail it contained. It was taken up by the British League of Nations Society which served as a conduit of ideas into the Foreign Office itself. The close connections of the metropolitan elite in London helped: Woolf and his wife, Virginia, who helped him write parts of the report, were close to Robert Cecil, who was to be the prime mover of the League idea inside the British government. Through him, Woolf's *International Government,* published in 1916, circulated widely in Whitehall and exerted such an influence on thinking in the Foreign Office that many of the early official blueprints for "International Government under the League of Nations" were basically cobbled together from Woolf's work.[21]

The case still had to be won at the highest levels, though, and as late as 1917 the outcome was in doubt. Early that year, the powerful secretary of the Imperial War Cabinet, Maurice Hankey, summarized the main postwar options for ministers as: (a) "some sort of international organization, such as league to enforce the peace"; (b) "a league of the character of the Concert of Europe formed after 1815"; and (c) "a reversion to . . . the balance of power."[22] Few openly argued for the third, which had widely been discounted in public speeches by politicians on all sides. The first option was based on ideas pushed by the American League to Enforce Peace, by Woolf, and by Liberals such as Lord Bryce, but it implied a doctrine of collective security that went far beyond what most advocates of arbitration had proposed. And it was bitterly opposed by Congress's British counterparts, conservatives like Lord Curzon, who worried that it severely limited British freedom to define its own foreign policy. Hankey himself opposed it for similar reasons. But within the cabinet there was also support for the idea, notably from Robert Cecil, who would go on to lead the British negotiating team at Paris on the formation of the League. Cecil had already circulated a memorandum of his own on "proposals for diminishing the occasion of future wars," essentially continuing an approach that his onetime superior, Edward Gray, had been working on from the very start of the war.

An obvious first step for these very historically minded diplomats was to analyze the strengths and weaknesses of previous schemes, and there was a surge of wartime interest in the Concert diplomacy of 1815. The Foreign Office established a committee to look into the entire subject, and this eventually produced a report—named after the committee chairman, Lord Phillimore—which backed the idea of arbitration within a "council of nations" and included a draft constitution for a new League of Nations with principles and procedures for the peaceful settlement of disputes that eventually found their way into the League Covenant.[23] While still focusing on conflict resolution, this was significantly different from the approach taken by the American legalists because it made a political body—the "council of nations"—rather than an international court the chief arbiter. The British wanted to get U.S. administration reactions to Phillimore's report—which remained vague about the specific structure of the new governing body—when it was finished in the spring of 1918, but Wilson gave instructions that there was not to be any public discussion and contacts were confined to his personal emissary, Colonel House. He rebuffed several British efforts to publish Phillimore, and his emissaries conveyed only the vaguest sense of his ideas. A year later, the British League of Nations Union bemoaned the fact that "we are still ignorant of the exact nature and scope of President Wilson's proposals."[24]

Meanwhile British planning continued, and in the run-up to the peace negotiations in Paris, Robert Cecil was able to hand the Americans a detailed blueprint for the League that outlined a secretariat, an international council of states, and an international court of justice. Much of the credit for this must be attributed to one other player on the British side, an absolutely crucial figure in helping design a League that could overcome Whitehall's objections to what was going to be, in all likelihood, a major departure from established diplomatic procedures. Remarkably, he was not British at all—indeed, he had fought against the British in the Boer War nearly two decades earlier.

The trim, upright figure of Jan Smuts bestrode the international stage for the best part of four decades. With a Cambridge degree in law, and a serious interest in botany to boot, Smuts was a brilliant Boer guerrilla commander who had accepted the reality of defeat, entered politics in the newly founded Union of South Africa, and become a leading theorist of imperial rule. Committed to forging a new white South African nation that would reconcile Boers and British and unite them in the mission of bringing civilization to sub-Saharan Africa, he was a leading advocate of the idea of the British Commonwealth—a paradigm as potent as Pan-Americanism for the new League of Nations.

It was primarily in South Africa that the idea of an organic melding of the (white) nations of the British Empire had developed. After the Boer War was over, young British intellectuals and policymakers were concerned to bring together Boers and English speakers; Smuts shared their desire. While Whitehall worried about India, they saw the future as an alliance of white peoples—bringing together Australians, Canadians, and New Zealanders—with the motherland in a fashion that would simultaneously respect their evolving national cultures and provide collective security. The threat they feared was not so much from Germany as from the restless peoples of Asia and Africa whose sheer numbers made them question their power to civilize the world. The same kind of reasoning explains why theorists of Commonwealth were also generally in favor of closer ties with the United States. Commonwealth was thus at once a product of racial anxiety and national prestige, a parliamentarian solution for an overstretched imperial power—internationalism as White Pride.[25]

From Smuts's perspective, creating the British Commonwealth would allow the new South Africa to combine a high degree of national autonomy with the security and commercial advantages of full participation in the life of the leading empire of the time. But Smuts did not stop there. An evolutionist in politics (rather like Wilson), during the war he saw the Commonwealth idea as a model for an even larger future political community, a League of Nations that would bring together all civilized peoples, healing Europe as well as helping Africa. This noble goal—which he, with his African mission firmly in mind, was well aware of—also had a very precise strategic purpose: in such a league, the destinies of the British Empire and the United States would be conjoined. The war had shown the weakness of the British position in Europe in the absence of American support; the League was the means of preserving their alliance into the peace.

The most realistic of idealists, Smuts threw his weight behind the League idea and argued publicly through 1917 that military victory must be followed by "moral victory" if "military imperialism"—something that "has drifted from the past like a monstrous iceberg into our modern life"—was to be replaced by a peaceful era of international harmony.[26] Smuts argued that this transition from force to cooperation between nations could be seen already happening in "the British Empire, which I prefer to call . . . the British Commonwealth of Nations." And he went on to make the connection even clearer:

> The elements of the future World Government, which will no longer rest on the Imperial ideas adopted from Roman law, are already in operation in our Commonwealth of Nations. . . . As the Roman ideas guided European civilization for almost two thousand years, so the newer ideas embedded in the British constitutional and Colonial system may, when carried to their full development, guide the future civilization for ages to come.[27]

According to Smuts, a league of democracies had effectively emerged in 1917 with the American entry into the war alongside Britain and France against the autocracies of Germany and Austria-Hungary. The Central Powers represented a "last effort of old feudal Europe to block human progress." Acting very deliberately as a kind of bridge between the Americans and the British, Smuts offered an appealing blend of morality and realpolitik. On the one hand, he argued that science (since the new League represented a new stage in man's political evolution, one that would accommodate the nation-state without superseding it) and right both lay on the side of the Entente powers. On the other, democracy promotion was an obvious tool to use to drain such support as still existed in central and eastern Europe away from the kaiser and the Austrian emperor.

This combination of philosophical ideals and sound strategy struck a chord with President Wilson. In December 1918, barely a month after the war's end, Smuts circulated a pamphlet entitled *A Practical Suggestion* in which he argued for a version of the League of Nations idea. It was radical on disarmament issues, proposed the tripartite structure of executive council, assembly, and secretariat that was eventually adopted, and argued for giving the new organization responsibility for the administration of former German colonies. It also suggested that it concern itself with drawing up principles of international law—an echo of the legalist agenda of the prewar era. This was much more sweeping than anything Cecil or Phillimore had proposed; indeed, at this time Cecil was still thinking only along the lines of a new Concert, with regular Great Power conferences and a permanent secretariat—much like an improved version of the 1815 system. It was also more radical than the draft Colonel House himself had drawn up at Wilson's request, which was much closer—in its stress on arbitration and appeal courts, and a Permanent Court of International Justice—to prewar American legalism. Wilson liked Smuts's radicalism, his decisive break with the past, and perhaps he liked his anticolonial credentials too. Reading his work as he sailed on the SS *George Washington* to Paris, keeping most of his own advisers at bay, he fell under its influence.

On the British side, it remained a hard sell. At the Imperial War Cabinet on Christmas Eve 1918, all those around the table recognized that the peace settlement would need to result in some kind of postwar security pact; at the same time, none present sought a superstate or world government. But whether the proposed League should be permanent or merely a new version of the old Concert, what the balance of power within it should be between small and large powers, how much executive authority it should possess, and how far it should be committed to defense of the postwar territorial settlement were all as yet undetermined. Both Smuts and the Phillimore committee had backed Taft's League to Enforce Peace idea of a system in which violations of agreed rules automatically triggered sanctions against offending nations, but many conservatives disliked the idea, and some of them opposed the idea of collective security altogether. They feared that British troops would find themselves putting out fires all over the world, and questioned whether the League's military arrangements would add anything to Britain's own defenses. Lloyd George as usual wanted both sides of the argument at once: he insisted the League must be effective and not, in his words, a "sham"; on the other hand, he ruled out its enjoying independent executive powers. His preferred model was one where authority remained in the hands of national governments. Although Lloyd George publicly supported Smuts, in fact support within the British cabinet was lukewarm for anything more than a permanent conference system—a kind of improved version of 1815. Such, at any rate, was the thrust of the instructions the cabinet gave to Robert Cecil when he and Smuts prepared to depart for the peace conference in Paris.

In Paris, however, personal diplomacy took on a life of its own. The Cecil-Smuts team basically ignored the instructions they had been given by the cabinet, and used the support of Woodrow Wilson to trump the objections of their own prime minister. Wilson himself came up with new articles—one on guaranteeing the rights of labor, the other on ethnic minorities and their rights—that like much of his thinking emerged suddenly to the consternation of his own advisers. But these, along with Colonel House's suggested permanent court of justice (which Wilson disliked), were accretions to a draft that was basically a British concoction, drawn up at Whitehall in a fairly systematic fashion over the previous two years. In a mere eleven days, a commission chaired by Wilson, and dominated by his adviser Colonel House and Robert Cecil, composed a draft agreement for discussion. Within two months the new body had been approved by the delegates.

ORGANIZATIONALLY, the League abandoned the legalist paradigm almost entirely—to the dismay of many American internationalists—and followed the preference of Smuts and Wilson in basing itself on the tripartite division of powers in a parliamentary democracy. There was the equivalent of a legislature consisting of an upper house, the council, which had Great Power permanent members and four rotating members of the lesser powers drawn by election, and a one-member, one-vote assembly. The office of the secretary-general was set up to be the League's weak executive, an administrative rather than a diplomatic post. All that was left of the legalist model was a provision—forced on a deeply reluctant Wilson—for the eventual creation of a new Permanent Court of International Justice to provide the League with a source of binding judicial authority over member states for interstate disputes.

This structure had obvious weaknesses. The assembly might look like a legislature, but it had no lawmaking capabilities, and any council member could veto action, rendering it unlikely that much would be done there. The secretariat was envisaged as a fairly weak coordinating body with no powers independent of the League's members. The court (eventually established in 1922) was certainly not the central all-powerful judicial mechanism Taft and Root had hoped to see. Most worryingly, despite members being obliged to uphold the territorial provisions of the peace settlement, the League lacked any standing forces of its own (a French proposal along these lines was rejected) or any machinery for enforcing the peace beyond a commitment by its members to submit any disputes among themselves to arbitration. If a member did resort to war in defiance of its League commitments, the most that was contemplated was boycott and sanctions. The council could recommend action to be taken against an offender but had no means of following through. From our perspective, the weakness is evident; yet from any perspective, the League was an extraordinary diplomatic innovation, a realization of the dreams of many nineteenth-century internationalists and a moment of truth for others. It dislodged the primacy of the international lawyers and circumscribed the role of arbitration: there would be no "array of wigs and gowns vociferating in emptiness," as Alfred Zimmern scathingly dismissed the legalist vision. But on the other hand, in its democratic dimension, and its emphasis on the role of public deliberation, public opinion, and the political participation of "social consciousness," it reached back to the radical impulses that had emerged a century earlier in the reaction to the Concert of Europe.[28]

THE AMERICAN WITHDRAWAL

On January 16, 1920, as the midmorning sun shone off the Seine into the Clock Room of the Quai d'Orsay, the new League of Nations held its first council meeting. It was almost exactly a year after the peace conference had agreed to set it up. Seated around the green baize, the world's statesmen heard the council's first president, French socialist politician Léon Bourgeois, proclaim the day as "the date of the birth of the new world." Still housed in Paris, the League already had more than forty members, including Liberia, India, Persia, and Siam. For the world's small states, membership in the League was a natural progression from their involvement in technical bodies and conferences earlier, but it also represented a guarantee of formal international equality: the Thai prince Devawongse, for instance, was a strong supporter of the League because it would guard "the safety of the smaller nation against the greater." But equally important was the fact that in this still limited manner, the new organization was gesturing to a globalism, a move beyond the conventional boundaries of a Eurocentric world.[29]

But one very large state was not present—the United States—and Wilson's absence was underscored by an empty chair at the main table. Although he had returned months earlier to Washington, the League's cause there was not faring at all well. The president, who had scarcely bothered to hide his disdain for the Senate while in Paris itself, had underestimated the task of persuading a Republican-controlled Congress, and his tactic of going over the heads of the politicians to the people did not work as well at home as in Europe. He made no real effort to reach out to members of his own party, still less the Republicans, and he infuriated many senators with his arrogance when he presented the treaty to them in the summer of 1919.

For what he had delivered in Paris bore almost no resemblance to what the American public expected. International law appeared to have been buried. Article 10 of the Covenant, which committed

League members to defend the Versailles borders, was widely denounced. The Covenant, declared Henry Cabot Lodge, the Republican leader in the Senate, was not

> what many of us had in mind when we talked of Leagues of Peace where international law was to be developed and the great feature was to be a strong international court to interpret and lay down the law and behind which the nations were to stand. The court has almost disappeared; international law, I think, is hardly mentioned; and the thing has turned into a plain political alliance.[30]

The League was in short nothing like the product of a third Hague peace conference, as some had hoped; nor did it resemble the proposals of the League to Enforce Peace. American legal internationalists shared Lodge's belief that Wilson had established the League on political foundations rather than legal ones. In their view, he had not merely ignored the arbitration tradition in American diplomacy, he had also put its existing achievements at risk. What they had been asked to sign up to was an alliance linked to a quasi-parliamentary sounding board with no lawmaking powers rather than a court with a clearly defined mediating role in defusing conflicts. They had placed their hopes in law rather than sanctions; the League, to judge from its Covenant, ranked the power of sanctions above the law. And to make matters worse: which sanctions? Nothing stronger than international public opinion.

Lodge himself claimed to favor joining the League provided that America could retain freedom of action. The real irreconcilables were against joining on any terms. While an ailing Wilson toured to speak in support of the League, Idaho senator William E. Borah toured against it and denounced the president for having sacrificed the peace of America without securing Europe's. The "European and the American systems," he argued, "do not agree." In a marathon speech before Congress at the end of 1919, Borah raised a number of powerful objections. It was not merely that Congress would be bypassed in the event of a League decision to go to war against offenders; it was also that unanimity in the League Council was itself no guarantee of the virtue of such a war. The American people should not be obligated to act just because the League told them to. Wilson had hoped to reform the Old World along the lines of the New; in fact, what he created threatened to let it back *into* the New in a different guise since the League would be bound to interest itself in American affairs. Above all, Borah recollected the founding fathers' warning against "entangling alliances" and declared in rhetorical horror:

> We are in the midst of all the affairs of Europe. We have entangled ourselves with all European concerns. . . . We are sitting there dabbling in their affairs and intermeddling in their concerns. In other words . . . we have forfeited and surrendered, once and for all, the great policy of "no entangling alliances" upon which the strength of this Republic has been founded for one hundred and fifty years.

Once a virtuous republic, the United States would now find itself committed "to a scheme of world control based upon force, . . . We may become one of the four dictators of the world but we shall no longer be masters of our own spirit." Americans would be contaminated with the taint of empire. "The maxim of liberty will soon give way to the rule of blood and iron."[31]

Borah's opposition, stirring though it was, was not the main reason why the Senate refused to ratify the League. The internationalists were divided, and the president himself, exhausted and ill, bore a large share of the responsibility for mishandling negotiations and precluding the kind of compromise that would have passed. But rejection did highlight the resistance in Congress to the idea of making a permanent commitment to a general international organization. Once Americans had come to see Europe as fallen and their own country as the moral alternative, the old arguments for remaining aloof were as powerful as those for missionizing abroad, especially since the negotiations in Paris had revealed that even as powerful and charismatic a figure as Wilson was obliged to compromise once the maps came out and the bargaining began. Wilson's claim that the League of Nations represented a distinctively American reshaping of international affairs went down well abroad, but not at home where it looked all too European.

The internationalist struggle continued long after the Senate defeated the idea of U.S. membership of the League in 1920 and Wilson's departure from the presidency the following year. Supporters of the League continued to press for ratification through the early 1920s, and in various ways a surprisingly large number of Americans participated in the League's activities. Buoyed by evidence that public support was stronger than the Senate battles suggested, and financed by private endowments like the Carnegie and the Rockefeller Foundations, supporters of Geneva founded think tanks, journals, institutes, and conference programs to train Americans in their role in the world. Between the wars, International Mind alcoves could be found in libraries across the country; International Relations clubs sprang up in hundreds of high schools. But winning hearts and minds is not a short-term strategy, and the memory of Wilson's humiliation remained vivid in the minds of his supporters for many years. As Democratic vice presidential candidate in 1920, Franklin D. Roosevelt had called for League membership with reservations. As president, however, he backed off entering the World Court, despite the evidence of strong public sympathy for this: the isolationist press and forces in Congress were too strong to be ignored. Such experiences explain Roosevelt's cautiousness once the Second World War presented him with a second chance to bring the United States into a world organization.[32]

Meanwhile, under Wilson's successor, President Warren Harding, U.S. foreign policy became actively hostile. In his acceptance speech as Republican candidate, Harding had referred contemptuously to the Covenant as "conceived for world super-government," but in his campaign he said just enough to keep the internationalists in his party hopeful that he supported some alternative to "the Paris League." The League to Enforce Peace remained silent during the election itself and faded away after Harding's election. After Harding's overwhelming win, Senator Borah called the result "an absolute rejection of all political alliances or leagues with foreign powers." Neither Harding nor his successor Coolidge were prepared to risk disagreement. On Wilson's death, in February 1924, the municipal authorities in Geneva arranged for a marble tablet to be set into the balustrade in the garden of the Hotel National to honor "the founder of the League of Nations." Prime ministers and heads of state of all the member states came for the ceremony. But there was no American presence, not even the consul in Geneva.[33]

STATESMEN AND EXPERTS

For many years after it was unceremoniously wound up at a final ceremony in Geneva in 1946, people forgot about the League. They forgot about the time capsule that had been buried before the war in the new Palais des Nations to celebrate its construction, and they ignored the League's own archives in the buildings that now housed organs of the United Nations. Occasionally a former official would write a memoir or prepare a briefing on its workings to help guide the transition to the new United Nations. But insofar as the League was remembered at all, it was under the sign of failure.

This was entirely understandable. Wilson had brought the United States into the war to make "the world safe for democracy," but the League saw Europe slide into dictatorship. It failed to bring about the general disarmament promised by the Covenant, and over time it came to look less like an alternative to Concert diplomacy and more like an adjunct to it.[34] Lacking the backing of some of Europe's most powerful states, it basically turned into an instrument of those that had founded it—Britain and France. Yet because neither power really placed much confidence in it, the actual impact it could make in security affairs was always very small. In the 1930s, under the French civil servant Joseph Avenol, the League was reduced to an embarrassing and even abject role. Avenol proved willing to sacrifice Ethiopia to keep Italy in the League in 1935, pushed out some Jewish officials, and tried repeatedly to bring Nazi Germany back in. Under his leadership, the League made no protest when the Third Reich took over Austria, and ignored Albania's request for an emergency debate when Italy invaded in 1939. It is not surprising that when Britain and France declared war on Germany that autumn, they did not even bother to invoke the League Covenant.

But there were also problems from the outset with the quasi-parliamentary model that lay at its core. The League devoted great attention to publicity—logically enough since its founders had believed the international public opinion was its most valuable safeguard—yet this encouraged statesmen to come to Geneva for theatrics rather than serious policymaking. When expectations were raised, as in the enormous 1932 World Disarmament Conference, the participants were less concerned to reach agreement than to avoid the blame for failure. Ever since the Hague conference of 1899 this feature of open diplomacy had been evident, but the League itself was damaged by the disappointed expectations that invariably followed. The unanimity rule on the council condemned it to impotence, and the lack of a credible deterrent—proposals for a League police force got no official backing—eroded the authority of the rules and laws whose importance it proclaimed, exactly as the American legalists had feared back in 1919.[35]

In power-political terms, therefore, the League was dealt an almost impossible hand. Its structure made action almost impossible, while the balance of forces was arrayed against it. To make matters worse, it was operating on a shoestring in an era of acute financial stringency: its total annual budget averaged a little over five million dollars a year—less than a thirtieth of the UN's half a century later. To the great urgent crises of the day—the world economic depression after 1929, disarmament, fascist aggression in Corfu and Ethiopia, and the rise of the Third Reich—it had no answer.[36]

Yet ironically, the very open-ended and unlegalistic structure that undermined its political authority fostered the extension of League influence in other areas, often entirely unforeseen by its founders. Outside the diplomatic limelight, its achievements were often durable and its organizational arrangement influential and long-lasting. In particular, its technical services took the organization of international humanitarian cooperation and science promotion much further than anyone had imagined possible before the First World War, and they turned out to be one area where American internationalists were still able to become heavily involved, gaining experience that would help shape the very different course of American foreign policy after 1945. As a diplomatic vehicle the League was a failure; as a source of expertise and international action, it became the agent or beneficiary of the kind of organic growth in cooperative behavior that Wilson, Smuts, and Zimmern had believed in. The international parliament—in the shape of the assembly—proved its value to Great Powers only by its impotence; but the international bureaucracy, the internationalism of technical, intellectual, and scientific specialism, proved its value through what it did.

ALL THIS HAD in fact been brilliantly anticipated in August 1919 by a young American named Raymond Fosdick. As he helped to set up the League's secretariat, he outlined what was to be an influential and persuasive assessment of the League's evolution:

> The non-political activities of the League are going to be immensely important and are going to furnish an admirable place to start the building of a new technique. . . . The world has had far too little practice in international activity. . . . We can establish a procedure and develop precedents; we can get the "feel" of international cooperation in pursuit of a common goal. Each step that we take, however halting, every decision that we reach as a result of frank discussion, will be a definite advance toward world peace. The result will be that when another Sarajevo comes, the world can meet it

with a system which has been developed and matured in many different areas and in many meetings of the family of nations.[37]

As Fosdick well understood, this evolution built on more than the prewar associationalism described earlier. It was above all a product of the First World War—perhaps *the* decisive moment in the shift from the nineteenth-century vogue for parliaments to the mid-twentieth century's love/hate relationship with bureaucracy. Total war had lent prestige to those civil servants who had organized the supplies, communications, and fuel without which the fighting itself would have been impossible. It had produced new forms of wartime cooperation, such as the Allied Maritime Transport Council, an unglamorous body for the coordination of shipping that exemplified an international executive run not by diplomats but by experts. In the international realm as much as domestically, government was reshaped by the wartime rise of this new class of bureaucrats; indeed it may have been *more* influenced by them since there was less institutional resistance from established agencies for them to combat. Was it coincidence that after the war ended, no fewer than four former Allied shipping experts landed in the League Secretariat, including the future architect of European integration, Jean Monnet? Functionalism—the idea that institutions emerge as a result of the logic of circumstances by demonstrating their practical utility—itself emerged out of these experiences.[38]

The composition and function of the secretariat itself had not been something that much bothered Wilson, certainly not once he definitely abandoned the thought of heading the new world body himself. Following Anglo-American consultations, it was agreed that a British civil servant should be put in charge and after Cabinet Secretary Maurice Hankey turned the job down, a reserved, methodical middle-ranking Foreign Office official, Eric Drummond, was appointed. The younger brother of the Earl of Perth, Drummond had been at the Foreign Office since 1900, his hard work and unassuming character appreciated by the foreign ministers, and by the prime minister, Herbert Asquith, whom he had served as private secretary. A Scottish Catholic, he had a strength of character and modesty that allowed him to build an international bureaucracy from the ground up. Since the history of bureaucrats rarely attracts readers, his is the kind of story that is easily overlooked. But his fourteen years in the position constituted a longer tenure than anyone after him, either at the League or the UN, and he must be regarded as one of the architects of modern international organization.

The start itself was unpromising. In London, in the summer of 1919, the secretariat consisted of Drummond, his assistant, a secretary, and a housekeeper working out of a single room. After a few weeks they managed to rent a mansion on Curzon Street, where under ceilings painted with cupids and water nymphs—the house had once belonged to the Duke of Marlborough—Drummond started to surround himself with an extraordinary team of much younger men, among them Monnet, Fosdick, a British economist named Arthur Salter, and an American press man named Arthur Sweetser (of whom more later).[39] Despite lacking funds, Drummond pushed successfully from the start for the creation of a professional international civil service organized into functional secretariats. This already represented a shift from wartime thinking in the direction of greater permanence and autonomy, since the few Americans and British officials who had actually bothered about the matter had assumed the League would be run like an inter-Allied wartime body with delegates representing their individual nations. The entire secretariat was tiny, less than 650 strong at its height, but Drummond's leadership and the dynamism of his younger colleagues fostered a bureaucracy far more powerful and diverse than the Pan-American Union or any other predecessor had achieved. (The legal section was headed first by a Dutchman and then by a Uruguayan, and it alone included members from Belgium, Cuba, India, Italy, and Spain.) More to the point, it quickly became much more powerful than the League's own founders had anticipated. The parliamentary model they had followed basically meant that the full assembly met only once a year; the result was that for the rest of the time, the League's civil servants were free to take the initiative.

They quickly found the world's problems being brought to their door. In war-torn Europe, fighting continued on the eastern fringes, strikes and uprisings plagued the industrial centers, and an economic slump increased unemployment and hunger; the Middle East was racked by disease and humanitarian disaster. Even as the new League set about establishing a new Permanent Court of International Justice, the International Labor Organization, and an international health bureau, and in general pushed ahead with the internationalist agency-building agenda of the past, it was handed the territory of the Saar and the Free City of Danzig to run under the terms of the peace treaty with Germany, and was asked to consider the international economic crisis, the plight of Christians in Turkey, and the status of Armenia. All this before the League even had a permanent home. Only in November 1920 did it relocate to Geneva—"a third-rate European city of little international importance," in the words of a contemporary journalist—in the heart of neutral Switzerland, where a large crowd welcomed delegates to the first assembly and heard speeches in front of the statue of Jean-Jacques Rousseau. The secretariat moved into the Hotel National on the lakefront and Drummond himself set up his office in the former bedroom of the sister-in-law of the Emperor Franz Joseph of Austria-Hungary.[40]

George Slocombe, a popular interwar writer who spent time in Geneva, was struck by the contrast between the venues for the new diplomacy of the triumphant democracies and the opulent venues of their discredited precursors. Switzerland itself, he wrote, seemed an almost deliberate slide into bourgeois dullness:

> For the palaces of kings and emperors and hereditary nobles which had witnessed the rise and fall of the Holy Alliance, the dispute between the Tsar Alexander and Metternich for the favours of the same lady, and the patient intrigues of Talleyrand, the modern Concert of Nations could find no substitute but a string of hotels with

> the same view of Mont Blanc behind a picture-postcard lake, with the same red and green plush furniture, the same imitation of French cooking, the same polished pinewood floors and white ripolined doors and lace curtains and German-Swiss managers and creaking lifts and double windows . . . hotels without history and without character, with symmetrical green or greenish gray facades, with cumbrous old-fashioned motor buses making three times a day the same monotonous journey to the Cornavin station.[41]

Yet the setting belied the enormous ambition and the geopolitical stakes. With the contagion of Bolshevism threatening to spread across Europe and the Middle East, and amid a global public health emergency graver than any before or since, the League acquired a new importance.

Two postwar crises in particular propelled the fledgling secretariat into the limelight. One was the plight of hundreds of thousands of refugees in eastern Europe and the Middle East, a humanitarian and public health disaster combining influenza, typhus, homelessness, and mass starvation that stretched older voluntary agencies to the limit and led the powers to ask the new organization to take charge. The other was the economic crisis in western and central Europe following the end of the war that forced reluctant statesmen to listen to the experts—leading economists and bankers publicized the gravity of the ongoing monetary instability at a conference in Brussels in 1920—and led them to agree to set up a permanent section for the study of economic and financial questions. Drummond was initially alarmed at this unforeseen expansion of the League's responsibilities, but his deputy, Jean Monnet, saw it as an opportunity. So did Monnet's friend Raymond Fosdick. Fosdick's appointment as undersecretary-general lasted only a few months before it became clear that the United States would not become a member. But in that time he helped establish the idea of "humanizing" the diplomacy of Versailles through "a systematic approach to international problems where everybody has everything to gain and nothing to lose." It was, he wrote, "a method of continuous international conference. . . . It provides not only for the centralization and coordination of international machinery but for its orderly and systematic development."[42]

Fosdick is one of those critical figures lurking in the shadows who helped turn around the setback of 1920 and later consolidated the internationalist thrust of American policy after 1940. Back in the States in time to witness Wilson's humiliation, he responded by helping to organize support for the League. Later on, as head of the Rockefeller Foundation, he played an important role in funding the League's technical operations. Other members of the new international civil service lasted longer but were equally energetic. Albert Thomas turned the International Labor Organization almost overnight into a powerful voice for the protection of workers' rights within a safely capitalist framework. Arthur Salter, who had worked with Monnet during the war on the Allied Maritime Transport Council, headed the new economic and financial section and oversaw both the monetary stabilization of Austria and Hungary and refugee resettlement in Greece and Bulgaria. Among Salter's younger colleagues was a Swedish economist, Per Jacobsson, who would end his career much later as head of the International Monetary Fund. Ludwik Rajchman, a Polish public health specialist, moved from fighting typhus in eastern Europe to founding the League's health section with financial backing from Rockefeller. These figures turned the League into the central agency of European reconstruction after the First World War and cemented the connection between internationalism and technical expertise. Contemporary commentators hailed "the discovery that Committees of Experts function more satisfactorily on an international than on a national basis."[43]

Long after the immediate crisis was over, the League's technical services remained impressively productive. They took advantage of Articles 23 and 24 of the Covenant, which specified League responsibility for opium trafficking, the white slave trade, and transportation, and provided that the League could gather under its auspices "all international bureaux already established by general treaties if the parties to such treaties consent." In this way the League rapidly became the umbrella organization and promoter of many of the international associations that had been formed before the First World War. Collecting data and issuing volumes of statistics was not the most glamorous of activities, but as Otlet had appreciated before the Great War, it laid the groundwork for future international problem-solving. Governments became used to League officials inquiring if not interrogating them and demanding information, and League officials played a critical role in brokering international agreements on the drug trade and prostitution. In these less glamorous arenas, as Fosdick had realized, cooperation could be wider: German and Soviet officials worked with the League's technical services before their countries formally joined, and American officials cooperated throughout the interwar years. Focusing mostly on Europe, it was chiefly through the technical side of its operations that the League reached into China, Singapore, and West Africa. The health organization alone, under Rajchman's direction, responded energetically not only to the public health crises of the 1920s but also to the impact of the Depression and of colonial rule on the health of Asian peasant farmers. While the colonial administrations themselves were forced by the crisis to retrench, French, Dutch, American, and Croatian doctors were sent to Asia with Rockefeller Foundation funding to report on the health aspects of agrarian reform. What its historian has called the "first Bandung conference," the 1937 League of Nations conference held in the "Paris of the East" in the then Dutch East Indies to discuss rural hygiene, did not just mark the emergence of international public health as a field of activity and intervention. It also crystallized the issues, still fought over today, among health professionals as to how far to attempt to address health problems through vaccinations against high-profile diseases and other top-down interventions, and how far to work through curative medicine on a wide front, connecting health to questions of poverty, land tenure, and political institutions more broadly. Impressive as it was, the public health side of Geneva's work was not unique. As the first such international body, the League was an ongoing experiment, accumulating new charges and constructing new professional networks and even new ways of thinking about the world's problems.[44]

Some League initiatives did not get off the ground, of course, or faltered: the International Institute for Intellectual Cooperation never really overcame an initial argument about when to readmit German members and was limited by a rather elitist conception of cultural production. For all the talk in the 1920s of rationalizing international life through scientific management, cooperation, and coordination, many conferences had little tangible result. Discussions over the criminalization of terrorism—a forgotten episode rediscovered by historians after the attacks of September 11, 2001—went nowhere as Europe fragmented ideologically and all hope of a common definition of the crime vanished. The international lawyers eventually succeeded in 1937 in getting the League to adopt a treaty for the establishment of an international criminal court, but not many states ratified it, and the entire scheme had to wait another sixty years to get off the ground. The creation of a European electrical grid was talked about briefly but had to wait until after the Second World War.[45]

Then at the end of the 1920s came the economic slump, which put an end to talk of the League as agent of an increasingly unified world and constituted its biggest failure of all. Albert Thomas's proposals for a European-wide labor exchange and a continental public works scheme that would produce an international communications and transportation infrastructure were discouraged by colleagues even before his death in 1932. The League's main economic strategy had been to stabilize capitalism, but there was no International Monetary Fund nor a World Bank, two institutions born later in response to these failures. Instead, a relatively powerful Financial Committee, largely run by bankers and treasury officials, was effectively entrusted by the British government and the Bank of England with the task of restoring monetary stability to east-central Europe, setting up new central banks, advising governments on budgetary discipline, and in return underwriting access to west European capital markets. Bank of England head Montagu Norman used the League to foster a practice of close central bank cooperation as the primary international means of coordination. Yet so far was this effort under British direction that the French developed their own parallel reconstruction effort entirely bypassing the League. In 1928, the governor of the Bank of France, Emile Moreau, confided to his diary:

> England having been the first European country to reestablish a stable and secure money, has used that advantage to establish a basis for putting Europe under a veritable financial domination. The Financial Committee [of the League of Nations] at Geneva has been the instrument of that policy.[46]

To make matters worse, the entire strategy was premised on a monetarist understanding of economic health, which made sound money and return to a modified version of the gold standard the priorities for the League. When the slump hit Europe at the end of the 1920s, the League became the cockpit for conflicting policy solutions. The French proposed federal union; the British and Germans opposed the idea because it implied a European challenge to the League itself, a detachment from the United States, and giving up on free trade. With the council torn, the League's inability to respond as the crisis shook the European banking system and encouraged a new round of protectionism led its members to look to the United States for leadership instead. But at the 1933 World Economic Conference that took place in London to stabilize exchange rates and boost international trade, it was in fact American policy—above all the decision of the new president, Franklin Roosevelt, to take the dollar off gold—that caused the meeting's failure and effectively ended international economic cooperation for a decade. Internationalism went into reverse and around the world the nation-state became the primary framework for economic policy for the next four decades.[47]

. . .

SECRETARIAT MEMBERS themselves had believed from the outset that it was important to be totally impartial: true internationalism meant the impartial gathering of facts, not bowing to the whims of political masters. They prided themselves on their ability to stand above national interests and valued their role in embodying and fostering that all-important guarantor of future peace—the "International Mind."[48] But there was of course a certain self-deception in all this. For all that they were couched as manifestations of technical administrative virtuosity, their numerous initiatives did not take place in some ideologically neutral zone. The League's currency stabilization packages were basically written, as a British Foreign office official put it, in order to keep places like Austria and Hungary "from throwing up their hands and going Bolshy."[49] The same anxiety lay behind its work resettling hundreds of thousands of refugees in Greece throughout the 1920s. Whether building new villages, or setting up independent central banks, the League's technical operations intervened heavily in member states' internal affairs as the price for assistance. As for the League's approach to health and sanitary regulation, this was staunchly paternalistic. Thomas's ILO had one of the most ideologically charged mandates of all in looking after workers' rights, and steered a precarious corporatist course between hostile capitalists to its right and revolutionary socialists to its left.

What is perhaps more striking is the staying power of this strand of interwar internationalism. By the late 1930s, more than half the League's budget was devoted to its so-called technical services. The crowds descended on Geneva every September for the annual theatrics of the assembly—much as they would do in Manhattan after the Second World War—but once they were gone, it was the international secretariat created by Drummond that remained at work. And although its leaders were mostly professional civil servants who had gained valuable experience in First World War policy coordination, they were surprisingly young—Salter was thirty-nine when he was appointed, Monnet only thirty-one. As a result, their internationalist careers were not ended by the Second World War, but continued thereafter and cemented the continuities with the UN: Salter would help run UN relief in postwar Europe; Monnet's friend, the Polish Ludwik Rajchman, set up UNICEF; Monnet himself of course was to become heavily involved in European integration. Overall, more than two hundred employees of the League Secretariat entered the service of the UN, and three of the closest aides of Drummond, Avenol, and Sean Lester went on to serve their successors in New York.

From this perspective, it is not the League's failures that we should focus on, but its enduring influence. A vehicle for world leadership based on moral principles and the formal equality of sovereign states, it preached the beginning of a new internationalist dispensation, repudiated the legacy of the Holy Alliance and the Concert of Europe, and offered the promise of democratization and social transformation through technical expertise. In fact, the League was the first body to marry the democratic idea of a society of nations with the reality of Great Power hegemony. This could be seen, for instance, in its decisive rejection of the possibility of a robust international law regime—something the UN would take even further—a rejection explained by the preference of its founders to preserve the political discretion of its members. It can be seen too in its deeply ambiguous attitude toward sovereignty and empire, embodied above all in the mandates system. Flexible and multivalent, this was a model of international government that would not only survive the Second World War but be greatly expanded and refined thereafter.[50]

CHAPTER 6

The Battle of Ideologies

Today we think planetarily and in Great Spaces.

—Carl Schmitt[1]

THE LEAGUE OF NATIONS embodied a paradox: it spoke the language of the brotherhood of man but existed as the result of a military victory. Like the older Concert of Europe, which it defined itself against, it was the instrument of a triumphant alliance of Great Powers and a means to preserve their domination of Europe—and their values—into the peace. But it was not alone. In the spring of 1919, as the League was born in Paris, the Communist International was established by the Bolsheviks, and the old conflict between Mazzini and Marx reemerged on the world stage. The two bodies basically existed as rivals, but in 1934 when the USSR entered the League, they were pushed uneasily together in the face of a common threat from the most radically anti-internationalist of all the Great Powers, the Third Reich. Vehemently opposed to both the League and Bolshevism, the Nazis were extreme nationalists. Yet even they were obliged, once Europe lay at their feet in 1940, to articulate their own vision of international order, almost against their will. A third internationalism—the fascist variant—was thus born, and it is in this ideologically charged context of competing visions of world order that we need to set the League's own understanding of the relationships between empire and nation, territory and sovereignty.

LIBERAL INTERNATIONALISM

When Woodrow Wilson passed triumphantly through Italy in January 1919, vast crowds gathered for a glimpse of him en route to the peace conference gathering in Paris. It was the first time a serving U.S. president had visited Europe. In the city of Genoa, he made two acts of homage. The more predictable of these was to the house where Christopher Columbus had been born. But as we have already seen, he also laid a wreath before a monument to the city's other great native son, Giuseppe Mazzini, and spoke of his debt to the Italian radical:

> On the other side of the water we have studied the life of Mazzini with almost as much pride as if we shared in the glory of his history, and I am very glad to acknowledge that his spirit has been handed down to us of a later generation on both sides of the water. . . . It is with a spirit of veneration, Sir, and with a spirit I hope of emulation, that I stand in the presence of this monument and bring my greetings and the greetings of America with our homage to the great Mazzini.[2]

Like most educated Americans, Wilson was steeped in the political theory of Europe. Almost a century earlier, Mazzini had argued that the spread of the nationality principle would bring peoples together. Woodrow Wilson saw things the same way and welcomed the establishment of new democratic nations and built the League of Nations around them. Yet like Mazzini, Wilson took no account of ethnic complexity at all, and like Mazzini he had only the haziest notion of how to apply the nationality principle to ethnographically complicated places like eastern Europe. Only belatedly did it hit him that what the principle of national self-determination did, as nineteenth-century critics like Lord Acton had pointed out long before, was to open a Pandora's box of competing claims and turn minorities into a political problem.

THE DARK SIDE OF NATIONALISM

"The exaggerated nationalism that creates the refugee and also creates most of the difficulties which beset him in the country of refuge has, however, been partly offset by the halting development of international solidarity," noted the author of the interwar period's major survey of "the refugee problem." "It is an astonishing fact that the refugee may have to consider as a practical problem whether he should seek refuge in Manila, Melbourne or Paris. It is no less astonishing that, in September 1915, when the final Armenian tragedy began, Ambassador Morgenthau should cable for assistance six thousand miles away and get it."[3]

Ethnic cleansing had emerged as a deliberate military strategy in the Balkan Wars of 1912–13. With the outbreak of continental war in 1914, the international dimensions of the refugee crisis grew quickly and worsened as fighting raged in eastern Europe and Anatolia long after the winter of 1918. By the time Wilson toured Italy it was clear that Europe faced a full-fledged humanitarian disaster and lacked the institutions to cope with it. Meanwhile, the peace conference in Paris and its embrace of nationality politics actually made things worse as east European leaders rushed to strengthen their claims to territory by forcing out members of those groups—Ukrainians, Hungarians, Germans, and Jews—whom they did not wish to include in their new states.

At Paris, refugees scarcely figured at all in the discussions over the founding of the League, and there was no mention of them in the Covenant. Traditionally it had been to church and missionary groups that governments entrusted their care. But the scale of the postwar problem dwarfed the capacity of such groups, and in February 1921 the Russian Red Cross Committee appealed to the League for help on the grounds that it was "the only super-national political authority capable of solving a problem which is beyond the power of exclusively humanitarian organizations." From the League's perspective, the hope was—and would remain for the next thirty years—that such problems were temporary. The Norwegian explorer Dr. Fridtjof Nansen was appointed high commissioner for Russian refugees. He was given a small staff and a budget dependent on contributions from member states and told to coordinate refugee care and resettlement. In such straitened circumstances, organized humanitarian internationalism was born.[4]

Nansen's long-term problem were the numerous White Russian refugees scattered across the world. A Soviet decree of December 1921 had stripped them of their nationality and they therefore required a new legal status. The solution he devised was an internationally recognized Certificate of Identity—the so-called Nansen Passport, in effect the first international identity paper—that allowed the holder to gain admittance to countries demanding proof of identity, and to travel. It is not surprising that when the White Russian Cossack officer Ivan Soboleff quit his regiment in Chinese Turkestan, flitted through the Chinese army, and spent two years traveling around the world by bicycle and motorbike, he called the book of his exploits *Nansen Passport,* in homage to the piece of paper that had made it possible.[5]

The emergence of the Nansen Passport was a striking demonstration of how rising nationalism and ideological conflict could prompt more intensive internationalism. In the late nineteenth century, the trend had been to do away with passports. It was the 1914–18 war that brought about their reintroduction. In 1920 the League sponsored one of its first technical conferences on the subject of passport standardization. Nansen's improvisation thus fitted into a more general rethinking of the relationship between mobility and security in the modern world. As new nation-states introduced citizenship laws that excluded minorities or (in the Russian case) political opponents, people were stranded by the fortunes of war, possessing only temporary papers or a birth certificate issued by some now defunct empire. The Nansen Passport offered one way around this new problem and eventually some 450,000 of them were issued. That an identity document with authority recognized by national states could be issued by a body like the League showed how far the reach of international government now suddenly extended.

At the same time, the League was overseeing emergency relief in the wretched camps and shantytowns housing Russian, Armenian, and Greek refugees in the Balkans. Together with charitable groups like the Near East Foundation—along the Kaisariani road out of Athens the Near East Foundation playing field is still visible—they ran and financed vast tented encampments and brought in health experts to stop infectious diseases. In 1923, the League helped the Greek government raise a loan to resettle the hundreds of thousands of refugees from Asia Minor and then set up the Refugee Settlement Commission, which built new neighborhoods and indeed entire small towns. This too was new: before 1914, humanitarian assistance had mostly been the domain of charities. Now it had become important enough to become the prerogative of governments.

The League's impact in such cases was enormous, but the problem was even bigger, and there were growing signs of donor fatigue. In an effort to regularize Nansen's position, his office became the Refugee Service of the International Labor Organization—thus providing some kind of home in the international bureaucracy. But governments refused to admit—as they would again after 1945—that refugees might be a permanent feature of a world order based around the nation-state, and this remained a constraint on international action under the League (and later the UN). The Refugee Service remained poorly financed, and when Nansen died in 1930 much of the energy went out of it. In his memory the ILO service became the Nansen International Office for Refugees, but it was an autonomous body and not formally part of the League at all. The League's—and its members'—unhappiness at the thought of any permanent association with refugee welfare could not have been more obvious. The Nansen Office received an annual subvention from the League along with instructions to wind up its work within a decade.

Yet far from disappearing, the refugee problem was about to grow significantly worse. The international depression, gathering pace after 1929, made it harder for refugees to seek work, and charitable support dried up. Soviet membership of the League from 1934 led to continual efforts by Soviet delegates to obstruct work on behalf of White Russians. And with the outbreak of the Spanish Civil War in 1936, refugees from the fighting, and from the triumphant Franco regime, became the largest single refugee group in interwar Europe. In addition, large numbers of Jews and leftists were either forced out of the Reich or chose to flee while they could. The League created a special high commissioner for refugees from Germany, then refused to give him proper support, and intergovernmental talks on balancing an "orderly emigration" with the "absorption capacity" of possible hosts got nowhere. Making matters worse, other east European states started to see in the Reich an alternative pole of attraction to Geneva and a model to emulate. Long before the Nazi New Order became a reality, schemes of forcible mass resettlement and large-scale deportation were in the air. Europe's refugee problem was clearly just beginning.

MINORITY RIGHTS

International oversight was also born in a closely related arena—that of minority rights. This arose also in Paris, where Jewish lobbying groups in particular urged the Great Powers to impose on the new states of eastern Europe the obligation to grant minorities certain rights. Clearly, to have any chance of success, such a policy required international policing in some form. By February 1919 versions of a minority-rights regime were being drafted by British diplomats who were well aware of the potentially explosive implications of the idea. Foreign Office expert James Headlam-Morley, who sat on the so-called New States Committee, asked his superiors for guidance as to what was meant by guaranteeing the "cultural, linguistic and political rights" of minorities: "I assume it implies definite clauses to be entered in the treaties, by which the new states are to be recognized, and that if the substance of these clauses is not observed, there will be a right of appeal to the League of Nations by whom the treaty will be guaranteed. Would it not be a good thing to ask the Legal section to draft clauses so that we might know more precisely to what we are committing ourselves?"[6]

Because the new international organization was to be allowed to monitor the behavior of sovereign states within what had generally been regarded as their own jurisdiction, the whole idea was bound to be deeply controversial. Moreover, in what was becoming an established pattern where international law was concerned, the Great Powers who were keenest for strategic reasons to impose these new legal obligations on the east Europeans were insistent that they should not be subjected to them themselves. Here, as in other areas, the League emanated the breathtaking civilizational self-assurance of nineteenth-century liberalism and the hierarchical world it took for granted. To British, American, and French delegates it was obvious that the maturity of their political institutions and the wisdom of their governing elites obviated the need for any such measures. Equally obviously, in their view, the new states of central and eastern Europe lacked the common sense to bring together their own fractured and divided societies without external supervision. When disturbing news arrived from Poland of anti-Jewish violence perpetrated by Polish nationalists in the spring of 1919, they felt confirmed in this view.

Headlam-Morley himself suggested that there were at least two aspects to this potentially most explosive of legal innovations. The first was substantive: rights for whom and which ones? In the case of Czechoslovakia, he observed, one might distinguish Germans in western Bohemia who had "always" lived there from Czechs who had chosen to move relatively recently to, say, Vienna. ("Surely when people of one nationality, for private reasons of this kind, choose to take up their residence in a foreign city, there is no claim of any kind to receive exceptional treatment.") In other words, not all members of an ethnic minority were equally worthy recipients of cultural and national rights—to use one's language in public as well as private, perhaps to ensure that it was taught in schools and allowed to be used in the press, and by extension to have a range of cultural activities safeguarded.

The second issue was procedural: what status should such rights have, and who could grant them and provide the guarantee that they would be respected, without which they would likely be meaningless? At Paris separate treaties were drawn up and eventually signed between the Great Powers and the states of eastern Europe. These granted international recognition to these states and their borders and in return guaranteed their inhabitants not only equality before the law and freedom of worship but the right to use their own language and to private and public education. The first such treaty, signed with Poland, incorporated a right of appeal to the council of the League; others, signed with another seven states, followed suit. It was in vain that diplomats from these small nations protested that the guarantees would make internal government harder and create states within states.

For all the obvious double standards, the minority-rights regime represented an enormous advance over any previous international effort to tell states what they should do in their internal affairs. The trouble was that it was set up in a way almost guaranteed to alienate all sides. Nations accused of misconduct were aggrieved at being singled out for international attention. At the same time, the League could not do much for those who complained. It refused to admit individual complainants and scrutinized all accusations so carefully that scarcely any were admitted for consideration by the council. Frustration therefore built up among representatives of the minorities and their supporters. They mobilized in a new lobbying group, the European Congress of Nationalities, but this did not have much success in improving procedure.

To complicate matters further, the largest single minority in interwar Europe was ethnically German. Stranded by Germany and Austria-Hungary's defeat on the wrong side of the new borders, millions of German speakers found themselves citizens of Poland, Czechoslovakia, and Yugoslavia. For them assimilation was far slower than the diplomats at Paris had envisaged and many of them faced pressure to leave their homes. Poland was especially assiduous in trying to force German farmers out; only the Estonians made a serious effort to incorporate minorities into their national life. But because the two major revisionist powers—Germany and Hungary—also made support for their conationals a key part of their interwar diplomacy, protection of minorities became bound up with a larger set of complaints about the justice of the Versailles settlement. And this in turn of course made countries like Poland, Romania, and Czechoslovakia dig in their heels. Since the British and the French needed strong supporters in eastern Europe against the twin threats of Germany and Soviet Bolshevism, they were unenthusiastic about making sure that their allies were observing the minorities provisions they had signed up to. Indeed as time went on and the threat from Germany grew, their pressure on the "New States" evaporated. Even before Hitler took power in 1933, therefore, most people in Europe had ceased to place much hope in the League as a defender of minorities. As in the case of refugees, the League promised more in the case of minorities than it was capable of delivering in the brief period when it enjoyed any kind of authority at all.

HIERARCHY AND RACE

Wilson's messianic rhetoric had electrified millions not only in Europe. Intellectuals in Cairo, Bombay, and Peking all praised his commitment to the rights of "small nations." In this "Wilsonian moment," they scarcely believed that he intended for independence to be granted to the peoples of Europe alone. The year 1919 brought swift disillusionment as the British clamped down on unrest in the Punjab, Afghanistan, and Egypt with no more than a murmur from the

Americans, Wilson's star waned quickly, and Mao Zedong, Jawaharlal Nehru, and Ho Chi Minh were just some of the young nationalist activists around the world pushed left by the return of empire.[7]

In Paris that February, the first Pan-African Congress convened in a hotel in the Boulevard des Capucines, with delegates from Africa as well as from the United States and Britain. Its rather moderate demands included the use of the League of Nations to supervise native rights, a program of graduated self-government, equal rights for "civilized Negroes," and the promotion of mass education in Africa. It was entirely ignored by the powers. The sociologist W. E. B. Du Bois, who had proposed a new Central African state under native control, was kept at arm's length by the American delegation, which was much more sympathetic to the case made by the British and the South African Smuts, for continued, indeed extended, white control of the continent.[8]

Equally revealing of Western attitudes to the rest of the world was the dismal fate of the 1919 Japanese racial equality clause proposal. Unlike the Africans, Japan's presence at Paris was invested with great symbolic significance: it was the one non-European, non-Christian country to be accepted as a major power, and consolidating this recognition was a preeminent goal of Japanese diplomacy.[9] Yet there was considerable anti-Asian feeling among many of the English-speaking delegates. Canada's 1910 Immigration Act had denied entry to immigrants "belonging to any race deemed unsuited to the climate or requirements" of the country. In New Zealand, politicians called for preventing the country being deluged with "Asiatic Tatars." Perhaps most virulently anti-Asian of all was Australia, whose White Australia policy followed South African models in using language tests to exclude nonwhite immigrants. In the United States, the Californian press ran anti-Japanese campaigns, an Asian Exclusion League was formed, and in 1913 the Californian Alien Land Act had specifically targeted Japanese immigrants and restricted their property rights. Smuts's vision of an Anglo-American League was rooted in these racial anxieties.[10]

When its delegation left Tokyo for Paris, the Japanese were

unsure—forgivably—how committed the Americans and the British were to setting up a League at all, and so they gave their delegates only the vaguest instructions to make sure "to secure suitable guarantees against the disadvantages to Japan . . . from racial prejudice." As a result, Japanese policy was basically made up on the spot by its delegates in Paris. In February they suggested to "secure the equality of nations" who were members of the League by guaranteeing the equal treatment of their nationals. As was clearly understood at the time, this would not be a commitment by the League to general racial equality around the globe but rather a discreet way of addressing the Japanese grievance over the discriminatory and humiliating immigration policies confronting them around the Pacific Rim. Everyone but the Australians (with the South Africans discreetly cheering them on) agreed to a preamble being inserted in the League Covenant endorsing the principle of racial equality, and when the Japanese tabled their draft, a majority actually voted in favor. Yet President Wilson, who was chairing the session, ruled that because the motion had not passed unanimously, it could not be adopted. Flouting his own procedures, Wilson evidently feared that the issue was simply too sensitive domestically and internationally for the motion to be allowed to pass. As for the Japanese, what upset them was not only the stunning diplomatic rebuff but also the fact that their initiative became known as the "racial equality" proposal—since the last thing they knew would help their cause was to be identified with the lesser peoples of the world. The only consolation was that Wilson had said they could take over the former German claims to the Chinese province of Shantung. To the dismay of the Chinese, Wilson thus effectively bought off the Japanese by violating his own principle of self-determination. Better the extension of imperialism, one might say, so far as Wilson was concerned, than any commitment to global racial equality.[11]

THE MANDATE SYSTEM

The Japanese proposal had certainly touched a nerve, because Western commentators were increasingly worried about "the Tide of Color" and a worldwide "awakening of race consciousness." Fear of "Asiatics" fueled scaremongering race tracts in the United States and the broader anxiety about race mixing even led to the emergence of an entirely new academic discipline—international relations—which in its earliest incarnation was very largely about how to think about the global implications of race tensions at a time when empire was increasingly in question. The prestigious journal *Foreign Affairs,* today perhaps the premier forum for commentary on international affairs in the United States, had actually been founded as the *Journal of Race Development* in 1910, the year before the Universal Races Congress in London, then turned into the *Journal of International Relations* (in 1919) before ending up with its present title.[12]

Race was not only an American concern. The British—with extensive colonial possessions to defend and a defense budget under constant pressure—were just as concerned. Revived by Du Bois at Paris in 1919, the Pan-African movement was about to enter its most active epoch, hosting congresses that attracted the likes of H. G. Wells. The following year, Marcus Garvey and his Universal Negro Improvement Association, emphatically linking together the plight of blacks in the United States and the continued grip of colonialism in Africa, held a much-publicized conference in New York's Madison Square Garden and issued a Declaration of Rights of the Negro Peoples of the World. Confronting powerful nationalist movements in Egypt and India, "the awakening of race consciousness," and increased organizational activity among "agitators" preying upon the credulous masses—and already anxious about the Bolsheviks' exploitation of the issue—British colonial officials anticipated the spread of multiple threats such as Pan-Africanism, Pan-Arabism, and Pan-Islam. "Asia is dreaming waking visions," wrote a British district commissioner, Captain J. E. T. Philipps (who would later be forced to quit the colonial service because of his outspoken criticism of indirect rule). "Africa is stirring uneasily in her sleep. To what world-conditions do we want them to become conscious?"[13]

In a world where preserving the standard of civilization through Western control seemed more important than ever, however, there was no easily applicable political model: a simple extension of colonial rule on nineteenth-century lines was simply unacceptable to European or American public opinion; on the other hand, allowing colonial peoples their freedom seemed equally preposterous. This was where the League's main contribution to the redefinition of Europe's relations with the colonial world—the mandate system—achieved its true significance. It took the old standard-of-civilization idea and recalibrated this for a world committed, eventually, to the Mazzinian paradigm of a society of nations. It extended imperial control in a less overt form. Nothing showed better the extent to which the League of Nations remained part of a worldview that took the virtues of empire for granted.

THE IDEA that uncivilized peoples would benefit from an internationalized regime within an imperial order went back at least to the radical British journalist J. A. Hobson, who had argued in the aftermath of the Boer War for international oversight of African peoples based on "a supreme standard of moral appeal, some conception of the welfare of humanity as an organic unity." Insisting that the war had been triggered by private finance capital in search of profitable resources to plunder, he went on to postulate three conditions for "sane imperialism":

> Such interference with the government of a lower race must be directed primarily to secure the safety and progress of the civilization of the world and not the special interest of the interfering nation. Such interference must be attended by an improvement and eleva-

tion of the character of the people who are brought under this control. Lastly the determination of the two preceding conditions must not be left to the arbitrary will or judgment of the interfering nation, but must proceed from some organized representation of civilized humanity.[14]

Oversight by an impartial and representative international organization thus became in Hobson's conception the key to justifying continued colonial rule. Internationalism was not the antithesis to empire but its civilizer. The work of this ardent follower of the tradition of Cobden—Hobson went on to write a biography of his hero entitled *The International Man*—represented a striking shift from Cobden's anti-imperialism, and evidence of how far the spread of empire had been accepted by the turn of the century even on much of the European left so long as intentions were pure and the goals disinterested. In Hobson's updating of Cobden, the supervision of "lower races" became one of the chief goals of international government, a trope that would help shape League policy and lingered on into the twenty-first century in the form of UN trusteeships and in the much later idea of an international "Responsibility to Protect."

The war itself gave Hobson doubts, however. As a supporter of the idea of a League of Nations, he feared that excluding the non-European world from participation might create an international version of cooperative imperialism "which would in the long run prove not less dangerous to the peace of the world than the national antagonism of the past, in that it was the expression of the joint ambitions and pretensions of a group of powerful white nations masquerading as world government." Yet there was no alternative: for Hobson, as for most liberal and progressive thinkers of his era (W. E. B. Du Bois was no different), participation in civilized life required national consciousness, and he saw no sign of this in Africa or elsewhere. Colonial peoples were, in effect, children to be educated in trust for civilization as a whole.[15]

Internationalization in this spirit offered a vocabulary for imperial policymakers to acknowledge the overt wartime opposition in Britain in particular to any further annexations of territory. Annexations, wrote the *Guardian* in 1917, were disreputable, as "populations ought not to be bandied about without regard to their own wishes as if they were property." In Parliament that May, Prime Minister Lloyd George said that Britain had no annexationist desires and would leave the fate of Africa to be determined at the peace conference. The Labour Party was even more outspoken and called for the formation of a new Super National Authority to run *all* African colonies, and the Arab provinces of the Ottoman Empire as well. If competition for resources led to war, perhaps the creation of an international economic body to supervise their exploitation could contribute to the peace.[16]

Confounding such hopes, the First World War did not end the Scramble for Africa but extended it into the Middle East, which had been secretly split during the war itself into British and French zones of influence in the Sykes-Picot Agreement. Whitehall simultaneously talked up the emergence of "an independent Arab State or a Confederation of Arab States . . . under the suzerainty of an Arab chief." T. E. Lawrence and Gertrude Bell promoted the Arab nationalist cause and an Anglo-French declaration regarding the Middle East issued immediately after the end of the war talked of "the complete and definitive liberation of peoples so long oppressed by the Turks and the establishment of national governments and administrations drawing their authority from the initiative and free choice of indigenous populations." But this certainly did not mean what it sounded like it meant—that peoples in strategically vital regions would be allowed to decide their own fate. Imperial strategic needs remained paramount. So the question became whether there was a way of winning Arab nationalists to the British side while preserving control. The chief British administrator in Mesopotamia, Arnold Wilson, thought not. He believed it was "impossible in these days to create a new sovereign Mohammedan State by diplomatic or administrative means."[17] Others were subtler and saw League authorization as the means of squaring the circle. "As regards British interests," Mark Sykes minuted Robert Cecil in October 1917, "it is, I think, desirable . . . without in any way showing any desire to annex Palestine, or to establish a Protectorate over it, so to order our policy that when the time comes to choose a mandatory power for its control, by the consensus of opinion and the desire of the inhabitants, we shall be the most likely candidates." Or as Winston Churchill was to write, "There were to be no annexations but Mandates were to be granted to the Principal Powers which would give them the necessary excuse for control."[18]

There were still the Americans to be brought into line, however. Woodrow Wilson was on record as opposing annexation, although he had no concrete alternatives. His adviser George Beer had proposed international supervision of Africa, and a U.S. draft of the covenant described the League as "trustee" with the "sovereign rights of ultimate disposal" over all mandated territories. Beer himself thought this arrangement was nothing but an extension of the 1885 Berlin Conference on Africa and believed that his main innovation was to propose that the League would have an "unqualified right of intervention." But such an idea sounded dangerously radical to the European colonial powers. The French in particular wanted "annexations pure and simple" so that France could "continue her work of civilization in tropical Africa" unrestricted.[19]

Caught between the Americans, who wanted a break with the imperial past, and the French desire for more colonies, the British found a compromise. There would be three classes of mandates, corresponding to the supposed civilizational capabilities of their inhabitants. The Class A mandates (in the Middle East) envisaged "provisional recognition" of their independence; the Class B and C mandates—for supposedly primitive places in the Pacific and Africa—remained colonies in all but name. Everyone concerned was happy bar the inhabitants of the mandates themselves. The French (and the Australians, South Africans, and New Zealanders) comforted themselves with the thought that there was "no real difference between a colony and a mandated area." Wilson preserved the principle of international oversight, and got agreement to create a new Permanent Mandates Commission (PMC) to scrutinize the work of the mandatory powers on behalf of the League and demand an annual accounting from them.[20]

What powers did the League's PMC really enjoy? It is true that the commissioners themselves were prepared to push disputes even with their own national governments surprisingly far. Their main lever was international public opinion, and in 1922 when the South African government used airpower to suppress a rebellion in southwest Africa, they were actually rather effective in quashing Smuts's hopes of being allowed to annex the territory. In a small way, perhaps, by establishing the principle of international oversight and making it respectable, the commission paved the way for postwar decolonization. But it is worth asking how long the colonies might have remained under imperial or mandatory rule had the Second World War not intervened and American anticolonialism (and America's fear of Bolshevism) not been added to the mix. Others believed the PMC merely had the effect of legitimating the existing colonial order. The future Indian premier Jawaharlal Nehru himself had no doubts, writing in 1942 that "so far as the League is concerned, it looks forward to a permanent dominance by these Powers over their empires."[21]

Moreover, however much liberals congratulated themselves on the impact of the Mandates Commission, it clearly did not do much to satisfy people in the mandated territories themselves. The Samoans, for example, who had a highly organized political structure of their own, found that their complaints about New Zealand rule were largely ignored. Almost no one bothered with the real grievances of Papuans under Australia. French mandatory rule in Syria—supposedly a Class A mandate—was hardly an advertisement for the standard of civilization either: only by bombing the center of Damascus were the French able to put down a nationalist uprising in 1925. Thus just over a decade before Guernica was flattened in the Spanish

Civil War to international consternation and outrage, French tanks, guns, and planes obliterated an old quarter in the Syrian capital. The death toll was several times higher than in Spain. Yet there was almost no international reaction and the Permanent Mandates Commission simply asked the French to explain themselves at a special session.[22]

Similarly unchecked, the British were equally fond of airpower. Churchill himself urged not merely aerial bombing but the use of mustard gas against "uncivilised tribes" in India and Mesopotamia. Only transport and production delays prevented their use, before a series of pioneering international conferences that discussed outlawing the use of chemical weapons led him to back down. Meanwhile, what was euphemistically known as "air control" remained the chief operational means of holding down large areas of the Middle East. The nationalist revolt in Iraq in 1920 cost nearly one thousand British lives; the Arab death toll must have been at least several times higher. About all that can be said in favor of the Permanent Mandates Commission is that Iraq was granted independence in 1932 (with no reference to Geneva as there should have been) because the British believed the newly independent kingdom would be even easier to rule than as a mandate.[23]

The mandate system had been too obviously part of a victor's peace to survive the fascist challenge. In 1935, when Italian troops invaded Ethiopia, Mussolini brushed off calls for conciliation or suggestions to legitimize Italian control by asserting the principle of League oversight; instead he called for direct rule pure and simple. Fascism in this sense represented a return to a cruder and less internationalized model of colonial order. Nevertheless, even for some Nazis, the value of legitimizing colonial control through the League appealed. A final coda reveals the malleability of the mandate concept. When the Third Reich's Jewish experts in the German foreign ministry drew up plans in the summer of 1940 for turning the island of Madagascar into a reservation for Polish Jews, they talked about this too as a possible mandate in a League now serving German ends rather than British. For a few seconds, the possibility evidently flashed across the mind of an ambitious Nazi civil servant, as France fell and Europe lay at the Germans' feet, of a League of Nations transformed into an instrument of fascist rule. How far-fetched this seemed was really a matter of perspective: what looked ludicrous from the viewpoint of London or Paris, a travesty of a more high-minded reality, seemed—as we know from the wartime correspondence of Indian nationalists and others—a relatively unremarkable proposition in Africa and Asia where what mattered was less the identity of the imperial master than the brute fact of European colonial rule itself.[24]

There were even in the 1920s, however, signs of resistance and opposition, efforts to coordinate international anticolonial action against the liberal empires that in some ways resembled the similar struggles that had taken place in Europe before 1848 against the empires of the Holy Alliance. Outrage at the 1925 French bombardment of Damascus had called forth a Committee Against Atrocities in Syria, and wider disappointment with the League's colonial policy led a Congress of Oppressed Nationalities to meet in Brussels in February 1927—a forgotten precursor to the much more celebrated Bandung Conference almost thirty years later. Among the participants was the Indian National Congress, participating in an international meeting for the first time, and representatives of another dozen African and Asian countries. A few months later, a short-lived League against Imperialism was headed by Jawaharlal Nehru, the representative of the INC and a striking contrast with the British-appointed stooge who spoke for India at the League in Geneva. Indeed a sympathetic journalist dubbed the 1927 congress "the real League of Nations."[25]

Behind this brief surge in anticolonial cooperation there was one organizer, the brilliant Comintern agent Willi Münzenberg, and thus one essential point of reference: the USSR. The Brussels conference was in fact initiated by the Communist International—as was the League against Imperialism. Nehru himself visited Moscow a few months afterward, and although the experience did not turn him into a communist (indeed later he was to say his visit was what had prevented him becoming one), it deepened his admiration for the Soviet stance against imperialism and demonstrated its global appeal. The League against Imperialism was not—could not have been—a serious counterweight to the Geneva mandates system, especially after 1929 when its noncommunist representatives came under attack from the Comintern itself. But it was of some historical significance because it represented the intersection of two forces: looking to the future, it indicated the alliances and connections being forged among colonial activists that would culminate in their domination of the UN in the 1960s and 1970s; looking backward, it was a last gasp, faltering and ineffectual, of the once vast revolutionary ambition of the Communist International, an organization that had emerged at the same time as the League of Nations, and for a moment threatened to rival it.[26]

COMMUNIST INTERNATIONALISM

The British writer and journalist Arthur Ransome had spent much of the First World War in Russia when in March 1919 a Bolshevik contact got him into a meeting being held in the old courts of justice in the Kremlin. Having made it past the two Red Army soldiers guarding the door, Ransome found himself in a large room, whose walls and even floors were entirely decorated in red. Banners proclaimed "Long Live the Third International" in various languages. He was struck by the sight of Trotsky in leather coat, breeches, and gaiters, with a fur hat bearing the insignia of the Red Army, for he remembered him as one of Europe's most ardent antimilitarists. Behind a red-covered table on a platform at the end of the room sat Lenin, "speaking when necessary in almost every European language with astonishing ease"; delegates representing mostly European socialist movements sat in rows in the hall.[27]

Ransome had stumbled, as he quickly realized, into the founding congress of the Third International. Thanks to Marx's participation, the International Working Men's Association of 1864 had been retrospectively dubbed the "First" International.[28] The Second had been formed in 1889, six years after Marx's death, when socialist and labor parties were becoming a real parliamentary force for the first time: it had established May 1 as an international holiday, created an effective international bureau in Brussels in 1900, and spearheaded the campaign for the eight-hour workday. It had also served to disseminate socialist and especially Marxist ideas around Europe with extraordinary success. But its internationalist credentials had been shattered by the outbreak of war in 1914 as workers went off to fight for their respective countries. A shadow organization based in Berne in Switzerland staggered on through the war, and it was the effort to revive it that had spurred Lenin to call for the meeting of this new body in Moscow.

Founded in the midst of the Russian civil war as a means of asserting Lenin's leadership over the European socialist movement, the Third International lay entirely in the hands of the Bolsheviks. In theory it was conceived as a supranational organization to which all national communist parties would be subordinate.[29] In fact, its members had to pledge allegiance to a list of twenty-one points drawn up by Lenin himself. These demanded that they break with "reformist" socialism, subordinate parliamentary activity to the needs of the revolution, base themselves on the principle of democratic centralism, and recognize the authority of what became known as the Comintern. In effect, adherence implied becoming a loyal instrument of the leadership of the Russian Communist Party. Always the centralizer, Lenin aimed to prevent the new organization turning into "the wreck of the Second International." In fact, despite these uncompromising words, tense negotiations went on until early 1923 to try to bring the members of the Second and Third Internationals together, but even as fascism gained power in Italy, they broke down and the European left remained fractured for another decade and more.[30]

For Lenin, the ultimate enemy was not the traitors of the Second International but the forces of capitalism and those who would defend it. In the words of Point 6 of his program:

> Every party that wishes to belong to the Communist International has the obligation to unmask not only open social-patriotism but also the insincerity and hypocrisy of social-pacifism, to show the workers systematically that, without the revolutionary overthrow of capitalism, no international court of arbitration, no agreement on the limitation of armaments, no "democratic" reorganization of the League of Nations will be able to prevent new imperialist wars.

In this way, the revolution from its inception positioned itself as the true heir to nineteenth-century labor internationalism, and denounced the League of Nations as nothing more than a continuation of the old Metternichian counter-revolution.[31]

Leninist and Wilsonian internationalism were thus in competition from the very start, and each man recognized the novel element in world affairs that the other represented: the competition started off with something of the intensity of a sibling rivalry. Lenin's denunciation of secret diplomacy was what had prompted Wilson's Fourteen Points, with its commitment to "open covenants of peace" and its prominent appeal to the Russians themselves to enter "the society of nations under institutions of their own choosing." In 1918, Wilson still hoped to be able to persuade "the peoples of Russia" of his good intentions. But the outbreak of the civil war, the Allied intervention in the Russian Civil War, and the spread of radicalism not only across much of Europe but across the United States in 1919 as well forced the two sides much further apart. Bolshevism now became a kind of raison d'être for the League itself. Wilson himself had confided to Lloyd George in March 1919 that "if we are to offer Europe an alternative to Bolshevism, we must make the League of Nations something which will protect neighbors and punish predators." When the League was founded, Russia was not invited to join, and the official American position was that diplomatic recognition of the Bolshevik regime was impossible.

The Comintern itself was thus formed not only to take advantage of "the gigantic pace of the world revolution" but also to prevent that revolution from being defeated by "the alliance of capitalist states which are banding together . . . under the hypocritical banner of the 'League of Nations.'" It had to serve as a means of cementing allegiance to the Russian Bolsheviks since they were the leaders of this "new era in history." Yet the International had a wider significance as well. As a decidedly antievolutionary Marxist, Lenin was conscious—and happy to discuss the fact publicly—of how odd it was that the revolution had broken out in Russia, and how important it was to ensure that it would spread globally. If the coming of a socialist society was inevitable, it would happen through the spread of the revolution. The Comintern thus served a second purpose, which was to develop revolutionary forces abroad. Alongside Lenin, much of the Bolshevik leadership was well traveled, familiar with exile, and polyglot; the Comintern was run by them as a means of consolidating the ties and connections that they had already forged in the years before the war.[32]

In short order, therefore, the Bolsheviks came to identify the defeat of the Second International with victory in a much larger struggle worldwide. The war, they believed, had become a catalyst for the long-awaited global revolution. Leading Bolshevik Nikolai Bukharin hailed the "contradictions of the capitalist world system" that had broken out in a "gigantic explosion." The imperialist system was in collapse. Only the proletariat could save humanity: "It must destroy the rule of capital, make war impossible, abolish state frontiers, change the entire world into one cooperative community, make a reality of the brotherhood and freedom of the peoples." The main obstacle was world capital itself, mobilizing behind the League of Nations, "pouring out torrents of pacifist words." The West's talk of peace was a fiction, another Russian delegate argued. The British and the Americans talked about "democratic foreign policy," but they were still the old imperialists. "Alsace-Lorraine has been incorporated into France without consulting the population; Ireland, Egypt, India have no right of national self-determination; the Yugoslav State and the Czechoslovak republic were established by armed force." As for the League of Nations:

> If it should come into formal existence, it will only play the part of a Holy Alliance of the capitalists to suppress the workers' revolution. Propaganda for the League of Nations is the best way of introducing confusion into the revolutionary consciousness of the working class. Instead of the slogan of an international union of revolutionary workers' republics, the slogan of an international association of sham democracies is being put forward, to be attained by class collaboration between the proletariat and the bourgeoisie. The "League of Nations" is a delusive means by which the social-traitors, acting on behalf of international capital, split the forces of the proletariat.[33]

Lenin himself referred to the League as a "stinking corpse" and "an alliance of world bandits against the proletariat." It seemed as though the Marx-Mazzini clash of the 1860s was playing itself out afresh, this time for much higher stakes: indeed, in a sense the entire Cold War was a continuation of the same struggle between rival nineteenth-century conceptions of international order once articulated by impoverished exiles in London but now espoused by the world's most powerful states. Except that what happened in practice was rather different. The Comintern lasted officially for more than two decades. But as Bolshevism consolidated its grip over the USSR and the immediate prospects for world revolution outside the Soviet borders faded away, official attitudes by Soviet diplomats toward the League and its members sounded a more measured and even conciliatory tone.

The war between the Bolsheviks and the Poles and the stalemate that followed was really the turning point, though it took Lenin a little while to realize that revolution in the rest of Europe was a doomed enterprise. When the British tried to broker an end to the Polish-Soviet War in 1920, the Soviet commissar for foreign affairs welcomed the initiative but turned it into a struggle for recognition. He protested that Russia could not recognize the intervention of "the group of governments called the League of Nations," and could certainly not accept the League's claim to act as an arbiter in international affairs over matters involving nonmembers. "The Soviet government cannot in any circumstance agree to a group of Powers taking on themselves the functions of a supreme court over all the States of the earth."[34] This relatively conciliatory message was strengthened two years later when Russia was invited to take part in a conference on international economic reconstruction at Genoa. Commissar of foreign affairs Georgy Chicherin, the multilingual scion of a wealthy aristocratic family of diplomats and jurists, shrugged off memories of his brief stint in Brixton jail, preached cooperation and coexistence between "the old social order and the new order now being born," and offered to participate in a "revision of the covenant of the League of Nations so as to transform it into a real League of the Peoples."[35]

Nothing came of this idea. But the era of Soviet irreconcilability was over. By the mid-1920s, not only did capitalism appear to have stabilized in Europe, but it was clear that the League would not in fact be able to bring down the revolution. In India and Egypt, the global revolutionary wave appeared to have subsided: Comintern expectations that the struggle for socialism would break out in Persia, Armenia, Turkey, and above all China—the failure there in 1927 was an especially severe blow—had been belied, and party memberships in these countries fell steadily. The Comintern's Negro Bureau exhorted Africans to rise up, but outside South Africa there was no Communist Party and no revolutionary movements. Its efforts to mobilize black Americans behind the slogan of national self-determination for them in the southern states was hopeless. As the logic behind the Comintern became less appealing, Soviet trade delegations spread out across Europe and governments began to recognize the Bolsheviks as the legitimate authorities in the country. Inside the USSR, the rejectionist school of Bolshevik international law gave way to accommodation and pragmatism, and at the end of 1925 Moscow responded positively to a League invitation to help plan a general disarmament conference.[36]

This was not to say that the Comintern was completely sidelined. On the contrary, Lenin's heirs tried to have their cake and eat it too, regularizing diplomatic relations with the European powers, even as they fostered relations with communist parties and anticolonial nationalists worldwide. In the mid-1920s, as we have seen, under the direction of master showman Willi Münzenberg, anticolonialism moved to the center of Comintern activity. The Brussels conference—Münzenberg had chosen the venue to publicize Belgian crimes in the Congo—and the Berlin League against Imperialism briefly brought together European anti-imperialists, fellow travelers, and colonial nationalists like Nehru and Chiang Kai-shek. But this masterful propaganda exercise had little of substance beneath it and was not taken seriously by Stalin and those closest to him.[37] In the mid-1920s, it was not just that Moscow was disappointed in the prospects for revolution in one Asian country after another; by this point many of the inhabitants of Central Asia in particular had already been forced to appreciate what others would come to see later, that for Moscow security came above revolution, and that this would always make the balance of forces in Europe the greatest concern.[38]

That Stalin's priorities did not lie in the colonial world became clear in the early 1930s as Hitler's rise brought the League and the Kremlin closer together. In September 1934, the USSR was admitted to the League and became a permanent member of its council. The Soviet commissar for Foreign Affairs, Maxim Litvinov, who was the chief exponent of the pro-League line within the Kremlin, welcomed the decision and even likened the League to the USSR itself, which he described as a sort of League of Nations of its own. Stalin for his part had few illusions about the League, placed no trust in "collective security," and did not seriously believe there was any prospect of closer understanding with any capitalist powers. But he had even fewer illusions about the Comintern. After all, it was imperative to have allies in Europe, and League membership signaled the Soviet Union's desire for these and its willingness to play by Western rules. Even before Stalin killed off its leadership in the Terror, this left the Comintern a shadow of the organization it had aspired to be. The final Comintern congress of 1935 devoted almost no space to anticolonialism at all, and one of the most striking things to emerge from

Stalin's interview with the American journalist Roy Howard the following year was his outright denial that the USSR had any plans to export world revolution, or even believed that this was possible. That the leader of the USSR should go deliberately on the public record on this point was remarkable to anyone who remembered the fiery internationalism of his predecessor. This certainly did not mean Stalin had given up faith in the idea of revolution, but in his mind this was linked now to the war he saw coming and the success of the Red Army, not to the fate of an organization he had always mistrusted.[39]

Stalin's basic outlook on matters of international coexistence emerged with exemplary clarity in a famous interview with H. G. Wells. Usually this is cited as an example of Wells's credulousness, and certainly the British writer comes across as embarrassingly self-centered and naïve. But Stalin himself was fairly forthright. Respectful toward Roosevelt, he made it clear that the American New Deal, in seeking to save capitalism, could not in his view escape its contradictions. He was unimpressed by Wells's idea that engineers and scientists might become the organizers of a new world order. Engineers do what they are told, Stalin told him; scientists are as capable of doing immense harm as good. People who serve the cause of profit are not the ones to "reconstruct the world." That can only be done through the possession of political power, and the only power capable of driving this through are the toiling masses and their representatives. In this vision, which placed the working classes of the developed world and the political leadership of the Soviet Union in the vanguard of change, there was no mention at all of empire and the anticolonial struggle.[40]

THE PROBLEM WITH INTERNATIONALISM

Although it is always tempting to write off Nazi ideology as the irrational expression of madmen, in the context of the larger twentieth-century story of international governance, nowhere else offers a more sustained critique of the dominant assumptions of liberal internationalism. It was not just that National Socialism disagreed with the terms of the peace settlement. Revisionism is too weak a term for the sweeping nature of the Nazis' objections: they believed their guiding philosophy represented an entirely different view of the world, one that exposed the League's internationalism for the sham it really was.

For National Socialism, there were several things fundamentally wrong with the League. One was its mystification and idealization of international law, as if this existed in an abstract realm independent of the power relations it reflected. In reality, all the League had done, Germans argued, was to freeze a moment in which liberalism, in the shape of Britain, France, and the United States, was temporarily dominant, and then rewrite the rules in its image. But behind all the talk of a new organization in which all states were equal, in reality some remained more equal than others. The major powers had permanent seats on the council, for instance, and they did not have to worry about being bound by things like minority rights treaties. Real power lay, as legal theorist Carl Schmitt put it, in the power to set the norms and to decide when they applied and to whom. The League was just another alliance, therefore, and as other states with different philosophies gathered strength, states like Fascist Italy and the Third Reich, the waning of the League's power would be reflected in the fact that people ceased to take any notice of its rules.

International law itself was to become, they hoped, much less central in the conduct of interstate relations. The League had led to a "juridification" of international life because it had attempted to craft perennial rules for state behavior and to freeze the territorial status quo established at Versailles. In the Nazis' organicist vision of world politics as a constant struggle for life this was implausible. States could not be expected to refrain from seizing opportunities to expand through conquest any more than a plant could stop growing; they could not be expected to do what lawyers said—the ideal of the arbitration movement and the new Permanent Court of Justice—

since there was no "common measure of justice"; rather, law should be expected, as in the Third Reich, to flow from the will of the people as expressed in the policies of their rulers.[41]

The Nazis took from an older German school of thought the view—common to nineteenth-century conservatives elsewhere too—that instead of trying to subordinate national states to international control, it was individual states whose will and autonomy was sacrosanct; at extreme moments, this led some German lawyers to deny the very possibility of international law, a denial that gathered force with the rise from the mid-1930s of an avowedly racist reading of law. If politics was a struggle between races, each unified in its own state, then there could in reality be nothing they shared, or should. Each state must on this reading develop its own conception of law. It followed that treaties were only to be observed insofar as it suited the signatories to observe them: they were "scraps of paper," as one German lawyer admitted in print, which could not be allowed to hold the well-being of the race hostage. Or in the words of another, "Generally recognized international legal principles and international customs are recognized by Germany only when they coincide with the legal concepts of the German *Volk*."[42] If blood was the basis of political belonging, then boundaries counted for little and ethnic Germans in Poland or Czechoslovakia owed a primary allegiance not to those states but to the Reich. Nazi lawyers worked hard to peddle this view not only because it allowed them leverage over the political organizations representing the ethnic Germans across eastern Europe, but also because they hoped to use it to pressure neighboring governments to cede rights over these minorities and thus allow the Reich to start interfering in their domestic affairs.

As these ideas germinated, the League ceased to be an organization intended to encompass Europe in its entirety and became one side in an ideological war. Germany had left Geneva shortly after the Nazis took power, but as late as 1936 it still seemed possible to British Tory supporters of the League that Nazi Germany might be brought back in, and that the quarrel with Mussolini over Ethiopia might be solved. The following year that became an impossibility. As the British and French governments publicly lost faith in Geneva, the two major fascist powers came together in their self-proclaimed Axis. Mussolini announced that Italy would withdraw from the League at the end of 1937 and described the League as "the tottering temple"; the German government declared that a return to the League would never be considered. The anticommunist alliance between the Third Reich, Italy, and Japan emerged, its function, according to its spokesmen, to "create a world-order in which the really vigorous nations can live together."[43]

What then did the Nazis propose in terms of world order in place of the League of Nations? Carl Schmitt, the most prominent and interesting legal mind on the German right, who had long been a vehement critic of the League, explained this at the very moment, in April 1939, when the German occupation of Prague for the first time demonstrated that Hitler aimed to do more than merely unify all ethnic Germans in a single state. Schmitt singled out the League's purported universalism for criticism. Airy claims to universal laws were at best hypocrisy, at worst recipes for instability, and those who claimed to make universal rules always demanded exceptional treatment for themselves. If universalism itself was bogus, what produced stability were legal regimes based on power over a clearly delineated territory. Schmitt gave the example of the United States: a Great Power that ruled the Western Hemisphere on the basis of the Monroe Doctrine, prohibiting any other major power from interfering in its zone of influence.

This transatlantic reference set off a brief flurry of interest in what the Monroe Doctrine really did imply. Before and after the fall of France, Hitler himself stated that world peace could be secured by an understanding among major powers that each would run their own particular "Great Space." "America for the Americans, Europe for the Europeans," was how he was quoted in June 1940. The following month Roosevelt's press spokesman briefly seemed to confirm the idea when he incautiously remarked that the U.S. government believed in the application of a "Monroe Doctrine for each continent." Two days later, he was emphatically overruled by Cordell Hull, the secretary of state, who clarified that the Monroe Doctrine "contains within it not the slightest vestige of any implication . . . of hegemony on the part of the United States." (A year later, shortly after the Atlantic Charter had spelled out the Anglo-American commitment to universalism, self-determination, and the reconstruction of a new liberal order, British foreign secretary Anthony Eden was still feeling it necessary to spell out that the Roosevelt-Churchill proclamation "excludes all idea of hegemony or zone leadership in the east or the west.")[44]

Schmitt had touched a nerve. For what his conception of the Monroe Doctrine pointed to was the critical importance of hegemony, and whether or not it fitted the American case—and of course plenty of non-Nazis believed it did—hegemony was the central idea around which the Germans in the Third Reich initially developed their distinctive conception of world rule. A heavyweight analysis of the topic, *Die Hegemonie* by Heinrich Triepel, a retired conservative professor of international law, had been published in Berlin in 1938, and together with Schmitt's work this provided the underpinnings for Germany's vision of Europe in the heady months after the fall of France. Triepel saw leadership by one or more states as the sole means to reestablish unity in Europe. This task fell to the Reich, in partnership with Fascist Italy, allying itself with some smaller powers, establishing protectorates elsewhere. Hegemony thus ideally reflected the inegalitarian constitutional structure of the Nazi New Order. Nazi politicians were of course less scholarly or mealy-mouthed than Triepel. There would be no question in the future, according to propaganda chief Joseph Goebbels, of some "crummy little state" acting independently or forgetting its place in the New Order.[45]

But this was no time for thinking of Europe in isolation, and Schmitt himself talked about the need to "think planetarily." In September 1940, the full global diplomatic implications of the new doctrine were spelled out in the Tripartite Pact between Germany, Italy, and Japan—an achievement of "those who tomorrow will preside over the reorganization of the world" (to use the commentary of France's Marshal Pétain). According to the pact's preamble, a condition precedent of any lasting peace was that "all nations of the world be given each its own proper place." That this rather vague formulation implied a system of hierarchy rather than equality among states was clarified in the first two articles, in which the leadership of each signatory in a specific region—Italy and Germany for Europe, Japan for "greater East Asia"—was acknowledged by the others. But it was an uneasy alliance: Hitler appears genuinely to have believed that Germany's goals were compatible with America's traditional hegemonic role in the Western Hemisphere and with Britain's continued control of its overseas empire. He thus felt deeply ambivalent about Japan's success and Britain's failure in Asia in particular and always shied away from playing the anticolonial card in Asia and the Middle East.

As for the Japanese themselves, they welcomed the new regionalism, since the prevailing attitude across the political spectrum there toward the League had become very critical. Much like Schmitt, interwar Japanese Pan-Asianists denounced the League as a fig leaf for what they called "the status-quo-maintenance" group. The British and French, they argued, held up "so-called democracy as their shared leading principle, and they use the League of Nations, which is no more than a puppet for their domestic issues, to rush about protecting their own vested interests." The Marxist philosopher Funayama Shin'ichi was among those who argued that the League's purported universalism was nothing but an instrument to prevent the countries and peoples of East Asia from coming together. His proposed "new internationalism" would transcend the League's version, which merely pitted state against state, and place it within a framework of regional integration. Such men saw the Japanese war against China, and then its entry into the larger world war, as the opportunity to create a powerful "progressive" East Asian model under Japanese leadership that would provide an alternative regionalist paradigm for the organization of the world as a whole.[46]

What the idea of hegemony as such did not clarify, and what

remained opaque in the highly formal language of the Tripartite Pact, was the nature of the rules to be laid down by a hegemon such as the Third Reich within its zone of influence. What each Great Power would actually do with or to the subordinate peoples in its "Great Space" was left up to them. At the theoretical level, neither Schmitt nor Triepel had said much about this question, perhaps deliberately as neither believed in National Socialist racialism. But the achievement of German hegemony made it necessary to think this through. A pragmatist in many administrative matters, Hitler preferred to leave all such considerations until after the war. But as the conflict started to turn against Germany, others felt it could not wait.

Fascist Italy—especially its diplomats—pushed hard for a kind of fascist internationalism: fusing Mazzini and Mussolini, they wanted to make it clear that the Axis was fighting for the rights of European nation-states. There was, after all, a fascist claim to Mazzini that was at least as tempting to make as the liberal one; as a commentator had noted in 1936, Mazzini was "at once the Democrat and the Nationalist, the Liberal and the Fascist."[47] Thus even as antifascists in New York founded a Mazzini Society to fight for liberal values, Mussolini invoked Mazzini's name. By 1943 there was a worked-out Italian vision of a fascist European confederation that was supported by many German diplomats as well, hampered only by Hitler's resolute rejection of any scheme for Europe based upon permanently acknowledging the sovereign rights of small states. A more sinister racial version emanated from some of the intellectuals clustered around Himmler in the SS. Focusing on race in a way Mazzini had never done, their basic conception was to stabilize Europe by turning each state into an ethnically homogeneous whole. In some cases this would mean population exchanges and expulsions; in others, more violent solutions. They believed that since minorities had been a source of international friction between the wars, their eradication under the hegemony of the Third Reich would suffice to bring peace to interstate relations in Europe by creating a continent of "race-satiated states." And since having numerous tiny statelets under the Reich's sway was easier than controlling larger states as junior partners, they favored splitting up not only Poland, but also France and the United Kingdom as well.[48]

WHAT'S WRONG WITH INTERNATIONAL LAW?

Nazi rule in occupied Europe brought to the surface the ideological priorities and contradictions of the Third Reich's anti-internationalism. More importantly for the future, it undermined some of the old liberal assumptions in the minds of Nazism's foes as well. In particular it led commentators in the UK and America to wonder out loud what the future held for international law. "What's wrong with International Law?" asked one émigré law professor in 1941. It was not that the Nazis were thought to be right in their arguments but rather that their rise to power had thrown into question many of the most cherished axioms of interwar internationalism, above all the desirability of trying to regulate interstate relations through law. Quincy Wright, a leading American supporter of the League, noted with dismay that "totalitarianism has unmasked the inadequacy of the philosophical and political foundations of international law." Law as an unquestioned fount of impartial authority lay in tatters. For some, the lesson was to establish an international authority stronger than the League had been with the power to make and enforce its own laws. But others wondered whether there existed the necessary shared values among states to make this possible, or whether very divergent social conditions and ideologies would preclude it. The old shared confidence in the nineteenth-century standard of civilization was thus mortally wounded by the rise of Nazism itself. If there was not a single European society, could there be a common standard of binding law? It was in this very precise sense that the war marked "the end of the European era."[49]

To make matters worse for those who wished to see international law become an effective supranational force, the war seemed to reaffirm the value of sovereignty. Early in the war there was a momentary impulse to see the nation-state in Europe as the problem and to argue for federalism as the solution. But this did not last, and by 1942 at the latest, precisely because the Nazis had trampled over the rights of small nations, enthusiasm for recasting the map of Europe and creating a continent of large federations had vanished. Emigré politicians took the lead in demanding the restoration of their independence and pointed to the Atlantic Charter in support of the restoration of self-determination. Stalin was their most powerful supporter in the Big Three. But there was no real opposition. Ironically, therefore, at the end of a war that had demonstrated nationalism's destabilizing potential, and its tendency to lead to the oppression of minorities or to outright mass flight, the war's victors reaffirmed the centrality of the nation-state in modern life, and prepared new international institutions that would create far more of them and work more fully through them than the League had done.

PART II

Governing THE World THE American Way

CHAPTER 7

"The League Is Dead. Long Live the United Nations."

In the distant lands the battle rages
Will this bleak horror never cease?
Can we, who fought through all the ages,
Make lasting Peace?
. . . .
Blind not the mind with ancient fears.
Time turns the glass, the sands have run,
Dawn on another million years
Has just begun.

—James Shotwell, "Is It the Dawn?"[1]

TO AMERICA

In the summer of 1940, the Nazis overran Paris, and the fate of the League of Nations hung in the balance. At this moment in which so many old and ingrained assumptions were abruptly overturned on both sides of the Atlantic, disturbing rumors came out of Geneva that the League's secretary-general, a former French finance ministry official named Joseph Avenol, was ready to collaborate. Nazism may have been anti-internationalist, but the leaders of the Third Reich were certainly not unaware of the value of working through international organizations. Joseph Goebbels had welcomed an international congress of prison experts in Berlin in 1935. In 1938, Germany had taken over the Vienna-based International Criminal Police Commission—Interpol, its successor body, does not advertise this Nazi interlude—and in the summer of 1940 Himmler's deputy in the SS, Reinhard Heydrich, had himself declared ICPC president. The Reichsbank remained an active member of the Bank for International Settlements throughout the war, despite the fact that it had essentially been founded at the behest of the Bank of England and had an American president. But the League of Nations was altogether a bigger and ideologically vastly more loaded proposition, and Avenol, who did put out feelers to Pétain, completely misjudged the situation. By August, he was gone, having alienated all sides, a figure of embarrassment in the history of the League.[2]

It was in such strained circumstances that the American connection provided a lifeline for what was left of the League in Geneva. American interest in the League after Wilson's great defeat in 1920 was always more sustained than the conventional story of disengagement and isolation suggests: there were more than two hundred Americans who worked for the League, including in some senior and prominent positions, and the Rockefeller Foundation in particular supported it financially through the 1930s. From time to time there were initiatives to forge closer relations, although these were buffeted by the economic crisis and by the collapse of international economic cooperation in 1933. Arthur Sweetser had been the first American to have been appointed to the secretariat back in 1919: he had helped set up the League's press office and would go on to become the first head of the UN Information Office. On the eve of the Second World War, he had discussed closer ties between the League and the United States with President Roosevelt, and Roosevelt had advised him to concentrate on economic and financial rather than political cooperation. Sweetser himself hoped to bring together the League's technical services with the Americans in some kind of new economic and financial organization.[3]

Arriving back in the United States from Europe in May 1940, Sweetser quickly drummed up support for the idea of bringing over the secretariat's economists and statisticians. His good friend Raymond Fosdick, now head of the Rockefeller Foundation and as ardent a supporter of the League as he was, was helpful as was the head of the recently established Institute for Advanced Study in Princeton, a body that already had close connections to the League and had given a home to leading émigré scholars such as Albert Einstein, John (Janos) von Neumann, and the mathematician Kurt Gödel. The two main obstacles were Avenol himself, who was reluctant to allow the League's offices to be dispersed, and the Roosevelt administration, worried in what was an election year about an isolationist backlash if the United States was seen to be welcoming the League. But both were overcome, and in August twelve key secretariat members, along with their families and files, made their homes in New Jersey. The Rockefeller Foundation paid the costs of the move, and the dining hall of the new Institute of Advanced Study in the Princeton woods became the hub of wartime League of Nations activities in America. Apart from the International Labor Organization in Montreal, this was the only functioning part of the League machinery through the war. While the rump secretariat remained under wraps in Geneva, these transplanted social scientists played a small but central role in the American discussion that now began about the challenges the postwar world would face.[4]

Sweetser and Fosdick had worked hard to bring over the League's economists because they were convinced that this would help ensure that the United States itself joined the League once the war was over. As Sweetser wrote in June to the head of the League's economics bureau in Geneva, "It is my belief that, if this country gave asylum now in this moment of emergency, it would be integrated forever. Our people are sentimental, as you know; the fact of coming to aid would create a bond which would be permanent." In the League's technical personnel, in particular, he and Fosdick saw the kernel of an approach to internationalism—practical, global, scientific, humanitarian—that could help Roosevelt succeed where Wilson had failed.

GETTING THE AMERICANS IN

The British were working in the same direction. In this second wartime incarnation of the Anglo-American partnership, their priority was simply to get the Americans committed—and not merely to entering the war, but this time to the peace after it too. Planning in detail was a secondary consideration and Prime Minister Winston Churchill personally regarded speculation about the peace as a waste of effort. Yet while he focused on getting Britain out of the dire predicament that faced it, the Foreign Office itself was already looking ahead and emphasizing the importance of the American connection.

In cabinet, the sluggish initial discussion on war aims was helped along by the eminent historian Arnold Toynbee, a man never shy of grand vistas. In addition to his scholarly distinction, Toynbee had played a critical role in discussions of the League idea in the First World War, and since then he had headed England's leading think tank on foreign affairs, the Royal Institute of International Affairs. Strongly Atlanticist in orientation and yet another recipient of Fosdick's Rockefeller Foundation largesse, Toynbee warned that the future of the world would be decided in the clash between "the Continental versus the Oceanic Pattern of World Organization." Drawing on old tropes in liberal political thought, he identified the choice between militaristic imperialism or maritime federalism—a "democratic Anglo-American world-commonwealth." But the democratic path would need to be stiffened with a dose of leadership; it would require nothing less than a "world directorate" "of the United States and the British Commonwealth" . . . a "World-Hegemony temporarily in the hands of the English-speaking peoples."[5]

Toynbee's world-historical mode of looking at things articulated Whitehall's deepest anxieties. Concluding that neither Europe nor the empire offered the resources to guarantee Britain that it would remain a major power, the Foreign Office hammered away at the importance of forging a partnership with the United States. "The future of the world depends on close Anglo-American cooperation," noted one diplomat in 1940. Almost no one on the UK side dissented; the only uncertainty was whether the American public would like the idea. The new ambassador in Washington, Viscount Halifax, warned that it might seem obvious in London but "for Americans it is a new and startling doctrine." Aware of their hostility to the idea of permanent alliances, Whitehall moved cautiously. But as it happened, the Roosevelt administration had its own reasons for reaching out to the British. Once the Soviet Union entered the war, it became nervous lest Churchill and Stalin make the kind of secret commitments that had hindered peacemaking efforts in the First World War. It was to prevent this that Roosevelt sent his invitation to Churchill to their secret rendezvous at Placentia Bay in August 1941.[6]

There the British were presented with a draft set of general principles that formed the basis for the so-called Atlantic Charter. Churchill grumbled, but it was already clear to him that without American support Britain could never prevail in Europe: the Wehrmacht was just too strong. On securing such support, therefore, the "future of the whole world" depended. Indeed the preamble to his joint declaration with Roosevelt talked of the "dangers to world civilization" posed by the Nazi lust for conquest. At this delicate point, with the United States not yet in the war, Roosevelt was still very cautious about any kind of permanent peacetime institutional commitment. The British side wanted the proclamation to pledge to build an "effective international organization" after the war, but Roosevelt watered this down. Determined not to share Wilson's fate, Roosevelt preferred to leave aside the question of a new League of Nations until the United States and Britain had policed the world for a few years and disarmed their enemies. On returning to London, Churchill told the cabinet that the Atlantic Charter contained "a plain and bold intimation that after the war, the US will join with us in policing the world until the establishment of a better order."[7]

Thus on the organizational front nothing concrete was agreed at all, and Churchill himself discouraged criticism of the League "until we were in a position to make positive suggestions for something to put in its place." What he was sure about was that no arrangement could work unless based on close continued cooperation between the wartime Big Three. For someone with his historical perspective, this meant a return not so much to the League—the old doctrine of collective security had brought no security at all—as to the principles of Concert diplomacy that had been established by Castlereagh, Alexander, and Metternich in 1815: Europe's stability depended on effective Great Power control.[8] As he told Stalin in January 1944, the three major powers were "the trustees for the peace of the world. If they failed, there would be perhaps one hundred years of chaos. If they were strong, they would carry out their trusteeship." He was therefore attentive to the Anglo-Soviet relationship, moving swiftly in the spring of 1942 to sign a mutual assistance treaty with Stalin that would last not only for the war, but for twenty years after it, and freely discussing spheres of influence in eastern Europe with the Russians, despite the disapproval of the Americans and the anger of east European exile statesmen.[9]

Privately, Roosevelt shared the view that any new world organization would have to be compatible with the idea of a high degree of Great Power control. He shocked one of his most senior diplomats, Sumner Welles, by writing off the League of Nations Assembly and talking about a police directorate of powers instead. In great secrecy, the State Department began drafting plans for an international organization along these lines. Publicly, Roosevelt's strategy was to shift American public sentiment back toward internationalism by steering clear of any discussion of organizational questions and highlighting instead the achievements international cooperation could make in areas like the struggle against hunger and poverty. In this sense, Fosdick and Sweetser's arguments made complete political sense to him and in 1940, he publicly welcomed the arrival of the League's personnel in the United States. In October 1941, he went further by making a point of attending the final day of a conference organized by the International Labor Organization, another refugee Geneva outfit. If permanent remedies to the world's woes were to be found, the president told the conference, the fullest cooperation between all nations would be required. Social and economic problems were not separate watertight compartments in the international any more than in the national sphere. The outlines of a version of postwar internationalism premised on a kind of New Deal for the world thus emerged.[10]

Only a few weeks later, the Japanese attack on Pearl Harbor brought the United States into the war, and British efforts to—as they put it—"mix up" the Anglo-American war efforts (in other words, coordinating them so closely as to lay the foundations for an enduring postwar relationship) went into overdrive. There were good practical reasons for formalizing cooperation, not only with Britain but with America's other Lend-Lease recipients. But as military cooperation intensified, Roosevelt searched round for ways of rendering the alliance more palatable to American public opinion. One of these was by recasting it as part of a much larger coalition.

It was during the British prime minister's visit to Washington in December 1941 that Roosevelt hit upon the term "United Nations" as a more inspiring alternative to the then current "Associated Powers." His assistant Daisy Stuckley recalled how he sold Churchill on the idea:

> FDR got into his bed, his mind working and working. . . . Suddenly he got it—United Nations! The next morning, the minute he had finished his breakfast, he got onto his chair and was wheeled up the hall to WSC's room. He knocked on the door, no answer, so he opened the door and went and sat on a chair and the man went out and closed the door—He called to WSC and in the door leading to the bathroom appeared WSC—a "pink cherub" (FDR said) drying himself with a towel and without a stitch on! FDR pointed at him and exploded: "The United Nations!" "*Good!*" said WSC.[11]

Before the United Nations became a peacetime organization, therefore, it was a wartime alliance.[12] Born in Churchill's bedroom, it saw the light of day the following month in a declaration in which Britain and the United States were joined by twenty-six countries, including the dominions and India, Central American and Caribbean states, European governments in exile, and the USSR. They pledged jointly not only to fight on until victory but to defend the principles enshrined in the Atlantic Charter, signed months earlier by Churchill and Roosevelt. From this point onward, the term "United Nations" came to connote the wartime alliance against the Axis and Japan, and was frequently referred to in this sense by Allied politicians and propaganda. It also crept in this form into legal and diplomatic usage. Starting with the Italians in 1943, surrender documents routinely referred to the victors as the "armed forces of the United Nations"; the Romanian armistice the following year noted that Romania "had withdrawn from the war against the United Nations," and in May 1945 President Truman noted that the "forces of Germany have surrendered to the United Nations."[13]

Meanwhile, the first public hints of a broader peacetime role emerged. In Washington, planning for a new permanent world organization to succeed the League was in full swing: the State Department's Russian-born Leo Pasvolsky, an aide to Cordell Hull and the principal figure involved in drafting what would become the UN Charter, had been entrusted with setting up a top-secret Division of Special Research early in 1941 that had initiated work on the subject. By late 1943, he had seen off rivals and their schemes for a world body divided into heavily regional subgroups and outlined the unitary conception that hewed more closely to the League structure, while preserving the new principle of tight Great Power control. All this put the Americans far ahead of the British, whose diplomats started focusing seriously on what they called the "World Organization scheme" only in early 1944; it was the previous November that they had learned their American counterparts wanted to discuss "the subject of a new League"—and even then they emphasized that "the entrance of the US and the USSR into a permanent organization is more important than the exact form of the organization itself."

When, on the eve of the crucial Dumbarton Oaks conversations in the summer of 1944, the British planners finally had the chance of extensive conversations with the State Department, they were amazed that the Americans had come up with "such far-reaching suggestions." They should not have been: these had been brewing in the State Department for the past two years, and before that in think tanks like the Council on Foreign Relations and Pasvolsky's home, the Brookings Institution. But the reversal with the situation in the First World War was striking.[14]

Another of the key differences between the wartime discussions in 1914–18 and 1940–45 was the shift in register. As planning moved from London to Washington, a generation accustomed to thinking in classic Oxbridge common-room style about the eternal wisdom of ancient Athens was superseded by a new cohort of policymakers more comfortable with discussions of comparative legal systems, farm economics, or business cycles. Still populated by historians and classicists rather than American-style social scientists, Whitehall had been thinking mostly in terms of a revival of the old Concert diplomacy. It is striking that second only to the mandarin Gladwyn Jebb, the Foreign Office official most closely involved in postwar planning for international organization was Charles Webster, a diplomatic historian of the Congress of Vienna. Webster himself liked the boldness of American thinking, particularly the way it continued and expanded the work begun by the League's technical services. The goals of the New Deal, as Roosevelt had anticipated in his Four Freedoms speech, also provided a potential program for global action, and the war itself had made the broader struggle against hunger and poverty seem more acute. But as civil servants and technical experts began planning for the serious humanitarian and refugee crisis that would undoubtedly greet the victors after Nazism's defeat, some British diplomats mocked the American "New Dealers . . . and their 'Tennessee Valley Authority' nostrums for the organization of international society which they tend to urge with missionary fervor."[15]

Those attentive to the American scene understood the political rationale to this dimension of the planning. If Roosevelt believed that the best way to bring the American public around to support peacetime internationalism was to demonstrate its humanitarian potential even before the war was over, then as British foreign secretary Anthony Eden observed in a critical memorandum, it was in Britain's interest to follow along:

> It must be obvious that for the success of any postwar relief scheme the contribution of the US will be all-important. . . . But I fancy that there is much more than postwar relief in question. The US Administration appear to be acting on the thesis that the more international machinery that can be got into operation with their participation before the end of the war, the greater the likelihood of American public opinion being ready to continue with international cooperation after the war. It would perhaps be putting it too high at this stage to say that the Administration definitely intends to try and establish under the aegis of the "United Nations" the embryo of the international organization of the future. American postwar cooperation in the international sphere being so vitally important, I submit that we must play up to any scheme of theirs tending to turn the United Nations into an operative piece of machinery.[16]

In 1943 the Roosevelt administration announced planning for the postwar international economy and war crimes trials. The same year, the first United Nations conference was organized at Hot Springs, Virginia, to discuss food needs, resulting in the creation of a small body that later became the UN's Food and Agriculture Organization. From Washington, Halifax, the British ambassador, underscored the reasoning:

> The President wished First United Nations Conference to be held in the United States and to be on a subject which should be humanitarian rather than political with object of accustoming American public opinion to United Nations Conference and presumably of preparing

> way for further conferences on more difficult subjects if first conference is a success.[17]

Before 1943 was out, another body, the UN Relief and Rehabilitation Administration, had also been formed, headed by Herbert Lehman, a former Democratic governor of New York. UN planning took on a still longer-term character the following year when attention turned to an area of vital concern and interest to the United States: the rewriting of the rules of the international economy. In July 1944, at the United Nations Monetary and Financial Conference, more than seven hundred delegates from the forty-four members of the United Nations gathered in the New Hampshire resort of Bretton Woods to draw up a set of rules and institutions that would regulate international monetary activity and prevent any return to the slump of the 1930s. Economic nationalism, which had helped bring about the collapse of the League of Nations, was to be kept at bay by a major cooperative international effort. Speculative capital flows were to be checked through capital controls, while trade was to be encouraged by lower tariffs and by maintaining convertible currencies at fixed exchange rates. British and U.S. treasury teams had been working in parallel, and their blueprints provided the basis for the two major new international bodies that would—some decades later—come to play a critical role in global governance. There was an International Monetary Fund to help tide member countries over temporary balance-of-payments problems, and an International Bank for Reconstruction and Development (later known as the World Bank), primarily intended to provide funds for the financing of postwar reconstruction projects in Europe. Delegates also agreed to set up an International Trade Organization, although negotiations for that collapsed four years later, leaving only the General Agreement on Tariffs and Trade as the forum for international trade liberalization. All of this represented a concerted intervention to manage international capitalism far beyond anything the League had ever attempted. For there was general agreement that in this area in particular the

League and its chosen techniques of stabilization had failed. Meanwhile, as new institutions were set up, old ones were to be wound down. The Bank for International Settlements, which had played a key role between the wars facilitating the central bank cooperation that lay at the heart of the League's approach to international finance, was actually dissolved because of its involvement with the Germans during the war—a decision that was only reversed in 1948. The minorities section of the secretariat too faced an uncertain future, as the minorities of eastern Europe themselves disappeared through deportation or genocide.

This ambitious complex of initiatives was welcomed by supporters of the League. Speaking at Oxford in November 1943, the classicist Gilbert Murray, who had founded the League of Nations Union many years earlier, got to the heart of the matter—the changing role of the modern state and the transformation in the nature of internationalism. Comparing Europe in the Thirty Years War with the situation around him, he noted:

> To see how enormous is the difference between those times and these it is enough to glance at one or two recent state documents: say, the Report on the Hot Springs Conference on plans for the organization of the agriculture and food supply of the world, and the more critical Report on the Transition from War to Peace Economy published by the Economic and Financial Commission of the League of Nations at Princeton. You are in a different world. The modern state, even though now for the moment definitely organized to the last button as a killing machine, is far more at home in the work of constructive organization, economic research, social service, care of health, provision against fear and want. The sort of work that we shall have to undertake, amid many dangers and on a gigantic scale, is just the work for which, in contrast to these earlier times, we are splendidly equipped.[18]

Murray made an unlikely advocate of planned, state-driven international cooperation of this kind. As a Hellenist and a Victorian liberal, his priority had always been the realm of the spirit. But he was astute enough to realize that the age in which the values of ancient Greece could presume to govern the world had passed. What was needed was no longer the League with its prewar faith in the power of civilized European values and its unreflective appeals to humanity, but an international coordination of scientific expertise for democratic ends. The torch was passing from England to America, and Murray and his son-in-law Arnold Toynbee were among those English intellectuals happy to help it along.

It was in 1943 that the first concrete public indications emerged that the Big Three were committed to returning to some kind of permanent world security organization when the war was over. Roosevelt's administration appeared to be on the way to winning the domestic public opinion battle, and polls indicated strong support for the idea of joining a postwar world organization, whether this was called the League of Nations or something else. To be sure, the League's reputation appeared to be irrevocably tainted—the League of Nations Association had already changed its name—and a public relations effort behind the promotion of the United Nations brand was in full swing: advertisements, Hollywood showgirls, musical anthems were all serving the cause. That autumn, two congressional resolutions called for the creation of international machinery after the war and passed with large majorities.

In the Big Three meetings that took place in late 1943 it was finally agreed to create a permanent international security organization. At the Moscow conference in October, shortly after the collapse of Mussolini's regime in Italy, representatives of the Big Three (joined by China) proclaimed that they recognized "the necessity of establishing at the earliest practicable date a general international organization, based on the principle of the sovereign equality of all peace-loving states, and open to membership by all such states, large and small, for the maintenance of international peace and security." This body did not yet have a name, and the same document used the term "United Nations" in its wartime sense to refer to the coalition of powers who would be consulted by them. That December, the leaders of the Big Three met for the first time at Tehran and declared that they and the United Nations would work toward "an enduring Peace" based on their own close cooperation and on "a world family of Democratic Nations."

Roosevelt gave Stalin one possible blueprint for the new world organization based on Pasvolsky's work in Washington—a worldwide assembly with no fixed headquarters; an executive council of the Big Four as well as six or seven other delegates selected by region; and an enforcement body dominated by the Big Four that was authorized to deal with any threat to the peace. This meant greater Great Power control than the League had permitted, and a heavier stress on enforcing their will.[19] Roosevelt also outlined for Stalin the kinds of threats he envisaged the new organization dealing with. One was when a small country was embroiled in revolution, or civil war or a border dispute with a neighbor—such issues could be dealt with by trade embargos or other "quarantine" measures. But the other was when aggression by a powerful state needed to be met with the threat that the Four Policemen would bomb or invade in retaliation. Prudently, Roosevelt avoided the thorny question of what was to be done when one of the Big Four were the aggressors. He wanted at all costs to avoid the question of Big Four veto power, which he thought Stalin would insist upon and which he feared would condemn a new organization to impotence.

Churchill's interest in the subject waxed and waned; Roosevelt, in his elliptical and cautious way, was now fully committed to it. Of all the major figures involved and their thinking on the subject, it is Stalin we know least about. In the 1920s he had sharply attacked the League of Nations as an organization of imperialists masquerading as peace-lovers. But he had never had much time for the Comintern, and after 1933 he had made sure that the USSR entered the League. Marxist ideology allowed considerable latitude for maneuver. Stalin's anticolonialism was predictable, as was his desire to make sure the Red Army had a free hand in eastern Europe. On the other hand, his overriding goal was to preserve good relations with the British and the Americans as long as possible after the war to give the USSR the time it would obviously need to recover from Nazi occupation: so long as membership of the UN helped Soviet security and did not jeopardize it, therefore, there was no reason not to go along with this latest expression of Anglo-American internationalism. What we do know is that in late 1943 he was desperate to get a second front opened the following year; one of the reasons why he had wound up the Comintern was to send a reassuring signal to his partners. Perhaps he was reassured in turn by Roosevelt telling him that American troops were not expected to play a police role in postwar Europe and that the decisions of the proposed new UN Executive Council would not be binding. In these circumstances, there was every reason to support the UN idea and few evident drawbacks.

The real opposition to Roosevelt and his Four Policemen idea came not from Stalin but from public opinion back home in the United States, which accused him of everything from being a nineteenth-century imperialist to appeasing Bolshevism. One newspaper reported that the administration preferred having the major powers acting together to revive the "fruitful Pax Britannica" of the previous century in a "heavily organized, bureaucratic world organization." Conservatives were appalled at the idea of an alliance that included Communist Russia, while Wilsonians saw it as a return to the Holy Alliance—animated by an imperialist disregard for the rights of smaller nations.[20] Upset by these reactions, and by congressional calls to wait for peace to be signed with Germany and Japan before any new organization was established, the administration used the cover of the D-Day landings to release an abbreviated version of its plans that was light on detail and heavy in its denial of any attempt to create "a superstate with its own police forces."

Much changed in those summer months of 1944. The blinding success of the Soviet offensive in the east—which in scale and impact dwarfed what was happening on the beaches of Normandy—drove the Wehrmacht back hundreds of miles and brought the Red Army deep into Poland and to the borders of the Balkans. Necessity brought first Eden and then Churchill to Moscow to clarify spheres of influence on the continent, an approach that was hard to square with the universalist language of the Wilsonian dream. At the same time as the ring of steel around the Reich was tightening, crucial secret discussions took place in Washington at Dumbarton Oaks (a Georgetown estate owned by one of Cordell Hull's aides), where British, American, Russian, and Chinese delegates began to put flesh on the bones of a peacetime UN security structure. Four key issues occupied most of their time. One was to what extent the new organization should cover more than security affairs: when the United States proposed, for instance, an Economic and Social Council to promote "the fullest and most effective use of the world's resources"—the kind of global New Deal the administration had been working toward—the Soviet delegates objected that this was exactly the kind of thing the League had wasted its time on. The "primary and indeed the only task" ought to be the maintenance of peace and security by a small and streamlined body. Other tasks could be handled by other organizations that need not be under the UN. But the United States got its way, and indeed the UN would preside over a vast expansion of the realm of international governance into areas of welfare and social policy that the League had initiated.

Second was the question of whether actual forces should be at the disposal of the new organization. The Soviet side promoted the idea of an international air force, in this way seeing the new UN as a continuation of the wartime alliance. To the British, this smacked of a world state, while the American side, keenly aware of the need to win over Congress, proposed that each power should make a general commitment to supply forces as and when they were needed. But in different ways, all three accepted the basic point that the new United Nations Organization should have a military force of some kind at its disposal. Third, there was membership. The USSR initially wanted this to be confined to the January 1942 signatories of the first UN Declaration, accepting that other "peace-loving" countries could eventually be admitted too. The United States, on the other hand, wanted as universal an organization as possible, with few ideological barriers to membership. To the Russians any such scheme raised the prospect of being outnumbered and outvoted: after all, the British could rely on their dominions falling into line, the Americans on many of the South American states. If fascist or quasi-fascist states such as Spain, Portugal, and Argentina were admitted, the Soviet position would be even worse. Hence their desire not only to prune the size of the General Assembly but also to insist that all sixteen Soviet republics be separately admitted—a demand that at one stage threatened to derail the negotiations entirely. A compromise made it clear that the organization was to aspire to universality, and that the only criterion for membership was to "love peace"; the Soviets were allowed a small number of obedient voting members (their number was whittled down from the sixteen Stalin demanded to two).

All of this had an obvious bearing on the utterly critical issue that nearly torpedoed the new organization before it had gotten under way: veto rights in the new Security Council. On the old League Council *every* member had enjoyed a right of veto, but the Americans worried that carrying this system over would simply condemn the new organization to the impotence of the old and prevent it from ever doing anything effective. On the other hand, doing away with the veto altogether was not something any Great Power could countenance, and certainly not the Russians. Stalin was worried that with the war approaching an end, Britain and the United States were starting to question the alliance, and by extension the Soviet role in eastern Europe. On October, 7, 1944, when the Dumbarton Oaks conference ended, the unresolved veto issue represented a ticking time bomb at the heart of the entire venture.

There were, of course, other ways of establishing Great Power cooperation. Two days later, Churchill met with Stalin in Moscow. Together with their foreign ministers, the two men negotiated the infamous Percentages Agreement that allocated a leading role to Britain in Greece and to the USSR in much of the rest of eastern Europe.[21] Whether this was a plan for informal long-term spheres of influence, or merely an effort to avoid short-term misunderstandings, its secretiveness smacked of a nineteenth-century mode of diplomacy at odds with what the United Nations was supposed to stand for. It was certainly hard to reconcile with the declaration that would be issued at Yalta, in February 1945—on the last occasion the Big Three met—promising freedom for the peoples of liberated Europe to choose their form of government. More meaningful than the declaration was the compromise that was finally thrashed out at that meeting on the veto: proposed sanctions or the use of force could be blocked, but not discussion of a matter that a sufficient number of other Security Council members wanted placed on the agenda. Once Stalin accepted this, it became possible to go ahead with planning the international conference to set up the new world body, and it was agreed that this would take place that April in San Francisco.

In a massive marketing blitz in the months after Dumbarton Oaks, State Department officials presented the proposals to the American public in a fashion that stressed their value for national security. Isolation had failed America, they preached, and with the development of German rockets, the oceans no longer guaranteed America's safety. There was precious little in their speeches about the rights of small nations and much about how American sovereignty would be preserved. "The thought of fashioning any kind of superstate is repugnant to us," declared the new secretary of state, Edward Stettinius, on New Year's Day 1945, "and no such thought has entered or can enter into our counsels." Officials preached a pragmatic realism—the new international organization was a vital necessity, even if it would not solve all the world's problems.[22]

This was all directed at deflecting isolationist criticism, and it appears to have worked. According to Gallup, 81 percent of Americans in April 1945 favored entry into "a world organization with police power to maintain world peace," even though many of them believed America would probably find itself fighting another war within several decades. But the response of longtime internationalists was ambivalent. The major American organizations backed the proposals—this was America's "second chance" and there would not be another. But privately, they were worried. Where was the commitment to human rights, or to decolonization, or the rule of law? "Dumbarton Hoax?" was one reaction. Many wondered what had happened to the rights of small states. The British *New Statesman* saw the proposals as justifying a new form of "Holy Alliance," and it was not alone. In the privacy of his diary, even the British historian-diplomat Charles Webster described their creation as "an Alliance of the Great Powers embedded in a universal organization."[23]

Roosevelt himself believed the San Francisco conference could not come too soon to head off the evidence of growing Anglo-Soviet hostility. He wanted to act "while the forge of war was still hot enough to fuse the nations together." It was thus vital to meet, if possible, before Germany was defeated. What the conference could actually contribute was, on the other hand, moot: a reporter noted three days before it opened, in a faithful rendering of the president's own thoughts, that it would be a chance to divest the Big Three of "some of its power, *at least ostensibly,* by giving a voice and a *feeling* of responsibility to smaller nations." Roosevelt knew that his much-vaunted "democratic organization of the world" would depend in the peace not on the power of command but of leadership and persuasion. He thus planned an event that would be not a peace conference but something like the constitutional convention that had cemented America's unity after the War of Independence. His real concern was not the smaller nations of the world, who ultimately would have little choice but to accept what the Great Powers agreed, if they wanted a world body at all, but the U.S. Congress. Keen from the start to avoid Wilson's errors in 1919–20, he continued the bipartisan approach he had followed on international questions throughout the war, and made sure that the U.S. delegation to San Francisco would include leading figures from both sides of the House.[24]

Roosevelt's death overshadowed the opening ceremonies at San Francisco but made delegates even keener to make the occasion a success. Skating over the very substantial continuities in form and concern with the League, pundits hailed the new organization as internationalism's second chance. This idealism had been whipped up by the U.S. government in particular, and was propagated by American nongovernmental organizations, but it also spoke to the mood of hope in the American public and elsewhere. Yet Roosevelt's loss did matter. If the UN had had a single architect, it was the man one of his biographers aptly termed "the juggler," keeping its disparate elements aloft with enormous skill. Even had he lived, to have held the Big Three together in 1945 would have been an enormous task, far harder than preserving the anti-Napoleonic coalition in 1815. For ideological differences were not the only disintegrative force; there was also the sudden revelation of the power of the atomic bomb, and above all, the emerging realization that Stalin really did propose to dominate the whole of eastern Europe after the war was over—an issue Roosevelt had always tried to downplay. Harry Truman, who needed to establish his authority in the presidency at the outset, took a tougher line with the Soviets; his advisers warned the Kremlin early on that differences in eastern Europe could jeopardize "the entire structure of world cooperation and relations with the Soviet Union."[25]

Among the smaller nations, the main misgiving was not that the Great Powers might fall out. On the contrary, they feared that the UN represented a step backward, and that the Great Powers were seeking, under the guise of internationalism, to create a new world directorate, far more frightening than the old Holy Alliance because of the awesome technology at its disposal. At San Francisco they therefore redirected attention back to the rights of the General Assembly, the commitment to human rights, the plight of colonial peoples, and the veto issue, asking precisely which "procedural matters" (in the language of Yalta) were to be exempted from its effect; it took a special envoy to Stalin to smooth over the difference and save the UN. The suspicion lingered that the UN represented not an advance on the League but a return toward the bad old nineteenth-century way of doing things. There was a stream of criticism from Canada, Australia, and others at the unrepresentative and undemocratic nature of the new world organization, but the Great Powers closed ranks—the memoirs of British delegate Gladwyn Jebb give a sense of their disdain—in the justified belief that whatever the complaints, small states would eventually fall into line for want of an alternative. And so they did. In June, President Truman addressed the conference's closing session, and a month later, the U.S. Congress voted by eighty-nine votes to two to ratify the UN Treaty. There would be no repetition of the humiliating reverses that had followed Versailles. With America now committed to the new body, and Britain and the USSR signed up, it enjoyed one advantage over its predecessor—the backing of the world's major powers.

THE FUNERAL was carefully orchestrated. One year after San Francisco, in April 1946, the last assembly of the League of Nations took place in Geneva. Lord Cecil—who had addressed the first assembly back in 1920—praised the League for having made the new world organization possible. "The League is dead. Long live the United Nations," he concluded. By this point, the handover had quietly been arranged. The magnificent Palais des Nations, on which Avenol had lavished so much attention, now became the UN's European Office. League bodies—the Health Organization, the Nutrition Committee, the Committee on Intellectual Cooperation—metamorphosed into better-funded UN entities—the WHO, the FAO, and UNESCO. The UN took possession of the remaining League assets, including its human capital—former League officials said farewell to Princeton and played a crucial role in staffing the new organization. Arthur Sweetser, the man who had helped engineer this outcome, described his feelings on being asked to compare the League with the UN as akin to a man on his second honeymoon being asked to speak about his first wife.[26]

But in fact the second wife looked uncannily like the first. Although the aura of failure that hung over the League made it essential in public relations terms to assert a clean break with the past, the truth was that the UN Organization was based on the fundamental tripartite structure pioneered by the League—legislature, executive, and governing council—and in many respects simply continued the ongoing League experiment. As one recent commentator on the subject has astutely noted, it is very rare for international organizations to die: they either dwindle into obscurity or, if they are fortunate, evolve with the times.[27] This is what happened in this case, thanks to the reengineering of the League that Pasvolsky and his colleagues had carried out during the war. And the changes they wrought were certainly sufficient to guarantee a long life for its successor. A Security Council, dominated by a veto-wielding Big Five (no statesman reared on the realities of nineteenth-century diplomacy could seriously dream of keeping France out), had exclusive jurisdiction for keeping the peace. The General Assembly existed primarily as a discussion chamber—although there would be moments when, thanks to the Cold War standoff between the two superpowers in the years ahead, it would play a more central role than anyone imagined possible in 1945. There was a new Economic and Social Council—a key achievement of American New Deal internationalism, which had been recommended in 1939 by a League report but had been impossible to achieve because of the war—that became the engine for international cooperation by experts on a much wider scale than in the League. More negatively, there was a new draft statute for the International Court of Justice, successor to the old Permanent Court of International Justice, and based like its predecessor at The Hague: time would show that it had even less to do. And while the preamble to the charter offered a belated peroration of faith "in fundamental human rights, in the dignity and worth of the human person, and in the equal rights of men and women and of nations large and small," binding obligations that actually committed members to anything such as the minority-rights treaties of the League were jettisoned.[28]

The truth was that the UN was above all a means of keeping the wartime coalition of Great Powers intact at whatever cost was necessary to avoid the fate of its predecessor. Its intensely hierarchical character reflected this, and so did its provision for military forces to be placed at its disposal. Strikingly, not only were all members of the UN expected to obey the decisions of the Security Council but even nonmembers were as well: Article 2 of the charter stipulated that "states which are not Members of the United Nations [shall] act in accordance with principles affirmed by the UN so far as these may be necessary for the maintenance of international peace and security."

In effect, the Big Three had ended up creating an organization that combined the scientific technocracy of the New Deal with the flexibility and power-political reach of the nineteenth-century European alliance system. Churchill, Stalin, and above all Roosevelt preserved the form of the League but turned back via the United Nations to the era Woodrow Wilson claimed to have rejected. Had the Big Three alliance remained intact after the end of the war, little would have prevented the UN from turning into the rather alarming international police power that at various times had appealed to Churchill, Stalin, and Roosevelt. Yet even by the spring of 1945, disagreement and suspicion were profound. Plans for a UN Military Staff Committee were an early casualty, and failure to reach agreement on this issue meant that even the limited collective security function envisaged in the charter for the UN Organization became impossible. Yet to old League hands like Sweetser, all of this was more than acceptable and the endless arguments about how the United Nations differed from the League were secondary. The League had been reborn, and could thus be buried with dignity. Through the United Nations, an organization it had done more than any other power to set up, the United States was back in the world, fully committed to a new version of the internationalist principles it had betrayed in 1920.

CHAPTER 8

Cold War Realities, 1945–49

There are fads in scholarship as well as in fashion. Just now, the current fad, with respect to American diplomatic history, is to belabor what is called "Wilsonianism" with all the sarcasm and dignified invective at the writer's disposal. . . . Only now, and belatedly, we are told, is the United States beginning to come down from the clouds of illusion and to survey realistically the true nature of the world.

—Grayson Kirk, "In Search of the National Interest" (1952)[1]

With little dissent, Americans have come to take it for granted that the counterpart of the League, the United Nations, is to be what Allen Dulles has called "our workshop of peace."

—Charles Seymour, "Woodrow Wilson in Perspective" (1956)[2]

One can read entire histories of American foreign policy in the Cold War without coming across a single reference to the United Nations. Usually the passage from the early to the late 1940s is portrayed in terms of the collapse of wartime cooperation and the rise of hawkish sages like George Kennan and Dean Acheson. Kennan in particular presides over the historiography, generating endless discussion of the complicated relationship his writings and especially his doctrine of containment bore to actual policy. He is an attractive figure to historians, partly because he was a consummate stylist and a considerable historian himself, even in his policy advice. Yet U.S. Cold War diplomacy revolved rather more around the question of what use to make of the United Nations than we think or than Kennan ever liked to admit. It is true that wartime internationalism was on the wane in policymaking circles by mid-1946 and that the UN—still finding its feet amid considerable bureaucratic disarray—was indeed marginalized as the Cold War was fought out in Europe. But the phenomenon was only temporary and only lasted as long as the attention of the United States was trained on Europe. From 1949 onward, as the battle shifted to Asia, the American rise to globalism turned international agencies into an indispensable Washington accessory. President Truman's second term in particular signaled the rise of a new, complex, and deeply ambiguous approach to American diplomacy, one that saw international institutions become a vital instrument for Washington in its pursuit of global power. This new approach did not repose as much faith in international law, world courts, or the rise of the International Mind as previous generations had done. It blended ideals and appetite, the call for freedom and offers of technical assistance, with the construction of naval bases in dozens of areas never previously deemed of peacetime concern to the United States. To a surprising degree given their novelty, it worked through international institutions. In short, the Cold War did not derail the project of internationalism; rather it redefined it and established its limits and goals and its relationship to American power.

LIVING WITH THE UNITED NATIONS

> The war was won not by any one country but by the combined efforts of the United Nations, and particularly by the brilliantly coordinated strategy of the great powers. So striking has been the lesson taught by this unity that the people and Government of the United States have altered their conception of national security. We understand that in the world of today a unilateral national policy of security is as outmoded as the Spads of 1918 in comparison with the B-29 of 1945 or the rocket planes of 1970. We know that for the United States—and for other great powers—there can be no humanly devised method of defining precisely the geographic areas in which their security interests begin or cease to exist. We realize, in short, that peace is a worldwide problem, and the maintenance of peace and not merely its restoration, depends primarily on the unity of the great powers.[3]

This assessment was sent to President Truman by his secretary of state in June 1945, when the San Francisco conference had ended, but the new United Nations organization had yet to come into being: only in October, once a sufficient number of states had ratified their membership, would it officially do so. Nevertheless, the centrality of the new organization to American security could not have been more forcefully asserted, nor the basic importance of preserving the understanding among the Big Three. Behind the scenes, American civil servants and military planners were helping to map out the structure of the new United Nations system—from War Department blueprints for an embryonic international armed force to public health specialists laying the foundations for what would become the World Health Organization. With relatively little corresponding work on the same scale on the British or Soviet sides, the United States could rightly claim parentage of the new world organization.[4] Yet even then a tantalizing question hung in the air: with U.S. national security being redefined so sweepingly that it had to be defended at potentially any point on the globe, what was the United States to do if the Big Three understanding broke down? And a second question followed: if the purpose of creating the United Nations Organization had been above all to educate the American public in the need to accustom itself to a global peacetime role for its country, how vital was the UN to the maintenance of that role? In the past, the country had set itself against permanent alliances. Would that attitude of reserve and aloofness continue?

THE AMERICANS had consented to let the first General Assembly meeting take place in London in return for British agreement to hold the founding conference at San Francisco, and so it was in the depths of a notably gloomy London winter that delegates assembled in the shabby grandeur of Central Hall, Westminster, in January 1946. They had two key items to discuss. One was to appoint a secretary-general and the other was to determine where the new organization should be based.

The League's chief civil servants had been first Drummond, a Scotsman, and then Avenol, from France. (The third, Irishman Sean Lester, essentially kept it alive during the war and was presiding over its winding up.) It had eventually been accepted by the powers that such an arrangement could not work any longer, and after what was to become a characteristic process in which the council's Big Two shot down each other's preferred candidates, Trygve Lie, a prickly, irascible former Norwegian foreign minister and a labor man with a taste for the nightlife emerged as the compromise choice. A career politician rather than a bureaucrat, Lie was an unexpected victor. Scarcely a household name, he had thought the Americans were backing him to preside over the General Assembly; suggesting him as secretary-general was in fact an afterthought on their part. To make matters worse, no sooner had he taken office than he learned that the five big powers had already agreed that they should get an assistant secretary-generalship each. The autonomy Drummond had enjoyed in building up his own executive administration was clearly not going to continue.

Before Lie had even been thought of, British Foreign Office mandarin Gladwyn Jebb—the man who had headed London's wartime unit on the "World Organization"—had been putting together the high-powered nucleus of the future secretariat from his still sandbagged offices in Dean's Yard, Westminster. Once the General Assembly was over, Lie sailed to New York with these new recruits and moved into the Waldorf.[5] The new organization was to be set up on a much more ambitious scale than the League, more than four times the size of the old secretariat. But this was not necessarily a good thing: in the rush of recruitment that followed, the original group of highly capable officials was swamped by less qualified newcomers. It did not help that Lie deliberately avoided seeking the advice of many former League specialists; the prewar body had fallen into such disrepute—especially with the Russians, who had been expelled from it after the invasion of Finland in 1939—that he feared even the appearance of continuity would be harmful.

Where Lie did do well was to sort out the thorny question of a permanent headquarters. The Europeans wanted to keep the League's successor in Europe: no longer being at the center of world affairs was almost unimaginable to them. "If the seat is in the New World, it is the end of Europe," warned the French delegate during a discussion in Andrei Gromyko's rooms at the Park Lane Hotel. On the other hand, for most of the non-European powers, Europe had had its day.[6] Hoping to keep the UN out of European affairs entirely, the Soviets particularly liked the sound of an American location, and the Swiss helped by hedging any future use of their country with so many preconditions that they effectively ruled themselves out. Eventually the Americans decided they welcomed the idea too, and the Senate blessed it. The British civil servant Charles Webster consoled himself that the Americans could not now say this had been forced on them: they would have to assume responsibility for the new organization's success.[7]

In late 1945, once a preparatory committee announced it would be recommending a U.S. location, offers immediately flooded in from municipalities as diverse as the Black Hills of South Dakota, Niagara Falls, and Hawaii; no fewer than half a dozen major cities also lobbied. Lie himself wanted New York. But because the original plan was to build an entirely new International City—along the lines of how an older generation of internationalists had imagined the future of Brussels and The Hague—three rural locations near major East Coast cities were shortlisted instead, eliciting angry protests from the wealthy residents of Greenwich, Connecticut, and Westchester County, New York, that they kept up for months. Only at the end of 1946—well after the new world body had begun to make its mark in international affairs—did the Rockefellers come to the rescue once again when the General Assembly agreed to John D. Rockefeller's offer of a gift of eighteen acres, mostly occupied by former slaughterhouses, on the down-at-heels Manhattan site of Turtle Bay on the East River.[8]

Before 1952, therefore, when the UN's gleaming new modernist headquarters emerged, matters critical to the preservation of international peace were discussed in a sequence of makeshift venues, including a converted gymnasium belonging to Hunter College in the Bronx and a former skating rink in Flushing Meadows, Queens, that had been erected for the 1939 World's Fair. The massive Sperry Gyroscope plant at Lake Success on Long Island housed the secretariat. The 1948 General Assembly met in Paris at the Palais de Chaillot, and voting on the Universal Declaration of Human Rights and Genocide Convention thus took place in the very building that had hosted Hitler during his brief dawn visit eight years earlier to the French capital. Such temporary expedients did not enhance the UN's authority. Neither did Lie's evident inadequacies as an organizer. A top bureaucratic troubleshooter, Robert Jackson, was sent in to sort things out, but he lasted only a few months before being forced out by bureaucratic stonewalling and Lie's own reluctance to restructure an already problematic secretariat. By early 1947 the secretariat itself was in open revolt over working conditions, and morale plummeted further when Senator Joseph McCarthy started investigating the political views of its U.S. employees. Considered against this background alone, it is easier to understand the Truman administration's misgivings about entrusting the new organization—which had at this point a budget somewhat smaller than that of the New York Fire Department—with handling some of the country's most pressing foreign policy priorities. In fact it is remarkable just how much was in fact initially handled through the UN at all.

The new secretary-general might have been chosen at the last minute, but he did enjoy one advantage over his predecessors, and that was the right conferred on him by the charter to bring matters before the Security Council on his own initiative. Drummond and Avenol had been silent presences at council meetings of the League: their task was not to set the agenda but to facilitate it. In the new UN, Lie could in principle do both, and in that first year he seized the opportunity. When the ambassador of Iran came to him because Soviet troops had failed to withdraw from the country, Lie took the decision, after some hesitation, to have the Security Council discuss the matter. Interestingly, it was not only the Soviet delegate who was discomfited. Both Edward Stettinius, now U.S. representative on the Security Council, and his successor as Truman's secretary of state, James Byrnes, believed Lie had gone beyond his powers. Rebutting them, he won an acknowledgment that he had not. Regarding Palestine, he was equally active.[9] Appalled by the UN's failure to impose the partition plan its own commission had recommended, he did something unusual by going before the General Assembly and introducing his own proposal to create a UN military force. Because discussions in the Security Council over how to find troops to commit to the UN Military Staff envisaged in the charter had become bogged down, Lie suggested to the assembly as a way out that he be allowed to recruit a much smaller force on his own account. This got nowhere, but it did convince policymakers in both Washington and Moscow that Lie was a little too unpredictable for their taste. His subsequent forays into the Berlin crisis and on the question of who should represent China after the communist victory on the mainland also opened him to criticism. A brave man but vain, highly emotional, and suspicious, Lie was not a natural diplomat.

Then there was his sense that it was his historic role to bridge the divide between the superpowers, which led him to badly misread his own importance. His impulse was understandable, for the Cold War immediately had a dampening effect not merely on the Security Council, which was deadlocked, but on the UN as a whole, where progress on a range of issues was sacrificed to the antagonism between the two superpowers. Lie proposed to solve this with a twenty-year plan that he kicked off with an ambitious "peace initiative" that took him—uninvited—to London, Moscow, Paris, and Washington. It was hard to say which power came to mistrust him more. When Stalin misguidedly withdrew from the Security Council in 1949 over its refusal to recognize Communist China, the Soviet Union's absence allowed Washington successfully to get UN backing to intervene in the Korean crisis. Once Lie came out in support, the Russians openly dismissed him as an American puppet, "humbly aiding Truman and Acheson to wreck the United Nations."[10]

AWAY FROM THE MONKEY HOUSE

The Russians were wrong, of course: the United States had invested too much in the UN to want to wreck it. They had not only set up the new world organization but staffed it at the highest levels with men who acted as a rather effective bridge between the secretariat and the State Department. But they were right that Washington had moved far from Roosevelt's pursuit of Great Power cooperation and had decided it needed a new strategy to confront Bolshevism directly. Almost as soon as Harry Truman replaced Roosevelt in April 1945, the tone toward the Russians had begun to change. Truman himself remained committed to the United Nations in a general sense, but foreign policy in his administration in these years was guided by men who despaired of the chances of cooperating with the USSR and thus of the UN itself as an important instrument for the pursuit of American interests. Undersecretary of State Dean Acheson, who had been involved getting the Senate to ratify UN membership in 1945, and had worked alongside John Maynard Keynes earlier at Bretton Woods, came at some point in 1946 to regard the UN as "the monkey house" and later wrote it off as the hopelessly idealistic creation of "that little rat Pasvolsky."[11] George Kennan had not much higher an opinion of it and wrote characteristically, in 1948, that

> we still find ourselves the victims of many of the romantic and universalistic concepts with which we emerged from the recent war. The initial buildup of the UN in US public opinion was so tremendous that it is possibly true, as is frequently alleged, that we have no choice but to make it the cornerstone of our policy in this post-hostilities period. Occasionally it has served a useful purpose. But by and large it has created more problems than it has solved.[12]

These men disagreed among themselves about how far the United States should abandon its older, rather limited role in world affairs and take on the trappings of a superpower. But whether, like Kennan, they feared overextension or, like Acheson, they believed the country had no choice but to take over from the British Empire as a global hegemon, they were of one mind in abjuring the United Nations and wishing they could draft a foreign policy based more on nineteenth-century European precepts than on the ideas of Woodrow Wilson.[13]

Kennan's restraint about how far American ambitions should extend was in fact a minority position within the administration. The real question for most senior policymakers was whether global power should be projected multilaterally or unilaterally. The war years themselves had seen the apogee of the One World tradition of Henry Wallace, Roosevelt's left-leaning vice president, who favored cooperation with the Russians. But as the Cold War heated up, and alarm grew at the speed of postwar American disarmament, some of Truman's closest advisers began arguing that American public support for the UN had gone too far and that it was time to educate the American people about the grim struggle that lay ahead. This did not necessarily mean abandoning the UN, but it might mean circumventing it.

With President Truman seated next to him on the platform, former British premier Winston Churchill sounded the alarm as early as March 1946—barely one month after the first UN General Assembly had finished—in his speech at Fulton, Missouri. Best remembered for its famous warning about an "iron curtain" descending across Europe, Churchill's references in the speech to the United Nations are generally forgotten. He actually called for the immediate creation of a UN armed force, and insisted on the need to make the new world organization a greater success than the League had been. But this sounded like mere piety next to the rousing call to arms, in which he urged the closest possible partnership between the Americans and the British to resist Soviet tyranny. This vein of Atlanticism was highly reminiscent of Jan Smuts's conception thirty years earlier of an Anglo-American condominium that would save civilization. Then the enemy had been Teutonic militarism, now it was Bolshevik tyranny, but in most other respects the vision was unchanged. As Smuts had done, Churchill argued explicitly that such a policy would not run counter to the charter but would in fact serve it.

Churchill had had a long chat with Truman before his Fulton speech and they had discussed the need for Anglo-American military collaboration, at least until the UN was in a position to pull its weight. In any case, the British leader was only confirming Truman's own instincts about Stalin. Two months earlier, the president had privately raised his concerns about the Soviets with his closest advisers, and the following month Washington had received the famous Long Telegram from George Kennan, then stationed at the Moscow embassy. Its alarmist diagnosis of the deep roots of Soviet behavior fell on receptive soil and led to Kennan himself being invited back and brought in eventually to head a new think tank within the State Department—the Policy Planning Staff. Although the Policy Planning Staff included at least one UN expert, its lengthy papers reflected Kennan's own skeptical perspective. Outside Kennan's office, other more powerful and influential figures—men such as Truman's adviser Clark Clifford, Secretary of War James Forrestal, and former Moscow ambassador Chip Bohlen—were also pushing the harder line. Through the summer and the autumn of 1946, the outlines of a new strategy began to emerge, gathering pace as a strongly anticommunist Republican majority emerged in Congress.

That September, a memorandum the size of a not insubstantial book thudded onto the president's desk. Truman had asked his aide Clark Clifford for an overall assessment of the character of the USSR and recommendations for an American response. Clifford's memo (actually written by aide George Elsey) shows that Kennan was far from the only Cold Warrior arguing that the Big Three idea behind the UN was finished. It depicted a Soviet Union bent on "world domination" in the name of Marxist ideals that were incompatible with American values. At great length, the report detailed the Kremlin's global ambitions and listed its violations of international agreements. Its conclusion—that mutual understanding between the two superpowers was impossible—implied that it would be dangerous and irresponsible to place America's future in the hands of the United Nations. America would have to chart its own course, and that course would have to be a global one.[14]

At about the same time, the new Soviet ambassador in Washington, Nikolai Novikov, was sending his assessment of *American* policy to the Kremlin. This too depicted a radical change of direction since Roosevelt's death, with the United States under Truman "striving for world hegemony," looking to take over Europe as "the stage on the road to world domination," and frustrated at continued Soviet power and its influence in eastern Europe. Novikov noted the huge increase in U.S. military appropriations, the plans for hundreds of new bases worldwide, and behind all this the newly "offensive nature" of U.S.

strategic thinking. Administration talk of modifying the United Nations to nullify the Security Council veto, which would continue on and off for several years, was intended, Novikov warned, to turn the United Nations into "an Anglo-Saxon domain in which the United States could play the leading role." The Novikov telegram was intended deliberately as a response to the Kennan telegram earlier that year, and in retrospect it reads as a more concrete and persuasive analysis. While the Soviets continued to think in traditional power-political terms (ironically, Kennan himself, having sent the dogs in the other direction, would belatedly try to insist on this), through the creation of a security buffer in eastern Europe, the Americans were revolutionizing their strategic vision by committing themselves to the quite unprecedented and unrealizable objective of containing "communism" worldwide. Operating like a nineteenth-century Great Power, Stalin was relatively unconcerned about the United Nations and did not regard it as an important diplomatic vehicle, whereas Truman did. The question was whether it could help in the containment of communism itself.

In October 1946, Truman welcomed the second UN General Assembly—the first to take place on American soil—with a strong defense of America's commitment to the new world body. Yet by this point skepticism about the political feasibility and military wisdom of relying on the UN had permeated the Truman White House. Churchill had poured scorn on the idea that such a new organization could be entrusted with handling the delicate question of atomic energy, for instance, and American efforts to internationalize the problem—the Baruch Plan for an International Atomic Development Authority—simply elicited a Soviet counterproposal for the complete outlawing of atomic weapons. The result was deadlock. Talks to form a UN military staff in fulfillment of the charter had broken down and the official appointed to head its new enforcement unit was soon looking for another job. In the critical areas of disarmament and enforcement, the original conception of the world security organization had thus already been found wanting by the end of 1946.

Equally important—because of its implications for Europe in particular—was the U.S. decision to wind up the UN Relief and Rehabilitation Administration. Since its establishment in 1943 to tackle the postwar humanitarian crisis, UNRRA had become a powerful multilateral aid vehicle run by Democrat Herbert Lehman, with the energetic Australian Robert Jackson as his effective deputy. By the summer of 1946 it employed more than twelve thousand staff in Europe and Asia, and disbursed hundreds of millions of dollars' worth of aid. But in the face of growing congressional criticism, Lehman was ousted and shortly thereafter the program was terminated. It was a critical moment, but the administration had decided it would be more likely to get appropriations for foreign aid passed by the new Republican Congress if they could be presented in terms of the struggle against Bolshevism. The trouble was that UNRRA provided aid to communist-dominated eastern Europe, and indeed to Soviet Ukraine and Belorussia too. And whereas UNRRA was most useful in south and eastern Europe and in China, it was the structural problems of the advanced economies of western Europe that increasingly preoccupied Truman's administration and worried Kennan and Acheson. Helping *them* implied an organization with a much more circumscribed geographical focus than UNRRA. Arguing for a new recovery package for Europe, Assistant Secretary of State William Clayton emphasized to Secretary of State George Marshall in May 1947 that what was important was that "we avoid getting into another UNRRA. *The United States must run this show.*"[15]

Clayton himself had in fact just come back from the first meeting of the new UN Economic Commission for Europe, which was busily planning its own recovery program, and his comments were thus pointedly directed at those who believed American aid to western Europe should go through that. But the administration was simultaneously realizing the full scale of Europe's postwar reconstruction needs. In the winter of 1946, it went back to Congress for several hundred million dollars in what it called "post-UNRRA" relief aid. And then, before the winter was over, came the unpleasant news from Greece, where the British had been propping up an unpopular right-wing government, that financial constraints would end the British presence there in a few weeks.

London's decision to withdraw troops abruptly from Greece—a country that had never before featured as a peacetime national security concern for the United States—became the catalyst for the Truman administration's new course. Having wound up UNRRA, the State Department was really out of its depth. UNRRA officials had already told them that they had failed to appreciate the sheer scale of the European reconstruction problem. In March 1947, therefore, Truman went before a joint session of Congress to request a further tranche of aid—nearly equivalent again for Greece to what had just been granted. (Turkey was mere window dressing to avoid too heavy a focus on Greece itself.) Except that what was really a conventional aid request was dressed up in apocalyptic terms as a struggle between good and evil, requiring American intervention to prevent a communist victory in what was about to become a Greek civil war.

Although historians have often regarded the Truman Doctrine as the moment when the Cold War began, the reaction of American public opinion worried the administration. White House officials must have had an inkling that people would be concerned by the scheme's failure to go through the United Nations, because they added some emollient references to it at the last minute. But the president was still roundly criticized: a Gallup poll showed that a sizable majority of Americans felt Truman had been wrong to bypass the world body.[16] The fact that Truman almost immediately became the first president since Monroe to have a doctrine named after him did not work in his favor, since the contrast between the geographically bounded goals of the original Monroe Doctrine and the limitless implications and militarism of Truman's rather vague commitment to defend freedom was widely denounced. The "Monroe Doctrine for the world" as some journalists dubbed it, was compared very unfavorably with the old. Commentator Walter Lippmann excoriated the speech for losing sight of the real strategic objectives of the United

States: it set Americans off chasing hares on the borderlands of the USSR—the policy of containment—when they should have been thinking how to strengthen their natural partnership with western Europe instead.[17]

Lippmann regarded the Marshall Plan scheme for European reconstruction, on the other hand, announced by Secretary of State George Marshall that summer, as a return to the right path. In his view, it had the right area in mind—Europe as a whole—and it chose the right way to run things by inviting European governments to propose uses of American funds. Like several other commentators, Lippmann foresaw Marshall's new plan extending entirely across Europe: he believed that the continent's economic interdependence would force this to come about and he saw it as something close to the recovery program that UN experts themselves had been drawing up inside the UN's Economic Commission for Europe. But Marshall's aides had not been aiming at this at all, and fortunately for them Stalin made sure it would not happen. Alarmed at what he saw as an American strategy of winning Europe for capitalism, he forced the Czechs to withdraw from Marshall Plan participation, tightened control in Prague, and moved rapidly in the autumn of 1947 to cement bloc unity in eastern Europe with the creation of the Cominform. The Kremlin started talking pointedly about the division of the world into two camps. After that, the UN's Economic Commission for Europe was forgotten, its dreams of bridging the East-West divide ignored by those who counted, and the Marshall Plan emerged much as Marshall and Kennan had wanted it, as a means of generating recovery in western Europe to provide an economic and security partner for the United States.[18]

Europe—the critical battleground of the first phase of the Cold War for both sides and the progenitor of nineteenth-century internationalist thought—was thus fought over largely outside the framework of the United Nations. It was one of the key initial differences between the UN and the League, whose entire raison d'être had been the consolidation of the Paris peace settlement. Instead the continent turned into a laboratory for the rather different international organizations that both superpowers created early in the Cold War. First, Congress backed the European Recovery Program that emerged out of General Marshall's speech, and an Organization for European Economic Coordination was set up, helping to lay the foundations for the later integrative process that the west Europeans themselves would initiate in the early 1950s based on heavy industry, trade liberalization, and central bank cooperation. The next step was even more dramatic in terms of American diplomatic precedent—a full-blown peacetime military alliance with the west Europeans.

The model for this was the 1947 Inter-American Treaty of Reciprocal Assistance that had opened by talking about the UN and the need to avoid war among the signatories but was really a military alliance against a threat from outside the hemisphere. The real likelihood of a Soviet invasion of the Americas was of course negligible: the threat, however, was helpful as a means of cementing bloc loyalty around the principle of anticommunism. Two years later, Washington took the unprecedented step of signing the North Atlantic Treaty and creating NATO. Ratified overwhelmingly by the Senate that July, the North Atlantic Treaty marked an enormous break with American diplomatic tradition, since for the first time in its history, the United States committed itself in peacetime to a military alliance with European powers. The size of the Senate vote—eighty-two to thirteen—was a sign of the radical change that had taken place in American thinking. As in the Inter-American version, the alliance was justified by reference to the UN Charter, which provides for the right to collective self-defense, and administration officials argued that its signing did not mean the UN was no longer important. Indeed, they insisted at great length that it was not a traditional kind of military alliance. But that was fundamentally what it was. Once Dwight D. Eisenhower, a man with much less time for the UN than the Democrats, took office, more regional alliances were crafted, enhancing American influence in Southeast Asia and later the Middle East, prompting fears in those regions of being sucked into a Cold

War they wanted nothing to do with and thereby inadvertently encouraging the emergence of a new force in global affairs—the nonaligned movement.[19]

WORLD FEDERALISM

The complexities of the Truman administration's evolving attitude to the United Nations reflected the delicacy of the U.S.-UN relationship. If the new world body looked too obviously like an American creation or an American puppet, its usefulness would suffer. Turning it into an explicitly anti-Soviet coalition, for example, was likely to produce a more focused but perhaps less powerful body. In 1948, this issue cropped up when Secretary of State George Marshall testified before the House Foreign Affairs Committee. Radical options were in the air. Some committee members wanted the president to propose a general UN conference for charter reform to make "the United Nations capable of enacting, interpreting and enforcing world law to prevent war." Others wanted to abolish the UN veto, returning to the Baruch Plan of a UN atomic development agency and establishing an international police force. Against the backdrop of widespread fears that a third world war was imminent, such proposals sought to turn the UN into a more effective guarantor of world peace.[20]

But they did so by proposing measures that could never have obtained Stalin's approval and that in fact mostly implied turning the UN into an anticommunist alliance. Speakers decried the extensive Soviet use of the veto, pointing out that it had deployed this no fewer than twenty-four times (the United States had not used its once), and one of them described the Soviet Communist Party as "the only functioning international agency in the world." Not surprisingly, red-baiters like the youthful new congressman Richard Nixon were among the hearing's organizers. But equally influential was a breed of idealists with a very different agenda, preeminent among them a group that rose and fell with astonishing speed in the late 1940s—the United World Federalists.

On the whole, as this book has attempted to make clear, world government in the sense espoused by Saint-Simon, H. G. Wells, or Paul Otlet has always been a minority taste. Believing in the compatibility of nationalism and internationalism, what most nineteenth-century internationalists sought was a coordinating agency that would empower nation-state members. But in the 1940s, world government momentarily seized the imagination of an astonishingly large number of people. The reason was simple: the atomic bomb and the question of how to control its use. As early as 1940, in his prophetic short story "Solution Unsatisfactory," science-fiction writer Robert Heinlein had seen that the development of radioactive weaponry would force the debate about world government: imagining Hitler's defeat, Heinlein depicted top American officials arguing over whether to impose a "military dictatorship over the whole world" or to use the opportunity to create a "worldwide democratic commonwealth" with police powers to control the use of these alarming new weapons and prevent proliferation:

> "League of Nations," I heard someone mutter.
>
> "No! . . . Not a League of Nations. The old League was helpless because it had no real existence, no power. It was . . . just a debating society, a sham. This would be different *for we would turn the dust over to it!*"[21]

Five years later, Hitler had been defeated and atomic fear was everywhere. Who controlled atomic energy was obviously the crucial question. The bombing of Hiroshima and Nagasaki cast a pall over the San Francisco conference, and on both sides of the Atlantic many erstwhile supporters claimed that the UN itself was now an answer to yesterday's problems and that a move to worldwide federation was urgently needed if mankind was to avoid a third and final world war.

Foremost among them were the physicists themselves. In October 1945, Albert Einstein signed a letter to the *New York Times* that predicted the UN would fail as an instrument of peace because it was based on "the absolute sovereignty of the rival nation-states"; he called instead for a "Federal Constitution of the world, a working worldwide legal order, if we hope to prevent atomic war." The following month, the Los Alamos scientists issued a public statement that called for world government as the ultimate goal. Einstein himself agreed to become chairman of the Emergency Committee of Atomic Scientists. For them, the Truman administration's plan to create a powerful new International Atomic Development Agency—presented to the first meeting of the UN's Atomic Energy Commission in 1946—opened up the possibility of making the UN the powerful international controlling force over atomic energy they desired; its failure, after an argument with the Soviets over the organization of inspection, left them despondent and the movement split as most scientists then accepted the need to continue their research for Washington. Once the House Committee on Un-American Activities began investigating scientists with international connections, a chill settled over further discussion. By the end of 1947, the scientific federalists were in unmistakable decline.[22]

Other leading American intellectuals had also moved in a federalist direction. Based at the University of Chicago, some responded to the Bomb by meeting to draft the outline of a constitution for a world government. What this self-appointed Committee to Frame a World Constitution wanted was not merely safety from the terrors of nuclear war but a return to the idea of a World State undergirded by World Law—the creation of a just international order. They believed that a "general movement for World Government" was growing, and wished to point the way. In 1948, after numerous meetings, they produced their report. Written in a spirit of defiant optimism, the report predicted that a powerful world government ("this is practically the consensus in this generation") would come within half a century at the most. It opened with a Declaration of Duties and Rights and proposed a federal convention with each delegate being elected by between half a million and a million voters. The whole thing was—as one might have expected—unmistakably American in inspiration.

Taking as its model the U.S. voting system, it provided for regionally organized electoral colleges—including Europa (Europe "outside the Russian area"), Eurasia (to include Russia and eastern Europe), Afrasia (extending from the Maghreb to Pakistan), and sub-Saharan Africa (but not necessarily including South Africa itself). A single language was to be designated by the new World Government within three years, and a federal calendar. Despite the distinction of the signatories, it was a staggeringly implausible document, and after its publication it sank almost without trace save for a few vitriolic commentaries in the anticommunist press. (The *Chicago Tribune* warned readers that its combination of "Franklin D. Roosevelt and Karl Marx" would "abolish the United States and all other countries.") But the report's very formulation, and the hard work behind it, indicate the strength for a brief moment in the United States of a small but vocal group that believed the United Nations had not gone far enough and feared that it would look to the rest of the world like "an American device for maintaining the status quo."[23]

Compared to such groups the United World Federalists were realists. They were not maximalist utopians like the Chicago professors, and they argued that the UN needed to be reformed rather than replaced. But they were for a time unwilling merely to fall in line behind the administration like the more mainstream UN supporters were doing. Founded in February 1947 on the eve of the Truman Doctrine, their origins lay in the wartime vogue for international federalism that had erupted in 1940 and 1941 and was still a powerful subcurrent on both sides of the Atlantic. The UWF also owed much to its dynamic young president, twenty-six-year-old Cord Meyer, a highly intelligent and articulate former marine who had served in the Pacific war and had lost an eye in Guam before going on to attend the San Francisco conference in 1945 as a junior official. Meyer toured the country drumming up support for world federation, and he turned the UWF into the largest federalist pressure group in the world. In September 1947, a Gallup poll showed that 56 percent of those questioned supported the view that "the UN should be strengthened to make it a world government"—a striking indication of the political danger the Truman administration faced in appearing to be looking outside the UN for America's security—and the UWF started the effective lobbying of Congress that led eventually to hearings in the spring of 1948.

Public alarm among supporters of the UN had been aroused in 1947 when the Argentinians—certainly with American approval—announced that they would ask the General Assembly to examine abolition of the veto. (The Argentinians themselves had only declared war on Germany in March 1945 in order to squeak into the UN.) No single measure was more likely to result in Soviet withdrawal. Marshall himself suggested the formation of a study group to look at changes to the veto and, most controversially of all from the Soviet viewpoint, the formation of a new body that could deal with security issues when the Security Council was deadlocked. All this aroused a furious response from Moscow, and the Soviet representative Andrei Vyshinsky insisted that both the Truman Doctrine and the Marshall Plan already constituted violations of the UN Charter. The Cominform was established in eastern Europe, threatening—or so it seemed from the outside—to mark a Soviet decision to break away from the UN and return to Leninist revolutionary internationalism. It was at this point that Marshall himself began to reconsider, and when he went before Congress in 1948 he argued that the reform of the UN needed to be handled carefully to avoid the organization splintering and meeting the fate of the League.

Speaking at the same hearings, the UWF's Cord Meyer disagreed. Reform would not wreck the UN: it was already on the rocks and the veto was not the only problem. The UN could be made much more effective if it was given greater enforcement powers, with more authority for the International Court of Justice and its own police forces. But what was really needed to counterbalance this and make it work was a sincere and comprehensive overture to the Soviets. Meyer impressed the committee, but Marshall carried the day, and the final bill, drafted by the committee itself, set out simply and blandly "to strengthen the United Nations and promote international cooperation."[24]

The UWF was never again to achieve such prominence. In fact, it became increasingly supportive of official policy. At the high point of its membership in 1949, when this stood at around forty-seven thousand, it backed the North Atlantic Treaty ratification. Then came the Korean War, which it also backed, and by 1953 membership had fallen to fifteen thousand. A hard core of several thousand remained loyal for decades, but they did not include Cord Meyer, whose subsequent career was even more extraordinary than the exploits of his youth. Having begun to work with the new Central Intelligence Agency to combat communist infiltration of the UWF in the late 1940s, Meyer joined the CIA full-time in 1951 at the invitation of the director, Allan Dulles. Fending off FBI charges that he was a security risk, Meyer quickly moved to the right. In the 1950s, he headed the CIA's International Organizations Division, channeling funds clandestinely to a variety of journals and lobbying groups. From 1962 onward, he was in charge of covert operations. When he retired, he wrote his account of his movement from wartime internationalism to the heart of the American national security state. It was an epitaph for one form of American internationalism that had flourished briefly for a short few years after the war.

THE UNREALITY OF REALISM

Kennan's influence on policy has often been overrated, but it is impossible to overrate his skill or influence as an analyst. In February 1948, now heading the Policy Planning Staff in the State Department, he identified two contrasting approaches to international affairs—the *universalistic* and the *particularist*. The former, which he disliked, focused on solving conflicts through the application of general rules and procedures, through law rather than politics, above all through international agencies and institutions. Kennan's innate skepticism about American democracy and his rather un-American view of diplomacy as an elite art emerged in his denunciation of the escapism and wishful thinking that lay behind popular support for the United Nations. In its place he proposed a case-by-case approach that relied on alliances of like-minded states with a "real community of interest and outlook" rather than on "the abstract formalism of universal international law or international organization." The problem with internationalism was not only that it led to false expectations. More worryingly, it could reduce American freedom to act and enmesh the country in "a sterile and cumbersome international parliamentarism."[25]

Kennan's analysis, from inside the policymaking machine, articulated a new "realism" in thinking about international affairs that had its counterpart in the commentariat outside Washington. Former Trotskyist James Burnham had just published his bestselling *The Struggle for the World*, an anti-UN call for a preemptive war that would pave the way for the triumph of American values. Echoing Heinlein's fiction, he preferred an American monopoly over atomic weapons to world government. But books like Burnham's were comets that flared briefly and died away, repelling as many people as they persuaded by the violence and crudity of their argument. Much more influential in the long run was the shift in overall orientation masterminded by a small number of intellectuals.

The rise of what later generations would call realism had started with the war and was bound up with the collapse of the League of Nations and the rise of Nazism, especially after the invasion of Czechoslovakia in early 1939. E. H. Carr, the British journalist and historian, had paved the way in a slim volume entitled *The Twenty Years' Crisis, 1919–1939*. Still regarded as a foundational text in the theory of international relations, Carr's book attacked the wishful thinking of the League and its supporters. They had confused how things were with how they felt they ought to be, Carr argued. One could not simply assume as Woodrow Wilson did that states shared a community of interest in the pursuit of peace. Instead, he urged a return to the wisdom of Machiavelli. As he put it bluntly, "Morality is a product of power."

In the United States, the transformed balance of power in Europe from the summer of 1940 upended traditional American strategic assumptions about the safety of their sea-girt hemispheric position. Pioneering strategist Edward Meade Earle (a founder of the discipline of security studies and a fan of Carr's) was one key figure, running a highly influential seminar in Princeton that brought in Carr himself, Kennan, and many other luminaries. In a sparkling but critical piece on H. G. Wells, Earle pinpointed Wells's error in thinking that scientific progress had made political institutions and processes irrelevant: a world state such as Wells wished for would not come into existence, asserted Earle, merely because we could fly faster around the globe. On the contrary, rapid scientific change created new threats that advocates of One World preferred to ignore.[26] Theologian Reinhold Niebuhr was another of the early realists, warning what he called "the Children of Light" in a series of wartime lectures not to underestimate the forces arrayed against them: a world community was not inevitable merely because technology seemed to demand it. National allegiances remained strong and so did the will to power: "a potential world community announces itself to history by the extension of conflict between nations to global proportions," he wrote in 1944. "The pride of nations is not easily brought under the dominion of the universal principle." Before genuine universalism could triumph, "corrupt forms of universalism must be defeated." Wise policy required going beyond the naiveté of those who had believed "a new definition of international law which denied the principle of the absolute sovereignty of nations, would serve to annul the fact." It also meant taking on those who believed founding global institutions was enough to "overcome international anarchy."[27]

Expressed in a rhetoric of gravitas and ethical responsibility, Niebuhr's work was immensely influential, spilling over from theology—the 1940s saw theologians exert unparalleled authority over the public debate about the direction of American policy—into academia and the world of policy. But the basic idea he outlined—that international institutions could have no value independent of the national interests of states—was already being developed in a much more systematic fashion by the social scientists and theorists. A cluster of émigré German lawyers in particular were critical in the dissemination of this view: brilliant scholars like Georg Schwarzenberger, John Herz, and Wolfgang Friedmann, having learned the hard way through the coming of Nazism and their own exile, believed that the older generation's simple faith in international law needed rethinking. To take account of power, and the basic human desire for it, one needed a new way of thinking about international affairs that subordinated law to the study of politics. This discipline was the infant social science of international relations.[28]

Hans Morgenthau was perhaps *the* critical figure in this cohort. In his widely read 1946 *Scientific Man versus Power Politics,* Morgenthau echoed Earle, attacking the naiveté of technocratic dreams of human improvement and the faith in universal reason that underpinned them. No international institutions, he wrote, could survive unless they accepted the reality of constant political struggle. *Scientific Man* criticized international law in particular as a kind of parallel universe to the world of political reality; like it or not, war was an integral part of the fabric of international life, and wise statesmen were preferable to well-meaning but impotent lawyers: "The question to be answered is not what the law is but what it ought to be, and this question cannot be answered by the lawyers but by the statesman. The choice is not between legality and illegality but between political wisdom and political stupidity."

Two years later, Morgenthau's textbook *Politics among Nations* made his name and virtually single-handedly recast the Cold War discipline of international relations in the United States from out of this disillusionment with international law. Drawing on cautionary wartime lectures that he had delivered when popular American enthusiasm for the UN was at a fever pitch, Morgenthau developed his opposition to the old internationalist certainties, warning against applying universal moral principles to the behavior of states and depicting the pursuit of national interest as the motor of international politics. This view rendered international cooperation as a secondary and at best fortuitous phenomenon rather than the evolutionary endpoint of human affairs. Anxious about the excessive moralizing that was emerging out of America as it groped toward a new world role—a moralizing found among both enthusiasts for and skeptics of the new United Nations—Morgenthau's chief goal was to get policymakers in Washington to think clearly about the national interest and to understand the Cold War not as a moral crusade but as a power struggle.

In fact, like Earle and Carr (and for that matter Kennan himself), Morgenthau's own thought on the subject of international cooperation was considerably more complex and nuanced than many of his followers acknowledged. What he opposed was not any appeal to international law per se so much as the idea (previously dominant through the teachings of the Austrian giant of the discipline Hans Kelsen) that law could and should be detached from the realm of politics. Supporting the UN was all very well, but it was important not to lose sight of the basic importance of the balance of power, especially in Europe. Earle, for his part, warned of the vagueness of the concepts of national security and—still worse—national interest, and the need to define these in wide terms to include not merely military and geographical factors but ideological and moral ones too. The neglected John Herz's masterly *Political Realism and Political Idealism* went furthest in charting a middle course for those, like the author, who believed that even in an international state system dominated by the struggle for power, collective security, values, and international law would still play a necessary role. Herz wanted a "realistic liberalism" that would provide theory and practice of "the realizable ideal," and he suggested that there had been too much debunking of the League of Nations, which had in fact pioneered collective security arrangements still worth taking seriously. Once one accepted the premise of Herz's "realistic liberalism," there was in fact much common ground between the two extremes, above all in the more pragmatic and practical world of policy.[29]

Away from the ivory tower, the pursuit of American security and support for international institutions certainly did not seem incompatible objectives. After all, the United Nations—with its Great Power condominium—was a very different instrument than the League had been, and not bound to the legalist internationalism that had prevailed in the early decades of the century. Even Kennan, unenthusiastic as he was, recognized that supporting the United Nations could have some value: he backed the decision to refer the issue of the Soviet blockade of Berlin there in 1948, for instance. For others, participation in the United Nations was vital to the new global U.S. foreign policy for the same reason that these regional treaties were—they both cemented the United States into the world and precluded the return to isolationism that always lurked as a dreadful possibility in the minds of officials in the Truman administration. Internationalism was the only way for America to behave like the power it was destined to become. Kennan might dream of an America that behaved like Bismarck's Germany, but the American public would not stand for it: the United States could only break with decades of isolationism by wrapping itself in the mantle of some higher and less self-interested purpose. Bodies such as the still immensely popular UN lent themselves to this. Moreover, American policymakers were starting to realize how much power they had over it, and how little the new world body could constrain them. Even after it became clear that the American public would accept—indeed might prefer—new alliance systems directed from Washington, there was only flexibility to be gained from continuing to link these, rhetorically at least, to the development of the United Nations as well.

It is probably a mistake to try to identify a single individual as the architect of this more positive and instrumental approach to the UN, but if there was one, it was the future secretary of state Dean Rusk. Unlike the more intellectual Kennan, Rusk rarely went into print, and whereas Kennan's reputation soared as he became American foreign policy's greatest critic, Rusk's plummeted through his involvement in the Vietnam War, resulting in his current oblivion. Yet despite the carefully cultivated aura of dullness, American foreign policy from Truman to Johnson arguably owed as much to him as anyone else. A southern boy from a modest background who had gone to Oxford on a Rhodes Scholarship in the 1930s and served in the Pacific during the war, Rusk saw active service in India and Southeast Asia, and helped to build up a U.S. base system in the Pacific under the aegis of the United Nations before moving to the Department of State. These very specific wartime experiences in Asia—and his long-standing knowledge of the British and their empire—shaped his outlook.

Counterposing himself to the State Department's Europeanists, Rusk—who headed the department's UN desk—argued powerfully in the late 1940s for involving the new world body in American diplomacy. Arriving in his job only a fortnight before the Truman doctrine was proclaimed, he was immediately vindicated by the storm of criticism that greeted the speech for going round the UN, and he played a central role thereafter in demonstrating to Truman and General Marshall how useful it could be as a vehicle for American goals. He showed them how to exploit the large pro-U.S. majority in the General Assembly, embarrassing the Soviets over Greece in late 1947, and how to reconcile support for America's European partners with strong anticolonialism, using the UN to help bring independence to Indonesia the following year, and in the process forging closer links between Washington and India. Rusk had no difficulty reconciling the need for regional security alliances with commitment to the UN itself; he supported development of the hydrogen bomb as well, but he believed the UN itself could be an effective instrument of anti-Soviet pressure. He even brought Republican John Foster Dulles, another internationalist, onto the U.S. delegation to the UN to ensure the maximum bipartisan support for his policy, which thus continued despite the pressures of McCarthyism.

Increasingly appreciated by Marshall and by Truman himself,

Rusk pushed this strategy to the limit during the Korean War. As soon as he learned of the North's invasion of the South, he persuaded the president to take the issue to the UN. Because the Soviet representatives were boycotting the Security Council, they were in no position to use their veto. Truman himself was appreciative: he understood how different the position would have been had the United States intervened in Korea alone. What makes Rusk's contribution so fascinating is its blend of idealism and military ambition. On the one hand, Rusk believed in the power of international law. And his commitment to anticolonialism became more vocal in the early 1950s as he started to make speeches calling for the United States to support anticolonial nationalist movements in Asia in line with the UN Charter. At the same time, he negotiated regional security pacts and base agreements, seeing American military and naval power as indispensable to the overall internationalist mission embodied by the UN.

If the Truman administration's realists owed much to the influence of interwar German thought, Rusk's very different approach can perhaps be traced back through his student days in Oxford to the worldview of English imperial internationalists. Two of his professors, both heavily involved with the League of Nations, had influenced him. One was the international lawyer James Brierly, whose defense of international law and strong criticism of the doctrine that a state's national interests always come first stayed with Rusk. Like Brierly—indeed like most good British liberal imperialists—Rusk believed that law, morality, and power went hand in hand. His old professor of international relations, Alfred Zimmern, who had played such an important role behind the scenes in 1917–18 in drafting British plans for the League of Nations, had similar views. By the early 1950s the elderly Zimmern, who had retired from Oxford and was teaching in a small college in Connecticut, was publicly urging his former student to take over the role in the world once played by the British Empire—to work through the UN where possible, and around it where necessary, exactly as he had believed Britain itself should do with the League between the wars. In Rusk, men like

Zimmern saw an American to whom they could hand on the torch of freedom and secure the standing of civilization in the world. America itself the former classicist saw as a new Athens, the leader of a modern commonwealth of freedom.

Rusk's version of internationalism would be continued by his colleague John Foster Dulles, while Rusk himself would support it in other ways through the 1950s as president of the Rockefeller Foundation (thus becoming the spiritual heir, as it were, to Raymond Fosdick, who had brought him onto the board in 1948 as trustee). Out of office, he showed as much interest in the spread of ideas as in policy—much as one would have expected from a former college professor. In 1954, for instance, he chaired an extraordinary meeting of scholars and policymakers under the aegis of the foundation—the participants included Walter Lippmann, Hans Morgenthau, Reinhold Niebuhr, Paul Nitze, and journalist James Reston—to discuss the future of theoretical research in international relations. Ranging over such abstruse questions as the nature of social scientific theory, the importance of morality in policymaking, and the definition of the national interest, the conference has been hailed as a critical moment in the rise of international relations as discipline in the United States. Later, Rusk would also use the foundation to publicize the importance of foreign aid and technical and welfare internationalism, continuing the tradition Fosdick had inaugurated before 1939.[30] In 1962, having thus nurtured the American investment in the internationalism of technical expertise and social science, Rusk would return to government, durably serving both Kennedy and Johnson as secretary of state. Only with the rise of Henry Kissinger would Rusk's instrumental internationalism finally be challenged. But by then, as we shall see, the relationship between the United States and the UN had changed fundamentally.[31]

CHAPTER 9

The Second World, and the Third

The future historian may regard as the greatest "revolution" of the twentieth century not Lenin's overthrow of the short-lived free regime in Russia in November 1917, but the less conspicuous . . . and yet more far-reaching process which brought Europe's four hundred years old dominion of the globe to an end.

—Hans Kohn, "The United Nations and National Self-Determination" (1958)[1]

I have lived seventy-eight years without hearing of places like bloody Cambodia.

—Winston Churchill, 1953[2]

FROM THE SECOND WORLD TO THE THIRD

It was a striking fact that as the Cold War opened, the USSR, widely regarded for much of the twentieth century as the internationalist state par excellence, felt itself to be lagging behind. "A rather strange picture has emerged," Stalin's chief cultural ideologue Andrei Zhdanov confessed to delegates at the first meeting of the Cominform in September 1947. "Representatives of the widest variety of activities—scientists . . . trade unions, youth, students—consider it possible to maintain international contact, exchange experiences and consult together about problems of their work, hold international conferences and gatherings, but the Communists, even of countries that are allies, shrink from establishing friendly links among themselves." As striking as this admission was what Zhdanov did not say. Left out of the speech he delivered was a paragraph in which he talked about the "bright page" of the Soviet role in setting up the United Nations, and praised the idea of the latter as an organization to strengthen "genuine cooperation between peoples."[3]

The truth was that by this point the Soviets were having serious second thoughts about the UN and toying with the need to return to a policy of centralized ideological control. When they had finally wound up the Comintern in 1943, they had abandoned revolutionary internationalism for the Great Power version, but the results were worrying. The new world organization was becoming a place of public embarrassment. In discussions of Iran and Greece in 1946, as in the Security Council debate about Berlin in 1948, the very successful American strategy was to attract publicity to issues Stalin would have preferred to keep out of the limelight by forcing the Soviets to use their veto. And there was a structural problem too. Within the UN Secretariat, a number of the secretary-general's closest advisers were Americans, mostly men with close ties to the State Department; in contrast, a scanty one percent of the officials in senior posts were from the USSR. In the assembly, there was an effective built-in American majority on most issues; combined with the nations of the Commonwealth, the large number of west European and Latin American states easily outvoted the Poles, Yugoslavs, and Czechs who marched alongside the three Soviet delegates: this was why the Soviet Union used its veto in the Security Council no fewer than forty-seven times in a mere six years, while the United States never had to use it at all in twenty. "As the United Nations and the cold war have simultaneously developed," noted two American analysts, "it is hardly too much to say that the United Nations has become a reflection or even an instrument of the policies of the western powers, almost always supported by a large majority of the other members." Rusk's strategy seemed to have prevailed: the USSR had entered what some called the "permanent opposition."[4]

To a large extent this reflected the lack of interest the Soviets had shown in the whole world organization idea from the start. Stalin had participated in the founding of the UN on the assumption that it represented a formal recognition of the special rights of Great Powers in preventing another world war. Critical of how the League had ended up, he had no great hopes for it in other respects, frowned on the multiplication of the specialist agencies, and mostly kept out of them. In areas where Stalin discerned no vital interest—Palestine, Kashmir, Indonesia, the Italian colonies—Soviet delegates did not block Western initiatives. The veto itself was chiefly wielded when matters that the USSR regarded as lying within its own sphere of interest came into play. For this reason, the preservation of sovereignty was Moscow's paramount consideration, and nothing excited the Kremlin's contempt more than "bourgeois apologists" for a federalist world government. Even in the early critical discussions at Dumbarton Oaks, Gromyko had made it clear to his American counterparts that the USSR would rather have a world without the UN at all than one in which it was denied the right to veto any dispute touching on its interests.[5]

All it could try to do therefore was to use the veto to paralyze the new world body and to stop the Security Council or the General Assembly from becoming powerful enough to constitute a threat. Stalin watched with perplexity as the Americans proposed shifting power out of the Security Council and giving the assembly and the secretary-general more authority. When the Americans proposed reforming the charter, the Russians emerged as its most stalwart defenders. With Mao's victory in China, Stalin blocked the UN's further growth, threatening to hold up any expansion of the membership of the General Assembly until the communist regime in Beijing was recognized. His logic seemed validated when the Americans proposed giving the General Assembly greater power to act whenever the Security Council was deadlocked on a matter of international peace and security. This move—which was not of course in keeping with the original conception behind the charter—generated what a commentator called a "cold fury" in Moscow toward the organization, and led eventually to Trygve Lie's replacement as secretary-general. "The United Nations Organization," Stalin fulminated in February 1951, "is being turned into an instrument of war, into a means of unleashing a new world war. . . . [It] is now not so much a world organization as an organization for the Americans, an organization acting on behalf of the American aggressors." As two astute American commentators noted the following year, what was surprising after all this was not Soviet hostility toward the UN but the fact that it remained a member at all.[6]

One reason no doubt why it stayed in was that the Kremlin's efforts to establish alternative organizations were such a failure, for although it suited both communists and anticommunists throughout the Cold War to draw attention to the ideological power of Marxist internationalism, its actual postwar achievements were remarkably small. The creation of the Communist Information Bureau in 1947—the occasion for Zhdanov's speech—saw the Soviets responding to the Marshall Plan by trying to impose ideological uniformity on its strategically vital east European satellites. Revealingly, the Cominform's birth took the form of a meeting of communist parties, not a conference of allied states, and although it claimed to mark the birth of a "democratic and anti-imperialist camp," in fact all the invitees at its founding conference were European. Less than a year later, it all but blew apart when the main watchdog of ideological conformism, Tito's Yugoslavia, showed unexpected signs of independence of mind. The Cominform scarcely survived the Tito-Stalin split and the east European show trials, and it was dead within a decade, having lasted less than half as long as its predecessor, the interwar Communist International.

The Soviet effort to construct assemblies of "peace-loving"

citizens from below was even less fruitful: although such bodies as the World Peace Council and the World Congress of Partisans of Peace were heralded in Moscow as potential alternatives to the United Nations, they lasted an even shorter time. Later efforts by the Russians to bring together communist parties from around the world in periodic conference were deeply troubled affairs and merely demonstrated how much resistance there was by the 1950s among even supposedly friendly states and parties to accepting a leading role for Moscow of the kind Lenin had demanded in 1919. First Yugoslavia, then far more threateningly and durably China, emerged as ideological rivals and made such meetings more trouble than they were worth: they required painstaking preparation and never resulted in anything more tangible than embarrassingly vague communiqués. By the early 1960s, even the Cubans were emerging in Africa as a revolutionary competitor to Moscow. Meanwhile, the UN was proving its staying power. As Zhdanov virtually admitted back in 1947, even though the international institutions that counted through the Cold War were created, and run, by the Americans and their allies, the Soviet Union could not afford to remain aloof.[7]

The USSR therefore remained in the UN, and after Stalin's death his successors started to see new opportunities in it for extending its global influence. When in 1956 Hans Morgenthau described the UN as "a grand alliance" in opposition to the other "grand alliance" of the Soviets and their allies, this statement, which would have been close to the mark at the start of the decade, was already out of date.[8] By then the Soviet Union was participating in UN technical assistance work, had rejoined the ILO, UNESCO, and WHO, and under the new secretary-general, Dag Hammarskjöld, had helped negotiate an end to hostilities in Korea and played a small part in his remarkable personal mission to China to negotiate the release of downed American pilots. In 1955 there were serious talks for the first time in years on disarmament and the peaceful uses of atomic energy, the signing of the Austrian peace treaty, and the normalization of Soviet diplomatic relations with West Germany and Japan. Above all—and perhaps in the UN context most importantly—in that same year, the membership logjam was finally broken and the deal was done that allowed another sixteen members in, thereby ushering in the most dynamic decade in the history of the UN.[9]

The old interwar Soviet line of "peaceful coexistence" between communism and capitalism was now reinterpreted by Stalin's eventual successor, General Secretary Nikita Khrushchev, as the Kremlin looked beyond the Cold War division of Europe to the struggle for influence in Africa and Asia. For *the* major ideological issue of the time was, Moscow slowly realized, one where the USSR could hope to turn the UN to its advantage—the struggle against colonialism. Both the superpowers could claim the mantle of anticolonialism of course, but the Americans were hampered by the fact that the colonial powers were their closest allies, and in the 1940s in particular, they were loath to embarrass them publicly. The Soviets had no such constraints, for their main allies—the east Europeans—had no overseas colonies to lose. The USSR, declared Zhdanov in 1947, was "the only true defender of freedom and independence for all nations and an opponent of national oppression and colonial exploitation in any form whatever." In one of his last speeches, Stalin himself abandoned the old division of the world into "socialist" and "imperialist" camps and acknowledged the existence of a third "peace camp" that was vital to winning over to socialism.

Stalin himself remained largely focused on overcoming the division of Europe. But his young colleagues were impatient to look farther afield. In France at this time, the demographer Alfred Sauvy was coining the term "Third World," singling out the colonial world of Africa and Asia and its growing importance in the Cold War as a zone of global transformation. After Stalin's death in 1953, and especially under Khrushchev, the Soviet appeal to the colonial world, reduced since 1934 for power-political reasons to a whisper, now reemerged as the chief expression of the old Marxist internationalism. As the United States responded, the old battle between Marx and Mazzini was restaged globally, and the United Nations became the chief institutional theater of this contest.

DECOLONIZATION

It is, in retrospect, startling just how rapidly Europe disgorged its colonies after 1945. Decolonization was a process that went back a long way, of course, having begun fitfully at the end of the eighteenth century in the Americas before going into reverse with the Scramble for Africa and the Middle East from the end of the nineteenth century. Even during the Second World War, few Europeans anticipated that within a couple of decades their empires would have shrunk to almost nothing. They were, of course, aware of the rise of nationalist opposition to European rule, especially during the war itself, but Churchill, Smuts, and others saw the proposed new international security architecture centered on the UN as a way to cement white rule, not give it up. Churchill himself had dampened speculation that the freedoms mentioned in the 1941 Atlantic Charter would apply beyond Europe. The Dutch government in exile, equally adamant, insisted that it had found a "doctrine of synthesis" in which East and West were combined under their patronage, ruling out any talk of independence for Indonesia or Surinam. When proposals were mooted by the Americans to hand the ultimate responsibility for all colonies to the new UNO, Europeans were shocked. René Pleven, secretary for the colonies for Charles de Gaulle's Free French, led the charge on behalf of the civilizing mission:

> At this very moment, when France is certainly more aware than ever of the importance of her Empire . . . a new doctrine is being put forward whereby colonial responsibilities should be assumed no longer by those nations who for centuries carried them out . . . but by some international organization which, one has to assume, is credited with the cardinal virtue of justice . . . and of competence and diligence. Neither the interests nor the wishes of the colonial populations would be served by a reform which would transfer to a caretaker organization, acting under a collective name, the continuation

> of the colonizing work which is liberating the primitive societies from the great calamities which are ravaging them and which are called: disease, ignorance, superstition, tyranny.

Yet there were powerful countervailing forces, and not just in the United States and the USSR—which both supported colonial demands for independence. The fascist powers in Europe were too European and too fascist to recognize the potential global appeal of anticolonialism until it was far too late. But in Asia, the crumbling of Dutch, French, and British rule was hastened by the Japanese willingness to play the anti-European card. The march to the 1955 non-aligned conference at Bandung, one historian has written, in fact began with the Japanese takeover of 1940–42, and Japan's wartime cooperation with nationalists in Asia was part of the reason for the widespread dissatisfaction in the region with the European effort to roll the clock back in 1945, especially in the Dutch East Indies and French Indochina, where colonial rule was reimposed by armed force. Even before that, India's Congress Party mounted a wartime campaign of unrest and civil disobedience to British rule and thousands were arrested. Gandhi and Nehru took matters no further while the war was on—but they made it clear that their struggle was part of a larger effort to resist the restoration of colonial rule by European powers after the war: "Our struggle is only a phase in the struggle of the oppressed peoples all over the world."[10]

To combat these pressures, the Europeans responded with both conceptual inventiveness and force: "natives" became "autochthons," empire turned into "Union," and protectorates—a colonial notion discredited by the fate of Czechoslovakia under the Nazis—were rebranded as "associated states." The civilizing mission thus refused to die. "British imperialism is dead, insofar as it ever existed, except as a slogan used by our critics" ran a Whitehall propaganda brochure in 1946. According to the Colonial Office, the "colonial system was a practical illustration of democracy under tuition." France's 1944 Brazzaville Declaration on the future of the empire insisted that "the overseas populations do not want any kind of independence other than the independence of France."[11] When natives behaved in ways suggesting this was not true, the clampdowns were bloody. Tens of thousands were killed by the French in Algeria in May 1945; the repression in Syria and Madagascar was equally vicious.

But the rulers of empire could take heart from American backtracking. Roosevelt's assistant secretary of state, Sumner Welles, might have hailed the end of "the era of imperialism."[12] But in the War Department, Henry Stimson could already see the need for American bases overseas. Even as the State Department in Washington drafted plans for the UN to take over *all* colonies after the war, the U.S. Navy was identifying certain Pacific islands as too important strategically to be allowed to go their own way. Here, already in 1944, was the beginning of a postwar American empire based not on colonization but on the acquisition of military and naval bases and enclaves.

It was therefore not surprising that in the months before the San Francisco conference, the question of colonies and trusteeships was striking by its absence. The Dumbarton Oaks proposals, for example, said nothing on the subject, and over the winter of 1944–45, the British beat back an American proposal to extend UN supervision to all colonial territories and made sure the new organization could do little more than gather information. The Big Three eventually agreed that the UN would concern itself with former League mandates and other territories taken from the enemy. (It could also encompass territories that chose to place themselves under trusteeship, but in practice there was no chance of any of the European powers agreeing to this.) The American navy got its bases, which were now designated "strategic trust territories." It all amounted to a huge defeat for the anticolonialists in Washington, and an acceptance that European rule would return to Southeast Asia.

Even the more open environment of the San Francisco conference failed to change the fundamentals. The UN Charter avoided any clear commitment to the right of all dependent territories to full independence. Trust territories were placed under UN oversight. But Article 76 defined the goal not as independence but something far weaker—"their progressive development toward self-government or independence as may be appropriate to the particular circumstances of each territory and its peoples and to the freely expressed wishes of the peoples concerned." The "strategic trust territories" were to be supervised, not by the General Assembly and its Trusteeship Council, but rather by the Security Council. Existing colonies were rebranded "non-self-governing territories," and here all the colonial powers had to do, according to the charter, was to "recognize the principle that the interests of the inhabitants of these territories are paramount and accept as a sacred trust the obligation to promote to the utmost . . . the well-being of the inhabitants of these territories." The colonial powers did accept the obligation to transmit information regularly on their colonies to the secretary-general and went away from San Francisco confident that the new world body was compatible with continued imperial rule.

It is true that some changes from the time of the League might have given them pause. The General Assembly was made responsible for the trusteeship system—a contributory factor to the later rise of the assembly that we will discuss below. The charter also gave the UN a foot in the door of the European colonial system in general. The Trusteeship Council itself was to be composed not of civil servants—as in the old Permanent Mandates Commission—but of representatives of UN member nations, thus politicizing empire, putting the colonial powers in the minority, and increasing the likelihood of extensive public discussion of their policies. On the other hand, the charter recognized self-determination as a principle not a right, and chose not to second-guess the imperial powers as to when independence might occur.

THE RISE OF THE GENERAL ASSEMBLY

The apparently feeble new trusteeship system did not then look at first glance as though it would produce results any more dramatic than the League's commitment to mandates had done. The General Assembly was not very effective in badgering "administering powers" to set timetables for independence and to boost native participation in the running of their colonies. On the Trusteeship Council, imperial powers predominated at first, since those administering trust territories numbered half the council's members, and in addition other permanent members of the Security Council had a seat. Minor irritations aside, the European empires looked safe.

And had this been the old League of Nations they might have been: the League's assembly, hailed at the time as the embodiment of Tennyson's "Parliament of Man," had in fact been dominated by Europe. Forty-eight countries had sent delegates to the first assembly meeting in Geneva in 1920, but there were only four from Asia (including the Raj), and none from the Middle East: Islam was scarcely represented, nor Buddhism or Confucianism. The UN was different—and right at the outset representatives of the empires, men such as Britain's Ernest Bevin and France's Georges Bidault, had been struck by Europe's relative lack of weight in its deliberations. Twenty-seven of the original fifty-one members of the UN had once been colonies, and others were east European People's Democracies with no liking for empire. Anticolonialism was boosted in 1947, when the Latin American states established a Conference of the American Committee for the Dependent Territories to "fight colonialism in all its forms no matter where it is found." A growing number of Arab and Asian member states also sympathized with ongoing struggles for self-rule across the swath of territory from Tunisia to Burma. Led by the Philippines (granted independence by the Americans in 1946) and the Indians (independent from the British the following year), the assembly itself took up the anticolonial cause.[13]

Its very first session in 1946 was a sign of things to come as the Indian delegation charged South Africa with discriminating against citizens of Indian descent. In theory, the attack was inadmissible, since the domestic jurisdiction clause of the charter supposedly ruled out discussion of such issues. Yet not only did the assembly disregard this, but the Indians were not even yet fully independent. In the process of breaking free of British imperial tutelage, they clearly saw the assembly as an attractive and productive forum to make their mark, since the more traditional course—given that both India and South Africa were part of the British imperial system—would have been to allow London to adjudicate the issue quietly. Instead, the Indians presented the General Assembly with what they regarded as an egregious case of racial discrimination. The assembly's powers might be limited, but what the Indians wanted was "to expose the wicked policy of General Smuts in all its nakedness before the world," and for this it was the ideal forum.[14]

Given that both international law in its nineteenth-century incarnation and the charter had clearly been drawn up to serve imperial interests, it is not surprising that politics rather than law proper or the letter of the charter drove the assembly. American suggestions to refer the South African issue to the International Court of Justice were dismissed on the grounds that where racial prejudice was concerned the issues were inherently political and should not be handed over to judges. Traditionalist claims that the issue was really one of minority rights, something that the UN was wary of resurrecting, were rebuffed by the Indians, who insisted that this was not about minorities but about race. The Indians won their vote, and the South Africans, who had never expected the United Nations to involve itself in their internal affairs, were shocked. The result was hailed as a victory for democratic values. But it was a double-edged victory all the same: denunciations of South Africa's internal policies became an annual feature of the assembly, intensified of course after the declaration of apartheid. But the assembly had little power in this case beyond denunciation, and the value of this soon depreciated.

The liquidation of the British mandate in Palestine the following year demonstrated the limits of its influence more emphatically. This after all was an issue where the assembly was the primary decision-making body, and in November 1947 it voted for partition in a resolution that placed Jerusalem under trusteeship and put minorities under the protection of the UN, a resolution that would have represented—had the provisions come into force—a striking revival of minority rights. Once again, politics trumped law, and the idea of asking the International Court of Justice to adjudicate—this time proposed by the Arab countries—was turned down, just as it had been in the South African vote the previous year. After the fighting the following year between Jewish and Arab forces rendered the 1947 partition plan moot, the General Assembly voted to appoint a mediator, under whose auspices an armistice agreement was eventually signed in 1949. But the Palestinian case suggested that although the UN could shine a bright light of publicity on colonial rule, it lacked the military force necessary to enforce its own policies. It also showed that in 1947 the Third World vote was still too limited and divided to carry the assembly: the Arabs opposed the partition plan but could muster only thirteen votes. Above all, it showed that when the superpowers chose to act—the United States was the first to recognize Israeli independence de facto, the USSR de jure—there was little the rest of the UN could do.

It was, of course, obvious that the Security Council was a deeply politicized body, but this revealed that the assembly was as well, not in the sense of cleaving to one side or the other in the Cold War but in the more specific sense of believing that the world's political representatives not the lawyers should make the fundamental decisions. In effect, the rise of the General Assembly meant the triumph of the Wilsonian vision of global governance through parliamentary deliberation and the final defeat of half a century and more of legalist internationalism. Law's demise had already alarmed commentators analyzing the Dumbarton Oaks proposals. Things did not improve with time. By the 1950s, students of the World Court warned that in contrast to the interwar experience, it was being sidelined: "the picture is bleak." Eisenhower's secretary of state, John Foster Dulles, who had attended the 1907 Hague conference with his lawyer grandfather, came to see international law as yesterday's dream. Fending off press magnate Henry Luce in 1957, Dulles told him that "the World Court is unemployed. . . . There are lots of arbitration agreements around but they are never used." The old Institute of International Law was alarmed at the politicization of elections to the court; though it could scarcely admit it, what really alarmed it was the sharp decrease in the number of European judges. By the mid-1980s, commentators speculated that the creation of "a much-publicized but virtually ineffective court" had actually set back the cause of world peace by helping to discredit the role of international law.[15]

The truth was that the General Assembly would not only not bind itself to legal judgments, it would not even necessarily bind itself to the charter itself. Based on the pure parliamentary procedure of majority voting, this made it an inherently unpredictable instrument so far as the Great Powers were concerned. In a now forgotten illustration of its assertiveness, the assembly voted down an agreement reached among the British, Americans, and French to carve up Libya into three trusteeships for them to run: after the defeat, British foreign minister Bevin muttered testily about the emergence of an "Arab-Moslem-Asiatic bloc." Instead Libya was run by a UN commissioner appointed through the assembly; the following year, another was appointed to the former Italian colony of Eritrea.

Watching these events from his perch in the State Department, George Kennan warned Washington that the General Assembly might not turn out to be as faithful a servant of American wishes as some seemed to believe. It gave decision-making power to the majority of its members, even though they lacked any uniformity either of size or of political complexion. All kinds of polities were being recognized as sovereign entities, and the criteria for recognition were vague and far looser than in the past. It was, in short, "a fortuitous collection of social entities which happen at this stage in human history to enjoy a wide degree of acceptance as independent states." He estimated that even then only about one-quarter of them were reliable supporters of the United States and that whereas in major questions of peace and security Washington had gotten its way, in colonial issues it was already regularly being outvoted. His prescient conclusion—reached even as Dean Rusk was winning the first round of the policy battle—was that the assembly's utility to Washington lay primarily in the Cold War struggle with the Soviet Union, and insofar as that gradually gave way to other concerns, it would cease to offer the same advantages. To anyone who knew Kennan the conclusion was not surprising: temperamentally, he disliked any subordination of foreign policy to the demos, and the UN Assembly seemed equally problematic since it removed power from the hands of diplomats and made it subject to "the parliamentary drama" on an international stage, an altogether "new, more complicated and more hazardous theater of operations." Kennan's fault was not so much that he was wrong as that he saw too far ahead. What seemed alarmist as the UN and the United States went to war together in Korea looked increasingly obvious a decade or so later on.[16]

THE MAIN REASON for this was the swift and unforeseen expansion of the General Assembly's membership after 1955. Four new members joined the original fifty-one at the UN in 1946, but only one state a year was able to join between 1947 and 1950, and none at all were admitted between 1950 and 1955. Stuck between Soviet obstruction and McCarthyism in the United States (the red-baiting investigations reached even into the secretariat), the UN seemed paralyzed; Trygve Lie's constant calls to make the organization a genuinely universal one sounded merely plaintive. But Stalin's death and the appointment of Dag Hammarskjöld as secretary-general helped to unblock the stalemate, and although the Chinese issue was not resolved—representatives of the People's Republic of China would only replace Taiwan at the UN in 1971—intensive diplomacy and the evident impatience of the majority of the UN's members with the obstructionism of both the superpowers allowed in another sixteen new members in 1955—among them the newly independent states of Cambodia, Laos, and Libya. After this, expansion was startlingly rapid. A further twenty-three members were added by 1961, thirty-three more over the following decade. By this point, the Afro-Asian bloc dominated the General Assembly.

The Bandung Conference in 1955—the year that the General Assembly voted to make the right to national self-determination the centerpiece of any future human rights covenant—marked the Third World's arrival as a political force and the moment when the world's fundamental division shifted from West-East to North-South. The conference itself brought together twenty-nine Asian and African states and colonies that had been invited by Indian prime minister Jawaharlal Nehru and Indonesian president Sukarno: the participants included anticommunist allies like Thailand and Sri Lanka, Communist China (to Washington's dismay), and neutrals such as India. The extension of the Cold War into Asia with the U.S. creation of the Southeast Asia Treaty Organization in 1954 had been one of the prime motivations for the conference: SEATO, Nehru stated at the time, came close to "declaring a kind of Monroe Doctrine, unilaterally over the countries of South East Asia."[17] Alarmed by the rise of the Warsaw Pact in the Soviet bloc and Eisenhower's new regional military alliances not only in Southeast Asia but also in the Middle East, the participants at the conference demanded to remain above the fray, and to speak out for a world whose basic survival was threatened not so much by the Cold War as by nuclear armageddon. Even American allies such as the Philippines and Iraq argued powerfully in favor of self-determination. The conference itself debated whether Soviet rule in eastern Europe constituted a form of colonialism—reaching no clear conclusion—but ended with a sweeping condemnation of "colonialism in all its manifestations." It urged immediate UN membership for newly independent nations such as Cambodia, Ceylon, and Vietnam and reaffirmed its members' desire to help the

UN itself work more effectively, by making membership in it universal and freeing it from the grip of the Great Powers.

Western observers were distinctly nervous. In a lecture he delivered at the London School of Economics, the British theorist of international affairs Martin Wight sounded a note of alarm. What he called "the Bandung Powers" were nothing less, he said, than "a Mazzinian revolutionary league" that had managed to turn the United Nations into an "organ of the anti-colonial movement, a kind of Holy Alliance in reverse." Another British commentator correctly foresaw that the newly independent states would "use the success of the conference as a means of asserting the Arab/Asian point of view and of claiming that the Bandung countries were entitled to a far bigger share of the world authority (as represented by the UN) than they had had when the UN was founded."[18]

Beset by the emergent civil rights movement at home and prey to fears of a global race war, some in the Eisenhower administration felt equally threatened. Secretary of State John Foster Dulles worried that Bandung would encourage "communist engulfment" of the Third World and wished he could have stopped it. He was plagued by the old fears of Pan-Asianism: like many another internationalist, he had grown up in a world where such anxieties about global race conflict were commonplace. Eisenhower himself was less perturbed and put his finger on the central point: nationalism had grown rapidly throughout the world since the end of the Second World War, yet the Soviets had managed to be far more successful than the United States in utilizing "this new spirit of nationalism in its own interest."[19] Once the conference was over, the postmortem in Washington was a little more reassuring. Communist China had not dominated the event, and most of the results had been in line with American policy, or not too far from it.[20]

In the immediate aftermath, Eisenhower felt vindicated in his view that empire had had its day. Even before the Suez Crisis the following year, which allowed him to make the point very publicly, and to force a dramatic acceleration in the pace of decolonization in

Africa, he was thus coming around to accept the need to embrace nationalist elites in the Third World. An African American congressman who had attended Bandung returned home and warned Dulles and Eisenhower that "we [had] to move fast." Asked how the United States could increase its influence in Africa and Asia, Congressman Adam Clayton Powell Jr. responded, "Quit taking the side of colonialism in the UN; clean up the race problem in the United States as rapidly as possible, and get across the tremendous progress we've already made; appoint more Negroes to our foreign diplomatic posts." Dulles himself talked about organizing a "Bandung Conference in reverse" with British foreign secretary Harold Macmillan to publicize plans for orderly decolonization and thus take the wind out of Soviet sails. Or would have done had the British allowed it to happen. "It is universally admitted that the colonial era is dead," American analysts noted in January 1956. "Yet in the current phase of the Cold War we are saddled, in the minds of millions, with the onus of colonialism." From this perspective, the Suez Crisis came as a gift because it allowed the Eisenhower administration to assume the role of leader of the anticolonial world against its European allies. In 1956, Eisenhower welcomed it when the General Assembly again asserted its prerogatives—this time in the face of likely British and French obstruction on the Security Council—and he allowed UN secretary-general Dag Hammarskjöld to create an ad hoc UN Emergency Force to send to the region. Here was perhaps the high point of the anticolonial UN-U.S. symbiosis, a venture that marked the origin of UN peacekeeping and showed once again how far the organization's successful growth depended on American support.[21]

Le Monde noted in October 1956, after Suez, that "the Americans do not intend to lose by default the battle they have started with Moscow for the control of the underdeveloped countries, popularly called the 'uncommitted third.'"[22] Yet Eisenhower moved cautiously, and the formal U.S. position in the UN on the question of self-determination remained constrained by what the Europeans would allow. For many British and French observers, the reversal of empire had gone too far too fast and if allowed to continue unchecked would destabilize what they called "international society." In Wight's words:

> Some of Eden's critics seem to argue that the right policy is to grant independence to the rest of Asia and Africa as quickly as possible, and let the newly enfranchised members of international society settle down to industrialise themselves and practice democracy. . . . This may be the dream-transformation of the historical experience called Balkanisation, which means a *Kleinstaaterei* of weak States, fiercely divided among themselves by nationalistic feuds, governed by unstable popular autocracies, unaccustomed to international law and diplomatic practice as they are to parliamentary government and a battle-ground for the surrounding Great Powers.[23]

Other British and French commentators were even more outspoken. They defended colonial rule outright, some on the grounds that the new nationalist elites could not rule, some on the more plausible grounds that they knew how to rule all too well but were wedded to a kind of integral nationalism that spelled a dismal future for their own minority peoples and border tribes. Bandung, after all, looked very different from Tibet or Papua New Guinea than it looked from New Delhi and Beijing. And it was not only died-in-the-wool imperialists who worried; so did thoughtful liberals like the African American writer Richard Wright, whose account of Bandung in *The Color Curtain* remains one of the most provocative discussions of what had been achieved there.[24]

Officially, the American line talked of "evolutionary self-determination"—a very Wilsonian-sounding slogan that allowed the United States sometimes to support their European allies and sometimes, as in Indochina and at Suez, to rebuff them. But there was none of the Wilsonian uplift. "Our desire," stated Dulles, "is a world in which peoples who want political independence shall possess it whenever they are capable of sustaining it and discharging its responsibilities in accordance with the accepted standards of civilized nations."[25] As this suggested, Dulles still seemed to hew to the old idea of civilization as a criterion for statehood. Stalin's successor, Khrushchev, relished the challenge. Keen to show that the Soviet Union could compete technologically with the United States, he sent Sputnik into space, reaffirmed Bolshevik modernity, and sent out promises of support to the Egyptians, the Indians, and many others. In the first ever visit by a Soviet leader to Africa, he told the All-African People's Conference in Accra in 1958 that the USSR fully supported the principle of "the right of nations to self-determination." Not surprisingly, when Africans were asked which power they most sympathized with in these years, about 25 percent named the USSR as their favorite compared with just 3 percent for the United States. Democracy was much less important to them than scientific expertise and a sense of solidarity with the underdog.[26]

How little room this left American diplomats was graphically revealed at the very end of the Eisenhower administration in November 1960 when the UN General Assembly voted on a Declaration on the Granting of Independence to Colonial Countries and Peoples. The original idea had come from the USSR, but it was the rival draft proposed by a group of twenty-six African and Asian countries and largely based on the Bandung principles that was overwhelmingly adopted. Not only the Europeans, however, but the United States too abstained. This was a personal decision of Eisenhower's, made after the British prime minister appealed to him, but it appalled his own side. "For the record," wrote the U.S. ambassador to the UN, "I am shocked and disheartened." Even the secretary of state had been unable to persuade the president.[27] It seemed further confirmation to Eisenhower's critics that he had ended up allowing American policy to be made by Europeans. The declaration itself—which stated that all peoples had the right to self-determination and called for immediate steps to be taken to grant independence in the colonies—had no binding force. But it was the most powerful call yet from the UN against a continuation of the European empires. The following year, the assembly agreed, at the Soviet suggestion, to set up a special committee to monitor progress in the colonial territories toward independence.

It was against this backdrop that we should evaluate the rise of the General Assembly. The Cold War had left the Security Council deadlocked: an average of eighteen council resolutions a year in the late 1940s had dropped to fewer than five through the 1950s. Instead, helped by the Uniting for Peace resolution, which allowed business to be shifted there from the council, the limelight shone on the assembly. The expansion of 1955 increased its impact, and so did the rise of the nonaligned movement later in the decade. Thanks to its influence even the Security Council was reformed—a successful campaign resulted in 1965 in the expansion of its membership from eleven to fifteen. The assembly itself publicized the cause of national liberation movements from the FLN in Algeria to the PLO, and the political impact of this publicity in the 1960s was sometimes enough to offset military inferiority and even defeat. There is little question, for instance, that the FLN's highly effective use of the UN did much to keep pressure on the French and hasten independence. De Gaulle was furious and described UN meetings as "no more than riotous and scandalous sessions where there is no way to organize an objective debate and which are filled with invectives and insults." But his anger reflected the pressure from New York, as de Gaulle supervised France's withdrawal.[28]

John F. Kennedy himself had been a passionate voice for anticolonialism from the 1950s. Conscious of this shifting balance of forces, his administration came into power in 1961 determined to win the struggle for hearts and minds in the Third World. Kennedy liked to run his own foreign policy. But it was indicative of the new course that he picked as his secretary of state the understated Dean Rusk, the man who had spearheaded Truman's UN strategy, and who, as president of the Rockefeller Foundation, had continued to advise John Foster Dulles on the need for an internationalist approach to the Third World. A 1959 article Rusk had penned while still at Rockefeller described "the broadening base" of international cooperation as both a "realist" and an "idealist" necessity. [29] Two years into his service under Kennedy, Rusk spoke more explicitly about the way the United States was working with the developing nations of Latin America, Africa, the Middle East, and Asia as they embarked on the "great revolutionary process" of modernizing their societies:

> Where colonialism still exists, it will pass from the scene. Where political and social power—and land—is still held by a few, it will give way to the assumption of power—and of the ownership of land—by the many. In the cities new generations of men and women will be coming forward, asserting new ambitions for themselves and for their nations, demanding and achieving the right to assume political responsibility. We cannot expect this process of modernization to take place smoothly in all nations and at all times. There have been and will be upheavals; but behind them are powerful, constructive forces: the determination of citizens that their lives and the lives of their children shall be enriched and that their nations shall have a place of dignity on the world scene.[30]

To outsiders, the ambitions—after the relative restraint of the Eisenhower years—were breathtaking. The former colonial world was to be entirely remade in the image of modernity as defined by Americans. As counterinsurgency morphed into social engineering, and technical assistance and development aid handed foreign policy over to engineers and economists, American national interests were defined with an expansiveness that shocked commentators such as Kennan. Declared Rusk in 1965, "We can no longer secure the blessings of liberty to ourselves and our posterity by isolating our nation, our continent or our hemisphere from the rest of the world. The speed of modern communications and transportation and the range and destructiveness of modern weapons have erased the margins of distance and time which until the end of the Second World War contributed greatly to our security. Today we can be secure only to the extent *that our total environment is secure*" (emphasis added). It was a redefinition of American national security that made outer space, or the struggle for the Mekong Delta, as important as Cuba, Europe, and Japan. But it did so in the name of the United States of America as a nation whose unique understanding of the struggle for independence positioned it to help other developing nations around the world along the path of freedom and democracy.[31]

Much of this effort was to be directed through American institutions—including new agencies such as the Peace Corps and the Agency for International Development. But as one would have expected under Rusk, the UN system was not neglected. The United States could not be the world's policeman, Rusk explained, and if the construction of a genuine "world community" was an American necessity, working through the UN was vital. After all, he admitted candidly that "an international organization is often more acceptable politically than any of its members acting individually. The flag of the United Nations is the emblem of a world community. It can be flown in places where the flag of another sovereign nation would be considered an affront." What this implied, then, was accepting the world trend toward nation-states and leading it. As he put it in a speech on "The Bases of United States Foreign Policy," "Our foreign policy is directed toward building the kind of world community called for in the United Nations Charter—a community of independent nations, each free to work out its own institutions as it sees fit, but cooperating effectively in matters of common interest."[32]

It might thus have seemed that the realignment in American foreign policy toward a stronger anticolonial position, started tentatively under Eisenhower and pushed forward with greater energy under Kennedy, would cement the already close relationship between the United States and the UN. Khrushchev's Third World honeymoon was fizzling out with little to show for it as the Russians tiptoed between détente on the one hand and warding off the ideological challenge of the revolutionary Chinese on the other. Their Third World clients were quickly dissatisfied—they did not even manage to persuade the sultan of Zanzibar, who preferred to look for help from the Chinese. (One of the elements in Khrushchev's downfall was internal Kremlin criticism that he had not bothered to plan his Third World strategy ahead of time, and had wasted resources for no obvious gain.)[33]

And yet despite the lack of ideological competition, the close cooperation between Washington and New York fractured in a few short years in the 1960s, dooming both the Ruskian vision of the UN at the heart of American foreign policy and the UN's own capacity to occupy the center ground of world politics. The rigidities of the Cold War mindset that saw communism everywhere, confronted by the dramatic changes occurring within the UN, produced a fissile mix.[34]

One reason for this was to be found in the increasingly powerful role assumed by the UN secretary-general. Trygve Lie had fallen foul of the Soviets because of what they interpreted as his excessive subservience to American wishes. Dag Hammarskjöld's very considerable diplomatic achievement in the 1950s was to take advantage of the opening provided by the convergence of improved superpower relations and the simultaneous acceleration of decolonization to bring new authority to his post, while remaining in a much quieter and less obvious way than Lie aware of the fundamental importance of good relations with the Americans. Hammarskjöld's posthumous sanctification was probably a necessity for an organization in dire need of heroes. But it allowed his acute sense of political strategy and his attentiveness to Washington to be overlooked. Uninterested in the struggle for human rights, and not much more concerned with the UN's specialist and technical agencies, which were in any case scarcely under his control, Hammarskjöld understood that turning the United Nations into an instrument of international administration with the secretary-general as chief executive took it into a new area that, precisely because it had been unforeseen by the UN's founders, was shrouded in ambiguity and therefore an opportunity for a politically agile secretariat to expand its own power. With the invention of peacekeeping in Suez and Lebanon, he showed how rapidly he could respond to colonial crises and demonstrate the UN's usefulness as stabilizer and buffer.

The Congo Crisis—in which he was to lose his life—was a step further, an intervention in the name of the international community and the people of Congo in a postcolonial civil war. Here there was no peace to keep, and although neutrality was an indispensable flag for the UN in this situation, in reality it did not exist. Although Soviet anger with Hammarskjöld's actions in the Congo escalated to the point where Khrushchev publicly questioned his impartiality, Hammarskjöld brilliantly outsmarted the Soviet leader by presenting the UN's survival as dependent upon a strong executive. But in the broader sense, as the Americans themselves would soon discover, Khrushchev was right. Impartiality, the claim to stand above politics, was both rhetorically necessary and scarcely possible (and not only because one of Hammarskjöld's key aides had links with the CIA throughout the crisis). Once Hammarskjöld was gone, and his successor the Burmese diplomat U Thant used his post to criticize American policy in Vietnam, Washington's liking for the idea of a powerful UN secretary-general quickly waned.[35]

But a more important reason why the Americans soured on the UN was that the drive to self-determination was producing what Martin Wight had called "Balkanization" on a global scale. Already in the 1940s, American delegates had warned of the danger of creating large numbers of unviable microstates. "Unnecessary political fragmentation" was also one of the reasons American delegates had advanced in 1960 for not voting for the Declaration on the Granting of Independence to Colonial Countries and Peoples. In fact, from the 1960s onward, these proliferated. The League of Nations had ruled Lichtenstein, Monaco, and San Marino out of full membership because of their size, but the UN—and especially the Third World majority in the General Assembly—resisted this and opposed the idea of creating associate or secondary forms of membership. Indeed, the admission of very small states into the assembly was hastened by the anxiety among the former colonial powers that if they allowed multiple categories of membership in the UN, then they too might suffer. There was a real clash here between two arguments of considerable force: on the one hand, the idea that one tampered at one's peril with the concept of the sovereign equality of states; and on the other, the view that it would do the UN no good in the long run if a large number of tiny states were able to exercise a disproportionate influence in the assembly. As the UN's largest financial contributor, the United States was naturally inclined to the second view. Hammarskjöld had been rather unsympathetic to the self-determination campaign for this reason; always attentive to American concerns, he had worried that it would make it harder for him to act as peacemaker between the two superpowers without effecting any real improvement in the UN's effectiveness. But his replacement, U Thant, was rather different, and viewed developments in the assembly with equanimity. In 1969 the Security Council set up a committee of experts to review how the UN would be affected by the admission of sixty-five possible new members with populations under 300,000. But actually vetoing the admission of ministates was diplomatically unacceptable, and with the admission of Bhutan in 1971 and Grenada in 1974, the United States gave in.[36]

It did not help that the assembly in the 1960s equated self-determination with independence. A community could not, in other words, in the eyes of the majority in the assembly, conceivably want any other political outcome than complete freedom. Thus when the Cook Islanders voted for self-government under the protection of New Zealand, the assembly refused to admit that they had exercised their "right of self-determination" and pledged support in their continued struggle for full independence.[37] The result was that at the end of the 1960s there were some fifteen members of the UN with populations under one million, and many more in the wings. One had to wait for the end of the Cold War for the process to reach its ultimate conclusion. In the early 1990s, Monaco, Lichtenstein, and even Andorra were granted full membership.

With independence for the tiny Pacific island of Palau and its twenty thousand inhabitants granted in 1994, the Trusteeship Council was left without any territories to oversee. The extraordinary story of the international oversight of decolonization thus reached its uninspiring conclusion. Yet another microcommunity granted the full trappings of statehood and the privilege of a seat in the General Assembly could be seen not so much as triumph for the nationality principle as its reductio ad absurdum. Mazzini, Mill, and Marx, all of whom had seen nationalism as integrative not disintegrative, would have been appalled. Equally absurdly, the Trusteeship Council survived, despite having nothing to do, a casualty of the paralyzed reform process inside the UN itself. Its operations suspended, it today exists as a website. Meanwhile, the UN Special Committee on Decolonization monitors the Western Sahara, Gibraltar and the Falklands, the coral atolls of Tokelau, and the other mostly Pacific and Caribbean islands that make up the world's sixteen (in 2010) remaining colonies, and it marks important anniversaries such as the end of the Second International Decade for the Eradication of Colonialism.

In the United States, there was growing disenchantment with this situation. Reviewing what had happened to the noble principle of self-determination, a State Department historian in 1977 decried the proliferation of ministates and looked forward to conferences at which "the great landmasses would be numerically outranked by galaxies of miniature island-states" with the delegates of major powers rubbing shoulders not only with delegates from "Bahrain, Bhutan, Comoro, the Maldives, Qatar, the Seychelles and Surinam but also from such exotic places as Afars and Issas, Brunei and Ifni."[38] But the problem was not just the numerical one. Increasingly, the United States was finding itself on the wrong side of votes on a whole range of issues. After years of criticizing the USSR for its use of the veto, the first American veto in the Security Council came in 1970, when it stood alongside Britain in opposing a resolution urging more forceful measures to confront the rogue white settler regime in Rhodesia. Defending Israel soon required more and turned the United States into the main veto-wielding power in the Security Council: it exercised the veto seventeen times between 1970 and 1985 on the question of Israel alone. It is not surprising that a classified 1970 U.S. memo defined the basis of relations with the UN as "damage limiting rather than accomplishing anything in particular."

The growing self-confidence of the nonaligned movement that lay at the root of these developments was difficult for the Americans to accept. Dulles's 1956 critique of nonalignment and neutrality as "an immoral and shortsighted conception" was soon abandoned; but Washington's support never became more than lukewarm at best, and those who argued that the United States as an anticolonial power should be sympathetic were always sidelined. Instead, anticommunism made the United States look like a supporter of empire. At the same time, as the membership of the UN's Economic and Social Council rose from eighteen in 1946 to twenty-seven in 1965 and fifty-four in 1973, the Third World became dominant in the UN's core bodies. Leading figures in the nonaligned movement spoke strongly in favor of the UN in these years. "We think it would be a black day indeed for the world, and particularly for the smaller countries if the United Nations were to suffer the fate of the League of Nations," said the Burmese U Nu in 1961.[39] Seeing control of the UN as an issue that could unite the Third World against both sides in the Cold War, leading figures in the nonaligned movement fought to have Security Council meetings held outside New York (two took place in 1972 and 1973 in Addis Ababa and Panama), struggled for control of the UN budget, and aimed to transform the secretariat itself. At the end of the 1974 General Assembly, Algeria's president, Abdelaziz Bouteflika, is said to have remarked that "the only thing left now to decolonize is the Secretariat"; seven years later, the nonaligned movement was successful in bringing about the election of Peru's Javier Pérez de Cuéllar as secretary-general, despite American opposition. By then it was increasingly the Third World, and particularly the nonaligned movement, that was setting the agenda at the UN.[40]

In effect, what the globalization of self-determination and the successful struggle against colonialism appeared to have done was to reverse the positions of the Soviet Union and the United States. At the start of the 1950s, the former was on the defensive; by the mid-1970s, the USSR was making common cause with the nonaligned movement on many issues, and it was the United States that found the UN a hostile environment. The trouble for anyone who cared about the latter was that the UN needed the United States far more than the other way around. By 1970, the assembly represented 127 countries and it had a built-in African-Asian majority. It was, on paper, a more stable and more global assembly than anything seen before. Its expansion was a sign that the principle of national self-determination had triumphed and become the basis for the world's new internationalism; the Cold War, far from stopping this trend, appeared to have if anything accelerated it. But what were the consequences of this triumph? Not defection. On the contrary—and in striking contrast to the League's assembly before 1940—the General Assembly continued to grow and numbered 188 members as the century ended. But did it manage to grow correspondingly in importance? Clearly not. Decolonization brought not power but irrelevance. Far from becoming a greater check to the ambitions of the world's great powers, the General Assembly was increasingly written off as nothing more than a talking shop. Politics at the UN became ever more about symbols and ever less about substance. It was as though decolonization marked not only the UN's triumph but its world-historical culmination.[41]

CHAPTER 10

Development as World-Making, 1949–73

CARY GRANT: How do you feel about the untapped resources of the underdeveloped nations?

DORIS DAY: I think they ought to be tapped.

—from *That Touch of Mink* (1962)

The greatest development of the postwar era lies in the concept of international economic development aid as a permanent and inevitable feature of contemporary international organization.

—Wolfgang Friedmann, 1964

THE BACKGROUND TO POINT FOUR

Truman's surprise reelection in 1948 marked the moment when American policymakers began to look systematically beyond Europe and Truman himself returned to the United Nations, this time not to reach out to the USSR but to combat its influence. The idea that America had a special mission to transform societies across the world was an integral part of this new conception of its role. In the great ideological confrontation with Soviet communism, the Truman administration believed it had to demonstrate that capitalism had the better tools for improving the lives of the world's poor and underprivileged. It would show that whatever Lenin might have said, capitalism was not synonymous with colonialism, and that in American hands international institutions could help bring European imperial rule to an end, not perpetuate it, unlock the secret of growth, banish the memories of capitalism's failure in the 1930s, and change the world through the application of technology and expertise. This was the nineteenth-century heritage of scientific internationalism recast for an era of planners and experts, one that would build on the institutional legacy of the League of Nations and extend it further than anyone in the League had ever dreamed of.

In Truman's inaugural address in January 1949, development provided the keynote. Looking to wean countries off emergency American aid, the speech—known as the Point Four Program after the critical section—presented a stark vision of the global challenge that faced Americans and extolled foreign aid as a way to spread democracy and peace. In the president's words:

> We must embark on a bold new program for making the benefits of our scientific advances and industrial progress available for the improvement and growth of underdeveloped areas.
>
> More than half the people of the world are living in conditions approaching misery. Their food is inadequate, they are the victims of disease. Their economic life is primitive and stagnant. Their poverty is a handicap and a threat both to them and to more prosperous areas. For the first time in history humanity possesses the knowledge and the skill to relieve the suffering of these people. . . . I believe that we should make available to peace-loving peoples the benefits of our store of technical knowledge in order to help them realize their aspirations for a better life. . . . Greater production is the key to prosperity and peace. And the key to greater production is a wider

and more vigorous application of modern scientific and technical knowledge.

As Truman had previously showed no signs of attaching any great importance to this subject, the speech came as a welcome surprise both to the State Department's technical assistance experts, who were unused to such attention, and to American supporters of international institutions. Identifying global poverty as a threat to the American way of life, Truman promised that the United States would work through UN specialized agencies "wherever practicable." Arguing that supporting nationalist movements in the colonial world would enhance the UN's power, he presented his strategy as an American alternative to imperialism: "The old imperialism—exploitation for foreign profit—has no place in our plans. What we envisage is a program of development based on the concepts of democratic fair-dealing. All countries, including our own, will greatly benefit from a constructive program for the better use of the world's human and natural resources."[1]

Rarely has a speech about technical assistance had such an impact. Ignoring the fact that Truman was asking Congress—once bitten, twice shy following the scale of U.S. aid to Europe—for a miserly $45 million (and would end up with little more than half that), Soviet commentators immediately saw this as the "formation of a worldwide American empire," an extraordinary bid to "seize the colonies and underdeveloped areas of the world in toto."[2] If this exaggerated the resources Washington proposed to deploy, it was true that Truman had offered a breathtaking redefinition of the U.S. national interest. The country's security now apparently rested not merely in stabilizing Europe but in warding off the threat to the developed world posed by the rage of the world's rapidly breeding poor. This was to imagine a world role for the United States that went far beyond conventional strategic conceptions, indeed far beyond any conception of global influence that the British or any European power had previously embraced. It required simultaneously dismantling European empires and replacing them with teams of scientific experts, bankers, and technical advisers. Worried at the prospects of being swamped by "Oriental civilization," the United States would forestall this, not through the race war Hitler had forecast but rather by Westernizing the colonial world.[3]

Officials in the Truman administration had been fretting for months about the lack of a systematic policy toward Asia in particular. In early 1949 the civil war in China was not going well from the American point of view, and the economic outlook in Japan looked fragile. The European Recovery Program had shown the possibilities of regional planning but also made it harder to justify standing by passively while "the Orient falls apart."[4] However, the difference with Europe was that any "regional Asiatic Recovery Program" would have to involve not merely rebuilding existing institutions but helping peasant societies industrialize more or less from scratch, and this would require long-term commitment and extensive technological and industrial investment. The ultimate bill was potentially huge, but the starting point was modest. Worried that American policy abroad was seen as too negative and too focused on combating communism militarily, senior policymakers proposed to Truman "a substantial program of technical training . . . as well as economic assistance" in conjunction with international agencies such as the United Nations and nongovernmental organizations.[5]

One of the American participants, State Department economist Joseph Coppock, later summed up the new approach in an interview:

> **Coppock:** . . . [T]he U.S. decision was to go both ways, to use the U.N. and the specialized agencies to the fullest extent possible and to use the U.S. bilateral programs as a supplement.
>
> **[Interviewer]:** Was that based on political considerations?
>
> **Coppock:** No, I'd just say practical sense. See, you had these international organizations, so it was good to use them so that some country wouldn't be dependent upon a particular bilateral con-

> nection. There was a general attitude favoring the use of international channels in dealing with these problems. You would get your experts wherever you could get them to provide this aid. You would then supplement U.N. aid with U.S. aid, but the U.S. was the main reservoir for this kind of knowledge anyway. A lot of the people drawn by international organizations would be U.S. people anyway.[6]

In effect, the existence of the world body gave American foreign policy an alternative outlet, and although it had both advantages and disadvantages compared with operating unilaterally, it provided increased room for maneuver. Washington could decide when to work multilaterally and when alone, as the circumstances dictated.

It is this ambidextrous aspect of American internationalism, critical to understanding its continued support for UN institutions throughout the postwar era, that is missed when American foreign policy is broken down into idealist and realist strands. Most of the time it was both, and for the pragmatists in charge, the true realism involved using international institutions where possible. The strategy offered enormous symbolic capital and political cover, at absurdly little cost: the entire 1954 budget of the UN and its main agencies (FAO, ICAO, ILO, UNESCO, WHO) totaled approximately $83 million, of which the United States contributed $24 million, at a time when American grants to Greece alone were around $68 million and worldwide amounted to a massive $5.1 billion.[7] It is therefore not surprising that given the powerful American role in funding, staffing, and shaping the UN system, the line dividing global agencies from American ones was hard to trace from the start. Even once the Soviet Union started providing aid through the UN after Stalin's death, the sums involved were tiny compared with the American contribution—a mere $2 million pledged in the late 1950s, for instance, against around $38 million by the United States.[8] No other country came close to having the influence over international development that was enjoyed by the United States.

. . .

Point Four itself was presented by Truman in his Point Four speech as an internationalization of the achievements of the New Deal. Recalling the interwar Tennessee Valley Authority scheme, he boasted that "we are somewhat famous . . . for technical knowledge"; a little American know-how would turn the "undeveloped rivers and valleys all over the world" into economic dynamos. Historian Arthur Schlesinger argued that the TVA demonstrated America's ability to deploy the state to improve the life of millions without becoming a "total planner":

> No other people in the world approach the Americans in mastery of the new magic of science and technology. Our engineers can transform arid plains or poverty-stricken river valleys into wonderlands of vegetation and power. . . . The Tennessee Valley Authority is a weapon which if properly employed might outbid all the social ruthlessness of the Communists for the support of the peoples of Asia.[9]

It was an achievement that came naturally to the mind of Democrats in particular. But the roots of technocratic thinking extended a lot further back than the 1930s. Saint-Simon and Comte's vision of modernizing society through social science and expertise meshed easily with American exceptionalism to provide a perfect foreign policy script for a country that saw itself as benign, altruistic, and detached from any hint of imperialist politics and self-interest. Missionaries, charities and—not least—the occupation authorities in the Philippines had been spreading American expertise for generations. Between 1903 and 1923, ten major American foundations promoting social scientific research had been established, starting with the Rockefellers' General Education Board and ending up with the Social Science Research Council: despite their differing agendas, they shared an internationalist outlook and a fervent belief in the possibility of social reform.

The Tennessee Valley Authority itself, like the New Deal more generally, had certainly played an important ideological role in the highly charged world atmosphere of the interwar period. It had been conceived as an American answer to the challenge of totalitarian modernization, proof that capitalism could be directed to the collective good without abandoning democracy. This made it both a riposte to Stalinist planning—"why should the Russians have all the fun of remaking a world?" asked author Stuart Chase in 1932—and a counter to the grand infrastructural projects of the Third Reich. Seeing "the spirit of science introduced into politics and industry" in the Soviet Union in 1931, Julian Huxley, the British biologist and eugenicist who would later become the head of UNESCO, was relieved to visit Tennessee in 1935 and witness the exciting results of what he termed an "experiment in applied social science." Linking together agriculture, industry, and power generation, the control of floods and disease, and public health alongside education and urban planning in a single conception, the TVA embodied and endorsed America's claim to technical modernity.[10]

The world's slide into war in the 1930s only made that achievement seem more precious and significant. In eastern Europe, new states were caught in a trap of peasant poverty and rapid population growth that the League of Nations had been unable or unwilling to do anything about. Yet the east Europeans had little fondness for the Soviet model of coercive industrialization and collectivization of the land, and still less for the Nazi dream of permanently ruralizing them. The New Deal offered an alternative. But the trade across the Atlantic went both ways, for some distinguished and innovative economists from the region were thinking the problems of rural poverty through for themselves, and after the war American development theory was shaped to a striking degree by émigrés like the Austrian Paul Rosenstein-Rodan, the Estonian Ragnar Nurkse, Budapest-born Peter Bauer, and the German-Jewish refugees Hans Singer and Albert Hirschman.

In 1943–44, with the Nazis in complete control of his homeland, Rosenstein-Rodan was already publishing pioneering arguments for a "big push" through large-scale industrial investments to kick-start growth in overpopulated "backward" areas. His approach argued for going beyond the market, since he showed how, left to themselves, market forces could leave an economy in a state of underdevelopment. Capital from abroad might be needed to supplement domestic savings, but the model reflected the interwar experience in aiming to foster growth in a basically closed economy. These conditions were to be found not only in 1930s eastern Europe but in much of Asia, Africa, and South America after the war as well. Rosenstein-Rodan joined the fledgling World Bank in 1947, before helping advise governments around the world and developing the reputation of MIT as one of the major training grounds for Cold War development thought.[11]

A creature of the global interwar depression, developmentalist thought was bubbling up elsewhere too. In South America, export staples had collapsed in the 1930s, forcing governments to find new ways of boosting growth by expanding domestic markets and encouraging manufacturing. Remembering this experience, Latin American economists would become some of the principal advocates of import substitution and forced industrialization after the war: the clash between a relatively closed vision of domestic industrialization shared by many of the Latin Americans, Indians, and east Europeans and the U.S. vision of development within a more open economy, in which efficient agriculture was the key, was to continue for decades. And there was one last source of development expertise: empire. Between the wars, London and Paris studied ways of improving colonial economies—and reducing their own subsidies—through commodity marketing boards and minor infrastructural schemes. In Africa, the district administrator who "knew his natives" was replaced by scientific advisers and technical officers, whose expertise would be valued even after independence both by new nationalist elites and by the international agencies offering them advice. A generation of technicians thus emerged in European colonial services in the 1930s who would go on to staff the international development agencies of the postwar era.[12]

All these streams converged in the United States in the 1940s and made it a major center of development thought at a time when the war had made it possible—perhaps even necessary—to dream of a kind of New Deal for the world. In 1941, Vice President Henry Wallace, perhaps the best-known internationalist on the American left, asserted that modern science had "made it technically possible to see that all of the people of the world get enough to eat."[13] With the arrival of the League of Nations technical services in 1940 from Geneva, League economists mapped the world in terms of its calorific intake, and League statisticians produced internationally comparable macroeconomic data and national income aggregates. Such achievements allowed planners to respond to the immediate needs of the war but also to think about combating its deeper causes in poverty, hunger, and unemployment. Geographers worked on ambitious proposals for the planned international resettlement of the world's surplus populations. Demographers produced pathbreaking research on the impact of modernization on population growth. Even before the war ended, therefore, American social science had been internationalized to an unprecedented degree and the intellectual potential for a more ambitious foreign aid policy had grown with it.[14]

EARLY INTERNATIONAL COOPERATION

There was another way of coming to development in the 1940s, however, that ran not through theory but through the urgent practicalities of organizing military supply needs during the war. The modestly titled Middle East Supply Center (MESC), for instance, was an Anglo-American office that coordinated the logistics of the entire eastern Mediterranean; it was also an experiment in wartime international cooperation. Its young Australian boss, a thirty-year-old naval officer named Robert Jackson, ran it with awesome efficiency—at least one wartime British general is supposed to have received a message from his prime minister saying, "Do anything Jackson asks. Signed Churchill." When he was still in his twenties, Jackson had been entrusted with the defense of Malta, a task he carried out brilliantly and that remained with him thereafter as a memory and template of what a successful logistical operation of that kind required. The challenge was not only technical—how to preserve life in a closed environment with a very finite quantity of supplies—but human and social too: how to persuade the members of a society, each with very different interests, in a situation of extreme tension that they should work for the common good. At the MESC, Jackson ended up as tsar of wartime food production across the Arab lands. It was the first and so far the only time anyone has attempted to coordinate the needs of farmers and consumers in the region as a whole, and his success in those few years in boosting crop production and supplies for the troops without any breakdown in health or living conditions for the civilian population—a remarkable episode scarcely mentioned in most accounts of modern Middle Eastern history today—constituted a very powerful model of what targeted social and economic engineering within a still largely closed economy could achieve.[15]

Jackson himself was a powerhouse of an administrator and his promotion at the end of the war to help run UNRRA, the UN agency tasked with administering relief to a war-torn world, was a natural one. UNRRA's boss was the veteran American politician Herbert Lehman, whom Jackson revered, and while Lehman managed the domestic American politics, Jackson pulled together the operational side. As a result of the efforts of these very practical men and their thousands of subordinates, the world's transition to peace took place after 1945 without the sort of public health breakdown that had marred the end of the First World War. UNRRA's operations were vast and far-flung, extending deep into the USSR and East Asia. When opposition in the 1946 Republican-led "do-nothing" Congress forced Truman to close down UNRRA on the grounds that American money should not be going to support communism, both Jackson and Lehman were bitterly disappointed. But they had already demonstrated the potential for a genuinely international body to provide assistance, stave off social unrest, and even to become involved in developmental work as well. Had Jackson succeeded in his next assignment, to help UN secretary-general Trygve Lie make the new world organization more efficient, the subsequent history of the UN might have been very different. But Jackson was an administrator not a diplomat, and his style was suited to war and crisis, not to the black arts of peacetime international bureaucracy.[16]

After the disbanding of UNRRA, other aid agencies stepped in. Both the Food and Agriculture Organization (FAO) and the World Health Organization (WHO) were beefed-up reincarnations of League-era bodies, and both of them were driven by men whose wartime experience also encouraged them to think fast and big. But American money was crucial to their success too, and what their subsequent history showed was how far America's very specific priorities and aid orientation would shape their approach and constrain their ambitions.

The FAO was a creature of the war—it had been established with Roosevelt's blessing in 1943 and became fully operational in 1946—and its first secretary-general, the British nutritionist Sir John Boyd Orr, was a man who took wartime confidence in planning to a new level, picking up League of Nations work on global nutritional needs and arguing for the eradication of world hunger through the creation of a World Food Board that would enjoy compulsory powers to set food prices and purchase and distribute surpluses globally. The board was not to be run by national representatives at all but by experts: in Boyd Orr's mind, it basically represented a continuation and extension into the peace of the kinds of state rationing and redistribution mechanisms that had become commonplace during the war itself. Much of the colonial world welcomed the idea, but representatives of European and American food producers fought to torpedo it. It was congressional opposition that was decisive; the very idea of an international organization devoted to ensuring that the entire world had enough to eat ran directly counter to the free trade regime Washington envisaged—indeed nothing short of socialism could have been more calculated to enrage the Republican-dominated Congress of 1946—and the World Food Board was soon abandoned for more modest goals.[17]

The World Health Organization saw an analogous struggle. It was set up after UNRRA experts at San Francisco in 1945 persuaded the conference to found a serious international health organization. Even before it was formally established in 1948, its interim staff had helped combat a cholera epidemic in Egypt in 1947, developed a mass inoculation anti-TB campaign in Europe, and began training health professionals in countries like Ethiopia, Greece, and China. WHO too was held back by shortage of funds, but eventually it took over UNRRA's antimalaria program, a project closely associated for many development experts with agricultural improvement, and identified itself with the mission of its global eradication. This was part of a bigger battle between advocates of governmentally driven public health policies and American proponents of disease eradication through advanced pharmaceutical technology, a battle that was ultimately resolved in the Americans' favor.[18]

Given these initial arguments of orientation and policy inside the new UN specialist agencies, we can better understand the meaning of Truman's 1949 proposal to make technical assistance the centerpiece of development and to encourage the use of the UN for this purpose. For both the WHO and especially the FAO—and indeed for the UN as a whole—technical assistance offered a practical and modest alternative to the more ambitious and more socialized approaches to aid that had run afoul of Congress. Eased by the Democratic triumph, Truman's administration channeled new funds their way. For the underfunded FAO in particular, the result was transformative, and it embarked on dozens of country missions in the early 1950s, focusing on the training of Third World counterparts in American expertise. In a kind of Cold War magnification of the Saint-Simonian vision, American money thus paid for a proliferation of an international cadre of apolitical technical experts. At relatively modest cost, American knowledge ramified around the world, with huge implications for the way development was conceived.

As development turned into American social science, one of the consequences was that it became a more top-down affair and there were fewer real conversations with people from the countries concerned. Too much funding is not always a good thing, and in the prewar imperial order, development projects had mostly been halting, circumscribed, and often driven by the demands and ideas of colonial elites themselves; lack of money played a part in this, and so did the often intimate relationship between colonial officials and African and Asian intellectuals. In the 1930s, the Congress Party in India, for example, was running a planning committee to act as a kind of shadow government whose existence British officials could not entirely ignore. But from the 1950s, development as an international effort operated at a much greater distance from the realities on the ground. Enjoying far higher levels of funding—the postwar American economy was far more invested in higher and technical education than the British had been—development was also increasingly shaped by a one-size-fits-all approach to problem-solving. To take a typical example: at an agenda-setting 1958 American conference on Africa's development needs, there was no African present, and not even any African assessment of the continent's development needs. Africans, the organizers assumed, were poorly educated and likely to be partisan, unlike the scientifically motivated Western experts themselves.[19]

For all the self-serving scientific gloss, there was an anxious ideological subtext to the American embrace of developmentalism. The United States was at least formally against European empire, but this meant accepting a world less under Western control at the very time when all the experts predicted rapid population growth in the former colonial territories. Behind the new creed of development therefore lurked a Malthusian nightmare in which the civilized West was swamped by people with black and brown skins. Back in 1927, the head of the International Labor Organization had called controversially for "some sort of super-national authority which would regulate the distribution of population on rational and impartial lines." Two decades later, Julian Huxley, the first director-general of UNESCO (and a committed eugenicist) went further, proposing that the UN encourage the formulation of "a world population policy." After the defeat of the Third Reich, the idea of turning the UN into a kind of international eugenics agency was obviously bound to lead to trouble, and the secretariat sensibly let the idea drop. (Huxley went on to become president of the British Eugenics Society.) But Anglo-American population anxieties were not so easily allayed, especially once the UN began publishing the first regular data on world demographic growth. Through foundations, private organizations, and later through USAID, American population control enthusiasts went around the UN, eventually managing to set up what can only be described as a front organization within it—the UN Fund for Population Activities—which operated entirely outside the control of member nations.[20]

The preferred U.S. vehicle for multilateral development was the body that had been set up for something approximating this purpose at Bretton Woods in 1944: the International Bank for Reconstruction and Development (which came to be known in these years as the World Bank). As it happened, Truman's 1949 speech had stressed the role for private investment at the very moment when a rethink was taking place inside the bank. Originally intended to bring stability to war-torn Europe, the bank needed a new raison d'être when that task was taken out of the hands of the UN and reassigned to the Marshall Plan. The bank's directors eventually decided to return to their longer-term mandate—development—and to seek funds on Wall Street. Truman's embrace of development came at just the right time.

It was at this point that the World Bank as we know it began to emerge. Missions to southern Italy, India, and Colombia generated a series of overall macroeconomic assessments and prescriptions featuring large-scale projects—steel mills, dams—that were intended to have a transformative impact, galvanizing national economies and giving them the kind of "big jump" that economists like Rosenstein-Rodan and Ragnar Nurkse were arguing for. But the bank itself was conscious of the need to establish credibility with its lenders, and its own approach was cautious and conservative.[21] Cultivating an ethos of proud impartiality and technical expertise, it was critical of the Truman administration's willingness to make bilateral loans to potential clients like Mexico, Iran, and Brazil through the alternative Export-Import Bank, whose lending criteria were less prescriptive and more political.[22]

Within the UN itself, however, the American-driven development drive was viewed with mixed feelings. Many UN staffers, drawing on very different national experiences of their own, wanted much greater funding for the UN than the United States was willing to provide, and greater support for the industrialization strategies that would liberate the Third World from dependence on commodity exports. In effect, the debates that had taken place at Bretton Woods between the Americans and the British over the degree and kind of intervention needed to make world capitalism function continued into the 1950s, only now in the context not of European reconstruction but of global development.

After Truman's Point Four speech, therefore, the UN orchestrated several major reports on development, all of which implied a much greater and more systematic investment of American capital than the White House was willing to contemplate. The first argued for full employment policies to prevent a recurrence of the Depression by more extensive use of the World Bank and IMF; the second was an analysis of "the economic development of the underdeveloped countries" that called for capital investment across the underdeveloped world; and the third singled out the "special difficulties of the poorer underdeveloped countries" and argued for measures internationally to regulate trade markets and commodity prices. At the same time, in the General Assembly, the Indians and others pushed hard for concessions from the Americans. Even before the term "Third World" had been coined, therefore, the UN was emerging as the site of an alternative vision to Washington's—not an international economy fueled by trade liberalization, but one based on a redistribution of power between developed and underdeveloped parts of the world.

The question was whether with the very limited funding at its disposal the fledgling UN could push development in these more ambitious directions. Technical assistance was relatively easy and uncontentious, and the Americans were happy to help the UN set up an office to manage this, the embryo of its later far more extensive Development Program. But allowing the UN to disburse development funds of its own elicited less enthusiasm in Washington. UN development economist Hans Singer—described by World Bank president Eugene Black as one of the "wild men of the United Nations"—produced studies that supported the idea of the UN establishing its own soft lending arm. At the same time, UN experts were sent along to try to persuade Black to expand the bank's operations, a request that ran up against his overriding desire to gain a coveted triple-A rating for the bank's bonds, something not attained until the end of the decade. In fact, the bank's directors had deliberately kept the UN at arm's length, fearing its political influence would jeopardize their credit rating on Wall Street, and they brokered an agreement early on that ratified the bank's status as a specialized agency of the UN while preserving its identity as "an independent international organization." It is not surprising that the General Assembly was soon calling for the UN to develop its own development funding, and the demand was actually passed in the assembly in a vote that was regarded by American (and British) officials as a "serious defeat." Yet as with so many General Assembly resolutions, words were not matched by deeds: because funding depended chiefly on congressional support, such an agency could not emerge without American support.[23]

The arrival of a Republican administration in 1953 reduced the aid flow to a trickle and made the prospect of turning the UN into a major development promoter even less likely. Eisenhower was unimpressed by grand visions of global development or worldwide antipoverty campaigns. But the results were paradoxical. As American internationalists went into a kind of internal exile, awaiting the return of a more sympathetic administration, Dean Rusk left the State Department to head the Rockefeller Foundation, which he turned—

following the spirit of Raymond Fosdick—into a powerful funder of American expertise applied to global problems. Even more importantly for the UN, Paul Hoffman, who had run the Marshall Plan very effectively in Europe, joined the U.S. delegation to the UN (after a detour at the Ford Foundation where he became a powerful advocate of global development). In 1957 he published an article arguing, on the basis of his European experience, for more soft money to be made available at the World Bank, and the following year, when it was finally agreed in Washington to allow the UN its own funding agency, Hoffman himself was put in charge. In 1965, he became the first head of the new UN Development Program. His extensive bipartisan contacts in Washington secured funding from Congress, despite critics of the UN's "multi-billion dollar, giveaway carnival," and memories of his Marshall Plan days gave him credibility with European donor governments too. As a result, his Development Program soon amassed the lion's share of all UN funds on economic and social programs: by 1971, its annual disbursements ran to $290 million, a sum that dwarfed that spent by the UN on health, food, education, or any of the other specialized agencies. No longer bound by the old emphasis on technical assistance, Hoffman's UNDP worked very closely with the World Bank—an agency increasingly favored by President Nixon—funding surveys of mineral resources, the mapping of remote regions, and the establishment of pilot plants in new industries to pave the way for future capital inflows from the bank or foreign multinationals.[24]

The driver for all this extraordinary experiment in using international institutions to encourage global flows of investment capital—both at the UN and outside it—was Washington's fear of the threat posed by the Soviet Union's brief foray into aid diplomacy. Khrushchev had no sooner been confirmed as new party leader than he was off traveling to China, India, Burma, and Afghanistan, emphasizing the USSR's desire to assist in the "national development" of nonsocialist countries in Africa and Asia.[25] This was no longer the internationalism of the Comintern, in which Moscow dreamed of orchestrating world revolution through a network of communist parties. It was a much more eclectic and opportunistic vision in which the Kremlin reached out to new nationalist ruling elites, turning a blind eye as they crushed or marginalized communist parties in their own countries. The ties that bound now were not ideology or fidelity to Lenin's program, but rather a shared interest in resisting "imperialism" and promoting national growth through state planning. The year after the Bandung Conference, in the speech in which he denounced Stalin's crimes Khrushchev alluded again to the Soviet Union's special understanding of the Third World:

> The new period that Lenin predicted in world history when peoples of the East take an active part in settling the destinies of the whole world and become a new, powerful factor in international relations, has arrived. . . . In order to create an independent national economy and to raise the living standards of their peoples, these countries, though not part of the world socialist system, can benefit by its achievements. They now have no need to go begging to their former oppressors for modern equipment. They can obtain such equipment in the socialist countries.[26]

Although the actual sums the Soviets spent on aid lagged behind Washington's—a total of $1 billion in 1954–56, well under a fifth of the American level—it was enough to make American internationalists very nervous, especially as they knew the image of the USSR was more attractive to young Africans, and no doubt others, than the image of the United States itself.

Alongside the expansion of the UN's development programs under Hoffman's leadership, a new generation of American social scientists began to develop sweeping theories of societal transformation that went beyond anything advanced under Truman and that would have an enormous impact on U.S. foreign policy in the 1960s. With a strong sense of the Soviet threat and a belief in the American capability to respond, men like MIT economist Walt Rostow presented an alternative world-historical narrative to Karl Marx's. Their overarching concern was how to explain—and hence find the political recipe for—the rise of economically self-sustaining nations. Rostow himself saw the British Industrial Revolution, with its sudden leap from rural to urban and industrial societies, as the archetype for other modernizing nations, and he took the Marshall Plan (on which he had worked) as a model for how enlightened policy could build democracy at the same time as modern industry. He then extrapolated Europe's lessons and applied them to the world, modestly subtitling the 1960 book in which he laid all this out *The Stages of Economic Growth: A Non-Communist Manifesto,* as if to assert the Cold War competitiveness that drove the entire scheme. Pitting Walt Whitman (Rostow had been named after the poet) against Karl Marx, American idealism and energy against Germanic materialism, *Stages* rose to the Soviet challenge.

Offering a confident bridge to a better and more stable future, modernization theory posited a stark dichotomy between traditional societies and modern ones. History was the passage from one kind of society to the other, a passage that all peoples would eventually make but that could be accelerated with the right kind of advice, and that—without such advice—could go horribly wrong, as the Germans had already shown. Anthropologists could help shed light on the sticky residues of traditional practices and beliefs, the obstacles to a successful transvaluation of social values; the demographers could show how best to make the transition to a society able to reproduce itself without overly straining resources; economists could guide investment and planning strategies to maximize growth. The moral was clear: Third World governments together with American advisers should concentrate on accelerating the transition and ensuring that it happened on terms compatible with Western values and interests.

But the Rostows of this world are not content merely to write books; they aim to shift policy too, and as Rostow himself understood very well, modernization was a paradigm that posed a challenge to old-fashioned Republican statecraft. In 1957, along with his colleague Max Millikan, he criticized the Eisenhower administration for being too old-fashioned and superficial, writing that the United States had been putting too much of the emphasis on "pacts, treaties, negotiation and international diplomacy" and failing "to deal with the nature of forces at work in the world."[27] In cooperation with Paul Rosenstein-Rodan, Rostow and Millikan argued that expert-led development could promote democracy, transform societies, and galvanize the masses in a national revolution far more appealing than the Marxist version. There were cultural changes to consider, issues of village size and farming techniques, before one could map out the correct path to industrialization through a "takeoff" to self-sustaining growth. From Mao's victory in China, Rostow derived a sense of the importance of winning over and transforming the peasantry, whether by bombing them or by giving them seeds and advice and redesigning their villages. That way you could appeal to their own self-interest, reduce hunger, and above all slow down the drift to the cities of those large anomic masses of easily radicalized young men who were natural cadres for the communists. His base at the CIA-funded Center for International Studies at MIT became a social scientific laboratory for the modernization mandarins, and Rostow himself became a policy adviser to the staunchly anticolonial Senator John F. Kennedy and later a senior national security adviser in his administration.[28]

By the time Eisenhower's term neared its end, development economics had achieved a new prominence and respectability. The idea that the free market alone was inadequate to guarantee growth and improve living standards had entered the mainstream, and different versions of this critique circulated among activist Democrats in Washington and the Third World elites they were in touch with. Both the American technical assistance programs and the UN itself functioned as a kind of bridge between the two, a means for Americans concerned to foster the right kind of nationalism in the Third World to come into contact with African and Asian leaders and to offer their advice and assistance. In 1951, a UN group of experts had recommended that "the government of an underdeveloped country should establish a central economic unit with the functions of surveying the economy, making development programs, advising on the measures necessary for carrying out such programs and reporting on them periodically." By the end of the decade, such measures had become the global norm. Economists like Rosenstein-Rodan, W. Arthur Lewis, and Hans Singer moved between academia, the UN, U.S. government, and advising Third World officials, and drew up programs to train cadres of Third World bureaucrats. It was at this time that most governments in the postcolonial world established national planning agencies and industrial development corporations, and those in the West began creating development agencies and ministries of their own to channel bilateral aid in the way the Americans had been doing since the end of the war. In the 1950s, development economics appeared on the curricula of most major American universities, and articles and journals dedicated to the subject proliferated. Support for these trends ran across the party divide in the United States, especially after the Soviets launched Sputnik, the world's first artificial satellite, in 1957. When on top of everything Fidel Castro seized power in Cuba, and the Algerians won independence from the French, opening up the Maghreb to Cold War rivalry, the need to respond to the USSR through development was felt by Eisenhower himself: he not only supported the founding of an Inter-American Development Bank, and pledged nearly half its initial $1 billion in capital, but also supported health care, housing, and land reform through a new regional fund. In 1960, he backed the creation of a new soft loan facility at the World Bank, a means of demonstrating greater commitment to the world's poor, especially in Africa, within the framework of the bank discipline he prized.[29]

The subsequent green light for the UN Development Program was only one of the policies generated by the best and the brightest of the Kennedy administration, brash, highly educated, and convinced of the transformative power of ideas. Advised by Rostow and others, Kennedy was much more and more broadly committed to development ideals than Eisenhower had ever been. An avowed anti-imperialist, he was keen to show Third World leaders that American know-how would be made available to help them. The American people, he declared in the presidential campaign, "should be marching at the head of this worldwide revolution"; instead they had allowed the Soviets to steal a march on them.[30] Pushing forward the ambidextrous internationalism pioneered by Truman, Kennedy created USAID, on the one hand, as the major disburser of bilateral American aid, and on the other supported the ongoing UN development initiatives. In September 1960 he went to the UN and urged successfully that the 1960s be declared the Decade of Development. If the long-term results would be disappointing, the short-term reception was immensely popular: Hollywood took up the theme, and in 1962 Cary Grant impressed Doris Day in *That Touch of Mink* by delivering an impassioned speech at the United Nations in favor of raising the living standards of the world. The following year, at the FAO's 1963 World Food Congress, Kennedy called for a comprehensive approach to world hunger: the FAO budget increased tenfold. The new World Food Program, a compromise between the desire for a multilateral means of tackling world hunger and the American desire to deploy food surpluses to diplomatic advantage, offered a further example of the increased intimacy of the U.S.-UN relationship.

But the glitter of Camelot hid a much more brutal side of development thinking, which was always and above all so far as Washington was concerned a Cold War national security doctrine. Failure in the Bay of Pigs to overthrow the Cuban Revolution had left the Kennedy administration resolved at all costs not to "lose" another American state to communism, and this attitude led them to interpret development in an increasingly militarized mode. The key postcolonial question for Washington was not democracy or dictatorship but Cold War orientation. One key new ally were the generals, a fact acknowledged when a 1961 U.S. National Security Memorandum proposed relying on military officers in Third World countries to promote development. In Bolivia, to take one example, Kennedy's aides immediately channeled massive amounts of aid to the military, which they used to smash the unions, especially the well-organized and well-armed tin miners, rounding up leftists, and preparing the path to the 1964 coup that ushered in two decades of military rule. In Indonesia the military came to power in a horrifying bloodbath that left an estimated half a million dead. The Johnson administration not only approved—if the Bolivians paid the price for Castro's success in Cuba, the Indonesians paid for Ho Chi Minh's—it hailed the role played in the country's subsequent dictatorship by U.S.-trained Indonesian economists. As these "economists with guns" (as their historian has termed them) showed, the authoritarian and coercive side of developmentalism depended not only on American funds and initiative, but on the energy of native partners as well.[31]

Vietnam itself was the ultimate revelation of where modernization theory could lead. It was after all the region for which Rostow himself had responsibility within Kennedy's National Security Council, and it had been turned into a laboratory for all the modernizers' favorite ideas. There was Johnson's hope of building up a Mekong Valley Development Authority based on the TVA, and the forced relocation of thousands of farmers in the strategic hamlets scheme. None of this stanched the rise of the Vietcong. As the psychological war went from bad to worse, and the Americans and their allies were outfought, Rostow himself increasingly fell back on the mass bombing doctrine he had learned from his wartime service with the Strategic Bombing Survey in Europe. Thus war and development were shown once again to be naturally linked categories, and by the end Rostow had become one of the Johnson administration's leading hawks. Optimism and development had led in his case to escalation and war crimes. Neither his career nor modernization theory ever recovered.

Although it had not necessarily implied repression and authoritarianism, still less massive bombing on the scale of Vietnam, the top-down developmentalism typical of the early postwar decades had always risked hubris of one kind or another. The infamous Tanganyikan Groundnut Scheme, dreamed up by British colonial experts in East Africa to generate a profitable vegetable oil export sector, had created a dust bowl and destroyed indigenous farming. The Volta River Authority was much more successful, and became the chief source of electricity in postindependence Ghana (it still is), but the TVA-style scheme designed to transform Afghanistan's Helmand Valley simply wrecked traditional cultivation and irrigation systems and demonstrated the fatuousness of overambitious efforts to remake entire societies: the effort to defeat communism there caused such social dislocation that it helped it take over. The search for a single technological key that would unlock the secret of growth—a prospect American proponents of development seemed especially attracted to—also led to huge hopes being invested in the deployment of new strains of wheat and rice. Yet even the so-called Green Revolution—a Cold War propaganda term that credited U.S. technology with saving Asia from going Red—grossly simplified the many complex reasons why crop yields increased and exaggerated the benefits that seeds alone could bring.[32]

Nonwesterners tended to be keener on industrialization and import substitution than most Americans, less anxious about population growth, and less inclined to see food production as the most important goal. Most importantly, of course, they were more likely to understand the institutional and cultural realities of their situation. But American development experts found it hard to heed the views of the people whose lives they proposed to improve, and even after aid agencies began to analyze the likely social consequences of the projects they funded, indeed even after those analyses demonstrated the likely damage that would ensue, their mindset changed but slowly.[33] Yet for the first time, internationally comparable economic data were becoming available, and the message they conveyed was an uncomfortable one. If there was growth in the former colonial world it was dwarfed by the extraordinary postwar boom in Europe and the United States, and because population was growing faster in the developing world, a significant gap in per capita incomes—now for the first time measurable thanks to the spread of national income statistics—was starting to open up. To make matters worse, the expansion of world trade seemed, if not to be bypassing much of the Third World, then to be making much less impact there.

The UN development community had grown from modest origins in only a few years, but it was poorly placed to explain what had gone wrong or what to do about it. Some of the reasons for this emerged in 1969, when a devastating internal report questioned the effectiveness of the UN Development Program, and much more as well. Commissioned on the eve of what was planned to be a further increase in the UNDP budget, the report ranged far beyond UNDP itself and constituted probably the single most perceptive, hard-hitting (and amusing) analysis that has ever been produced of the UN approach to development as a whole. Written by a formidable team led by Robert Jackson (formerly of the Middle East Supply Center and UNRRA) and his collaborator, Margaret Anstee (later the first woman to rise to the rank of undersecretary-general in the UN), its verdict was all the more powerful in that it came from figures deeply committed to the cause of international cooperation.[34]

"The Capacity Study," as it was entitled, was in many ways a defense and justification of the UN. The authors applauded the UN's commitment to technical cooperation, and argued that there was no better organization available for helping developing countries. The trouble, according to them, was the disjointed way it had grown in the past two decades. With a relatively weak secretary-general unable in practice to exercise much oversight over its numerous component parts—a trend that had begun under Lie, accelerated under Hammarskjöld, and culminated with U Thant—and with an increasingly anti-American General Assembly as an alternative power center within the UN itself, new agencies had emerged without any overarching direction, all of them keen for a slice of the development pie. Within twenty years, at the behest of its members, the United Nations had turned into an institutional nightmare, with more than a dozen specialized agencies and a control machinery that was completely unworkable. In fact, there was no effective coordination at all. As a result, the world organization seemed "incapable of intelligently controlling itself" and its development effort in particular was over-centralized and too distant from the experts in the field. It was, stated Robert Jackson, the report's lead author,

> becoming slower and more unwieldy, like some prehistoric monster. . . . For many years I have looked for the "brain" which guides the policies and operations of the UN development system. . . . The search has been in vain. . . . The UN development system has tried to wage a war on want for many years with very little organized "brain" to guide it. Its absence may well be the greatest constraint of all on capacity. Without it, the future evolution of the UN development system could easily repeat the history of the dinosaur.[35]

The Capacity Study went on to warn that if the UN failed to reform itself in basic ways, its leadership of the development agenda was likely to be challenged from other bodies.

Whether the UN really did lead the development agenda even at this stage was a moot point, however. Bilateral American aid through USAID was—thanks to its function as safety valve for American farm surpluses and unwanted equipment—growing so fast that it dwarfed any international agency: by 1976, U.S. economic assistance to Egypt alone was three times as large as the total UNDP budget. Of the multilateral institutions, the World Bank was emerging under the leadership of Robert McNamara, Kennedy's former defense secretary, as the powerhouse that it was to remain for the rest of the century. Ambitious to move from grand infrastructural projects to tackle the causes of global poverty and backwardness, and blessed by the Nixon administration, McNamara abandoned the more cautious Wall Street–friendly posture of his predecessors. Kissinger noted to Nixon, probably in 1970, that while the UNDP was important to the United States, it had become "much less important than the World

Bank."[36] In the 1970s, while UNDP grant-giving rose from $239 million to $520 million, the soft loans disbursed by the bank's International Development Agency rose much faster, from $288 million to $1.278 billion. Nor did the numbers tell the full story: in practice, the UNDP under Hoffman tended to work very closely with the bank and even to carry out projects on its behalf. Thus it was in the course of this decade that the bank cemented its dominance over the agencies under the UN's own control as the most important player in the global aid drama.

The organization's own structural inadequacies—so unsparingly laid bare in the Capacity Study—were only part of the explanation for this. The bigger issue was politics, as the arguments and tensions over the meaning and purpose of development that had been evident from the late 1940s exploded into a new global contestation. As the decolonized world combined forces with the South and Central Americans, visions of the international economy that posed a significant challenge to American development thinking and implied a quite different path for the world economy gained ground at the UN.[37]

TOWARD THE NEW INTERNATIONAL ECONOMIC ORDER

"A conflict between two worlds—one rich, one poor—is developing," noted *Time* in December 1975, "and the battlefield is the globe itself."[38] In truth, this conflict had been in the making from the moment decolonization itself allowed the developed world to speak more powerfully than ever before in an international setting. By the early 1960s, West Germany and Japan were recovering strongly, Japan had been brought into the Organisation for Economic Co-operation and Development (OECD), and the European Economic Community countries were voting as a bloc in the world's main trade organization, the General Agreement on Tariffs and Trade (GATT). It was to confront all these challenges that in 1962 a group of nonaligned countries met in Cairo and demanded international action on trade and development. The so-called G-77 group of underdeveloped countries at the General Assembly later that year repeated this call and proposed a UN conference on the issue.

The battle lines between North and South were hardening. The combination of the Afro-Asian bloc and the Latin American states constituted an overwhelming majority in the UN, and despite European and American opposition a motion to hold a conference on the subject was passed and in 1964 the first UN Conference on Trade and Development (UNCTAD) took place. The conference itself was an important milestone in international economic history. With 118 countries represented—compared with the twenty-three that met in 1947 to discuss the formation of an international trade organization—it was an indication of the extraordinary transformation of the world.

In particular, it indicated the growing cohesion of the underdeveloped nations, now banded together in the G-77 group. Their solidarity impressed and disturbed Western diplomats. There had been Western opposition not only to the meeting, but to the choice of an Argentinian economist, Raúl Prebisch, as its organizer. Both had been overruled. Prebisch had previously turned the UN Economic Commission for Latin America into a prominent and critical voice in the international development debate and become a strong critic of American economic hegemony. His argument for global redistribution was based chiefly on the impact of international trade on internal development. There was no reason in principle, he claimed, why being on the periphery of the world economy need lead to dependency or prevent a country from pursuing economic policies to its own advantage. The trouble came with foreign trade, when in the absence of a countervailing power, advanced countries producing manufactures were able to keep up the prices of their goods vis-à-vis the primary products exported by most peripheral economies. Trade, Prebisch preached, was a kind of postcolonial servitude; the market needed to be the servant not the master, otherwise empire continued, even after its formal demise. The report he prepared reflected, in the apt summing up of a contemporary critic, "a philosophy of international economic policy that might be described as the internationalization of protectionism for less developed countries."[39]

Put in charge of organizing the 1964 UNCTAD meeting, and establishing it as an independent unit beyond all but the most indirect control of the UN Secretariat, Prebisch with his organizational flair and sense of drama made a success of the conference and publicized his ideas. Interestingly, a quite different explanation of the developing countries' difficulties in the international trade regime was being offered elsewhere at this time. Some said the problem was that they were deliberately being shut out of developed markets: the Common Market's new tariff barriers around western Europe, designed to protect French farmers, were a case for the prosecution. But the implications of these two approaches ran in opposite directions. Unlike Prebisch's, the second identified interference with free trade as the problem, not free trade itself, whereas the very title of UNCTAD suggested that reform of trade and the cause of global development were connected. For the former, the ongoing GATT negotiations provided an instrument for improvement; for the latter, far more radical measures were needed. Prebisch himself was a relative moderate. In a lengthy speech at the conference delivered on behalf of the victorious Cuban Revolution, Che Guevara warned delegates not to be taken in by the temptations provided by the capitalist West. Bodies like the World Bank, the IMF, and GATT had just one purpose: to save capitalism for the American dollar. Only a united front of the world's underdeveloped nations would allow the entire global economy to be changed so as to put an end to the "exploitation of man by man."[40]

This message fell on receptive ears in the UN General Assembly. The new states of Africa and Asia were suspicious of capitalism, and fearful of economic neocolonialism in which mining corporations and banks kept control of their resources. Uneasy at what was happening to the UN Development Program, they were growing more hostile to the role of the United States and the West, more drawn to

Marxist critiques of capitalism even while wishing to keep their distance from a Soviet model few found attractive, and they feared that trade liberalization would constrain their own development plans. Much more was needed than preferential access to Western markets or technical assistance—they called for cheap loans with no strings attached, commodity price support, and breaking up Western cartels that kept things like shipping costs high. Prebisch himself calculated that to be successful, the UN Decade of Development required a 5 percent minimum real annual growth rate, and an annual export growth rate of 6 percent. Alternatively, the West would need to provide a huge increase in capital inflows. The bill for Kennedy's promises was being presented.[41]

These estimates immediately became the target of criticism from U.S. undersecretary George Ball, probably the most powerful man at the conference. Yet politically the first UNCTAD meeting was surprisingly successful. It managed to win some IMF funds to finance balance-of-payments difficulties caused by sharp drops in commodity prices, and it took steps to improve Third World access to European markets. Above all, it emboldened the members of the G-77. Thanks to pressure from the underdeveloped world, it was agreed to create a permanent secretariat that would arrange a meeting every four years. This very effectively kept the North-South question in the spotlight for the next two decades.

Yet keeping it in the spotlight was not the same as winning concessions. Successive conferences endeavored to shame the developed countries into living up to the commitments they had made. But UNCTAD itself was a relatively weak organization, split between powerful caucuses of states with very different interests, and unable to enforce rules or even monitor their observance. The more it got into specifics—of commodity pricing, or shipping policy—the greater the disagreements emerged from within the G-77 group itself and the harder it became to find a consensus position. Hence its leadership tended to keep things at an abstract level. Yet this simply caused more frustration. By the time of the third UNCTAD conference in 1972 it was clear that radicals and pragmatists were divided on whether to embrace the new forum for cooperation or to use it as a means of fomenting class war.[42]

That same year, George H. W. Bush, then serving as U.S. ambassador to the United Nations, advised president Nixon that "we need to go on the offensive and show we support the UN." The Vietnam War had emboldened the radicals in the General Assembly and generated an increasingly anti-American tone. Entirely in keeping with the trajectory of U.S. diplomacy since the 1940s, Bush recommended emphasizing "economic and social conditions."[43] Yet the old approach no longer represented an easy road to international acceptance. On the contrary, as the war's extraordinary cost pushed up inflation and destabilized the international economy, many G-77 members now questioned American leadership and wanted action on more than commodity prices and terms of trade. They wanted to take on the power of multinational corporations, whose activities had begun to dominate world manufacturing, and to move the debate away from growth and toward inequality. In 1973, the OPEC oil cartel's price hike was cheered on by many of the developing countries since it was, as one put it, the first time that non-Western powers had taken the initiative in the world economy. A meeting of the nonaligned movement in Algiers that year revived Raúl Prebisch's old call for a New International Economic Order to improve the position of the Third World. The following year, the UN held a special session to debate the subject, and in the teeth of strong American opposition the General Assembly duly passed a Declaration on the Establishment of a New International Economic Order. Development was accorded a high priority, but the G-77 were really concerned about sovereignty and justice. States ought to be free to do as they wished internally without interference, to choose whichever development regime they thought best, and to exercise "full and permanent sovereignty over . . . natural resources and all economic activities." The United States, which had dreamed under Truman of standing for the fight against world poverty, was now reviled for defending the rights of large corporations and big business. To the dismay of American corporations, nationalization was described in the Declaration as an "inalienable right": Salvador Allende's Chile, which had hosted the 1972 Santiago UNCTAD meeting (to Kissinger's alarm), led the way, nationalizing massively profitable American-owned copper mines, cement producers, and banks. Within only a few years, 75 percent of the holdings of American raw materials corporations based in the Third World had been nationalized. When the United States retaliated by cutting off access to credit, this opened up a new line of attack: the demand for a new approach to international loans and for debate over the future of the American dollar as an international reserve currency.[44]

Implausibly, in the light of the Jackson Capacity Study report, the UN itself was envisaged as the vehicle for this new international economic order. As the declaration put it:

> The United Nations as a universal organization should be capable of dealing with problems of international economic cooperation in a comprehensive manner and ensuring equally the interests of all countries. It must have an even greater role in the establishment of a new international economic order.

This was less a statement than a battle cry to turn the UN into the means of engineering an international economy based on the developmental needs of the Third World. But saying it should be so did not make it so, and over the following decade, as we shall see, the United States responded energetically to what amounted to the most serious challenge to its global leadership since the end of the Second World War. The UN itself was the principal victim and slid into an obscurity from which it only reemerged, in a guise more acceptable to Washington, in the 1990s.

CHAPTER 11

The United States in Opposition

Symbolically, the United Nations compound on the East River in New York is coming to resemble the Guantánamo Naval Base in Cuba. Both are an affront to the principles and norms of the territories that surround them and both are vestiges of past power configurations.

—Stephen Krasner, *Structural Conflict* (1985)[1]

THE FIFTIETH ANNIVERSARY of Woodrow Wilson's death passed quietly. In February 1974, with Nixon embroiled in the Watergate scandal and Secretary of State Henry Kissinger shuttling around the Middle East, it seemed a very distant memory. Speaking in the house where Wilson had died, the head of the Woodrow Wilson Foundation dutifully urged young Americans to put Vietnam behind them, and to remain true to the idea that the United States had a special part to play in the world.[2] But down the road, a more memorable and bracing act of homage was being delivered to an audience at the Woodrow Wilson Center for Scholars in Washington. The speaker was the serving U.S. ambassador to India, but he was not one of nature's diplomats: Harvard professor, intellectual, and controversialist, Daniel Patrick Moynihan liked to think big and provocatively, and his speech constituted the opening shot in a bid to reclaim and update the Wilsonian heritage as America struggled to find a new leadership role in the world.[3]

Moynihan was a Democrat who had attracted Nixon's interest through his headline-grabbing writings on race in American cities, but he also had a longtime interest in international issues, and his unconventional mind had already led him to get NATO to start thinking about "challenges to modern society" such as the environment. Openly admiring of Woodrow Wilson and his appeal to universal moral values, Moynihan praised him for his confidence in America's mission and his willingness to use its military strength in the First World War to save "the liberty of the world" and lead "the concerted powers of all civilized peoples" in its defense. But, said Moynihan, Wilson's legacy had not been cherished. He had helped create a world of independent nations and free peoples, as well as the world order that "by legitimating and channeling these forces would sufficiently contain them." Yet recent evidence suggested that the latter achievement was under enormous strain and that the United States was losing enthusiasm for the world it had created. It was time for a rethink and a return to basic principles.

The problem according to Moynihan was that since the Second World War, American foreign policy had strayed from the true path: it had veered between a "reform-interventionist" mode, exemplified by such policies as the Truman Doctrine, and "a security-isolation" reaction. The Vietnam War had started as the former, thanks to Kennedy's modernization gurus, and ended up as the latter. Yet the original Wilsonian promise had lost none of its meaning for America or mankind. "The Wilsonian world view is already half achieved," Moynihan noted; most peoples in the world lived in independent states for the first time in history. But Wilson (and Mazzini before him) had been wrong to assume that this would automatically lead to a growth of personal freedom, for many of them languished under dictatorial rule. It was up to America to promote the struggle for liberty around the globe.[4]

Moynihan's call to inject morality back into American foreign policy was a none too subtle attack on the diplomacy of the Nixon-Kissinger team. His old Harvard colleague Henry Kissinger of course saw things very differently. If Moynihan's god was Wilson, Kissinger's luminaries were the European statesmen of the era of the Concert and the balance of power. Ever since his doctoral dissertation, Kissinger had testified to the virtues of the men who had created the century-long peace that followed the Congress of Vienna. Three years before entering office as Nixon's national security adviser, Kissinger had penned a revealing piece in which he contrasted the ideal figure of the Statesman—wary, rational, conscious of power's limits, gradualist and devoted to survival—and the Prophet—revolutionary, tempted to make his own reality, obsessed with what is right, with total solutions. The Statesman, said Kissinger, was a European phenomenon, a product of the scientific revolution, and as such it included Soviet leaders. The Prophet, on the other hand was prerational, ecstatic, and swept away by his own rhetoric: Kissinger clearly had Third World nationalists in mind. Statesmen could negotiate with one another, but there was no point talking to Prophets.[5]

Viewed as an attempt to conduct the Cold War on the basis of quiet tête-à-têtes among Statesmen, Kissingerian détente was a deliberate repudiation of the ambitious world-making diplomacy that had got America into Vietnam and into trouble. It involved a self-conscious attempt to return American foreign policy to nineteenth-century diplomatic norms—using summitry and personal understandings to bypass bureaucracies and those social forces and institutions that impeded Great Powers from getting along. Fear of nuclear armageddon was the overriding threat; avoiding world war the goal. Kissinger made it clear—to Moscow, to Beijing, to Mobutu and the shah of Iran—that he was basically not interested in what rulers did to their own people. Between 1971 and 1973, the Nixon-Kissinger team transformed U.S.-Soviet relations. But the outbreak of war in the Middle East suggested their overwhelming focus on Moscow and Beijing had led to other sources of conflict being neglected.

Kissinger's unremitting emphasis on military power—in particular on nuclear weapons—as the crux of modern diplomacy was now put in question. When George Kennan was asked in 1972 about how the Soviet threat compared with twenty-five years earlier, he responded that the USSR had weakened significantly, and that nuclear weaponry was a kind of "fantasy world." Détente was a sane development, in Kennan's view, but it could also start to look like the pursuit of yesterday's problem: he wished both the USSR and the United States would wake up to the limits of their influence and that the United States would scale back its global commitments. Moynihan thought by contrast that the fault lay in subordinating all of world politics to the East-West problematic. For Kissinger the North-South front opened up by decolonization was relatively unimportant, except to the extent that it threatened the understanding between the superpowers. Moynihan, on the other hand, believed that the real challenge for America came not from Soviet Russia but from managing the rise of the Third World.[6]

In March 1975, he published a blockbuster article entitled "The United States in Opposition" in which he explored what neo-Wilsonianism meant in a world in which the United Nations, the body that had come closest to realizing Wilson's dream, was becoming increasingly intractable. A new world society, he argued, was being born thanks to decolonization and the spread of national self-determination. But although this owed more to the sponsorship of the United States than to any other single power, the United States was no longer welcome inside the UN, where an overwhelming majority of Third World states, organized as a bloc, routinely attacked it, voted down its motions, and peddled their own collectivist nostrums. As Kennan had warned back in 1949, the UN General Assembly was set up like a parliamentary body and this could only eventually disadvantage the Americans. Worst of all, the State Department had done nothing about this barrage of criticism because it did not really believe the UN mattered.

Moynihan did. One could not walk away from it, as some American unilateralists urged—America had built too well. There were now international bodies such as the World Court, and normative regimes such as the international law of the sea, that had real power; pretending they did not exist or could not affect American interests was not an option. It was time to change course, Moynihan concluded, to acknowledge the ideological unity of the Third World and, rather than opting out, to do what a parliamentary system encouraged—that is, to move into "opposition." Accepting its relative isolation within international society, Washington could begin to collect its thoughts and to chart an alternative course for the world. Wilson provided a guide. Reclaiming what had really been at stake in his great struggle with Lenin, America needed now to speak, as Moynihan put it, for the party of liberty against the party of equality and to reassert the values of liberalism. The worldwide drift to radicalism and socialism needed to be fought. Free enterprise and the value of civil and political liberties needed to be reasserted. "It is time that the American spokesman came to be feared in international forums for the truths he might tell."[7]

The article made a splash and Kissinger himself is said to have missed an appointment in order to finish it. President Ford was enthusiastic—he had himself denounced the "tyranny of the majority" in the UN General Assembly the previous year—and he appointed Moynihan U.S. ambassador to the UN. It was at just this time that criticism of the world body, especially from American conservatives, was becoming louder. The conservative Heritage Foundation, established in 1973, was already advancing down the oppositional path that would lead it to mount an influential and highly critical United Nations Assessment Project and goad Congress into an ever more hostile relationship to the UN itself. Fresh from a stint as U.S. delegate, William F. Buckley Jr. wrote that the UN embodied "the most concentrated assault on moral reality in the history of free institutions." Australian novelist Shirley Hazzard, who had worked in the secretariat, wrote that it was unreformable and self-destructive; others were less flattering still. Yet the implication of Moynihan's argument was that with patience, energy, thought, and conviction, American foreign policy might be able to restore meaning to the body Washington had created. World leadership was still possible.[8]

It is not necessary here to dwell on the sound and fury that attended Moynihan's seven-month tenure as U.S. ambassador: the controversy was unparalleled until the appointment of the equally abrasive but less intellectually interesting John Bolton thirty years later. It did not help that the General Assembly passed the notorious resolution equating Zionism and racism shortly after Moynihan arrived. This was like a red rag to a bull (especially one—although he always denied this—probably already contemplating a run for the Senate as his next career move). Moynihan hit the headlines by defending Israel and describing Zionism as a "national liberation movement," while excoriating the UN's record on human rights and democracy. Journalists in New York loved it, but American career diplomats were unimpressed and so was Kissinger. When the British ambassador to the UN, Ivor Richard, asked for a "little more tolerance" and cautioned that the UN was "not the OK Corral and I am hardly Wyatt Earp," Moynihan assumed that Kissinger had sanctioned what amounted to an obvious attack on him. Ford persuaded him to stay on, but by February 1976 he was gone, preparing for the Senate race later that year. As senator for New York he would remain in office for twenty-four years.[9]

Moynihan's lasting contribution was to lay the intellectual foundation for a radically new multitiered American response to decolonization and its consequences. The emergence within the United Nations of a powerful bloc of states with a very different conception of global justice than that of the United States led Washington to move in the late 1970s from tacit opposition to outright counterattack on several fronts. One of these was the challenge posed by Third World calls for a New International Economic Order. Another was human rights; a third was on the environment. As Washington shifted gears from Kissingerian realpolitik to Carter's moral idealism, it resurrected Western economic solidarity against the South, and at the same time promoted human rights and the rights of the individual against the state. To be sure, Washington continued to support numerous dictators around the world. But the point was not consistency. It was the investment of energy in the construction of a new normative order, a kind of reshaping of world society of the kind Moynihan had called for. Moving away from Kissinger's traditional respect for the sovereignty of states, the United States shaped its policy to an unprecedented degree around what Moynihan's friend Norman Podhoretz called "sovereign individuals." The consequence was a marginalization of the core United Nations bodies, and a reorientation of American power toward support for a revival of market forces in the international economy and nongovernmental human rights organizations. As Congress and American public opinion became unprecedentedly hostile, the power of the UN to respond to truly global issues such as the environment was eroded.[10]

AGAINST THE NEW INTERNATIONAL ECONOMIC ORDER

Did the rise of the Third World mean the end of the West? That, for a moment seemed to be the prospect as the G-77's demand for a New International Economic Order threatened to splinter the precarious unity of the Atlantic alliance. While Kissinger's attention was elsewhere, focused on ending the war in Vietnam and détente with the Russians, European politicians reached out to the underdeveloped world. Already their aid policies were differing sharply from Washington's, and aimed to provide concessional access to the European Community's markets. An astonishingly acrimonious meeting between the European Commission's Dutch president, the socialist Sicco Mansholt, and a Nixon administration trade official in 1973 indicated Mansholt's desire to reorient Europe away from its close relationship with the United States to new ties with the South. "Relations with the U.S. [will] be decidedly secondary," Mansholt said bluntly. We should bear in mind that the enlargement of the

European Community that year had created a trading bloc larger than either the United States or the USSR. Helping forge a new international partnership between a newly reorganized Europe and a newly cohesive South seemed both morally right and strategically prudent, especially to the socialists and social democrats who dominated much of the decision making in the Community in the 1970s. They understood the world as a set of interdependent economic relationships rather than a zero-sum power struggle between states: Southern collapse would necessarily harm the North. And they were heirs to an older vein of European thought, some of it socialist, some of it fascist, that dreamed of a naturally symbiotic *Eurafrique* that would bring together the manufacturing Europeans and the resource-rich lands across the Mediterranean.[11]

Algerian president Houari Boumedienne, one of the leaders of the G-77, sought to exploit this opening. In an interview he gave to a Belgian newspaper in September 1973, he reached out to the European Community:

> If you look closely, we complement each other and can work together to our mutual advantage. Europe finds itself at a crossroads. It is slowly starting to assume a global role. If it accepts being a faithful ally of American imperialism, it will become our adversary; if instead, it opts for an independent role, it can, with our cooperation do great things.[12]

The implications for Washington were grim, and some felt the entire geopolitical structure of postwar American power was at risk. Nixon's willingness to devalue the dollar in 1971 had been criticized by many American globalists as a xenophobic act that threatened a return to the economic nationalism and isolationism of the 1930s. Kissinger was under fire both for having neglected Japan in his wooing of China and for having failed to appreciate the critical importance of western Europe in his eagerness to smooth relations with the Kremlin. His critic and rival Zbigniew Brzezinski—who would become Carter's national security adviser—warned of a breakup of the Atlantic alliance.[13] As a result, first informally and then more formally, the European relationship with Washington was patched up, and Japan was brought in. In 1973 three hundred politicians, academics, businessmen, and labor leaders were brought together in the private Trilateral Commission, founded by David Rockefeller and initially directed by Brzezinski. Its credo was summed up by one participant who noted, "Globalism and bilateralism offer little hope for success, but trilateralism does." The extensive involvement of Rockefeller himself recalled the continued influence of that family—from the age of Wilson to that of Fosdick and Rusk—in institutionally reinforcing the American commitment to global hegemony. The commission was written off by the evangelist Pat Robertson on the right as a proto–world government emerging "from the depth of something evil," and by the left as the revanche of international capitalism. The left certainly was close to the truth in that the recalibration of economic relations among the states and organizations of the West was what fueled the return of the United States to global leadership. Two years later, the establishment of what would become the G-7 made the process more official, and allowed the United States to shore up the relationships with western Europe and Japan that constituted the central axis of its postwar economic strategy. By 1980, the countries represented in the Trilateral Commission traded two-thirds of all world exports, and nearly two-thirds of world GNP. The effect was to weaken the bargaining power of the South, at the very moment that the latter's own internal cohesion was starting to splinter under the impact of the oil crisis. As Atlantic solidarity was reaffirmed, the gap across the Mediterranean widened: Boumedienne's death in 1978 signaled the end of the putative South-European alliance. It was all a perfect illustration of Brzezinski's point, made in the days after the critical 1973 Algiers meeting of the nonaligned movement, that "overt political acts and perhaps even the creation of new political structures" were needed "to cope effectively with what may appear to be now essentially technical or economic problems."[14]

UNCTAD and the UN's call for a New International Economic Order had, after all, been greeted quite differently in the United States than in Europe, and Washington's willingness to negotiate with the South was more tenuous. Moynihan, as ambassador to the UN, promised to improve access to Western markets and international measures to stabilize Third World export earnings. Kissinger himself offered to create an International Resources Bank during his first ever trip to Africa in 1976. But even these mildly conciliatory schemes went too far for men like Treasury Secretary William E. Simon or Ford's chief economic adviser, William Seidman, who warned against compromising "our basic commitment to the free enterprise system."[15]

Free-market ideologies fused with American pride and unwillingness to take any more of the anti-Americanism increasingly associated with UNCTAD. American attitudes toward the UN were changing and the high levels of public support that the world organization had previously enjoyed were dropping fast. For years Gallup had been asking Americans whether they thought the UN was doing a decent job, and between 1950 and the mid-1960s the figure responding positively never fell below 50 percent and was generally around 80 percent or higher. In 1967 it fell to 49 percent, and by November 1971 it was at an all-time low of 35 percent. When the new UN secretary-general, the Austrian Kurt Waldheim, met the U.S. ambassador, George H. W. Bush, in January 1972, he confessed that "the prestige of the United Nations [is] at a low ebb." Nixon himself was hardly reassuring: "We have the same problems in the United States about support for the UN. It is part of the general problem we have about American attitudes toward international affairs." In former State Department official Richard Gardner's words, "the United States is now on a collision course with the very international agencies in whose future it has an important stake."[16] The Ford administration delayed disbursements to the World Bank and announced in 1975, driven by congressional and union pressure, that it would leave the International Labor Organization.[17]

The idea that institutional reform could improve international governance through the United Nations no longer interested Washington. When the Dutch economist Jan Tinbergen proposed a scheme for "the optimal world order" that involved a radical expansion of UN power and a proliferation of new agencies—incredibly, he called for a World Food Authority, a World Agency for Mineral Resources, a World Energy Research Authority, a World Technology Development Authority, an International [Environmental] Control Agency, a World Disarmament Agency, and a World Trade and Development Authority—the reaction across the Atlantic was one of incredulity. Tinbergen, a socialist and a veteran of the Netherlands' powerful planning culture, simply did not see which way the wind was blowing. One U.S. Commerce Department official stated bluntly that "there are at this moment two international organizations that are quite useless: the UN and UNCTAD." American officials accused the latter of manufacturing "repetitive crises" and of generating "unilateral demands, and there is really no end to this process."[18]

This sense of exhausted patience was critical. There were many reasons why the developing world's call for a New International Economic Order achieved so little. But the primary reason was American opposition. Yet Moynihan had not only caught the mood but he also urged Washington to find an alternative. He was, after all, a Wilsonian. Still, it had to be an open question whether an alternative was even possible. Such were the forces of fragmentation in the mid-1970s, both within states—as the postwar corporatist compacts between organized labor and capital broke down—and between them, that it was quite unclear whether the old Bretton Woods monetary order that had collapsed in 1971 could be replaced at all. Some American observers believed that the age in which a hegemonic United States was able to impose economic rules and institutions on the world was past. "The quest for global rules is bound to be futile," declared Robert Rothstein, a scholar of UNCTAD, at the end of the 1970s. He foresaw the emergence of a "system with great potential for conflict and disintegration into hostile fragments."[19] Others welcomed the prospect of some "loosening" of the system. In 1977, the brilliant young British economist Fred Hirsch had mused about whether what he called "a controlled disintegration of the world economy" might not be "a legitimate objective for the 1980s." He was thinking about how a looser set of international monetary arrangements that allowed currencies to float would have the benefit of allowing national governments, following the collapse of fixed exchange rates, much more room to choose their own policies.

But what would the implications of "controlled disintegration" be for American world leadership? Hirsch's dramatic phrase caught the attention of the American banker Paul Volcker. Already a man of considerable influence, Volcker was heading the Federal Reserve Bank of New York when he delivered a lecture in Hirsch's memory in November 1978 (Hirsch had died prematurely that year). "A crisis can be therapeutic," he told the audience. "It demands a response." But it did not, he argued, need Hirsch's. Volcker understood the conflict between the desire for greater global integration, on the one hand, and the goal of modern democracies, on the other, to shape their own destiny—the very conflict that would erupt with even greater force some three decades later. But he approached the problem, as he admitted, as an American, and as a member of the policy elite of the country searching for a new way of bringing stability to the world economy. From that perspective, increasing the autonomy of national governments as Hirsch (and the UK Labour government) wanted looked like a way to stop trade and financial liberalization and turning back the clock. The great fear was of a return to the 1930s. The "fabric of discipline is fraying," warned Volcker; it was important to resist "the pressures to turn inward."[20] To protect an open world economy in an era of floating exchange rates would require greater coordination among bankers and treasury ministers. Stability would come in the long run not from intervening in the currency markets but from pursuing the right kind of policies at home. Thus Volcker reached the opposite conclusion from Hirsch: there was no substitute for international fiscal discipline. The unspoken corollary was that the guardians of the world's money would in the future have a greater role to play internationally—and national legislatures and electorates a smaller one.[21]

Less than twelve months later, Carter appointed Volcker chair of the Federal Reserve Board. With extraordinary speed he raised interest rates to 20 percent and at the cost of soaring unemployment (and havoc with the economy in neighboring Mexico) reduced inflation in the United States from 13 percent to 3.2 percent by the early 1980s. Once he had slain the inflationary beast, rates could be brought down again and the world made safe for capital. But it was not only inflation that was slain, it was the hopes of the developing world for an alternative international economic order run through the United Nations. Instead the dollar's status as international currency of last resort was safeguarded and the surplus OPEC oil profits that some developing countries had hoped might be the weapon to break American power ended up being recycled instead by Wall Street and the City of London and restoring their control of the international economy: the South had split, just as Che Guevara had warned it might. At the World Bank, Robert McNamara mused in 1980 that discussions on a New International Economic Order were "last year's fashion." UNCTAD was defanged with the appointment of a Washington-friendly secretary-general in 1984, and turned into a harmless accessory to the extraordinary transformation of capitalism that now took place under President Reagan and his successors. With not only UNCTAD but the UN itself sidelined, and international economic coordination run through the World Bank and the IMF—two institutions firmly in the control of the West—the United States emerged out of opposition.[22]

THE RISE OF HUMAN RIGHTS AND THE NGO

Rights, the cause that Moynihan had identified as the second arena of battle, were never a straightforward concept and they were always understood internationally in multiple ways. In the nineteenth century, freedom of conscience had been the main right to attract diplomats' attention. Between the two world wars, the League had focused on the collective rights of minorities. But in the early years of the United Nations, this effort had been abandoned in favor of a return to the rights of the individual, and the 1948 Universal Declaration was widely regarded at the time—and now—as enshrining this commitment. In fact, behind the scenes, the powers fought strongly to make sure it was not binding. The British feared embarrassment over the colonies, the Americans over segregation and civil rights. Stalin objected to any attempt to "turn the United Nations into a kind of world government placed above national sovereignty." On few other issues was there such unanimity in 1948.

With human rights paralyzed, decolonization shifted the rights debate again, away from individual liberties toward collective socioeconomic rights, above all to the right of national self-determination. At the 1955 Asian-African Conference at Bandung, delegates charged that the Universal Declaration was a neocolonial weapon that used the language of universality and individual rights to undermine the cultural integrity of nations.[23] "If human rights are sacred," the Lebanese delegate at Bandung declared in 1955, "the rights of nations themselves, no matter how small, to the respect of greater nations is at least just as sacred."[24] In the face of Western resistance, the General Assembly ordered that the right of national self-determination be incorporated in the planning of the UN human rights covenant that was to succeed and give force to the Universal Declaration.[25] After it was decided to split the covenant into two—one dealing with civil and political rights, the other with economic, social, and cultural rights—self-determination appeared as the lead right in both.

Through the 1950s, therefore, human rights were subsumed within the anticolonial cause. In the heat of the struggle for independence that could turn into the very Mazzinian demand that individuals should subordinate their own concerns to the general good of the nation. Writer and activist Frantz Fanon, participating in the Algerian struggle against the French, denounced the West's stress on the rights of the individual as an obstacle to revolutionary victory. "Individualism is the first to disappear," Fanon wrote in 1961 in *The Wretched of the Earth*: the "cleansing force" of violence would meld the "masses" into a unity in the struggle for national liberation—a struggle that would, he believed, so change their consciousness that in future no demagogues could pull the wool over their eyes. More or less as he wrote these words, the General Assembly was passing its Declaration on the Granting of Independence to Colonial Countries and Peoples, declaring "the subjection of peoples to alien subjugation, domination and exploitation" to be "a denial of fundamental human rights."[26]

Yet by the late 1960s, the right to self-determination was on the way to being won in most former colonial territories, and much of the Third World was sliding into dictatorship and one-party rule. The UN showed little enthusiasm for investigating, and its Commission on Human Rights averted its gaze. Apartheid South Africa remained the General Assembly's central focus, followed by Israel, Rhodesia, and the remaining African colonies. So far as the majority of UN members were concerned, rights remained a weapon in the continuing struggle against colonialism. When hundreds of thousands of East Pakistanis were slaughtered by the Pakistani army during the secession of 1971, or when civilians were bombed and starved in Biafra during the Nigerian Civil War, the UN's human rights commission was largely quiescent.[27]

In Washington, the view throughout the Cold War had generally been that none of this really mattered very much. Human rights were a "lost cause" that should be ignored, in order to conserve American firepower for more meaningful targets. As American modernization theory took an overtly conservative turn, other commentators argued it had been a dead-end creed in any case and that stability was more important for American interests than democracy.[28] In the meantime the United States was propping up numerous dictators for strategic reasons. The process had started with Franco and Perón but had intensified through the Cold War. By the early 1970s, the pantheon included figures such as Pinochet, Mobutu, the shah of Iran, Marcos, Suharto, and Salazar as well as the military juntas in Greece and Turkey. But then, quite suddenly, the sentiment in the United States changed, dictators started seeming more of a liability, and human rights acquired a new significance.[29]

THE PRECONDITION WAS DÉTENTE, the same geopolitical shift that had cut the ground from under the New International Economic Order. In Europe, a series of meetings on security and cooperation had been taking place through the early 1970s, bringing together the two sides in the Cold War. Human rights were initially of marginal significance in the discussions. For Brezhnev and the Soviets, the goal was belated international recognition for the borders they had established in 1945 in eastern Europe; the West for its part sought to foster détente and to improve humanitarian assistance and cooperation. When the culminating conference took place in Helsinki in 1975, its greatest achievement (at least in Soviet eyes) was its commitment to the inviolability of the existing frontiers. The Soviets were also delighted that the signatory states pledged noninterference in one another's internal affairs. The Helsinki Final Act was, from this viewpoint, a deeply conventional document. Tacked on more or less as an afterthought was a section pledging respect for human rights in conformity with the UN Charter and the Universal Declaration: neither Brezhnev nor many of the other diplomats attached much importance to it.

Yet while American rights activists were initially critical of Helsinki, there were some people who did take its mention of rights seriously. Extraordinarily courageous human rights groups sprang up in eastern Europe and the USSR, and activists in western Europe and the United States started to put pressure on Western governments to help them. The novelist Aleksandr Solzhenitsyn had memorably stated in his Nobel Prize lecture in 1970—which had to be smuggled out of the USSR—that "no such thing as INTERNAL AFFAIRS remains on our crowded Earth!" For Russian physicist Andrei Sakharov, himself awarded the Peace Prize five years later, human rights were coming to play an important part in his activism. A Moscow Helsinki Group was formed in 1976 in Sakharov's living room, and the Czech Charter 77 group emerged the following year. Both took advantage not only of the Helsinki provisions, but also of the fact that the communist bloc had just ratified the new UN human rights covenants. In the sense of creating a framework for action, the UN was actually more effective than some of its critics liked to acknowledge.[30]

This reconfiguring of rights, not as part of a larger political project led by the state but as an ethical alternative to the tyranny of the state, fell on receptive ears in the West. One key actor was the U.S. Congress, where in 1974 Senator Henry "Scoop" Jackson, a Democrat with a strong record of support for civil rights and environmental causes, sponsored a measure that linked trade to freedom of emigration in order to help Soviet Jews. Jackson was not the first Democrat to discover the issue: Minnesota congressman Donald Fraser had previously drawn attention to human rights violations in Chile and elsewhere, and growing congressional interest in the topic had led Kissinger preemptively to establish a new human rights section in the State Department. But Jackson was influential in suggesting how human rights could be linked to other diplomatic tools. Attentive to the unfolding Helsinki process, the newly elected President Carter took this a stage further and in his inaugural address in January 1977 made human rights a centerpiece of his presidency. Invoking the need for a new national spirit of moral self-belief, he insisted that "our commitment to human rights must be absolute."[31] He had no sooner entered office than he cut aid to Central and Latin American and African dictatorships for human rights violations, and warned the South Africans that apartheid was an affront to America's "profound commitment . . . to human rights": in general, he made it clear that internal repression was now viewed as a threat to American interests and values. The limits to American power meant that exhortation was often unmatched by results. And American strategic interests also undercut human rights and kept dictators in office. Yet there was no mistaking the shift. Carter was laying the foundations for the humanized version of liberal internationalism—with its stress on freedom, rights, and the spread of democracy—that would shape American policy for the next thirty years.[32]

THIS MOVE TOWARD HUMAN RIGHTS could not be divorced from the simultaneous rise of a new kind of player on the international stage. Even as American foreign policy was being reoriented toward values in the fashion Moynihan had urged, pressure on the United Nations and on its members to take individual human rights seriously was coming from another quarter as well—a very mixed assortment of groups lumped together under the heading of nongovernmental organizations.

They were not exactly new in the history of international affairs. To go back no further than the 1940s, the Roosevelt administration had encouraged citizens to mobilize in support of an internationalist peace. Religious and civil rights groups lobbied delegates at the 1945 San Francisco conference and by then NGOs were already an accepted, if limited, part of the landscape of international life.[33] Yet the Cold War also discredited many of them. Moscow had worked through front organizations since the 1920s, and the International Union of Students, the World Peace Council and the International Association of Democratic Lawyers were all either run by communists or supported by Soviet funds. The CIA was new to the game but caught up fast. The head of its new International Organizations Division was Cord Meyer, whom we have previously encountered as the youthful director of the United World Federalist movement. It was Meyer's disillusionment with the communist infiltration of internationalist movements like the UWF that led him to the CIA, where he became adept at creating front organizations for counterpropaganda.

At its height, the CIA was channeling money through more than sixty foundations to over one hundred organizations. When, for instance, the sculptor Reg Butler won an international sculpture competition organized by the Institute of Contemporary Art in London to commemorate the "Unknown Political Prisoner," it turned out that the prize money had originated with the American government, which hoped to erect a giant version in West Berlin to embarrass the Soviets. The International Commission of Jurists—regarded today as a reputable institution—started off as another CIA venture, built upon the foundations of the decidedly disreputable International Committee of Free Jurists in West Berlin, a body that had been set up by a former Nazi posing as a Jewish survivor.[34]

This shadow war of secret funding and Potemkin NGOs raised the question whether a genuinely autonomous nongovernmental organization was even possible in the Cold War. British lawyer Peter Benenson believed it was not only possible but necessary. A well-connected barrister who had gone to Franco's Spain to sit in as observer on the trials of union workers, Benenson understood that people were tired of "polarized thinking." In 1961 he published a long article in the British newspaper the *Observer* that reminded readers of the Universal Declaration's commitment to the rights to freedom of thought, religion, and opinion and called for pressure to be put on governments on both sides of the Iron Curtain to release those being held simply on account of their political or religious views:

> Open your newspaper any day of the week and you will find a report from somewhere in the world of someone being imprisoned, tortured or executed because his opinions or religion are unacceptable to his government. There are several million such people in prison—by no means all of them behind the Iron and Bamboo Curtains—and their numbers are growing. The newspaper reader feels a sickening sense of impotence. Yet if these feelings of disgust all over the world could be united into common action, something effective could be done.[35]

The response was extraordinary. As Benenson looked on in disbelief, local groups formed themselves and adopted their own political prisoners. Gradually he came to understand just how many people wanted to feel directly involved. Campaigning fulfilled an ethical, even a spiritual need for Western societies starved of the possibility of meaningful political engagement. The month after the article appeared he wrote a very frank letter to his closest colleague about the new movement:

> The underlying purpose of this campaign—which I hope those who are closely connected with it will remember but never publish—is to find a common base upon which the idealists of the world can cooperate. It is designed in particular to absorb the latent enthusiasm of great numbers of such idealists who have, since the eclipse of Socialism, become increasingly frustrated; similarly it is geared to appeal to the young searching for an ideal, and to women past the prime of their life who have been, unfortunately, unable to expend in full their maternal impulses. If this underlying aim is borne in mind, it will be seen that, *à la longue,* it matters more to harness the enthusiasm of the helpers than to bring people out of prison. . . . Those whom the Amnesty Appeal aims to free are the men and women imprisoned by cynicism and doubt.[36]

This conveyed an extraordinarily unpragmatic conception of political action in which results mattered less than the moral transformation of the activists themselves. Yet the results were sensational. Within two years the organization had a name, a structure, and an international dimension that expanded beyond western Europe to the United States and elsewhere. Growth was held back in its early years by bad leadership—one secretary-general nearly brought the organization down when his links with British intelligence were revealed—but by the early 1970s it had more than two thousand membership groups in more than thirty countries, and in 1977 it was awarded the Nobel Peace Prize. What had started off as a small office for Appeal for Amnesty 1961 turned into the world's largest human rights NGO, with an army of volunteer letter writers, backed by a well-regarded central information-gathering office.

Amnesty International quickly demonstrated the impact an NGO could make on the United Nations. In December 1972 it launched an international campaign to abolish torture, mobilizing public pressure to force governments to heed the prohibition on the use of torture in the Universal Declaration. A million people signed a petition that demanded that the UN condemn torture and an international conference brought together government delegates, UN representatives, and NGOs amid broad media coverage. The following years saw the coup against Allende in Chile and the collapse of dictatorships in Portugal and Greece, which uncovered evidence of widespread torture in both countries. Sustained lobbying by Amnesty International and other NGOs paid off—it was at this time that Amnesty increased the pressure on governments by starting its Urgent Action campaigns—and in 1977, as news came in of the death of Steve Biko in South Africa, the UN General Assembly called on the Human Rights Commission to draft a convention against torture. When this was passed in 1984 it represented the first major triumph in international legislation for the new human rights movement.

Amnesty International by this time was perhaps the best known and most influential human rights organization in the world, but it was certainly not alone. From the late 1960s, other bodies had also been emerging—chiefly in western Europe and the United States—that brought together activists keen to do something about the plight of individuals suffering at the hands of repressive governments. The Biafra War spurred the emergence of Médecins sans Frontières after a young French doctor, Bernard Kouchner, left the Red Cross in outrage at its refusal to speak out against the violence carried out by the Nigerian army. The Oxford Committee for Famine Relief had been formed in 1942 to help the Greeks starving under Nazi occupation, but it was the spectacular field operation it mounted in Biafra that turned Oxfam into a household name. Benenson seemed to be right:

European publics yearned for a cause, and sought to make a difference politically in a way that allowed them to eschew the tired polarities of the Cold War.[37]

Their example confirmed that the Cold War icepack could be broken, and that activism could make a difference. Ideas had power and governments could be shamed into action, even in the era of Henry Kissinger. Because these were important lessons, they could be learned by very different groups of people and put to different ends. In fact, the broad term "NGO" hides as much as it reveals. If Amnesty International was a kind of church, with its own congregation, its focus on good deeds and the individual conscience, other groups emerged in the United States that looked less like churches and more like lobbies with very different funding strategies and philosophies. These new NGOs focused on results, boasted a more intimate connection with congressional leaders, administration officials, and major foundations in Washington and New York, and appeared a lot more like the old Cold War versions than Amnesty did.

Working through and with Congress—to take perhaps the best example—a new organization called Helsinki Watch was established in 1978 to help dissidents behind the Iron Curtain. Today better known as Human Rights Watch, it is probably the premier human rights organization in the United States. But unlike Amnesty International, Helsinki was not formed atop an activist mass membership that provided contributions and energy, but rather as a centrally organized office that came into being thanks to a generous grant from the Ford Foundation. In fact, as its name suggested, its origins lay in the Helsinki process and in the official American response. A congressional committee had been established to monitor Soviet compliance with the Final Act. President Carter himself then appointed an outspoken lawyer, Arthur Goldberg, to head the American delegation to the follow-up conference that was scheduled to take place at Belgrade in 1977. Goldberg had once taken the young Daniel Moynihan under his wing, and like Moynihan he disliked the diplomatic approach. In Belgrade he launched an attack on Soviet rights abuses, making effective use of materials provided to him by NGOs. His brash style did not produce any notable results. Nevertheless, it was precisely his status as outsider to the traditional modes of statecraft and his appreciation of the usefulness of the press and public mobilization (in his past he had been both a member of the OSS and a union lawyer) that made him see the possibilities of a new kind of official-unofficial coalition of forces to enhance American interests.

After the conference, Goldberg suggested to the Ford Foundation that it would be a good idea to have an American monitoring group that could operate outside official circles.[38] His suggestion was sympathetically received by the foundation's president, McGeorge Bundy, who had been a long-serving national security adviser to both Kennedy and Johnson. Bundy reached out to a New York publisher named Robert Bernstein, already involved in free speech campaigns in the USSR, and invited him to submit a proposal for a new monitoring body. An initial $25,000 was requested for planning an organization that would help "consciousness-raising" in western Europe so that the U.S. delegation to the 1980 conference would not be as isolated as it had been at Belgrade. Within a few months, with Bundy's strong personal backing, Ford gave an enormous grant of $400,000 to set up the new organization. In its 1979 annual review, the Ford Foundation proudly but misleadingly referred to the fact that "in the United States, a group of private citizens has organized Helsinki Watch, Inc., to monitor U.S. compliance and to call public attention to cases of official mistreatment of Watch groups in other countries." In fact, the monitoring of U.S. rights abuses was distinctly secondary to the main task of reporting on eastern Europe and the USSR, and so far was this from being the initiative of a small group of private citizens that only the personal attention of McGeorge Bundy and his Washington connections could explain the award of a grant that was far larger than any other made that year.[39]

Helsinki Watch made an impact much more quickly than even Amnesty had done; it was, after all, a far more centralized outfit. The 1980 Madrid Conference on Security and Co-operation in Europe (CSCE) became the scene of "grand human rights theater," with the new NGO as one of the prime actors, introducing dissidents to journalists and providing information packs to government officials.[40] For the first time, a CSCE conference saw Western diplomats raising human rights issues with the Soviet and east European delegations. Not only would this pressure increase in the coming years, but through their extensive contacts with and support for east European dissidents, Helsinki Watch brought a new effectiveness to the monitoring network across Europe that could plausibly claim some of the credit for the collapse of communism. Anxious not to be seen as a poodle of Washington, the organization branched out in the 1980s and became involved in the Americas. Taking on the Reagan administration's support for human rights abusers there won it new supporters, bolstered its legitimacy and moral authority in important ways, and allowed it to transcend its origins.

Helsinki Watch thus pioneered—even more than Amnesty International—a new model of rights activism that brought diplomats, politicians, and NGOs together in a single concerted effort. If Amnesty's basic approach was pacifist, Helsinki Watch's was militant. The one relied on moral suasion and the power of shameful publicity, the latter on persuading congressmen in the world's most powerful state to enact legislative reforms targeting rights abusers. At the time, and even now, these differences interested only the specialists—the term "NGO" covered them both. With astonishing speed, NGOs of all kinds became part of the institutional reshaping of international politics—linked to national and international governments through funding, associational status, and meetings—and NGO activity proliferated. The UN welcomed more NGOs into its deliberations, and the number of major NGOs granted the right to participate in the Economic and Social Council rose from 132 in 1969 (a number little changed for twenty years) to 236 in 1979, 367 in 1989, and more than one thousand by the end of the century. This incorporation of the NGO into international life was claimed by the UN as an indication of its democratization and responsiveness to civil society in general, as well as a sign of its transformed attitude to human rights in particular. NGOs carried a legitimacy that national governments did not; they were said to embody the aspirations of ordinary people, the voice of "civil society." But as they became recipients of government funds as well as disbursers of advice, their moral position became more complicated. What civil society and which membership legitimated Helsinki Watch? Without American money and a shift in American foreign policy its emergence was inconceivable. Human rights was a struggle to defend the individual against the state. But its emergence as an international movement was inseparable, as Moynihan had preached, from the normative transformation of American power.

In fact, things were about to get muddier still, for a natural consequence of these developments was the creation of human rights and pro-democracy foundations by Western governments themselves. President Reagan himself was not, as some recent scholars have claimed, captured by the human rights movement; rather, he annexed it for his own ends. Even as groups like Helsinki Watch's younger sister, Americas Watch, denounced his administration for tolerating human rights abuses in the Western Hemisphere, President Reagan proclaimed his own "Project Democracy" to contribute to "a global campaign for democracy." Moynihan had called for this in his homage to Woodrow Wilson, and had criticized Kennan a few years later for portraying as a North Atlantic cultural outgrowth what was in fact "a well-documented and universal human aspiration . . . the desire to be free." Such sentiments now resonated in Reagan's address to the House of Commons in London in June 1982:

> We must be staunch in our conviction that freedom is not the sole prerogative of a lucky few but the inalienable and universal right of all human beings. . . . The objective I propose is quite simple to state: to foster the infrastructure of democracy, the system of a free press, unions, political parties, universities, which allows a people to choose their own way to develop their own culture, to reconcile their differences through peaceful means.

To support this "crusade for freedom," the same Congress that was withholding funds from the UN funded a new National Endowment for Democracy. Ideologically, this represented a neoconservative version of a human rights movement, one that took the old anticommunist left's idea of a democratic international and made it official policy for the right. Like several other neocons, the NED's president, Carl Gershman, had moved from the Young People's Socialist League through the civil rights movement to the circle of Democrat Scoop Jackson. What brought him and others to support Reagan was their shared anticommunism; what they brought the Republicans and the administration was conviction that America should lead a global fight for democracy, and that the struggle against totalitarianism had to be fought on the plane of ideas as well as arms.[41]

Its organizational arrangement bore their imprint too, and brings the NGO story right back to its Cold War origins. Funded by Congress and the State Department, the NED distributes its monies to four chief recipients—the official international foundations of the Democratic and Republican parties, the Free Trade Union Institute, and the Center for International Private Enterprise—which then work with foreign partners. In a fashion not entirely unlike the CIA-funded Congress for Cultural Freedom, this allows the NED to present itself and its work not as an outgrowth of the American state but as an expression and representative of trends in American "civil society." Bizarrely, the act that established the NED states that "the Endowment will not be considered an agency or establishment of the U.S. Government." Blurring the line that separates government from the world of civil society, gesturing toward a future democratic universe while itself embedded in the Cold War past, the NED updated Woodrow Wilson's Mazzinian vision and took the credit as the number of democracies in the world soared at the end of the century. In fact, its model for projecting American power and influence was such a potent one that it easily outlived the Cold War itself, and in 2011, still proclaiming its nongovernmental character, it hailed the Arab Spring as a sign that recent checks in democracy's advance might turn out to be only temporary. A nongovernmental body founded by government, an activist organization that in fact embodies a global mission for the United States itself, the National Endowment for Democracy through its ambiguities illustrates the deeply ideological character of the human rights revival.[42]

One further Kafkaesque twist must be mentioned. In 2007, *Foreign Policy* editor Moisés Naím wrote an article on "Democracy's Dangerous Impostors" in which he denounced the rise of a mysterious new phenomenon—the so-called GONGOs, and he cited Putin's Nashi and the Sudanese Human Rights Organization as examples of the "government-organized nongovernmental organization." Some GONGOs, he agreed, are harmless, but many of them are dangerous because they deploy the legitimacy of the NGO in order to advance the interests of their governments abroad. What then of the National Endowment for Democracy—a GONGO too, as Naím admits? Because he sits on the board of directors, he thinks the NED is a good GONGO and, like him, open about what it does. This confusing state of affairs Naím proposed to solve through a world rating system for NGOs. Yet why would ratings agencies themselves be able to escape the pressures, forces, and temptations that imperil the autonomy of NGOs? In fact, a ratings agency already exists for freedom, for example: it too is a GONGO—called Freedom House—that is based in Washington, almost entirely funded by the U.S. government, run by a board of trustees that believes that "the promotion of democracy and human rights abroad is vital to America's interests abroad and to international peace." In twenty-first-century Washington—and in many other world capitals too—civil society is no longer easily separable from governmental power, a separate privileged and morally superior vantage point to assess its Other. United by common interests and ideals, the two have in many cases become blurred.[43]

ENVIRONMENTAL POLITICS: THE TWILIGHT OF INTERNATIONALISM

As his obituarists would endlessly recall, the essence of Ronald Reagan's message was optimism. Critics felt this optimism was misplaced and saw America entering a world of denial, retreating into itself.

Carnegie Endowment president Thomas Hughes talked about "the twilight of internationalism." Asking what had happened to the American energy to remake the world that had impelled the pacifist millionaire Andrew Carnegie to found the endowment seventy-five years earlier, Hughes assailed Reagan for refusing to acknowledge the jurisdiction of the International Court of Justice, attacking the United Nations, denouncing treaties, and trampling on international law. Reagan was "whistling in the dark," wrote Hughes, as he redirected the force of American "optimism" toward rearmament, lawless interventions abroad, a bloated deficit, and an overvalued dollar.[44] Reagan's supporters took a different view of course, and not only in the field of democracy promotion and the arms race. They saw America returning to a position of world leadership, not withdrawing from it. But there is no question that Reagan's conception of world leadership left little room for the United Nations and handicapped its efforts to exert leadership on a variety of global issues. There was no better illustration of this than the environment.

ONLY TEN YEARS EARLIER, the United States had been leading international environmental policy at the United Nations and seeking to turn the world body into an effective leader on what was an entirely new issue in global affairs. While the postcolonial South looked forward to industrialization, emancipation, and increased prosperity, public opinion in the West was questioning the cult of growth, and asking whether the pursuit of technological and industrial progress had not exacted too great a toll on the environment. "Faith in science and technology has given way to fear of their consequences," noted *Time*.[45] Science fiction mapped the zeitgeist. Philip K. Dick's 1968 novel *Do Androids Dream of Electric Sheep?* envisaged a future in which World War Terminus, fought decades earlier, for reasons no one can remember, has left San Francisco in toxic ruins and ended civilized life on earth: national governments have collapsed, the UN has resettled survivors elsewhere in the solar system, and humanity's long association with the planet has all but ceased. The following year, the *New York Times* reported that student anger over Vietnam was about to be eclipsed by even greater mobilization around "the environmental crisis." Then came the first Earth Day, in 1970, when millions of Americans—a million were estimated to have gathered in Central Park alone—took part in an environmental teach-in that was probably the largest single demonstration in American history.

Environmental fears were connected to older anxieties about global overpopulation that reached their height as neo-Malthusian fears spread and new international programs of population control were disseminated. Demographers had popularized the idea that curbing population growth was a precondition for prosperity; indeed the idea gathered ground that societies only entered modernity once they made the transition to low fertility. World Bank president Robert McNamara stated bluntly that rapidly growing populations were "the greatest single obstacle to economic and social development," and the 1966 United Nations Declaration on Population made much the same point.[46] In 1968, biologist Paul Ehrlich's bestselling *The Population Bomb* warned that hundreds of millions were bound to die of starvation in the coming decade. Secretary-General U Thant told the UN in 1969 that members had only a few years "in which to subordinate their ancient quarrels and launch a global partnership to curb the arms race, to improve the human environment, to defuse the population explosion and to supply the required momentum to development efforts." The Club of Rome's 1972 doom-laden *Limits to Growth* sold nine million copies in twenty-nine countries, using an early computer-generated world systems model to map the association between population, resource depletion, pollution, industrial output, and food. Into the computer went the data; out came exponential population increases, shrinking crop yields, and escalating levels of environmental degradation. Readers lapped up the message: the earth had become a lethal time bomb, primed by man himself.

The policy response at the international level was driven by the

Americans and by President Nixon in particular. Not terribly interested in the issues themselves, Nixon was alive to the potential political payoff. At home, he set up the Environmental Protection Agency and provided the funding that made it the largest civilian agency in the federal government within a few years. Once he realized that this risked losing him conservative votes and the support of corporate America, he decided it was time to "get off the environmental kick."[47] But internationally, different considerations applied, and his commitment lasted longer: there were no domestic votes to lose and plenty to gain in his mind by making America lead on the issue. More practically, American manufacturers were pushing him to toughen up regulation globally since stringent domestic controls would penalize American producers unless other countries fell into line. Contradicting those who advised him that there were no votes in it, Nixon told his chief environment policy adviser, Russell Train, to give the United States a "leadership role" in international discussions. Together with Train he saw environmental matters as a low-key way of consolidating the U.S. relationship with the Soviet Union, but the multilateral agenda was even more important. And this was where an institution like the UN had its uses.[48]

Even before Earth Day, the United Nations General Assembly had decided to hold a major conference on the environment. It was a new venture—the initiative came from the Swedes—for a body that until this point had been more concerned with growth and development. A few protective measures had passed into international law since the war, but most, like the antiwhaling convention of 1946, had achieved little. The 1972 Stockholm conference was headed for the same neglect, until U Thant appointed an energetic Canadian businessman, Maurice Strong, to run it. But in the run-up to the conference itself, it rapidly became clear that not everyone shared the sense of imminent danger. As a Brazilian diplomat stated in 1971:

> Environmental deterioration, as it is currently understood in some developed countries, is a minor localized problem in the developing

> world. . . . Evidently no country wants any pollution at all. But each country must evolve its own development plans, exploit its own resources as it thinks suitable, and define its own environmental standards. The idea of having such priorities and standards imposed on individual countries or groups of countries, on either a multilateral or a bilateral basis, is very hard to accept.

A delegate from the Ivory Coast put it more simply: more pollution would be fine if it meant industrialization.[49]

For all the North-South tensions, the conference itself managed to get environmental protection in the headlines. It produced the usual high-sounding declaration of principles—a grab bag of commitments with something for almost everybody—but its real significance was that it pushed environmental issues up the political agenda in the developed world in particular. After Stockholm, many governments set up ministries along the lines of the American EPA and national environmental legislation proliferated.[50]

Thanks to strong backing from the Americans, a small new UN agency—the UN Environment Program (UNEP)—was created too. Nixon had wanted something more powerful and visible but was slowed by UN turf wars and growing corporate opposition. Yet the case for a dedicated international watchdog unifying, researching, and promoting the cause of the environment had become compelling. None other than George Kennan, architect of America's Cold War containment policy and rarely thought of as an apostle of international organization, wrote in *Foreign Affairs* of the need for an international environmental agency. For Kennan, this was a cause that could bring together the superpowers and supply them both with a mission "to replace the waning fixations of the cold war" and reenthuse a disenchanted younger generation.[51]

UNEP was a tribute to American involvement and to the West's desire to win the support of the developing world: it was decided to headquarter it—a bold step symbolically—in Nairobi. But it was only an initial step: its budget was tiny, initially around $20 million annually—less than one-twentieth of the EPA's—and it lacked anything like the EPA's regulatory powers. The EPA had come about through bottom-up pressure on the American political system; UNEP was the product of a top-down response to international public opinion. The EPA emerged before opposition to it was fully mobilized; UNEP, on the other hand, emerged at a time when that opposition—both from developing countries anxious not to have their own growth derailed and from developed-world corporations—was gathering steam.

In fact, developed-country governments were doing more domestically for the environment in the 1970s than ever before. Green parties did well in northern Europe (even as interest waned in the United States, Japan, France, and the UK), and soaring oil costs in 1973–74 helped make their case for energy efficiency. Able to push things through the European Economic Community more easily than the UN, Europeans started regulating everything from acid rain to noise pollution. Thus the 1970s saw significant environmental diplomacy: as many treaties were drawn up in a single decade as in the previous forty years. One consequence was that the seas became markedly cleaner as agreements were reached to control marine dumping and land-based sources of marine pollution as well. In the Mediterranean, for instance, untreated sewage, industrial effluent, and oil had pushed up pollution to "a critical level." Titanium dioxide was being dumped in its sluggish waters and tourists were coming down with hepatitis. The UNEP played a part in helping turn this around, and under its leadership, Israel and the Arab states, Greece, and Turkey all participated in the cleanup. It was not a route to a larger regional peace. But pollution levels were stabilized, and water cleanliness improved despite the rapid growth of cities and industries around its shores.

At the same time, American public opinion and scientific research propelled international cooperation over the ozone layer. Despite pressure from the aerosol industry, U.S. lawmakers banned CFCs in aerosols, and after American companies protested that any future action needed to be international rather than unilateral, the UN again became heavily involved. UNEP-sponsored research uncovered a vast seasonal hole over Antarctica that was growing each year, and at Montreal late in 1987, UNEP brokered an agreement. It fell short of a total ban. But it was remarkable all the same for being the first time that countries committed themselves by treaty to protect the atmosphere even at some cost to their own economies.[52]

But these achievements, striking though they were, were not matched elsewhere. The fight against the dumping of toxic waste at sea did not fare well. The London Dumping Convention was so ambiguous in its wording that it might have made the situation worse by allowing many of the worst offenders to continue to offend with impunity. And one of the major targets of environmental protest in the West—the nuclear energy industry—was scarcely affected: it was one area where scientists tended to oppose protesters over the question of the risks, whereas they supported action on other issues. There was spectacularly little progress in law of the sea negotiations over mineral resources on the ocean floor, or on desertification. As for the international conference mode pioneered at Stockholm, it was producing less and less the grander it got. Bringing together the development and environmentalist agendas—a necessity if the developing countries were to be brought behind the latter cause, and if Western countries were to fund improved levels of Third World development aid—the main impact of the Brundtland report on *Our Common Future* was to publicize a phrase: "sustainable development."

It is true that the issues were getting tougher to deal with. In 1972, the key environmental concerns were primarily local or national and could be dealt with effectively by willing individual governments, pushed by domestic public opinion. In contrast, later international meetings focused on matters that were regional or global in character—regional water wars, desertification, global poverty, and above all climate change—and achieved almost nothing. Bureaucratic chaos did not help. And the UN Environmental Program, which for all its limitations continued to provide extraordinary value for money, remained too small to be effective. But bureaucratic confusion and the growing complexity and scale of the issues under discussion only hinted at the real problem. Politically, the decisive fact was that the United States had swung dramatically from being the primary promoter of international environmentalism in the 1970s to emerging as its chief opponent.

REAGAN'S OPTIMISM had a history of its own. Even as the Green movement blossomed in America, others had been critical of the endless recitations of doom and preached good news. Economist Kenneth Boulding in a widely read 1966 piece on "The Economics of the Coming Spaceship Earth," accepted that the limitless frontier had been replaced by an understanding of the planet as a single closed system but argued that human ingenuity made it possible to preserve mankind's quality of life. Techno-optimists like Buckminster Fuller viewed science as the world's savior. Vietnam-era America saw a striking intensification in this kind of positive thinking in counterpoint to the pessimists. Much of it came from California, where countercultural entrepreneurs like Stewart Brand, author of the best-selling *Whole Earth Catalog,* saw the planet as an ecological system but possessed a powerful faith in the idea of networks—whether electronic or market-driven—as a liberating force from the tyranny of the institutions of politics and the state. Devotees of the idea of personal empowerment, when the personal computing revolution arrived in the 1990s they were prophets of the coming digital utopia, harbingers of that era's devout faith in the infinite potential of human technology who would go on to become, in late middle age, advocates of the power of corporate philanthropy to tackle the world's ecological problems.[53]

Nuclear strategist Herman Kahn, formerly of the Rand Corporation and the Pentagon, made an unlikely complement to Stewart Brand. Yet both possessed confidence in the openness of the evolutionary process and the transformative power of both capitalism and technology, and prided themselves on their optimism.[54] Kahn, allegedly the prototype for Peter Sellers's Dr. Strangelove, argued that even nuclear war was winnable—a nuclear winter could be survived with the right preparations, he claimed—and enthusiastically fought the pessimists on every front with considerable political success. With Julian Simon, an economist, Kahn wrote *The Resourceful Earth* in 1984 to combat the gloomy forecasts that the Council on Environmental Quality had produced for President Carter. Simon himself was probably the most ardent "doom-slayer" of them all. Arguing that innovation was "the ultimate resource," he made a bet with fellow academic Paul Ehrlich of the *The Population Bomb* that the price of commodities would fall rather than rise during the 1980s—and won. But Simon and Kahn won more than that: with the victory of President Reagan, many of their ideas on everything from the possibilities of entrepreneurial individualism to the winnability of nuclear war entered the bloodstream of the administration. "A decade ago doomsters painted a chilly picture of a planet ticketed for disaster," noted *US News & World Report* in 1983. Now what seemed to lie ahead "could well be a renaissance for the US in political prestige and technological power."[55]

Reagan's election was a rout for the neo-Malthusians, the end of the road for the Club of Rome purveyors of gloom. Domestically, his administration rolled back legislation from the previous decade and slashed the EPA budget by a third in two years. Yet popular environmental consciousness was by now deeply entrenched in the developed world, and his assault on the new regulatory apparatus in fact prompted more Americans to join conservation groups. When asked by pollsters, Americans for the first time ranked a clean environment above a good sex life. Huge numbers of Americans were now members of the major Green NGOs, and their own lobbying prowess, if not a match for the money available to the corporations, was still sufficient to stall a really serious counteroffensive at home.

Internationally, however, Reagan's administration led a wholesale retreat from environmental protectionism at the very moment when Green politics was on the rise almost everywhere. In eastern

Europe—thrown into turmoil by a series of communist planning failures of which Chernobyl was the worst—environmental protest groups played an important part in hastening the collapse of Soviet power. In Brazil, Central America, eastern Africa, and India, coalitions of farmers began to mobilize politically and to forge connections to Western environmental NGOs. In fact, environmental NGOs were the fastest-growing of all categories of NGOs in the 1980s. Yet none of this had any traction in American domestic politics, and there was virtually no lobby for environmental internationalism in Washington. On the contrary, as Congress turned ever more hostile to the UN, the forces bearing down on the Reagan White House prompted an increasingly critical approach to international institutions.

Reagan appointees openly scorned multilateral environmental initiatives for their excessive "doom and gloom." The administration withdrew from the jurisdiction of the International Court of Justice, an important forum for the settlement of environment-related disputes It also quit UNESCO and undermined the Law of the Sea Convention. Opposed to regulation on principle, its overall philosophy was conveyed to Congress in 1982 by administration appointee Richard Funkhouser, an oil specialist and former diplomat who had been made the director of the EPA's Office of International Activities. According to Funkhouser, it was pessimism that led to the mistaken reliance on government, optimism that promoted scientific and technological breakthroughs:

> The US is committed to the premise that the free market approach can play a constructive role in the protection of the environment though it may need to be accompanied by complementary government action. Technological innovation and economic incentives are the foundation for the resolution of future environmental problems. . . . There must be more optimism and credence given to the roles and contributions of science, technology and human ingenuity, in addressing environmental and resource problems.[56]

What Reagan started, George H. W. Bush and Bill Clinton continued, as the United States abandoned its role as global environmental leader. At the UN's disappointingly unfruitful major environmental conference in Rio de Janeiro in 1992, the U.S. stood in the way of accords to protect the world's wetlands and forests: about the only environmental issues on which it joined in were banning CFCs and protecting the Antarctic. The Clinton administration preferred to work through the World Bank—an "ecological Frankenstein," as it was dubbed by opponents—and turned international environmental politics into an adjunct of the development debate, a move encouraged by Congress's increasingly anti-UN direction. The UNEP was doomed to an endless round of meetings, but efforts to reform it—either by increasing its powers or doing away with it altogether—got nowhere: it remained a small, fragile, poorly funded, and marginalized body.[57] Meanwhile, the antiscientific mood inside the United States intensified. The *New York Times* might describe the environment, as it did on the twentieth anniversary of Earth Day, as "a modern secular religion." But in a way that was the problem: protecting the environment was now being reinterpreted as a matter of belief rather than science, and there were plenty whose faith led them in another direction entirely.

The cause of global warming was perhaps the most important casualty. Created by UNEP and the World Meteorological Organization, the Intergovernmental Panel on Climate Change has become one of the largest and best-funded scientific programs in history and certainly the most international in scope, its forecasts increasingly authoritative. It is a testimony to the century-old vision of scientific universalism, but also a reminder of its political limits. For while European governments pressed for action as early as 1990, the Reagan and Bush administrations temporized, and under George W. Bush the United States opposed ratification of the Kyoto Climate Change Convention, the biodiversity convention, and the Law of the Sea Convention, among others. American obstruction is not the only reason for the lengthy gestation and subsequent difficulties of the

Kyoto Protocol. But it is a continuing reminder of the decisive move away from multilateralism that has taken place since the late 1970s, and of the continued role of American domestic politics in framing the possibilities for concerted international governance. Where Congress pushed—as in the realm of human rights promotion—American internationalism developed and mutated. Where it objected and resisted—as in the realm of the environment—it languished. The memory of Woodrow Wilson, so ardently evoked by Moynihan, carried a double message.

CHAPTER 12

The Real New International Economic Order

> We all had the feeling it could come apart in quite a serious way. As I saw it, it was a choice between Britain remaining in the liberal financial system of the West as opposed to a radical change of course because we were concerned about Tony Benn precipitating a policy decision by Britain to turn its back on the IMF. I think that if that had happened the whole system would have begun to come apart. God knows what Italy might have done; then France might have taken a radical change for the same direction. It would not only have had consequences for economic recovery, it would have had great political consequences. So we tended to see it in cosmic terms.
>
> —senior U.S. State Department official William D. Rogers, on British negotiations with the IMF in 1976[1]

AFTER 1945, American leadership had been critical in salvaging international capitalism from the wreckage of the interwar depression. The League's greatest failure had been in the realm of international economic cooperation; as a result, remedying this became a priority at Bretton Woods. The institutions that emerged there—the World Bank and the International Monetary Fund—replaced the failed, weak bodies that had existed under the League of Nations with more powerful and influential agencies that were able to oversee financial markets and to prevent a return to monetary anarchy and protectionism. Washington's wartime vision was not fully realized: the International Trade Organization so dear to the heart of Cordell Hull failed to materialize, and the central bankers' club, the Bank for International Settlements, which was supposed to be dissolved, in fact survived. Nevertheless, the new institutions—and others—buttressed a period of extraordinary prosperity in the West.[2]

Geographically, American economic power after 1945 was not dispersed equally across the globe. The old interwar hemispheric connection was overshadowed by two new nodal points, both with military occupations at their heart: Japan became the nucleus of an East Asian regional trading system, and even more importantly, there was the rapidly recovering and integrating west European economy, with West Germany as the manufacturing dynamo and the City of London as the major financial center. This new U.S.–western Europe–Japan power bloc, although not invulnerable, was easily a match not only for the USSR and its satellites—much larger in extent but far weaker industrially—but for the emergent South as well.

Yet in the early 1970s, after twenty-five years of the most sustained and most equitable growth ever seen, the cohesion of this power bloc was tested. Productivity slowed in the developed world and distributional conflicts intensified. Internationally, America's previously unassailable dominance of world manufacturing and trade started crumbling even before the cost of financing the Vietnam War forced the dollar off the gold standard. Then came the OPEC crisis. Twenty years earlier, a U.S. State Department report had warned Secretary of State Dulles that "with the center of gravity of the world's oil moving from the United States to the Middle East, matters of price and supply may eventually be determined in the Arab world and the unpleasant day may come when Arab states can double oil prices and get away with it."[3] In the first oil shock of 1973, soaring fuel costs plunged the world economy into the first serious recession since the Korean War and the struggle against inflation and rising unemployment was joined. A new word appeared—"stagflation"—to describe the unprecedented and still mysterious fact that for the first time inflation did not seem to diminish when growth slowed and unemployment rose.

It was at precisely this time of troubles as we have seen, that the emergent Third World demanded a New International Economic Order. The terrifying worry to Washington was that differing European and American responses to this demand might break up the politico-economic alliance upon which the postwar revival of capitalism and the emergence of the United States as a global power had been based. In retrospect, such a fear seems almost preposterously overblown. Yet it did exist, and its existence pointed not only to the scale of the American achievement in reconstructing global capitalism since 1945, but to its speed. What had been built so quickly could perhaps fall apart equally fast. Never did the early 1930s seem so close as in the early 1970s.

Moynihan had argued in his seminal 1975 article, "The United States in Opposition" that the real foe was not Bolshevism (he concurred with Kennan on its weakness and unattractiveness as a model) but the global appeal of British socialism. Perhaps only someone who had (as he had) been educated at the London School of Economics could have seriously asserted that the Third World's call for global justice was the result of the Fabian tradition lingering on in the former colonies long after the Union Jack had come down. But from that perspective, the clash inside western Europe in the 1970s between business and organized labor, a clash which it was far from clear at that time that business would win, took on an entirely new—indeed a "cosmic"—meaning. If Britain moved far to the left, as seemed perfectly possible, and if Europe reached out to the Third World and turned its back on Washington because it no longer feared the threat of Soviet invasion, then what would remain of the alliances that had been built up since 1945? The United States would be alone once more, feeling the tug of isolation from the heartlands. An American assessment at this time described the prospect of Britain pulling out of its diplomatic and military commitments as "the greatest single threat to the Western world."[4]

The sterling crisis of 1976 is rarely remembered today outside British Labour Party circles. Yet it was a critical moment in the emergence of a new financially based form of American internationalism. In London, Labour prime minister Harold Wilson had unexpectedly resigned, leading to a bitter leadership struggle that pitted the party's powerful left wing against the pro-Americans. The oil crisis had caused a rapid deterioration in the balance of payments and a full-blown sterling crisis. The leftists in the cabinet wanted increased protectionism, exchange controls, and domestic reflation even if this meant moving against the powerful City of London. The new prime minister, James Callaghan, and Chancellor of the Exchequer Denis Healey were Atlanticists who were in favor of negotiations with the IMF, which had already provided temporary assistance. Further help, however, would only come with strings attached. When they prevailed, it was much more than a defeat for the British left, the unions, and the working class. It was the first step in the capitalist reconstruction of the West.[5]

Neoliberalism is a convenient label for what followed: the rejection of the postwar social corporatism that had underpinned Western growth, the turn to monetarism and to deregulation. But what it all amounted to was the construction of a New International Economic Order—mostly Made in the United States—that easily rebuffed the Third World version, set the Atlantic alliance on a powerful new footing, and remade the rules of the global economy. Some of this was planned; much was unforeseen. But thanks to the financialization of the American domestic economy, which became a vast recycling mechanism for global capital surpluses passing through Wall Street, unfettered capital flows became the new norm. And as a world of creditors and debtors required different institutions from one of producers and consumers, new sources of institutional authority emerged and old ones declined. Washington assigned a new global role to the IMF in particular, even as it withdrew support from much of the rest of the UN. In this way, within twenty years, the crisis of the West was turned into a new model of world governance. It even had its own ideology: globalization.[6]

BANKERS ABROAD

In the 1970s, there was more money, moving faster and less controllably than ever before. The world was awash in petrodollars as a result of the oil exporters' cartel OPEC's success, and this large OPEC windfall searched for lending opportunities. At this time the total funds in the global financial system amounted to approximately $165 billion, of which some $35 billion were lent each year. Suddenly oil revenues amounting to almost $100 billion made their way to banks and other investors in the developed world. The question was, would these enormous surpluses, which dwarfed the normal amounts of capital available for lending, be recycled by public or private lenders?

Private bankers bid for the business: led by Walter Wriston of First National City Bank, they lobbied Washington to remove restrictions on U.S. bank lending overseas. The Treasury, run first by George Shultz and then by William E. Simon—both committed free marketeers—was sympathetic and loosened capital export controls. "After that you could scarcely find a banker at home," commented an economist. International lending had provided one-third of the profits of the major U.S. banks in 1973; by 1976, it provided three-quarters. European and Japanese banks hastened to compete and so did brokers, mutual funds, the first hedge funds, and a range of other financial institutions. Wriston and others were on a high: "countries don't go bust," he famously asserted. His First National City Bank was renamed Citibank, and together with J.P. Morgan it took the lead, arranging many of the syndicated loans to mostly South American borrowers.[7]

The new "casino capitalism" (the phrase comes from one of the phenomenon's most acute observers, Susan Strange) unleashed by the mass of petrodollars was a bonanza for the banks and a new challenge for national governments and for the IMF too. While Congress worried about the impact on the balance sheets of U.S. banks, large sums flowed across borders, beyond anyone's control. Floating exchange rates turned out to be susceptible to speculative raids. For economies like the British mired in recession, defending the exchange rate was almost impossible.[8]

The IMF's managing director at the time of the British sterling crisis was Johannes Witteveen, an economist who had spent most of his career in the Dutch central planning bureau, and was not therefore by temperament or training a free marketeer. U.S. treasury secretary William E. Simon certainly was. He had been disturbed by the growing encroachment of the state on private enterprise at home and abroad, watching in horror as government spending as a proportion of national income rose sharply everywhere in the developed world from the early 1960s. As a staunch advocate of unfettered capitalism and as treasury secretary under both Nixon and Ford, Simon was determined to reverse this trend, and he understood the oil crisis and its reverberations as an opportunity as well as a challenge. Above all, he understood how an international institution such as the IMF could be reshaped to become a global enforcer of fiscal discipline.[9]

Until this point, the IMF had played a surprisingly minor role in international affairs. The Americans at Bretton Woods had not wanted unrestricted capital flows—they distinguished between "productive" and "speculative" flows, and even after the OECD codified some liberalization of capital movements in 1961, it remained entirely normal for countries to impose controls when they felt it necessary. The IMF's original function was providing liquidity to overcome dollar shortages and watching over the functioning of international balances of payments and exchange rates. Because capital mobility was restricted, it mostly tided developed nations over temporary balance-of-payments difficulties caused by overheated economies, the scarcity of dollars, or unfortunate shifts in the terms of trade. It made few demands on its borrowers to change their domestic policies and was sympathetic to their need for growth. And it had very little to do with the developing economies of the Third World.

In the mid-1970s, amid fears that monetary instability might trigger off another Great Depression, the IMF took on more systemic responsibility, managing the precarious new regime of floating exchange rates in an agreement brokered by the Americans and the French that gave it a mandate to "exercise firm surveillance" over members' exchange rate policies. The U.S. Congress was unhappy at the possibility of the IMF overseeing American policy but was eventually persuaded when a Treasury official warned of a return to the "beggar-thy-neighbor policies" of the 1930s if monetary matters were left to the market. Simon himself, despite his free-market beliefs, could see the need for institutional intervention. The first meeting of the future G-7 in Rambouillet in 1975 blessed the change, and thus demonstrated the importance of the new body and of international monetary policy for the restoration of Western unity.[10]

"Firm surveillance" meant different things to different people, even within the IMF. But the 1976 sterling crisis clarified what it meant for Simon, and clarified it for the British as well, who found themselves having to negotiate simultaneously with the U.S. Treasury and the IMF team that flew into London. If borrowing countries could not be trusted to carry out the necessary internal adjustment by themselves, the IMF would tell them how. And the first thing that meant was prioritizing the struggle against inflation over growth, setting limits to the public-sector budget deficit, forcing the government to accept higher levels of unemployment, and advising on tax increases and the exchange rate level.[11] Thus began the long era of the IMF as cruel doctor of fiscal health, providing loans that were only granted on condition that the recipients cut public spending, set fiscal and later monetary targets, and pledge not to impose new tariffs or capital controls. The IMF became not merely a funder but an engineer at the global level of significant domestic policy changes. Once it had tasted the power of "conditionality," there was no turning back. In the 1970s only 26 percent of IMF loans involved substantial conditionality; by the late 1980s the figure had risen to 66 percent. Even God only gave Moses *ten* commandments, the veteran IMF economist Jacques Polak later commented in astonishment as the number of conditions multiplied. Through increasingly radical interventions over an ever-expanding geographical area, the institution turned into a powerful sponsor of global financial deregulation.[12]

The money that benefited from this was sucked into the United States by high interest rates and recycled around the world by Wall Street investors and banks. Despite soaring American inflation and chronic deficits, the IMF did not intervene in the United States itself and left it to the Federal Reserve under Paul Volcker to restore the confidence of foreign investors in the dollar.[13] With money cheap, inflation reduced, and credit easy, private as well as public indebtness skyrocketed as rates came down, new financial instruments were invented, and American companies and individuals took advantage of new means of borrowing: household debt averaged a prudent 65 percent of disposable income in 1981; by 2008 it had grown to 135 percent. The financial sector was even more unrestrained: as a proportion of GDP its debt rose from 22 percent in 1981 to 117 percent by 2008.[14]

The increasing openness of global money markets—reinforced by growing pressure from the IMF and the OECD on countries to do away with capital controls—locked banks across the world into their current precarious interdependence. The value of the stock of foreign assets as a percentage of GDP rose for a large sample of countries from 36 pecent in 1980 to 71 percent in 1995 and exceeded 100 percent in the new millennium.[15] The value of foreign exchange traded in international money markets easily surpassed the total foreign exchange reserves of all governments. Moreover, the identity of the lenders changed over time in ways that made managing any crisis harder: governments, the principal lenders in the 1950s and 1960s, had given way to banks participating in syndicated loans in the late 1970s and by the 1990s to the purchasers of international debt securities. The United States gave up the attempt to regulate the Eurodollar market by 1980 in the face of resistance from rival financial centers, and this opened the way to a spate of further financial deregulation.[16]

It was thus both unsurprising and deeply worrying that as foreign indebtedness rose sharply, it precipitated increasingly frequent currency crises that proved ever more contagious and difficult to manage. Between 1945 and 1971 there were just thirty-eight banking or currency crises globally; between 1973 and 1997 there were 139. There were no banking crises in the developing world in the earlier period and only sixteen currency crises; after 1973 there were seventeen banking crises, fifty-seven currency crises, and twenty-one combined. As *Financial Times* columnist Martin Wolf has noted, "the age of financial liberalization was . . . an age of crisis."[17]

One kind of instability in the 1970s, floating exchange rates in the developed world, was thus replaced by another in the 1980s and 1990s, Third World sovereign debt. It was primarily in the context of the management of these international debt crises that the IMF emerged as the lead agency. President Reagan had been far from supportive of the IMF when he entered office, and some of his most senior officials were strong opponents, as they were of any international organization. Seeing foreign debt crises close up and realizing the havoc they could create with the U.S. banking system changed their minds. In the 1982 debt crisis in Mexico—described later by the Fed as "a threat of financial disorder on a global scale not seen since the Depression"—Paul Volcker urged the IMF to become "bankruptcy judge on a grand international scale." The reason was not so much to protect Mexico as to prevent a massive banking collapse that would have caused the entire global recycling mechanism to seize up.[18] The U.S. Treasury hid behind the Federal Reserve and the Fed hid behind the IMF, which thus provided valuable political cover for the U.S. officials who were the ones really dictating terms. A consistent laissez-faire position would in fact have allowed lenders to assume their own risk and suffer heavier losses, and there was strong and persistent congressional criticism along these lines. But Congress did not get very far, and from the early 1980s onward, Wall Street's interest was usually equated with the national interest in the minds of administration officials. More than 60 percent of all emerging market debt trading by 1994 was in paper backed by U.S. Treasury bonds, a sign of their importance in keeping the system liquid.[19]

The IMF's critical role in these arrangements was obvious. Other bodies played a role—notably the central bankers' association, the Bank for International Settlements. Codes of capital liberalization originated in the developed world, drawn up in bodies such as the OECD and the European Community. But the IMF was instrumental in globalizing them. Moreover, as an international organization, the IMF had a better chance of persuading South American or East Asian governments to push through unpopular political domestic reforms than the U.S. Treasury would have had. As one Republican senator emphasized in 1984, "If the United States were to embark on a very heavy-handed effort to try to change domestic policies within recipient countries, we would be viewed as the ugly American. But when the international community as a whole does so, then I think real changes can be put into place, and that is what is needed in a lot of those countries."[20]

But the IMF could only act as a buffer and enabler of American power in this way so long as it was regarded as both legitimate and authoritative. Fidelity to its founding articles and respect for the voice of the non-American members of its governing board were critical in this respect. Yet the extraordinary widening in its activities—from surveillance to an ever more intrusive set of demands and conditions—strained its claim to legitimacy. Although the IMF was routinely urging the liberalization of capital controls, its founding articles provided no warrant for such advice. This did not worry the U.S. Treasury very much—which was prepared to push the IMF to do many things that it would have preferred not to—but it did bother European members of the board, who sought a "managed globalization" on the basis of rules. Through the early 1990s, efforts were made to draft an amendment to ensure the constitutionality of what the IMF was now routinely demanding of debtors. One can chart the concern over the growing power and ambition of the IMF in the struggle over this amendment. Opposition to it united Third World governments and Wall Street banks, both of which were suspicious of any enhancement of the IMF's power. More telling, perhaps, was the criticism from its own former director of research Jacques Polak, then in his eighties. Polak, a Dutch economist, had seen close up the evolution of efforts to stabilize an open international economy since the 1930s. He had started out at the League of Nations before the Second World War, continuing with the economics section when it was transferred to Princeton in 1940, and participated in Bretton Woods and UNRRA: he thus had precisely the long historical macroeconomic perspective that most in the Fund lacked. Already worried at the direction the Fund was headed in, he feared that giving it the legal authority to demand capital liberalization would lead to it making even more ambitious demands, thus further eroding trust in the developing world. By 1998 opposition to the amendment had grown so powerful that it was scrapped.[21]

As for the authority the IMF derived from its expertise, this too came under strain as a result of the extraordinary expansion of its role. American power expressed itself not only in its control of institutions but even more in the successful spreading of its ideas about what knowledge was. Nowhere was this more obviously true than in the realm of economics. Modernization theory had been suffused with economics but had borrowed eclectically from other disciplines too: its basic framework was, after all, historical. But most of the economists in the IMF had little interest in history, nor in the other social sciences. Its staffers were mostly male, and almost entirely economists, trained in American and English universities. Entering the IMF and the World Bank in the 1980s, they were rational-expectations revolutionaries who based their prescriptions on in-house templates couched in the language of the highly formalized mathematical models that the profession was coming to prize. Practitioners of perhaps the most successful single discipline in the postwar American university, they existed in a state of more or less total ignorance of the cultures, languages, or institutions of the countries they had been told to cure, having been trained, as many economists still are, to believe that this ignorance—being a matter of "exogenous variables"—did not matter. The substance of their approach coalesced in the form of the so-called Washington Consensus, a phrase coined in 1989 by the economist John Williamson to identify a cluster of prescriptions: avoidance of large fiscal deficits; curtailment of government subsidies; liberalization of trade and investment regimes; privatization of nationalized forms; and deregulation. If development economics had been premised on the possibility that backward economies might need a different set of prescriptions to advanced ones, the new dogma assumed that universal virtue resided in the market. Its proponents had little time for alternatives: the choice, according to a Brazilian central banker in the 1990s, was "to be neo-liberal or neo-idiotic." Ironically, their psychological attitude to the world was almost identical to that of the modernization theorists of the 1960s: possessed of equal belief in the transformative power of their ideas, they now set about dismantling much of the work of an earlier generation of advisers. As one economist put it, what was needed was an approach that would be "disruptive on an historically unprecedented scale."[22]

The consequence was an extraordinary transformation of property relations throughout the world. With startling speed, water, electricity, coal, trains, and buses were among the nationalized industries sold off: in the developed world, the water supply and other public goods were often handed over to private corporations. These ran more than 80 percent of the French water supply by 2000 (up from 32 percent in the 1950s; in England, Chile, and the Czech Republic they served the entire population). Powerful unions like the British National Union of Miners were smashed and impediments to the investment and repatriation of capital removed. As a proportion of global GDP, the share of state-owned enterprises fell from above 10 percent in 1979 to under 6 percent in 2004—in the UK alone the drop was from 12 percent to 2 percent—while more than $1.25 trillion was raised from privatization worldwide.[23] The economic consequences remain highly debatable—there is still no consensus that productivity actually improved as a result—but the profits to those managing the process and the damaging broader social consequences in terms of income inequality and its consequences were obvious. Some two thousand government concerns were dissolved in seven years in South America alone, many of them either passing into the hands of foreign corporations or making the fortunes of a new class of superbillionaires like Mexico's Carlos Slim. In 1987 there was one billionaire in Mexico; by 1995, helped by the privatization of one thousand state industries, there were twenty-four. Yet in the same period, real wages slumped. It was, writes historian Greg Grandin, nothing short of the "third conquest of Latin America."[24]

Across the Soviet bloc, something similar happened, only in an even more acute and dramatic form as access to Western capital and soaring indebtedness brought about first the collapse of communism and then led to further massive economic restructuring after it was gone. Harvard's brightest economists, having won their spurs in South America and Poland, were invited by Russia's president, Boris Yeltsin, to advise on reform. Their approach was as totalizing, as driven and as rushed as that of the earlier generation of modernization theorists. Back in the 1960s, Walt Rostow had called for a "sustained lift-off" into growth; now the liberalizers called for a "big bang" to establish a functioning market economy. "What Is to Be Done?" was the Leninist-sounding title of economist Jeffrey Sachs's article in the *Economist* in early 1990 calling for "shock therapy." The Russians got the deregulation and the unemployment without the billions in foreign aid and welfare safety net Sachs had hoped would cushion the blow, and the results were to turn a previously egalitarian society into a deeply unequal one plagued by poverty. While the privatization of land may have helped cushion the plummeting living standards of many ordinary Russians in the countryside, the resultant selloff of the country's industrial and mineral base created a new class of fabulously wealthy "oligarchs." Meanwhile, national income collapsed and so did life expectancy. A widening income gap created the nostalgia for the days of the Soviet Union that helped propel Vladimir Putin to power. The chief political analyst at the U.S. embassy in Moscow at this time later recalled:

> The U.S. government chose the economic over the political. We chose the freeing of prices, privatization of industry and the creation of a really unfettered, unregulated capitalism, and essentially hoped that the rule of law, civil society and representative democracy would develop somehow automatically out of that.[25]

The impact of the neoliberal experiment could be gauged by comparing China's development over the same period—a doubling of GDP, rapidly shrinking poverty, and immunity to the financial crises that convulsed the international monetary system during the 1990s. China's starting point was very different, obviously, to that of Russia. Nevertheless, the reversal in their fortunes was striking. In 1989, Soviet GDP was estimated to be approximately $2.7 trillion, roughly half that of the United States but about six times the Chinese total GDP of $451 billion; by 1999 the Chinese figure had risen to over $1 trillion, and by 2009 it was close to an astonishing $5 trillion while Russian GDP—even after some years of rapid growth—was still only $1.2 trillion in 2009 (and even adding in the other former Soviet republics was unlikely to have topped $2 trillion). If shock therapy had not actually killed the patient, it had come very close.[26]

THE CRITICS had seen it coming. In September 1982 the outgoing Mexican president, José López Portillo—Mexico was particularly vulnerable to American financial experimentation—publicly denounced "the financing plague . . . wreaking greater and greater havoc throughout the world," and the "witchdoctors" (in the IMF) with their "blind hegemoniacal egoism." In the 1990s, as structural adjustment spread, this kind of criticism mounted.[27] Even internal reviews found it surprisingly hard to point unambiguously to positive results from the Fund's frequent interventions. Critics argued that its policy was flawed on various grounds. For some, better economics, combined with greater outreach to borrowers and to knowledgeable NGOs, might result in a more humane and more effective lending. For others, the validity of economics as the sole metric was in question: if institutions, values, and culture actually shaped outcomes, should not loan conditions include attempts to modify social policies, institutional behavior, and even cultural practices? But inside the IMF adaptation came slowly. Its staff had a hard time accepting that a crisis was not always the fault of the borrower but rather of the way markets were functioning. Market irrationality was not something IMF staffers liked to think too much about; they preferred to think of it as self-correcting exuberance. Most of them were also poorly equipped intellectually to think through the possibility that their own policies were themselves making things worse, whether through the slacker regulation of global financial markets, or by precipitating downward deflationary spirals through unnecessarily harsh austerity programs, or, worst of all, by the deficiencies of their own disciplinary formation.

The IMF's ascendancy was only really checked as a result of its handling of the 1997 East Asian crisis, which spread with astonishing speed from Thailand to Indonesia, South Korea, the Philippines, and Malaysia, eventually bringing down the Suharto government and leading to a staggering 33 percent drop in South Korean GDP in 1998. The countries themselves bore a huge share of the resulting adjustment, while private banks took a loss of an estimated $60 billion. When it applied its usual medicine there, however, the IMF itself emerged diminished in stature, attacked from all sides.

Even the very men who had supported its deployment twenty years earlier now came out publicly against it. In February 1998, George Shultz, William E. Simon, and Walter Wriston jointly authored an article in the *Wall Street Journal* entitled "Who Needs the IMF?" Taking issue with hedge fund manager George Soros, who argued that the private sector was not an efficient means of allocating credit internationally, the three American notables pushed their liberal principles further than ever before. There was no problem with markets or the allocation of information, they wrote. The real problem had become moral hazard. Financialization had gone further than any of them had dreamed of, yet not only was the IMF not doing anything to check it, but the very possibility of an IMF bailout had come to distort the risks for both borrowers and lenders. They concluded, "The IMF is ineffective, unnecessary and obsolete. We do not need another IMF, as Mr. Soros recommends. Once the Asian crisis is over, we should abolish the one we have."[28]

Their demand thus echoed the fundamental question often posed by a skeptical Congress: did America still need international intergovernmental institutions? After all, many of the most powerful institutions underpinning the operation of the global financial system were far more informal. Credit risk assessment, for instance, had been largely handed over—thanks to the imprimatur of the U.S. Securities and Exchange Commission and the acquiescence of everybody else—to two major private U.S. ratings agencies, Moody's and Standard & Poor's, that had started out in the nineteenth century assessing railways. They were newcomers to international risk evaluation (as late as 1980 they routinely rated only about eleven sovereigns), yet the entire system of global finance was based on the assumption that they knew what they were doing. Only a few critical studies pointed out some of the problems with the mixture of guesswork, statistics, and ideological preferences that constituted their methodology.[29]

Things had changed enormously over the twenty years since Simon and Shultz had run the U.S. Treasury, of course, notably the shift from brokering intergovernmental lending to trying to keep track of the vast and increasingly rapid flows of the private sector. But the fundamental argument *for* the IMF, and the one that kept it afloat even through the most hostile Congress in living memory, remained unchanged. Precisely because of its intergovernmental character, it allowed the United States to exert an influence it would otherwise have found impossible to acquire; at the same time, it made it easier for the politicians of debtor governments to enact unpopular domestic policies. The payoff for Washington was enormous. While for the rest of the world, financialization brought the discipline of the market and the risk of surveillance, for the United States it brought apparently unlimited inflows of capital and an abundance of credit. Stabilizing this system with the aid of the IMF was a small price to pay. The IMF itself was still, in the admiring words of a 1999 *Time* article, the "fire brigade" of the "Three Musketeers" who comprised the "Committee to Save the World": U.S. treasury secretary Robert Rubin, Fed Reserve chairman Alan Greenspan, and Rubin's deputy at Treasury, Larry Summers. New rules of the game defined by the world's most powerful states; a powerful intergovernmental institution empowered to enforce them—on such statist foundations rested the liberalization of global finance.[30]

ORGANIZING WORLD TRADE

In the autumn of 1981 President Reagan arrived at Cancún, where his host was the same José López Portillo who would quit the Mexican presidency so furiously the following year. An official photographer captured the new American president, seated in his shirtsleeves at the end of a row of dignitaries with the pale blue waters of the Caribbean behind them. Next to him is the foreign minister of the Ivory Coast, behind him the president of Yugoslavia. François Mitterrand, Kurt Waldheim, and Indira Gandhi are there too, together with Zhao Ziyang of China and Crown Prince Fahd of Saudi Arabia. Of all the participants, only Mrs. Thatcher would have liked the message Reagan delivered, for even before the financial revolution had really gotten under way, he was about to signal a radical change of course in North-South relations.

By the start of the 1980s, G-77 calls for a New International Economic Order were languishing, and former German chancellor Willi

Brandt himself believed a large transfer of resources from the wealthy North to the impoverished South was essential and needed to be routed through international organizations to meet the South's demands. In fact it was at Brandt's behest that the Cancún meeting had been called. Writing this off as an attempt to globalize the values of European social democracy, Reagan saw it quite differently. Noting that in the United States "our government has overspent, overtaxed, and overregulated," he made it clear that international organizations were equally problematic and that he was opposed to setting up "some gigantic new international bureaucracy." He did not criticize the United Nations, but the only institutions he singled out for praise were the World Bank—now in its post-McNamara swing back to fiscal conservatism—and especially the International Monetary Fund. Above all, Reagan connected development to the cause of economic freedom, private investment, and the liberalization of world trade. At a time when trade as a proportion of U.S. GDP had doubled in a decade (in 1970 total imports and exports had amounted to under 11 percent of GDP, lower than the figure in 1929; by 1980 this had risen to over 20 percent), this amounted to a redefinition of development itself, placing trade back at the heart of American internationalism. Foreign aid as a proportion of U.S. GDP now dropped away to record lows. Instead, as trade grew, so did the country's deficit: dollars were now being recycled abroad chiefly through the deteriorating trade balance.[31]

Reagan's speech spelled the end of the Third World's New International Economic Order and with it of any hope for a new powerful UN agency to redistribute resources globally. President Clinton continued what Reagan started, and it was under the Clinton administration in particular that trade liberalization became the watchword of U.S. foreign policy and that a brand-new World Trade Organization was created in 1995 to promote this. The new body—a striking political achievement considering the growing suspicion of multilateral institutions on Capitol Hill in those years—came close to realizing what American policymakers had hoped for nearly half a century earlier when developing-country opposition, combined with lack of any real support from the war-torn economies of Europe, had doomed the original International Trade Organization to failure, even before it fell in Congress. Since then the General Agreement on Tariffs and Trade had proven its durability. Now commentators hailed GATT's metamorphosis into the WTO as another sign of capitalism's continued advance: the Berlin Wall had come down, communism was defeated, and there was a new global agreement to preserve free trade.

But at what price? There was a certain symbolism in the fact that the new organization was headquartered on the shores of Lake Geneva in an opulent neo-Florentine villa that had once housed the International Labor Organization. Paintings from the 1920s still decorated the walls—*The Dignity of Labor, Plowing the Soil,* and *Work in Abundance*—harking back to the very different priorities of an earlier era. Between the two world wars, capitalists had worried about money and trade but they had had to worry too about workers and their allegiances. By 1995, the Soviet Union had collapsed and the workers of the world no longer really worried anyone in power.

Like GATT, and unlike the new UN agency that Brandt had hoped for, the WTO was essentially a club of the developed world. It was secretive, and most of its decisions were made in a smoke-filled Green Room from which journalists, public, and even many of the WTO's own members were excluded. It talked the language of globalization, but this was a globalization that emanated from the North and remained under its control: yet the model was attractive enough for both Russia and China to seek to join, accepting some liberalization of their own economies in return for access to the markets of the West. It was a new kind of international organization—regulatory and thinly staffed, capable chiefly of brokering and enforcing agreements. Like the OECD, its chief role was in establishing new commercial norms, and the growing importance, for instance, of international commercial arbitration—and hence the increasing role of private lawyers in trade—was one of its achievements. Emerging as it did at a time of global growth, its supporters were euphoric. Renato "Rocky" Ruggiero, the Italian businessman who became its third head, predicted the eradication of global poverty within a few years if trade liberalization continued. "We are no longer writing the rules of interaction among separate national economies," he declared in 1996, speaking before an audience of UNCTAD delegates. "We are writing the constitution of a single global economy." Che and Prebisch would have been appalled.[32]

It sounded like the fulfillment of Volcker's desire, articulated nearly two decades earlier, not only to see off the disintegration of the world economy but to manage its reintegration. Indeed, the WTO's emergence looked for a moment like *the* great institutional expression of the globalization era, banishing memories of the ITO failure of half a century earlier. To its numerous critics, on the other hand, the emergence of the WTO simply created the third of an "Unholy Trinity" of global economic institutions to set alongside the World Bank and the IMF. Coming on top of growing concern at the role of the IMF, the WTO became another focal point for an increasingly powerful counterglobalization movement. It did not help also that it was soon plunged into a debilitating succession struggle over the appointment of its director-general. And the mood soured as developing countries dug in their heels over a raft of proposals that seemed designed too obviously to promote American and European interests: the ghost of UNCTAD was stirring.

Most debilitating of all was the return of unilateralism after 2001 under George W. Bush. The Bush administration lumped the WTO in with all the other multilateral institutions it disliked and threatened to bypass it in a series of bilateral and regional treaties—precisely the time-consuming process GATT and the WTO had been intended to circumvent in the first place. "Nobody wants to invest political capital in global institutions," declared a journalist for the *Washington Post,* in a piece on "Why Globalization Has Stalled." In July 2006, the new WTO chief, Pascal Lamy, declared trade talks officially suspended.[33]

GLOBALIZATION: FOR AND AGAINST

Only six years earlier, President Clinton had delivered a State of the Union address that even by the standards of the genre was unusually euphoric. "We are fortunate to be alive at this moment in history," the president had proclaimed in January 2000. "Never before has our nation enjoyed, at once, so much prosperity and social progress with so little internal crisis and so few external threats." Hard work and prudent domestic policy had been partly responsible for this. But the achievement reflected Americans' willingness to embrace what Clinton called "the central reality of our time"—globalization.[34] This was, in his words, "the revolution that is tearing down barriers and building new networks among nations and individuals, and economies and cultures."

That this term, which had come to assume totemic significance, had achieved such popularity when it had been virtually unknown twenty years earlier was a striking illustration of the triumph of the American New International Economic Order. In 1983, a Harvard Business School professor named Ted Levitt had published an influential article on "The Globalization of Markets" in which he argued that the world had become a single market, with a single set of desires and aspirations. Transport costs were plummeting thanks to containerization, the electronics revolution was transforming both banking and manufacturing, and currency trading had become a lucrative business. The term caught on and soon companies rushed to prove their global credentials. British Airways marketed itself as "The World's Favorite Airline;" Carlsberg boasted it was "probably the best beer in the world." By the end of the century, globalization was the new buzzword and there was no ambitious corporation or university that did not vaunt its globality.[35]

To its advocates, of course, globalization was not merely a description of the world, but a prognosis and a prescription too. Building on older visions of cosmic harmony through free trade—visions going back to the nineteenth century—the new globalizers based their sunny forecasts on the collapse of Keynesianism and the rise of new technologies. They obscured the key decisions made by states upon which the entire edifice rested and extolled the self-regulatory functioning of the market. It was all both inevitable and *right* according to those economists for whom the Keynesian consensus that had held sway from 1950 to 1970 had been swept away by rational choice theory and a belief ("hypothesis" was how the profession cast it) in the efficiency of markets.[36] Like the most powerful ideologies, this one prided itself on its lack of ideology: it was just a recognition of the only laws that could not be questioned—the laws of supply and demand. Even as some in the economics profession and the business schools did start to question their basic theoretical assumptions, the sense of optimism spread. The Dow Jones kept rising, through occasional downturns. The ever-increasing complexity and pervasiveness of financial transactions—the nominal value of over-the-counter derivatives rose from an already astronomical $866 billion in 1987 to $454 trillion in 2007—seemed to be producing ever more value. In 1996, Paul Volcker's successor at the Fed, Alan Greenspan, had wondered for a moment whether stock markets might be suffering from "irrational exuberance." But the indicators continued to move upward and he stopped worrying once the East Asian crisis was behind him.[37]

Not everyone was thrilled, especially those whose internationalism was of an older and less banker-friendly vintage. In the last piece he wrote before he died, veteran UN civil servant Erskine Childers made a blistering attack on the globalizers' complacency. The United Nations, he wrote, was "under the greatest threat of extinction in its history," and the Security Council was "a little club of emperors without clothes or competence." Because the leaders of the North, meeting as the G-7, said that they were watching over the "global economy" (the quotation marks were his), they claimed the UN was no longer needed as its steward. The catchword "globalization," he charged, was trotted out in support of this idea as if everyone in the world were benefiting, and as if it were an alternate "system, at work across and for the world's peoples," when in fact it merely implied the forcing open of other countries' economies so that "people with available money" could profit.[38]

A prime example of the sort of thing that infuriated Childers were the writings of *New York Times* columnist Thomas Friedman, who marked the apogee of the globalization vogue with his bestselling book *The Lexus and the Olive Tree*. According to Friedman, globalization had replaced the Cold War and America had triumphed twice over. This was no passing fad, he wrote, but the new enduring reality of international life. In the latest version of a trope that went back to Saint-Simon, he claimed that technology itself was reshaping society. Like so many economic advisers and bankers, he presented conformity with market forces as evolutionary prudence. Modernity required donning what he called the Golden Straitjacket—a set of policies that sounded awfully like the Washington Consensus. "The Global Straitjacket is pretty much one-size-fits-all," he wrote. "It is not always pretty or gentle or comfortable. But it's the only model on the rack this historical season." America remained the end of History for Friedman as it had been for Hegel.[39]

Even as he wrote, however, the bank loans to the developing world that had been flooding in during the 1990s suddenly dried up. Then came 9/11 and the presidency of George W. Bush. Al-Qaeda took the gloss off talk of global villages and entrepreneurial magic. A new counterglobalization seemed to have emerged, and suddenly the world seemed about to enter a much darker era, one in which unending war between irredeemably hostile cultures replaced the sunny unifying projections of the globalizers.[40] The man who had coined the term "Washington Consensus" conceded not only that the term itself was now "a damaged brand name" but that the prescriptions themselves had disappointing results.[41] A gap opened up between the more traditional free traders—concerned chiefly with the circulation of goods and labor, making the old distinction between productive and speculative flows of capital—and the money managers who wanted the unimpeded circulation of capital as well. Economist Jagdish Bhagwati's 2004 *In Defense of Globalization* raised a note of concern about the "perils of gung-ho financial capitalism." When *Financial Times* journalist Martin Wolf published *Why Globalization Works* the same year, it had a worried tone. Had the globalization of capital perhaps gone too far? he asked. Reagan and his successors had wanted the world made safe for investors, but hot money and the transformation of executive compensation were making money managers—and indeed corporate America as a whole—look ever more to the short term. The entire system was becoming liquid, more dedicated to the immediate profits of a few moneymen, and less concerned with capital's real function, to create new sources of growth and employment.[42]

BACK TO DEVELOPMENT?

Meanwhile, a rift was growing between the IMF and the World Bank. The bank itself, which had vastly expanded its development work before 1981, had been placed on the defensive in the Reagan years as administration officials inquired whether it was exhibiting "socialistic tendencies" and right-wing critics charged it was "run like a Soviet factory." It preserved its position by falling in with the Washington Consensus, preaching Chicago School economics and supporting IMF structural adjustment programs.[43] Yet by the mid-1990s, as criticism of the IMF mounted, officials in the bank began to resent their subordination. The cash-rich bank had been forced by the U.S. Treasury to give huge sums to fund IMF bailouts, sums that rose from 2 percent of its total lending in 1996 to nearly 40 percent in 1998, at the height of the East Asian crisis. The new bank president, James Wolfensohn, resented playing second fiddle to the IMF in this way, and disliked the arrogance with which the U.S. Treasury assumed that his institution would fall into line to contribute to poorly designed rescue packages.[44]

His chief economist, Joseph Stiglitz, publicly criticized the IMF's philosophy. Attacking its secrecy and the standardized approach it adopted when confronted with global crises, Stiglitz argued that it had "failed in its mission": far from it stabilizing things, crises had become more frequent and more damaging, and the old goal of full employment had been sacrificed on the altar of ideology. In fact, he wrote, there was no evidence that liberalizing capital markets was essential for growth and plenty of evidence to the contrary. Wolfensohn himself felt that the bank should think outside the economic box. It should advocate democracy and argue against corruption as a drag on growth. It was "civil society" that would provide the discipline, not centralized treasuries, and openness would bring success. Thus in an era of Third Ways, he sketched out a third way between state socialism and right-wing laissez-faire that was especially attractive for the head of an institution often criticized from both sides of the political spectrum.[45]

On the streets, a far more radical critique was brewing, however, one that argued against globalization and the liberalization of trade and capital, that connected this to the increasingly secretive, high-level nature of international economic decision making, and that called for a revival of politics in the form of protest, direct action, and in some cases outright violence against the violence it discerned in capitalism itself. The ebullient Wolfensohn himself was in a sense a product of this movement: the protests in Madrid in 1994 when the bank celebrated its first half century had turned what should have been a celebration into a public relations disaster for his predecessor. Antipoverty rallies and protests outside IMF headquarters had become commonplace when in November 1999 the antiglobalization movement made world headlines as demonstrators battled police in the streets of Seattle during the annual meeting of the WTO. More than forty thousand protestors are estimated to have been involved, making this easily the largest protest ever to take place in the United States against an international institution.

The protest itself, some months in the making, was the work

primarily of a very loose coalition of NGOs from around the world. There were local anarchist cells and labor unions, protesting the exploitative sweatshop practices of multinational corporations. There was Jubilee 2000, a church-based movement that was calling for forgiveness of Third World debt, which had already organized an even larger demonstration in Britain against the G-8 the previous year, and had some success in forcing politicians to take action. And there were American and international NGOs concerned with the environment, consumer rights, and anticapitalist alternatives. By the standards of most countries at most times, the Battle of Seattle was a peaceful, even tame affair (the Genoa clashes two years later were far more brutal). But the event propelled the antiglobalization movement to prominence. Technology offered activists many of the same advantages it gave to Wall Street—instant intercontinental communication and the ability to focus resources momentarily on a single point and then to disperse them again.

Such direct action and grassroots movements represented their own version of internationalism, one deeply suspicious of power and institutions and committed to a contemporary reworking of older nineteenth-century visions of universal brotherhood. Yet like their forebears, they were movements dedicated to political and social outcomes, and as such they could not easily ignore the question of how to convert the energy of protest into real pressure and change. Jubilee 2000's success in persuading first Prime Minister Blair and then the U.S. Congress to make commitments to Third World debt forgiveness showed that such pressure from below could achieve tangible results—even if actual write-downs took a lot longer to emerge. Wolfensohn himself understood the political importance of reaching out to the NGOs and the activists. Under his leadership, the World Bank pioneered a process of incorporating very new kinds of participants, not so much in its decision making—they never achieved much sway over that—as in the public relations that shaped the bank's image.

Echoing Wolfensohn's attempt to redeem the World Bank for

humanity, a similar kind of rehabilitation—for different reasons—was under way at the United Nations itself. With the enforcers of global capitalism newly uncertain of their mission, and the forces of "civil society" ready to be mobilized, the UN's new secretary-general, Kofi Annan, aimed to reverse the marginalization that the UN had endured since the 1970s. The development battleground offered the obvious terrain. Even before his appointment, several UN agencies had argued forcefully against structural adjustment and for what a 1987 UNICEF report called *Adjustment with a Human Face.* Critical of the IMF's approach, and marshaling evidence that markets themselves did not spread benefits equally or end poverty, economists like the Indian Amartya Sen argued for prioritizing "human life" rather than the needs of some abstract "economy." One could not simply assume as standard economics did that all individuals were similarly situated to make life choices. Human development depended on the ability of individuals to act, and education and access to a decent standard of living allowed people to make choices.

On his appointment in 1997, Annan deployed these arguments in an effort to help the UN return from the virtual irrelevance of the past three decades. Development, now expressed in terms of the fight against poverty and disease, was central to his strategy. The two major posts in the overall UN system besides his own that were traditionally filled in accordance with American wishes were the leaders of the World Bank and the UN Development Program. This fact alone created an incentive for a politically sensitive secretariat to ensure that development was defined in ways that made sense to Washington. How precisely it was defined was shaped by a critical semantic shift that was taking place widely at that time as leaders in the era of the Third Way—Clinton, Tony Blair, Annan himself—sought to distance themselves both from the discredited big-government nostrums of the past, and from the failures of neoliberalism's no-government minimalism.[46]

The answer lay in taking over a concept that had emerged in business schools twenty years earlier. "Corporate governance" had started out life as an ambiguous concept that came in at least two models—a cuddly high-minded version that reminded CEOs about social responsibility, safety, and environmental consciousness; and a tougher no-nonsense strain that saw democracy as a problem and (bad) government as the chief enemy of (good) governance. The term conveniently faced both ways: it gestured to notions of inclusiveness, ethics, and obligation, yet it implied the deep suspicion of formal political institutions and big government that was characteristic of the era of Thatcher and Reagan.[47] From business the new concept spread rapidly into international life. The World Bank led the way, reporting on "a crisis of governance" in sub-Saharan Africa in 1989 and making "good governance" a theme at its 1991 economic conference. Barely a decade after the first books and articles on corporate governance appeared, the phrase "global governance" was everywhere.[48] In 1995 a Commission on Global Governance set up by the Swedes reported on *Our Global Neighborhood* and called for a rethink of the UN and its relationship to other groups and institutions. There was even a UN-backed academic journal called *Global Governance*. "We say 'governance' because we don't really know what to call what is going on," wrote an early contributor. Insofar as it did mean something, it connoted a move away from more formalized public institutions to norms and values, regulatory standards, and legal systems, and an attempt to win the UN new supporters by bringing social actors into its decision-making apparatus. This was not the old UN of states speaking to one another; it was—or so the term suggested—merely the central node in a larger global network, encompassing governments, experts, NGOs, and business. Meanwhile, the World Bank itself was busy; by 2000, its development committee reckoned that it had undertaken more than six hundred governance-related initiatives in ninety-five countries around the world. Governance thus represented not merely a new approach to politics in the developed world; through the activities of international agencies, it was a creed justifying far-reaching interventions in the public administration, law, and political systems of countries around the world.[49]

The pro-American Annan quickly preached the new message, reaching out to NGOs and antiglobalization groups on the one hand, and to corporate America on the other. The following year he became the first UN secretary-general to be invited to the Davos World Economic Forum for the annual corporate-sponsored conclave of policymakers and businessmen. Back there again in 1999, he spoke about forging a new relationship between the UN and the corporate world, a Global Compact of business responsibility to "give a human face to the global market." Anxious to emphasize the importance of humanizing capitalism, Annan underlined the anxieties that globalization had created and warned that without attention it could reawaken the ghosts of the past—dictatorship, terrorism, and ethnic cleansing. The enormous Millennium Summit that he called in New York in 2000, with more heads of state in one place than ever before in history, highlighted these perils and sought to promote a new central role for the United Nations as the world's development broker—between corporations and international agencies, between warring factions in war-torn states, and above all between the North and the South. He also encouraged efforts to coordinate the traditionally disunited and uncoordinated UN agencies in an ultimately unsuccessful bid to streamline Jackson's "prehistoric monster" and develop its "brain."[50]

Helped by Mark Malloch Brown, a former journalist and PR man with good Washington contacts, who was brought in from the World Bank to head the UN Development Program in 2000, development brought the UN back to life alongside its expanded peacekeeping role. The UNDP operational budget doubled in the course of the 1980s and doubled again in the 1990s, reaching a peak of $2.4 billion on the eve of the Millennium Summit. Relations with the World Bank and even the IMF were much improved.[51] But this was development in an entirely new context, targeted on poverty but far more broadly than the old structural adjustment approach in that it defined development as a total restructuring of social and cultural institutions, a matter of anthropology and law and not just economics. All of this was a little like the modernization strategies of the 1960s, only now emancipated from the Cold War and supposedly keener to harness the energy of the private sector and NGOs. In a fashion reminiscent of President Kennedy's Development Decade rhetoric, the UN now committed itself publicly to ambitious Millennium Development Goals that aimed at halving the quarter of the world's population that lived on a dollar a day or less.

The goals focused on Africa in particular. Growth in South America and East Asia was high and raising overall living standards; the Chinese powerhouse was eradicating poverty at an extraordinary rate with little UN input. In sub-Saharan Africa, in contrast, despite signs of economic vitality, the problems were grave: the conflict in the Congo alone had claimed more than five million lives, entire countries were ravaged by AIDS, and many suffered from spectacularly poor and corrupt leadership. The continent thus became—as to a large extent it remains—a laboratory and a reality check for the UN's new development strategies.

But Annan's attempt to rehabilitate the UN in the eyes of the American public and to use a humanized version of development to do so was derailed by the terrorist attacks of 9/11 and the growing international rift over what to do about Iraq. Development could now only command American attention if further redefined: poverty eradication took on an entirely new meaning as the optimism of the Clinton years vanished. National security experts now warned that even if globalization had elevated the lives of billions, it had also created a new security threat in the form of a dangerous gap—an entire zone of discontent stretching across the middle of Africa as far east as Pakistan and perhaps even Indonesia where rapidly growing populations of impoverished youthful proto-terrorists posed the kind of problem the globalizers had not even thought about. In the changed international environment, in short, poverty had assumed a threatening new form. Malfunctioning states, formerly merely a problem for their own suffering populations, were now transposed into a direct threat to American national security.[52]

Anxious to demonstrate its relevance to Washington, the UN responded by redefining development as a matter of the "human security" of the world's poor. But commentators in the months after the Twin Towers attack in the United States were generally more worried about what this global development failure might mean for the security of the United States itself and what the American response should be. Development and security had been closely conjoined from the start, and development had always ultimately been about making a safer world for those doing the developing, whether American or European. Indeed for some, 9/11 represented nothing less than a historic failure of development. In a 2002 *Foreign Affairs* article, for instance, financial journalist Sebastian Mallaby reproached the United States for its reluctance to act imperially. In his view, the historic alternative to foreign aid was imperialism. It was true that foreign aid—alongside globalization—had helped build nations, but there remained "an obstinate group of dysfunctional countries." The international agencies had run out of answers and globalization would not do it either: it was therefore time for the United States to assume the responsibilities of imperial power. Yet although the basic drive to meet what Mallaby called "a new imperial moment" had to come from Washington, he did not conclude that America should shoulder this burden alone. He recommended it should use international institutions to meet this new crisis as it had used them in the past, to provide legitimation and to share the costs. But all this should take place outside the formal auspices of the UN itself and would involve the creation of "a new international body . . . to deal with nation-building."[53]

It is, in retrospect, revealing how few of the proponents of a new forward role for the United States after 9/11 seriously considered complete unilateralism. For Mallaby was certainly not the only one recasting liberal internationalism in a new muscular guise. Woodrow Wilson's old university, Princeton, was the birthplace of a new Project on National Security, critical not so much of Bush's projection of American power overseas as of his stupidity in not working in a properly multilateral spirit. Like Mallaby, these commentators believed that the UN was not working—"the system of international institutions the United States and its allies built after World War II . . . is broken," they wrote—and they proposed a neo-Wilsonian "Concert of Democracies" as a new collective security organization to take on this global task. This would forge "a world of liberty under law" that would make the world safe for the "American way of life." Because poverty, it went on, made state collapse more likely with its attendant ills—authoritarian leadership, environmental catastrophe, and pandemic disease—foreign aid had to become an integral part of America's national security strategy.[54]

Such prescriptions sounded hard-nosed and tough-minded, but they ignored some fairly basic political realities. Development had indeed involved helping new nations come into being, but in the Cold War this had typically meant working through the machinery of postcolonial states and the focus had been on infrastructural improvement. The vision of modernization through electrification, planned towns, prestige steelworks, and entirely revised farming methods had of course been ambitious enough—so ambitious that a degree of failure was often preordained. But what was now proposed was more ambitious still. That the United States would commit itself not merely to building dams and bridges and towns and factories but to reshaping the values of entire societies was implausible enough. That it would do so in precisely those societies where the state's authority had collapsed was even more implausible. And to imagine that the United States, even in coalition, would be willing to commit the troops and sustain the losses over the enormous period of time and the vast geographical expanse required to turn these conflict-ridden failures into exemplary modern market democracies simply defied belief. The Rand Corporation dutifully trotted out a report that drew lessons from the successful U.S. occupations of Germany and Japan. But the truth was that the only lessons these successes provided were negative. Not only did those two countries represent two of the most advanced economies in the world when they were occupied, but both occupied and occupiers in the mid-twentieth century had worked through robust state agencies that were able to plan, rebuild, and cooperate over a very long period. Could a largely outsourced nation-building effort seriously help some of the poorest countries in the world, where such infrastructure as existed had often been deliberately dismantled, to come out fine in only a few years? To pose the question was to answer it.

The neoimperialist prescription was also doomed by its own amnesia. Mandating a return to the imperial origins of international institutions, it refused to recognize that times had changed. The world of the League, of Jan Smuts and Woodrow Wilson, lay on the other side of what was arguably international government's most striking achievement—the globalization of national self-determination. Insofar as the UN possessed legitimacy in the very countries where Mallaby and others now urged intervention, it was precisely because of its historic association with this ending of colonialism. The Europeans still retained the taint of empire in the eyes of the rest of the world; was it really prudent for the United States to join them? In fact, as hostility to American excursions abroad mounted, the nation-building moment came and went. After Afghanistan and Iraq, Washington's always limited appetite for this was exhausted.

Thus the imperial version of the development/security nexus never really got the chance to prove itself except in Iraq and Afghanistan, which demonstrated its impossibility. The truth is that the contemporary American national security state, with preference for the light footprint, airpower, and an extreme aversion to risk, lacks the staying power or the competence to reshape the field of development. It turns out that the UN still has much to offer. But so does something quite new. As a resurgent China takes on a series of state-led infrastructural projects in Africa and Southeast Asia, it promises a form of "South-South cooperation," premised on a new, distinctively Chinese model of development that offers other developing countries the benefits not only of its capital but its own experiences as a latecomer to capitalism. The funds are still relatively small but growing very fast, and they have already challenged Western lending to Angola and elsewhere. By early 2012, Chinese development lending to Latin America outstripped both the World Bank and the Inter-American Development Bank.[55]

As the state-led Chinese model emerges as a new global investor, directing increasingly substantial sums toward Africa in particular, a challenge is emerging to the IMF orthodoxies and a return to something looking strangely like the statist engineering that the neoliberal revolution was supposed to have ended for good. A new Scramble for Africa is under way and American commentators fret. But from the point of view of erstwhile African and South American clients of the World Bank and other Western development agencies, Chinese involvement—for all its limitations—may come as a welcome relief. For the evidence suggests that efforts to export Western ideas of the rule of law to rural societies with robust complex legal traditions of their own has been far from productive and has even created instability and violence. Rushed and poorly thought through, a sequence of Western policies—from modernization through structural adjustment to the sweeping societal reforms the Wolfensohn-era World Bank sought to implement—have created a trail of havoc that makes the more ideologically minimalist and pragmatic approach from Beijing look socially responsible. What looks alarming from Washington is not quite so threatening when viewed from the world's poorest countries. As the crumbling Pont Kennedy over the Niger is replaced by a new Chinese bridge, for instance, the waning power of America and its international economic agendas may even come as relief.[56]

China's rise in the international economy and the consequent emergence of an alternative development model illuminates the close relationship that existed previously between the United States and the Bretton Woods institutions. The entire shift to neoliberalism had been driven from the 1970s by American ideological preferences mediated through international institutions. Today those institutions are disoriented and marginalized, their ideas questioned globally as never before. The IMF has found a new role for now in responding to the

Eurozone crisis. But many of its former Third World partners want as little to do with it as possible, and demand a greater voice in its decisions. The World Bank has embraced transparency, collaboration, and modesty—another way of saying that its top-down approach may be over, and its own future role much more circumscribed. The era of deregulated markets and endless financialization was checked—it is too early to say whether ended—in the financial crisis that started in 2008 and continues to this day. What is clear is that the New International Economic Order that was imposed by the West, with Washington's leadership, in the late 1970s as a way of responding to the demands of the South is no longer sustainable. With Japan mired in stagnation and both Europe and the United States struggling to emerge from major recessions, the geopolitical balance of power has swung south—to China, India, and Brazil. Going back to UNCTAD or the days of Third World solidarity is not in the cards. But in the struggle between the proponents of free markets and the proponents of a more strategic role for the state, the former can no longer count on sweeping all before them.[57]

CHAPTER 13

Humanity's Law

The power to decide who is sovereign would signify a new sovereignty.

—Carl Schmitt, 1923[1]

State sovereignty, in its most basic sense, is being redefined—not least by the forces of globalization and international cooperation. States are now widely understood to be instruments at the service of their peoples, and not vice versa. At the same time, individual sovereignty—by which I mean the fundamental freedom of each individual, enshrined in the Charter of the United Nations and subsequent international treaties—has been enhanced by a renewed and spreading consciousness of individual rights. When we read the Charter today, we are more than ever conscious that its aim is to protect individual human beings, not to protect those who abuse them.

—Kofi Annan, "Two Concepts of Sovereignty," 1999[2]

"GOD HAS GIVEN you your country as a cradle, and humanity as mother," Mazzini once wrote. "You cannot rightly love your brethren of the cradle if you do not love your common mother." As we have already seen, the idea that the national and the international are fundamentally complementary provided the rationale for creating a society of nations. First the League of Nations and then the United Nations were intended to usher in a world in which democratic polities guaranteed rights internally for their citizens while the world body oversaw their cooperation at the international level. The idea survived the Second World War. But of course democracy itself was never made a criterion of UN membership, and the charter itself, *pace* Kofi Annan's words above, is a deeply ambiguous document that commits signatories both to respect for human rights and fundamental freedoms *and* to the equality of "nations large and small" and the principle of states living in peace with one another as "good neighbors." In 1945 the principle of state sovereignty predominated. But by the end of the Cold War it was obvious that the idea that nationalism and internationalism complemented one another was often incorrect: member states were capable of tyrannizing their own peoples and creating human rights catastrophes and humanitarian disasters that threatened international peace. New and much more conditional attitudes toward sovereignty, already evident through the human rights revolution of the 1970s, were now taken up within the United Nations itself, and it became the instrument of a new civilizing mission that, much like the old one from which it sprang, relied heavily on the language of international law and the appeal to universal moral values for its legitimation.[3]

The "New World Order" that emerged after the Cold War was thus characterized initially not by the assembling of large military coalitions—the war in the Persian Gulf was exceptional from this point of view—but rather by an unprecedented expansion of the UN's responsibilities and powers in the humanitarian realm. Its officials, protected by sovereign immunity, were put in charge in places like Kosovo, South Sudan, and East Timor. They were increasingly not merely peacekeeping in the original sense—caring for refugees or delivering supplies—but active political agents who could have people arrested, and cancel or mandate elections. They were, above all, nation-building: the Security Council sent missions to at least twelve states after 1989 to help draft new constitutions; another fifteen or more received similar offers of help.[4]

In the process, some of the world organization's foundational political conceptions were transformed beyond recognition. Sovereignty was no longer regarded as absolute. The trend that had become evident between 1945 and 1970 of giving more weight to sovereign rights and less and less to individual liberties and rights was reversed. But the reversal went far beyond the monitoring of individual human rights abuses alone. At stake now were the rights of entire peoples. With the creation of the so-called Responsibility to Protect and then access to the services of the newly established International Criminal Court, the United Nations has come close to realizing the Hammarskjöldian vision of itself as an international executive agency for the world.[5]

The erosion of sovereignty was also accompanied by the return of an older rhetoric of universal ethics. A series of appeals to the idea of an "international community" of the virtuous justified the UN's new interventions. Yet while couched in the language of self-evident moral truth and old Christian doctrines of just war, the idea that humanity's rights trumped those of states nevertheless masked complicated political questions. Humanitarian intervention—war by another name—asserted the conditionality of sovereignty and thereby loosened the rigor of the laws of war, allowing UN troops—and even more the forces of other alliances such as NATO sometimes operating entirely outside the UN—much greater freedom from international law than ever before. To critics, the Responsibility to Protect, a doctrine developed chiefly in relation to conflicts in Africa, looked like a resurrection of the old nineteenth-century idea that there should be one standard of sovereignty for the civilized world and another for the uncivilized. The appeal to morality particularly failed to acknowledge the acutely political character in practice of both the Responsibility to Protect and the International Criminal Court. The new humanitarianism constituted the most ambitious attempt since the Second World War to restore a language of morality to international relations; but it was for precisely this reason that it showed the real limits and indeed the dangers—ethical, political, and practical—of such a venture.

TOWARD HUMANITARIAN INTERVENTION

In December 1988, as the Cold War entered its final phase, UN secretary-general Javier Pérez de Cuéllar traveled to Oslo to receive the Nobel Peace Prize on behalf of the UN's peacekeeping missions. At a time when he looked forward to a bold new role for his organization, it was, he said, striking to note the contribution to world peace that had been made by the UN in a form that had not even been envisaged by its founders. There had been no mention at all of peacekeeping in the charter, and the concept had only really emerged thanks to the ingenuity of Dag Hammarskjöld at the time of the 1956 Suez Crisis. In the aftermath of the Congo Crisis in the early 1960s, there had been a falling away in the appetite for further UN peacekeeping operations. Even so, by 1988 soldiers of fifty-eight nations, all flying the UN flag, were keeping the peace across the world. Pérez de Cuéllar's Nobel speech hailed these developments and the new role of the UN as world policeman in the service of peace, justice, and law:

> The technique which has come to be called peacekeeping uses soldiers as the servants of peace rather than as the instruments of war. It introduces to the military sphere the principle of nonviolence. It provides an honorable alternative to conflict and a means of reducing strife and tension, so that a solution can be sought through negotiation. Never before in history have military forces been employed internationally not to wage war, not to establish domination and *not* to serve the interests of any power or group of powers, but rather to prevent conflict between peoples.

In fact, thanks to the strong support of the first President Bush, the UN was just growing into the peacekeeping role that would turn it into the second largest deployer of troops in the world after the United States itself. Peacekeeping ventures in Mozambique, El Salvador, and Cambodia signaled a new activism; all proved successful in easing the transition from war to peace, caring for refugees and those who had been internally displaced, and ultimately in restoring political stability. In the 1970s there had been three new peacekeeping operations authorized, and there were no more until 1988. But in the 1990s, the number rocketed to thirty-eight. Between 1987 and 1994 the number of peacekeepers in blue helmets rose from ten thousand to seventy thousand, and the peacekeeping budget swelled from $230 million to $3.6 billion, dwarfing the regular operating budget of the UN. The organization was being pushed by the Security Council into assuming what was effectively a powerful new world role.[6]

At its root was the problem of what were becoming known as "failed states." This term, a seeming oddity in an era in which the state seemed to be more popular than ever before (the number had quadrupled since the end of the Second World War), was problematic from several points of view. It ignored the fact that, as the eighteenth-century partition of Poland showed, many victorious imperial powers in the past had justified dismembering existing states by describing them as poorly managed. Indeed, the entire history of contemporary Europe was of some states failing—Austria-Hungary, Prussia, the USSR—and being replaced by others. But it was not such cases that the advocates of the term had in mind: they were concerned not with the deliberate dismemberment of old states in Europe but with the forces for disintegration in new ones in the former colonial world, the persistence of poverty and ethnic conflict, and the ways this might generate international instability by causing large refugee flows, massive famines, or—after 2001—allowing anti-Western terrorist groups a haven. By 2002, the term had entered the National Security Strategy of the United States, while the British foreign secretary, Jack Straw, speaking in the run-up to the invasion of Iraq, cited the attacks of September 11 as the reason why preventing states from failing and resuscitating those that fail is "one of the strategic imperatives of our times."[7]

It had all begun a decade earlier when the Security Council broadened the concept of "threats to the peace" in what even sympathetic observers described as a "strikingly intrusive" interpretation of the charter to encompass "non-military sources of instability in the economic, social, humanitarian and ecological fields."[8] Then came Somalia. In what British diplomat David Hannay has described as "the most astonishing single document to be agreed in the immediate post–Cold War period at the UN," the Security Council authorized forces in December 1992 to go into the country because of the "magnitude of the human tragedy." This was new, but it blazed a trail, because the following year the council mandated intervention in Haiti too on the grounds that the situation required "an exceptional response."[9]

The debacle in Somalia nearly ended humanitarian intervention before it was born. The U.S.-led coalition oversaw a successful initial relief operation, before the twenty-five thousand heavily armed American troops withdrew so fast that the new UN force came in at only a third of its planned strength. To make matters worse, a U.S. "over the horizon" force remained in the area and launched a botched attack on Somali warlord Mohammed Aideed in October 1993, in the course of which two American helicopters were shot down and eighteen soldiers were killed along with hundreds of Somali civilians. The Clinton administration blamed the UN, even though the assault force had been under American command and anti-UN sentiment in the 1994 Republican-controlled Congress intensified, precipitating a budget standoff over the funding of U.S. arrears to the UN that threatened to undermine the rapid growth of peacekeeping operations for most of the decade. In addition, the National Security Restoration Act sharply constrained the use of U.S. troops under UN command.[10]

The tragedies in Yugoslavia and Rwanda—tragedies that left

an estimated quarter of a million civilians dead in the former, and more than 800,000 in the latter—highlighted the limitations on UN power in the absence of strong American backing. Secretary-General Boutros Boutros-Ghali was keen to preserve the UN's impartiality—a peacekeeping mantra—and to avoid getting drawn into other civil wars. To ensure this, he handed over operational power to his special representative in the Balkans, a risk-averse Japanese diplomat, and kept the power to order airstrikes in his own hands. As news reached the West of the Serb-run prison camps dotted around Bosnia, and Serb artillery shelled Sarajevo with impunity, the UN's passivity aroused increasing criticism. The Rwandan genocide, which erupted suddenly in April 1994, was an even greater test. A UN peacekeeping mission had newly arrived in Kigali to enforce a cease-fire agreement, but the force at its disposal amounted to no more than three small battalions—entirely insufficient to do anything to stop the horrific anti-Tutsi massacres that the government unleashed. While the Security Council deliberated, and refugees fled across the borders, hundreds of thousands of civilians were murdered in a matter of weeks. The UN force was eventually expanded, but it was too late, and it was the rebel RPF that took control of the country and brought the killing to an end.[11]

Only once the Yugoslav conflict got to the point of threatening Western prestige did the attitudes of policymakers shift quickly. In the summer of 1995, approximately eight thousand Bosnian Muslim men were shot by Bosnian Serb paramilitaries in the Srebrenica enclave where they had supposedly been under the protection of a Dutch UN battalion. In the aftermath of the massacre, the UNPROFOR commander in Bosnia together with the UN official in charge of peacekeeping, a certain Kofi Annan, managed finally to get the authorization for the use of military force against the Bosnian Serbs. Boutros-Ghali, who had previously blocked this, was away; Annan was sympathetic to the case for intervention. The Americans, British, and French were brought around to support the use of force, because they now saw Serb defiance as threatening the standing of their own troops. It was over embarrassingly quickly. Within a few months, a NATO Rapid Reaction Force had lifted the siege of Sarajevo and brought the Serbs to the negotiating table.

Angered by Boutros-Ghali's previous recalcitrance in Bosnia, the forceful American ambassador to the UN, Madeleine Albright, called for his head. Since it was unprecedented for a secretary-general seeking a second term to be denied it, the so-called Operation Orient Express was hatched inside the Clinton administration to oust him. When this failed, the United States was forced to cast its veto publicly against him—the sole member of the Security Council to do so. But it had already settled on Kofi Annan as Boutros-Ghali's successor: if Bosnia destroyed Boutros-Ghali's reputation, it confirmed Annan's as someone willing to contemplate the use of force, and likelier to heed Washington's preferences. Under his leadership, a more intimate relationship between the United States and the secretary-general's office emerged, a basic precondition for the new humanitarianism that would follow.[12]

Bosnia and Rwanda showed that sometimes peacekeeping was wrong, neutrality meant conniving in crimes, and intervening was the only way to prevent them from happening. Enforcing an arms embargo on all sides, the "peacekeeping" UN had prevented the Bosnians from defending themselves, and blocked all talk of taking on the Serbs. This failure, compounded in Rwanda, was lambasted by journalists like Samantha Power and David Rieff in the United States and Michael Ignatieff in Britain. Raised on the lessons of the Holocaust, they were burdened by the historical weight of the moment, above all by the need to act in the face of genocide. The writings of the Polish Jewish scholar Raphael Lemkin, who had coined the term half a century earlier, were now rediscovered. The young Labour politician Tony Blair credited a viewing of Steven Spielberg's Holocaust movie, *Schindler's List,* with steeling his resolve to do something in foreign affairs. Flying out of besieged Sarajevo,

Kofi Annan's future deputy, Mark Malloch Brown, wondered how "to turbo-charge traditional humanitarianism with an aggressive political advocacy intended to take on the causes of conflicts and thereby find solutions."[13]

Yet what did that mean for the UN and the existing architecture of international affairs with its emphasis on working through states? "Never again" was an admirable resolution. But in the early 1990s, the UN seemed part of the problem. As several commentators had noted shortly after its founding, even had that organization existed in the Nazi era, it would have had no legal basis for interfering in Germany's internal affairs. A new generation's anxious determination to avoid collusion in mass murder thus collided with the structure of the United Nations itself. Lacking its own troops, hostage to the clashing views of the Security Council's members, poorly equipped in any case for rapid reaction to state-orchestrated violence, the United Nations could scarcely have lived up to the interventionists' expectations. But the latter understood very well that the UN was not an autonomous actor. Boutros-Ghali had done nothing in Bosnia because there had been no willingness in Washington, London, or Paris to act.

All this changed when the next round of the Yugoslav crisis erupted—in the autonomous province of Kosovo—because there had been a changing of the guard and the interventionists were now in charge. Madeleine Albright replaced the lawyerly Warren Christopher as Clinton's secretary of state. An unabashed advocate of backing U.S. moral leadership with force, she had described the United States in a TV interview the previous year as "the indispensable nation." "If we have to use force, it is because we are America," she famously remarked. "We stand tall and we see further than other countries into the future."[14] She berated General Colin Powell for his reluctance to get involved and found a staunch ally in British prime minister Tony Blair, whose enthusiasm for fighting the good fight marked a contrast with the caution of his predecessor, John Major. In April 1999, Blair gave a speech in Chicago. "We are all internationalists now," he asserted. Globalization, he argued, had transformed politics and security as much as economics, and defending human rights abroad mattered for security at home and required institutional reform and new rules of international behavior. "We are witnessing the beginnings of a new doctrine of international community," he argued. For Blair, America had to lead the world's democracies in spreading liberal values because defeating evil would make everyone more secure.

As for Albright, she was determined not to allow a repeat of Bosnia on her watch, and to forestall any further ethnic cleansing on the part of the Serbs through decisive action whether or not the Security Council backed it. As she knew, inside the council resistance to the new doctrine was strong. Annan himself was sympathetic (he gave a strongly pro-interventionist speech, scripted by his English chief speechwriter, and refused to condemn the NATO bombing when it went ahead), but the Security Council was deadlocked. This did not much bother Albright or for that matter Blair: both felt that if the UN would not give the go-ahead, the interventionists should go around it. In the teeth of strong Russian and Chinese opposition—the Chinese ambassador termed the operation "a severe violation of the UN Charter and established principles of international law"—NATO started bombing the Serbs without Security Council authorization. In this way a group of Western powers moved toward a view of the world in which the defense of humanity overrode not only the sanctity of state sovereignty but in certain circumstances the authority even of the UN itself, unless and until the UN could be brought around to embrace these new norms.[15]

THE RESPONSIBILITY TO PROTECT

A conditional attitude to the United Nations had often been found among some of its most ardent supporters. Because they regarded it as a means to a higher moral purpose, there was always the possibility when the body itself failed of looking elsewhere to preserve the spirit of internationalism. Intellectuals such as Alfred Zimmern had felt this way about the League of Nations in the 1930s and again about the UN in the Cold War: if it was really unable to act in the name of good, then it fell to those who could to lead the good fight. Dean Rusk had felt similarly in the late 1940s and 1950s. As a new generation of American globalists became disillusioned with the UN, they too pursued this train of thought and started thinking about an "alliance of democracies," whether as a caucus in the UN, or if necessary outside it. As early as 1980, this was urged on Carter by members of the Coalition for the Democratic Majority, a seedbed of future neoconservatives. Twenty years later, Madeleine Albright inaugurated a "Community of Democracies" in Warsaw that created a Democracy Caucus at the UN four years later. (It still exists: the chair is held at the time of writing by Mongolia.) But although UN secretary-general Kofi Annan praised its emergence, looking forward to the day when "the United Nations can truly call itself a community of democracies," in fact the development was double-edged, since it always carried within it the threat of establishing an alternative international coalition outside the UN itself. Plans for a Concert of Democracies that could emerge as a rival pole of American power and influence were proposed over the next few years by American commentators, both neoconservatives and liberal internationalists, and featured in the policy platforms of the main two candidates in the 2008 U.S. presidential election.[16]

It was to ward off such calls, mostly made by Americans and potentially so damaging to the authority of the UN, that middle-ranking Western powers such as the Canadians and Australians explored whether there was not a way of enshrining a new approach to sovereignty inside the UN itself. The original twentieth-century conception of sovereignty was that it was a right conferred de jure. An alternative view was that what really mattered was not legal recognition so much as whether a government demonstrated the capacity to look after its citizens. In the 1996 book *Sovereignty as Responsibility,* Sudanese diplomat Francis Deng and his fellow contributors argued that in Africa sovereignty could no longer be regarded as conferring an absolute protection against external interference but rather a responsibility that could be forfeited in cases of egregious neglect or outright criminality. Control of a territory, the traditional criterion for sovereignty, was less meaningful than care of "life-sustaining standards" for a nation's inhabitants. States that did not care for their own people might thus lose their legitimacy; in such circumstances, the UN would have the right, and perhaps the duty, to get involved.

Deng's proposal was taken up once a high-level commission was established by the Canadian government to find a normative basis for future UN action so as to avoid the legal problems that the Kosovo intervention had posed. The idea of a "Responsibility to Protect" (R2P in the jargon) had already been implicit in Blair's 1999 speech. The 2001 Canadian report offered a way to legitimize future interventions, even as it suggested giving up talk of "intervention" altogether. But the criteria it proposed were vague, and the idea itself looked less attractive after the U.S. invasion of Iraq was hailed as an example of Responsibility to Protect in action. Even so, both Annan and his successor as secretary-general, Ban Ki-moon, embraced the idea as a means of reasserting the moral weight of the UN and avoiding further rupture with the Americans. At the 2005 UN World Summit a watered-down version of R2P won general acceptance for political reasons as well as ethical ones: it constituted a counterweight to the unilateralism displayed by the Americans at a time when Bush's national security rewrite prescribed a worrying new doctrine of preemptive force. Reclaiming the right to determine the exercise of such force for the UN in the name of a higher morality, R2P argued for an international responsibility to protect populations suffering gross human rights violations.[17]

Yet even as R2P reasserted the centrality of the UN, the aftermath of the first Balkan interventions showed just how unpredictable the consequences of intervention could be. Toppling dictators and defeating tyrannical militias did not automatically usher in a transition to a democratic peace; sometimes it helped other dictators to power or paved the way for drug cartels to flourish. As all along the way in the story of postwar international social engineering—first with development, then with neoliberalism, and now with this—reality was messier than the theory, and "transition," a term beloved of late-twentieth-century political scientists, turned out to be an infinitely extensible process with no clear outcome. After a decade in Bosnia, international administrators had still failed to knit together a country fragmented by war. In Kosovo, the interventionists' first success, Slobodan Milosevic's departure left chaos and criminality in its wake. When the newly elected President George W. Bush toured the vast U.S. military base at Camp Bondsteel in Kosovo, *Time* wrote in apparent surprise, "It would appear that the existence of democratic institutions does not necessarily signal the dominance of a democratic, multiethnic political culture. And that would mean the nation-building project may be so long-term as to make the Balkan peace-keeping deployments a relatively permanent affair." And all of that was before the invasions and occupations of Afghanistan and Iraq.[18]

In an era when democracy promotion was winning new adherents and the UN was being asked to help build parliamentary democracies in parts of the world that had never known them, these cases had disturbing implications for those concerned with "failed states." According to *Foreign Policy* magazine, which published its own Failed States Index, there were in 2005 thirty-three failed states in a really bad way and another forty-three that were on the verge. Since then, the democracy index seems to have been headed in the wrong direction. A British civil servant at the European Commission, Robert Cooper, had warned of the threat posed by places where "the law of the jungle" reigned and argued that Western states should pull out of such places when their interventions did no good. But how could you just pull out when R2P was premised on making things better?[19]

Part of the problem was that the debate about sovereignty behind R2P had been driven far from its origins as a result of the West's obsession with intervention. Francis Deng's original concern had not been about military action at all but simply about how to prevent the kind of state breakdown that had led to such high levels of internal displacement in some Central African states. Post-Kosovo, however, much of the commentary had been concerned with establishing legitimate grounds for international military action, and American interventionism in the war on terror intensified this tendency. Hence although many members of the UN were unhappy about this, R2P did tend to be evoked in the context of possible or actual interventions. When the Burmese junta prevented international aid from reaching the people of the country after the 2008 cyclone, Bernard Kouchner, who was by then French foreign minister, argued for applying the R2P, generating a controversy that was only laid to rest when Ban Ki-moon clarified the issue the following year by arguing for a narrow but activist interpretation that would allow it to be triggered only for specific crimes—genocide, war crimes, ethnic cleansing, and crimes against humanity.[20]

Whereas Annan (speaking before Kosovo and Iraq) had said that "our job is to intervene," Ban Ki-moon has tried to distinguish R2P from the idea of "humanitarian intervention," insisting that "the responsibility to protect is an ally of sovereignty, not an adversary." But this is really diplomatic obeisance to the many critics of R2P around the world, and not how its most ardent proponents have understood its goal. For those who once called themselves humanitarian interventionists, R2P has been the ideal rhetorical vehicle because it speaks the language of universal humanity and international community rather than force and war. This made it invaluable to American liberals as they sought to bring the Bush administration, chastened by the postinvasion challenge of ruling Iraq, around again to multilateralism.

Two figures, both vocal after 9/11, and both destined for the Obama White House, exemplified the instrumental character of this way of thinking. The journalist Samantha Power was the author of a Pulitzer Prize–winning indictment of America's continued failure through history to prevent genocide. She criticized the invasion of Iraq on the grounds that the United States had failed to secure UN backing and hoped that strong leadership from the secretary-general's office would eventually allow the UN to play the energetic role she envisaged preventing genocide and preempting mass abuses of human rights. But when the cause was right, Power believed the United States should lead, even if the UN failed to follow. Fearful of a "human rights leadership vacuum" after the Iraq fiasco, Power advocated a "coalition of the concerned" to keep the flame alive if the UN let them down.[21]

Anne-Marie Slaughter, a Princeton political scientist, took instrumentalism one stage further. Unlike Power, Slaughter's primary concern was not genocide prevention per se, but the most effective deployment of American power. In her mind, moves like Bush's controversial appointment of John Bolton as ambassador to the UN showed what not to do in a networked world. Embracing R2P, on the other hand, offered a way of allowing the United States to take the moral high ground internationally once more. Slaughter herself even proposed trying out a new "collective 'duty to prevent' nations run by dictators from acquiring or using WMDs." This kind of suggestion showed that the language of moral obligation could be stretched far enough in the right hands to accommodate virtually any perceived national security need of the United States.[22]

In the Bush years, Slaughter also codirected a blue-ribbon bipartisan Princeton Project on National Security, which aimed to craft a new long-term approach to foreign affairs. What was striking about the project's 2006 conclusions was the way they brought together the national security concerns of the Bush era with the language of moral responsibility. Co-opting large numbers of the great and the good, the Princeton Project demonstrated the wishful quality of thinking current within the American foreign policy elite six decades after the rise to globalism. The authors invoked the ghost of George Kennan, who had died nearby, aged 101, the year before the report was issued, and they stated that they aspired to the influence of his famous "X article." Yet their findings were strikingly un-Kennanesque. Kennan had never tried to argue that America's values were the world's; his was an approach based simply on the national interest, and it was evident to him that different states would define their interests in different ways. The Princeton report, on the other hand, assumed that "a world of liberty under law" (what kind of liberty and which conception of law were never specified) had universal appeal. "What does the U.S. seek," it asked in a revealing elision, "for all Americans and all human beings?" Kennan had always criticized overly capacious definitions of the national interest, and because he had not believed that American security was jeopardized in places like Asia and Africa, he had strongly dissented from the proliferation of commitments that Washington had undertaken around the world after 1949. The report, on the other hand, was entirely of its time and milieu in seeing vital American interests everywhere, and urgent battles to be fought on multiple fronts—from global warming and terrorism to democracy promotion and the expansion of human rights. Yet at the same time, it described the post-1945 system of international institutions as "broken." The report recommended forcing UN member states to accept R2P, on the one hand, and developing a global "Concert of Democracies" on the other if the UN proved unreformable. It talked about leading through hope not fear, but then insisted that both liberty and law needed to be backed by force. It spoke about working with other nations. But at the same time, it talked about "defining our border protections beyond our actual physical borders."[23]

The Obama presidency saw the ascent of this new breed of moralist-realists. Samantha Power became an assistant to Obama himself and a National Security Council staffer with responsibility for genocide prevention. Slaughter was appointed to George Kennan's old job heading the Policy Planning Staff, and four other participants in her Princeton Project also found positions in the administration. Not surprisingly, Obama's 2010 National Security Strategy reflected their influence. There was less talk of military predominance than under his predecessor, and much more talk of values that were (as always) both American and universal. Strongly committed to supporting "an international architecture of laws and institutions" (in obvious contrast to his predecessor), Obama reminded Americans that "nations thrive by meeting their responsibilities and facing consequences when they don't." The "nation that helped bring globalization about" must fight for the rights that had made America great and that others "have made their own": there was explicit support for the idea of enforcing the Responsibility to Protect, and no discussion of the possibility that other nations might opt for other sets of rights and responsibilities entirely.[24]

The gap that had opened up in 2003 between the United States and the UN now closed again, at least so far as the office of the secretary-general was concerned. How far the views of the Obama administration converged with those of UN secretary-general Ban Ki-moon emerged clearly during the Libyan crisis in March 2011. After the Security Council backed NATO intervention to protect civilians, the two men hailed this as the moment in which R2P became a new norm in world politics. But others on the Security Council disagreed. Although Russia and China abstained rather than vetoing the measure, both powers were strongly disapproving and worried where the disregard for Libyan sovereignty might lead. China, Pakistan, and India all spoke out in debate against using the new principle to justify interfering in a state's internal affairs: yet that was precisely what was done on the grounds that it had been necessary to preempt a massacre of civilians in Benghazi.

Close cooperation between the United States and the UN on what amounted to a policy of preemption for the sake of human rights (or, if one was kinder, genocide prevention) thus risked further eroding the trust of other powerful UN members, a trust already strained by American policy in Kosovo and Iraq. There were many obvious differences between Obama's invocation of R2P and President George W. Bush's 2002 National Security Strategy, but what they had in common was that each took a single issue—genocide in the one case, and WMD in the other—as threats of such consequence that preemptive action was needed to eradicate them. The political consequences in both cases were left unspecified but implicit. Just as the search for WMD had not legally encompassed the killing of Saddam Hussein, so R2P did not authorize the removal of Colonel Muammar Gadhafi, as Obama admitted—yet it was impossible to imagine the mission ending before he was ousted. Did this mean then a legitimation of regime change for human rights abusers? Despite the official denials, R2P seemed to gesture in this direction.

And where did one draw the limits to intervention? When Obama in his speech on Libya accepted that not every episode of mass violence could be expected to evoke an American response, he implicitly acknowledged the prudential limits to a morality-based foreign policy. Was it then enough to say, as he did, that it would act when it could, especially since warding off genocide is only one of R2P's supposed aims, and ethnic cleansing, crimes against humanity, and war crimes, the other three, routinely go unremarked? Why Gadhafi and not Tibet? Or Gaza, or Bahrain? Supporters say a little intervention is better than none. But that may be quite wrong, and for reasons that go beyond the obvious reproach of double standards. The main point is that the way leaders treat their people is not the only problem that counts in international affairs. A world in which violations of human rights trump the sanctity of borders may turn out to produce more wars, more massacres, and more instability. It may also be less law-abiding. If the history of the past century shows anything, it is that clear legal norms, the empowering of states, and the securing of international stability more generally also serve the cause of human welfare.

The historical record is cautionary in other ways too. R2P looks like nothing so much as the return of the civilizing mission and the "humanitarian" interventions of previous centuries—from Britain's use of abolitionism to legitimize its aggressive policing of the high seas to Fascist Italy's cynical rationalization of its invasion of Ethiopia in 1935 as an intervention in the name of civilization to suppress the slave trade. Before 1914, Balkan insurgents appealed regularly to the West's humanitarian sympathies to help them throw off the Ottoman yoke much as the Kosovo Liberation Army enlisted NATO to get rid of rule from Belgrade. But the troubled historical antecedents of their own interventions were not something policymakers dwelled on. Few if any of the supporters of NATO's air war in Libya in 2011 recalled the Italian invasion of that country that had taken place precisely a century earlier, an invasion that originated both the theory and the practice of mass bombing. This Western amnesia was itself a problem. The objections other states mounted to the idea of R2P could be seen to reflect not a love for autocracy and dictatorship or indifference to the rights of the individual but rather the fact that, as Deng Xiaoping said of the Chinese to U.S. national security adviser Brent Scowcroft in 1989, they have long and bitter memories of earlier Western interference in their internal affairs and see the use of force for humanitarian ends as inherently uncontrollable and open-ended. They saw in short what European and American policymakers had apparently missed—that the old ghost of the standard of civilization, exorcised after 1945 by the United Nations, had risen from the grave. It remains to be established whether this represents a last gasp of the European civilizational certainties of the nineteenth century, or the beginning of a new lease on life for a once discredited concept.[25]

PURSUING THE PERPETRATORS

If international executive authority expanded after the end of the Cold War through peacekeeping, interventions, and international territorial administration, it achieved institutional form above all in the realm of international criminal law and in the establishment in particular of the International Criminal Court. This was a truly remarkable development, not least because the idea had had such a short and undistinguished prehistory. Some inconclusive interwar discussions for such a body had taken place at the League of Nations, and then came the war crimes trials at Nuremberg, which were followed by a series of criminal investigations and prosecutions in the two Germanys. But proposals for a permanent international criminal court had languished and by the 1980s international law itself had become a pale imitation of what it had once been.

It was therefore a striking departure—in truth, at the time, a substitute for the more decisive action the United States and other major powers were then unwilling to make—when in 1993 the Security Council established an International Criminal Tribunal for the former Yugoslavia (ICTY) and authorized it to prosecute "persons responsible for serious violations of international humanitarian law committed in the territory of the former Yugoslavia." The UN Security Council nominated a slate of judges who were then voted on by the General Assembly, and the prosecutor was appointed by the council on the nomination of the secretary-general. These provisions were important because they guaranteed the permanent members of the Security Council control over the composition of the court. A year later, warding off criticism for its inaction in Rwanda, the Security Council set up a second tribunal for the genocide there.

Both courts have been busy: the ICTY has indicted more than 160 individuals and sentenced sixty-four of them, ranging from ordinary soldiers to Slobodan Milosevic, who became the first sitting head of state to be indicted for war crimes. He had been charged for ethnic cleansing in Kosovo in 1999, and was transferred to The Hague in 2001, where he was also charged for crimes committed in Croatia and Bosnia. (Having begun in 2002, the trial was still under way in early 2006 when Milosevic was found dead in his prison cell.) The Rwanda tribunal proceeded with fifty cases and issued twenty-nine convictions. They have established the principle that perpetrators may have to answer for their crimes, they have provided a place where the victims of violence can be heard, and they have revealed an enormous amount of information, as trials generally do, about the events themselves.

Moreover, their eventual demise will certainly not take away from their real significance—to have paved the way for a general tribunal—the International Criminal Court. This was first discussed in detail in 1994 at the United Nations, and work on a draft statute resulted in the new court being established when the 1998 Rome treaty was adopted. By 2002, a sufficient number of signatories had ratified the treaty and the court came into existence, its jurisdiction limited to "the most serious crimes of concern to the international community as a whole." Controversially, this included—or will include once an agreement has been reached to activate the court's jurisdiction in this realm—the crime of aggression, which was finally defined to the satisfaction of the court's members in 2010.[26]

What is so striking about the emergence of a permanent International Criminal Court is that it took place in the teeth of powerful American opposition. The Bush administration in particular threatened to veto UN peacekeeping operations unless the Security Council gave any Americans involved immunity from prosecution, and it went further—to the fury of many of its own partners—by concluding numerous bilateral agreements with other countries not to surrender each other's nationals to the court. Congressional opposition was, if anything, even stronger and tried to preclude military assistance for any country that was a party to the court unless it reached such an agreement. Yet none of this has been sufficient to prevent the court from beginning its work.[27]

American anxieties about the ICC had been reinforced by the increasing use of American troops in international missions from Kosovo onward. Charges that the NATO bombing of Serbia in 1999 were illegal unnerved the Clinton administration and confirmed the Pentagon in its deep opposition to the entire ICC project. In addition, after 9/11 the Bush administration was particularly worried that the way it was carrying out the "war on terror" might lay U.S. personnel open to arrest and trial abroad. Following publicity about the CIA's extraordinary rendition program, an Italian court convicted twenty-three Americans in absentia, including the CIA station chief in Milan, for the kidnapping of an Egyptian cleric in 2003; more cases may be forthcoming following revelations of secret CIA interrogation sites in Poland and Romania. In other words, even as a majority of countries in the world accepted the idea of a supervening legal sovereignty in the court to uphold the law's sway in cases where member states could or would not prosecute, the war on terror intensified the long-standing American unwillingness to allow its own judicial autonomy to be even potentially subordinated. Whereas the international politics of global financial reform had largely followed American wishes and practices, and the international politics of development always had a de haut en bas character, the rise of the ICC represented, at least in the eyes of its many Washington opponents, a real juridical challenge, and the U.S. reaction was correspondingly intense.

In fact, unlike prosecutors in several national jurisdictions, the court itself has generally been anxious not to tread on American toes. On the thorny question of whether the Bush doctrine of preemptive war was illegal or not, the court sidestepped the issue. Having accepted the definition of aggression worked out in the UN General Assembly, a definition that did not seem to have room for preemption, the court declared that unlike other crimes that it regarded as universal in character, it would not exercise jurisdiction over the crime of aggression when committed by nonsignatory states: not only the United States, but China and Russia as well, thus remained safe from investigation.[28]

Also bringing it closer to American wishes is the way the court has come to play an increasingly political role: what started out as a creation of the UN General Assembly, emphatically detached from the Security Council, has gone on to forge an increasingly close relationship to the council. In 2005, for instance, it was the council that asked the court to investigate the situation in Darfur and compelled Sudan to cooperate with the ICC despite Sudan's not being a member. The outcome was a striking one: the United States, like China, abstained but did not veto the resolution, and thus two major nonsignatory powers sitting on the UN Security Council compelled another nonmember, Sudan, to work through the new international criminal justice system.

The U.S. representative claimed to be motivated by the desire to place humanitarian assistance above the need to circumscribe the court's influence. That was itself a revealing formulation. In fact, what seemed to matter most was that while the Sudanese could be investigated, Americans would not. The Security Council included, at the request of the United States, a provision that exempted persons of nonparty states in the Sudan from ICC prosecution. No U.S. person supporting operations in the Sudan would be subject to investigation or prosecution because of this resolution. That did not mean that there would be immunity for American citizens who acted in violation of the law, since the United States would continue to discipline its own people when appropriate. But it did mean that the United States could both use the court for its own purposes and remain immune to its jurisdiction. One would be hard put to find a more perfect illustration of the value of international law to a Great Power.[29]

One could write this off as American exceptionalism, except that it has evidently struck other powerful states that they might become exceptions too. In the spring of 2011, the Security Council decided to refer Gadhafi to the court. Unanimously backing the resolution were at least five nonsignatories of the International Criminal Court, including Russia, India, the United States, and China. And once again, the resolution explicitly exempted the personnel of nonsignatories from the purview of the ICC.

Is the ICC then merely a court for the weak to be used by the powerful at their convenience? This is a suspicion that has begun to gather pace in Africa in particular. The continent has been on the whole supportive of the ICC—and more than half its countries have signed. But it has not escaped notice that the court's chief prosecutor seems to have been exclusively concerned with investigating Africans: five indictments of leaders of the notorious Lord's Resistance

Army in Uganda, several Congolese politicians, Omar al-Bashir and other Sudanese figures, in addition to investigations in the Ivory Coast and Kenya. The indictment of Bashir in particular led to a rift between the UN Security Council and the African Union, which regarded it as jeopardizing the prospects for peace. Since then a heated debate about the impartiality of the court has continued. Defenders of the court protest that its focus on Africa reflects the fact that domestic judicial systems are weaker in Africa than elsewhere. Other critics suggest that donor funds would have been better spent improving national judicial institutions rather than being poured into the ICC. And there remains force in the AU fear that by relying so heavily on the idea of prosecution, the West has exaggerated the power of the law to bring conflicts to an end and allowed this to displace potentially more cost-effective if slower and more morally ambiguous political avenues to peace. Europe's reckoning with Nazism and fascism after 1945, for instance, suggests that while it was important symbolically to confront key figures of the old regime with their crimes, recovery also depended on preserving stable state institutions, limiting the scale of purges, and cutting investigations short for the sake of stability and growth.[30]

This power imbalance at the heart of the ICC tells us something important about the spread of "humanity's law" after the Cold War. The idea for the court was not driven by Washington—and indeed Washington's toleration of it was always highly conditional, dependent on its functioning as a servitor of the Security Council and premised on a complete exemption for serving U.S. military personnel. Yet its role in American foreign policy since its creation has emerged in a fashion characteristic of the longer history of the American deployment of international institutions, its "exceptional" sponsor extending the power of international law while remaining above and beyond its reach itself.[31]

Advocates of the "justice cascade" have talked about the importance of entrenching the new humanitarian norms in the UN system while American power remains unchallenged, and many human rights supporters hope perhaps that their universalist premises can be rescued by eventually getting the United States itself to join. Yet universalism is in the eye of the beholder. China, Russia, and others who opposed NATO's intervention in Kosovo in 1999 so strongly may now feel that the vague rhetoric of an "international community" dedicated to defending humanity is one they can live with. For, like the United States, they too can claim exemption for themselves while availing themselves through the ICC of a new international instrument for imposing upon smaller and weaker polities around the globe. The world's largest powers will have no reason to fear it; medium-sized powers will be glad, as medium-sized powers always are, to live in a world of rules and institutions; it is the world's weak states that are most likely to feel its effects, for good and bad. But what makes the entire edifice so imposing and so useful is that its legitimacy is guaranteed by the imprimatur of the UN and above all the permanent members of the Security Council. In this sense, the ICC should be seen as adjunct to the idea of a Responsibility to Protect: norm and institution combined have come to legitimate new forms of international intervention in those parts of the Third World that cannot resist it.

Despite the endless invocation of the "rule of law" by American administrations and international agencies, moreover, what international law in particular really stands for today is not at all clear. The bright line between war and peace enunciated in the UN Charter has been blurred. The old norm against conquest—so powerful in the Cold War era—is crumbling. In the case of atrocities as well as weapons of mass destruction, policies of preemption subordinate legal entitlements to intelligence assessments; the public becomes secondary to the secret and the private, the legislative to the executive. As for the laws of war, the initial terrain on which the lawyers of 1873 tested out the claims of their new discipline, the dream of humanizing warfare seems less plausible than ever. The boundaries between legal and illegal, domestic and foreign, civilian and combatant have become confused as never before. Sometimes states evade legal obligations by changing the terms—so that instead of talking about going to war or even declaring war they use the language of intervention and conflict instead. Sometimes they claim that new insurgencies make law irrelevant. When legal advisers raise complications, those in government hide behind executive privilege and official secrecy. Thus legal arguments are publicized when they are serviceable and buried when not, and this increases the sense of their purely instrumental nature and subordination to the authority of the political.

Meanwhile, war itself may be about to leave an already permissive law far behind. President Obama's administration has made unprecedented use of robot drones as aerial killers, while targeted assassinations across the world, justified as "self-defense," have increased dramatically. Some sixty military and CIA bases are now utilized in the American drone program everywhere from Nevada to a former French Foreign Legion base in Djibouti: "pilots" fly the planes from terminals in Langley, Virginia, Bagram, or Balochistan, while analysts watch hours of live-stream "Death TV" fed back from the drones themselves. While military lawyers fret whether the occupants of those drone bases may not themselves be regarded as legal combatants and hence legitimately targeted by their enemies, technicians are working on a new generation of unpiloted robotic drones, whose "hunt, identify, and kill" functions will be run out of preprogrammed software.[32] In 2010 a little-noticed UN report into extrajudicial killings warned of a "highly problematic blurring and expansion of the boundaries of the applicable legal frameworks—human rights law, the laws of war, and the law applicable to the use of inter-state force."[33]

Viewed through the pages of the journals of robotic engineers, new nightmarish paradoxes of humanitarian warfare become technical challenges. In 2007, the U.S. military ordered a study of how to build "an ethical control and reasoning system." As human soldiering on the battlefield is replaced by that of "lethal autonomous robots," engineers are doing their best to ensure that they are "moral machines" programmed with knowledge of the laws of war and ethical capability. They extol robots' freedom from human emotion and prejudice and their superior information-absorbing capacity, and argue that they may therefore "fight" more humanely than humans. But the software is of such complexity that it generates unpredictable outcomes, and there have already been friendly-fire fatalities involving robotic weaponry. Given the planned shift toward robotics across the U.S. military—and the likelihood that others will follow—we face the prospect of future humanitarian interventions being fought on behalf of humans by nonhumans. Conjuring up this world, in February 2012 a proposal was published in the *New York Times* to "halt the butchery in Syria" by setting up safe havens patrolled by drones.[34] As rights are extended to robots—the U.S. Air Force, for instance, argues that its unmanned drones have the right to fire in "self-defense"—they are removed from peoples and states. A future beckons in which powerful states armed with robotic drones with laser-guided missiles shoot down their enemies from computer terminals across the world in the name of humanity.

Jeremy Bentham envisaged international law two centuries ago as a way of spreading universal well-being, independent of nation or creed. Today, in contrast, the appeal to law has become a vocabulary of permissions, a means of asserting power and control that normalizes the debatable and justifies the exception. The former U.S. secretary of state Elihu Root, whose memory was evoked in 2006 at the American Society of International Law a century after he had helped found it, would have been astonished at the change. In his time, international law had been proclaimed as a creed of universal applicability, and he could hardly have imagined the enviable situation that would be enjoyed by his heirs in Washington, who routinely preach the virtues of law while exempting themselves from many of its constraints. But the political advantages that have accrued to the United States in this process, advantages inseparable from its rise from being merely one of the second-ranking powers of the world to its most powerful state, have also come at a cost. That old vision of international law, which emerged to shore up the sovereignty of states by establishing rules for the conduct of war and which aspired to replace politicians with judges as the arbiters of the world's affairs, will continue to be taught as though it still has meaning. But it no longer carries much conviction, and the idea of a law binding upon all states and those governing them seems as far away as ever.[35]

CHAPTER 14

What Remains: The Crisis in Europe and After

Thus, I think that the type of oppression threatening democracies will not be like anything there has been in the world before: our contemporaries would not be able to find any example of it in their memories.

—Alexis de Tocqueville, *Democracy in America*[1]

The technocratic, corporatist, non-democratic nature of these transnational regulatory networks would be disguised and lauded as the newest triumph of deliberation, one that by definition produces the best, most rational achievement of the shared values of mankind.

—Martin Shapiro, "Will the Globe Echo the EU?" (2005)[2]

SPINELLI'S DREAM: THE ONCE AND FUTURE EUROPE

Baked by the Mediterranean sun beating down on the Tyrrhenian Sea, the volcanic islets of Santo Stefano and Ventotene lie sixty miles off the Italian coast. Each is a few square miles of parched, treeless, and windswept rock, inhabited since Roman times chiefly by lizards, seagulls, and political prisoners. Santo Stefano is the smaller of the two, dominated even now by the weed-infested ruins of the extraordinary Bourbon prison that was built on perfect Benthamite principles at the end of the eighteenth century. The slightly larger island, Ventotene, was the administrative headquarters of the prison complex under fascism, and it was there with nothing but the sinister rock of Santo Stefano to break up the monotony of the horizon that a small group of Italian political prisoners came together in the early years of the Second World War to diagnosis the source of Europe's ills and to propose a better future. What emerged in the summer of 1941 would become known as the Ventotene Manifesto. Its main author, a young activist named Altiero Spinelli, who had recently broken with the Communist Party, would become a legendary figure in the pantheon of postwar Europeanism, a leading federalist and an advocate of integration who played a prominent role in the drive toward European union until his death in 1986.

The starting point for the manifesto was naturally the failure of the League of Nations and the rise of fascism and Nazism. It denounced both the League's naïve confidence in international law and fascism's idolatry of the state, and went on to argue that the national state was in itself now a threat to the peace: Europe required not another League of Nations but full-blown federation. The communists themselves were criticized—on Mazzinian grounds—for preaching the virtues of class conflict. But although Spinelli had renounced communism, what he offered was in many ways a kindred vision: those "progressive forces' who believed in federation were to act in the name of the "masses," but they would be that minority of "serious internationalists" that was capable of acting decisively in a Leninist fashion to provide guidance in the critical moments when fascism and Nazism crumbled, moments "during which the popular masses are anxiously awaiting a new message." The real struggle was not going to be against this or that ideological current; it would be against those "reactionary forces" who aimed to restore the power of the national state. The real task was to make federation work, and if individual states wanted to go their own way they would have to be compelled to see the truth. For only a European federation had the answers to the problems of mixed ethnicity and geography that had brought war to the continent and twice through Europe to the world. Instead of spreading conflict, Europe should unify itself, while mankind awaited "the more distant future when the political unity of the entire globe becomes a possibility."[3]

That document now lies more than seventy years in the past. But what Spinelli would think about the present crisis in Europe is not unfathomable. Early on, he recognized that the Common Market was becoming a powerful force and he opted to work through it rather than around it. He never really liked its dependence upon intergovernmental cooperation and he always sought to strengthen the more genuinely supranational institutions—the European Commission and the European Parliament—over the Council of Ministers. On the other hand, he certainly approved of the idea that economic union might lead to political union, and complained only at the length of time this was taking. Nor would he have minded the elite character of the drive to further integration, since he was convinced that ultimately the continent's peoples would come to appreciate its blessings.

Faithful to the means while envisaging quite different ends, today's European Union exists in a deeply ambiguous relationship to the principles of Ventotene. Integration has been driven by a bureaucratic elite that continues to see national sovereignty as an obstacle to be overcome, but this elite has largely lost sight of the principles of social solidarity and human dignity that Spinelli wished to resurrect. From the perspective of Ventotene, federation was an instrument that would allow the struggle against inequality and poverty to be won. A form of managed capitalism would place limits on the market and property ownership without doing away with them completely; there would be nationalization of key industries, land reform, and worker cooperatives. The result would be not communism but the realization of a simpler, more manageable, and perhaps nobler dream: a world in which economic forces would be guided and controlled by man rather than dominating him.

This is the world we have lost in a double sense. In the first place, the sublime confidence and optimism in political action and mobilization for a better future that existed on Ventotene in 1941 is no longer with us. In addition, the Ventotene ideals, which basically underpinned the managed capitalism of the years of the postwar miracle in western Europe between 1945 and 1975, were repudiated following the turn to neoliberalism in the late 1970s and abandoned at the European level with the embrace of global finance from the 1990s. From the perspective of early-twentieth-century Europe, the sentiments of 1941 represent a regime every bit as *ancien* as the decaying and abandoned Bourbon panopticon on the island of Santo Stefano.

We can chart the turning point fairly precisely. The 1960s and 1970s were a time of prosperity in western Europe, and trade and growth outstripped the United States in a system in which the European Community carapace overlaid powerful and largely autonomous nation-states buffered both from the outside world and from one another but brought together gradually through the horizontal integration of economic complementarities. For the Community's bureaucracy, however, always dreaming of driving forward to more perfect union, they were a period of institutional stagnation. Then, in the early 1980s, France's finance minister Jacques Delors witnessed at first hand through the travails of the Mitterrand government the impossibility of building socialism in one country, and as president of the European Commission from 1985 to 1995 he resolved to shore up social solidarity at the continental level while accelerating market integration. With another senior French civil servant, the economist Michel Camdessus, moving to run the IMF in 1987, there was a close interconnection between Delors's integration drive in Europe and the emergence of a rules-bound liberalization of international capital flows at the same time. Equally instrumental in this process was a third French mandarin, Henri Chavranski, who oversaw the drafting of the Code of Liberalization of the discreetly influential OECD. What one scholar has dubbed "the Paris consensus," in contrast to the much more loudly self-advertised Washington version, opened up capital markets across the Union and the world, a move that was perhaps the key economic shift in the globalization of the 1990s. Delors gambled that Europe could enjoy both capital liberalization and enhanced welfare. He would turn out to be wrong.[4]

The high points of the Delors years were the Single European Act of 1986 and the Maastricht Treaty of 1992. With the ending of the Cold War in particular, membership of the Union doubled within a decade, and indeed the peaceful incorporation of much of eastern Europe was a historic achievement. But the success was a Pyrrhic one, replete with unintended consequence as expansion, so desirable politically, complicated things. Redistribution was built in through help for poor regions, but the Union itself did not function effectively as any kind of welfare guarantor for the poor and disadvantaged in general: constrained by what was in reality a very small tax-raising capacity, "social Europe" always took second place to the higher goal of fiscal convergence and monetary union. Integration thus brought a shift away from redistribution toward the control of inflation and capital and labor mobility. Signed in February 1992, the Maastricht Treaty gestured decisively toward not a Europe of welfare and regulated capital but rather to an intensification of the single market and an acceleration of trade and financial flows through the creation of a common currency.[5]

At the same time, the idea of a citizens' Europe with strong representative institutions failed to materialize as both the European Parliament and its national equivalents were marginalized. This was not simply because of the general mistrust of parliaments that became evident everywhere from the 1970s onward; it was also because enlargement necessitated increased majority voting, which meant that member states often signed up—were *obliged* to sign up—for policies they had not wanted and had no intention of carrying out. For this very reason, monetary unification was made conditional upon national governments handing over much of their discretionary fiscal power. The so-called Stability and Growth Pact, with its strict limits on deficit spending and debt in theory at least locked national legislatures in. Electorates registered some disquiet when they were consulted, but in most cases they were not. What cushioned the impact of what was an unnecessarily rigid system, was that before 2010 Stability and Growth Pact rules were not properly enforced: by then almost every country in the Union with the exception of Luxembourg and the Scandinavians had been in breach at some point. But because the penalties were mild, monetary and fiscal policy was looser than it would otherwise have been and there was little popular opposition.[6]

If legislators were not driving integration, who was? Here is where the European Union really has pioneered a new kind of internationalism. One key agent has been the European Court of Justice, an oddly neglected body and far more powerful than any world equivalent precisely because the national courts of member-states (with the important exception of the Germans, who have preferred their own supreme constitutional court as the ultimate arbiter) have generally been willing to defer to its judgments. The court started out by establishing that European law could not be overridden by national law, and then went on to make a series of far-reaching interventions in the realm of social policy and industrial relations that went mostly unnoticed by the broader public. Supported by the legal profession, the court came as close as any body to establishing "a new order of international law"—binding, pervasive, beyond political discretion—in a world that had otherwise given up on the possibility of this.[7]

Even more powerful and pervasive than the court, but more nebulous and still less visible, have been the regulators. According to a process known to the cognoscenti as "comitology"—"an indispensable tool for interest groups and a nightmare for European studies students" was how one Belgian politician described it—Brussels lawmakers passed general administrative laws whose details were then fleshed out by small committees of regulators and national experts. Opaque and unrepresentative, hundreds of such committees have operated in the shadows, outside the formal oversight of the European Parliament or even of the Council of Ministers. The Treaty of Lisbon in 2009 was intended to rebut increasingly loud criticisms of the undemocratic character of this system. But although the treaty pledged explicitly to revitalize "the democratic life of the Union," it has failed to do so. Today comitology flourishes, its procedures more arcane than ever, generating administrative laws that it remains virtually impossible to revise or scrap. In short, Europe empowered the regulators and the rulemakers over legislators and their citizens, blurring the boundaries between the public good and private interest, and in the process, as the legal scholar Joseph Weiler puts it, rendering "the nation-state hollow and its institutions meaningless."[8]

The real costs of this model of international integration became visible with startling speed once the financial collapse of 2008–2009 metamorphosed into the sovereign debt crisis of 2010. As the fairytale ended, the euro was plunged into uncertainty. Keynesians argued that expansionary policies could probably have headed off the worst of the crisis since the overall sums required to deal with south European debt were far smaller than had been at stake, say, at the time of the Marshall Plan in 1947. But we will never know because such policies were precluded by Eurozone rules and German political resistance. Instead the countries in the eye of the storm have been forced into austerity: national income has contracted rapidly, wages have been slashed, unemployment has soared, especially among the young, and the welfare achievements of previous decades have been rolled back.

There has been only one significant exception to the ongoing marginalization of national legislatures and their political leaders—the German Bundestag. As for the German chancellor, Angela Merkel, she has played a far more decisive role than any of the leading European officials except the head of the European Central Bank: in contrast the European Commission president, José Barroso, and the president of the Council of Ministers, Herman van Rompuy, have been sidelined. But not even Germany has controlled the process. For in the preceding years, as the crisis demonstrated, enormous power has been handed over not only to European civil servants operating with little accountability or transparency, but also to even less accountable groups outside the European bureaucracy altogether.[9]

As politicians negotiated through 2010–11 to keep Greece inside the euro, the constraint that they all faced was the need to avert a "credit event"—the adjudication of which depended not on them nor on any elected officials, but on the deliberations of a committee of the International Swaps and Derivatives Association that is made up mostly of bankers. These are supposed to set aside conflicts of interest that might be generated by their own firms' positions and speak for the industry as a whole, but the process's lack of transparency makes it impossible to know.[10] Immense power was also granted to a few American credit rating agencies—latecomers to the business of global risk evaluation (and not notably successful at it). Neither grouping had automatically acquired this power; they had won it through effective lobbying and a series of political decisions in the preceding years that had allowed capital markets to largely regulate themselves.[11]

Only in 2008 did Europe's political class start to acknowledge, in the words of the German president Horst Köhler, that the financial markets were "a monster that must be tamed."[12] Just how jerry-rigged the entire structure was has begun to emerge via compelling evidence that a small number of banks colluded in fixing the calculation of so-called London Interbank Offered Rate (LIBOR)—the basic interest rate upon which an impressive $350 *trillion* of financial instruments depended. The lack of interest generated initially in this extraordinary story outside the pages of the *Financial Times* is itself instructive. If the acronyms of modern financial life are impenetrable, the issues technically complex, the terminology euphemistic, and the sums involved literally unimaginable, it is not accidental: such factors have functioned to enhance the mystique of the "market" in whose name these developments occurred and to obscure its imperfections and asymmetrical opportunities.[13]

Yet even as these elements became better understood, the crisis revealed the financial markets' ability to preserve private profits while socializing their liabilities. That socialization was on a breathtaking scale. Government bailouts to the financial sector in 2008–2009 were so large that they left many countries' debt/GDP ratios on average 20–25 percent higher than they would have otherwise been.[14] The paradox was that while governments were thereby weakened, and in many cases slid into crisis, market participants took the assistance while moving rapidly and successfully to prevent any real regulatory challenge. The politicians denounced the irresponsibility of the bankers, but fell short of an effective response. On the contrary, helped by cheap money made available by central banks—so-called quantitative easing represented an extremely crude form of pump priming, the only form of stimulus left to an age that no longer believed in planning—and unfettered by a global financial transaction tax or any significant new regulatory pressures, the derivatives market at the root of the problem has continued to grow and the financial sector has pushed ahead with many of the novel and uncollateralized instruments that contributed to the crisis. Alternately cajoling and threatening, its leaders showed a much greater capacity for collective action, self-assertion, and self-preservation than the leaders of Europe's states.[15]

Spinelli's vision of an economy run in the service of human needs has thus been turned on its head. If the human needs being served by the euro—the currency with which the very project of ever closer union has come to be identified—are not primarily those of its citizens, this is not surprising because they have had less say in the outcome than the bankers. In the war years on Ventotene, finance capital was seen as a force to be controlled and checked, and the speculators themselves were seen as at least partially responsible for the slump of the 1930s. By contrast, integration through financial liberalization and monetary union has produced wealth that European democracies cannot afford and problems they cannot answer, limiting their power and undermining the credibility of their institutions. No longer the fount either of political liberty (as nineteenth-century liberals once hoped), or of social welfare, European internationalism has moved a long way from its origins.[16]

THE MYSTIQUE OF GLOBAL GOVERNANCE

Europe has rarely been just about Europe. As Spinelli's manifesto testified, it also has often stood, sometimes formally, sometimes implicitly, for a much broader normative ideal, most recently when George W. Bush's abrasive approach to politics made it peculiarly tempting to look across the Atlantic to the Union, with its fledgling common currency and its "European model of society," as an alternative. Jeremy Rifkin wrote in 2004 about "how Europe's vision of the future is quietly eclipsing the American dream." Tony Judt's 2005 history *Postwar* ended describing a continental nirvana in which people opted to pay higher taxes in return for "free or nearly free medical services, early retirement and a prodigious range of social and public services." Writing in 2009, on the very eve of the sovereign debt crisis, the political commentator Steven Hill went even further, describing the continent as "the new City on a Hill."[17]

It was in these years that some American commentators hailed a sophisticated new form of internationalism emerging globally that was largely based on the European experience. They wrote enthusiastically about a "New World Order" that looked suspiciously like the European Union writ large, a world in which formal supranational institutions played a relatively minor role and loose but businesslike networks of middle-level government officials from different countries, often mingling with regulators and industry experts, got things done. In this world, there seemed to be no evident conflict, and rather little formality. Most of what went on was behind closed doors, humdrum, and technical but ultimately of real consequence. It was a quiet world of international standard setting, Internet governance, and spreading human rights. States remained important, but through the actions of bureaucrats not legislators or politicians. The era of large international institutions, formal treaties, perhaps of diplomats too seemed to be passing.[18]

As a description of what was occurring not merely within Europe but globally, the picture was compelling: old-fashioned political scientists had mostly missed the fact that international affairs was becoming less focused on large formalized institutions and more dependent upon informal clusters and horizontal interagency relationships that blurred the boundaries between officialdom, corporations, and NGOs. This perspective implied—as a leading theorist of this process argued more explicitly later—a relatively minor role for behemoths such as the United Nations:

> There is an entire infrastructure of global governance that is not at the UN, or at the World Bank, or at the International Monetary Fund or at the World Trade Organization. It is the networks of antitrust officials, of police officials, prosecutors, financial regulators, intelligence operatives, militaries, judges and even, although lagging behind, legislators.[19]

This kind of description, however, comes across rather like the one regulators and networkers would presumably like to give of themselves—earnest and professional, guided by considerations of something dull but respectable called "best practice." Efficiency and expertise rule. One would scarcely guess that anything so uncouth as political power could influence the discussions over the conference table. There is no fighting here, no blood, not even any really sharp clashes of opinion. In short, this is a rosy picture of a world governed, in legal scholar Martti Koskenniemi's words, by the "Supreme Tribunal of a managerial world."[20]

It is of course an old idea, this thought that all would be well if only the politicians could be kept at arm's length and the people who actually know something allowed to get on with things. Before the First World War, scientists, engineers, doctors, and bibliographers all embraced internationalism for this reason: it gave them a grand mission and appealed to their sense of the nobility of their calling. Yet experts are not always capable of standing above the fray of politics and they are as prone to see themselves as representing their own governments as anyone else.[21] Whether expertise in the abstract is political or not, is not the question; it is rather what kind of political order the claim of technical neutrality is being advanced to support. Some hope this order will be a democratic one, led by the United States and the West and spread globally through the inspiring example provided by professionals working collegially. But American leadership and values alone are not really a sufficient cure for most people for the deficit of democratic accountability at the heart of modern international governance.

If other forces are needed to reinject a degree of popular participation in what remains a closed world suited chiefly to bureaucrats and lobbyists and to rescue the old internationalist dream, where might these forces be found?[22] Perhaps in that civil society whose magical effects are widely credited with the dissolution of communism and the injection of ethics into international life. Ninety percent of international NGOs have been formed since 1970, and there has been a quickening of associational life on a scale not seen since before the First World War: a 1994 *Foreign Affairs* article referred to a "Global Associational Revolution." Many NGOs are now entrenched and institutionalized in UN agencies and elsewhere, and they are the recipients of large amounts of Western aid. Two-thirds, for instance, of EU relief goes through them, and by 2003 they were disbursing more money than most UN agencies or indeed member states: the budgets of major NGOs such as Greenpeace and the World Wildlife Fund run to over $100 million annually.[23] Yet funding can become a form of co-optation, and many NGOs now worry about how to prevent the funders dictating their mission so as to preserve their legitimacy. Their world has changed fast in the past three decades, and their own accountability and transparency have come under scrutiny. So has the process whereby they select the causes they fight for. Global civil society, writes political scientist Clifford Bob, who has explored the process by which some issues get taken up and others do not, is basically a "Darwinian society" of complicated relationships between mostly Western organizers at the top of the pyramid and mostly non-Western movements bidding for their attention. This is not to say that the rise of the NGO is necessarily a bad thing, but simply that the energies they bring to international life must be set against their relative opacity and the fact that their agendas are often established with little public rationale or justification. Lobbying for specific causes, they supplement but cannot substitute for the more holistic approach to the public good that governing institutions are designed to adopt.[24]

Even less plausible as vehicles of a democratization of international life are the huge charitable foundations that have been one of the major sources of the so-called civil society revolution, and that oversee disbursements of some of the astronomical private fortunes that have been made over the past thirty years—mostly through privatizations, the dot-com boom, and finance. The result of their emergence has been not merely an explosion in private charitable giving but a transformation of philanthropy itself.[25] The new "philanthrocapitalists" are often impatient with the old global institutions, and they like to take an active advocacy role, pushing hard to solve society's problems in predetermined ways that reflect the personal views and preferences of the very wealthy individuals whose munificence they advertise. In classic fashion, they are inspired by their own success to empower new "social entrepreneurs" around the world. But they have a downside. Applying business methods to social problems, they exaggerate what technology can do, ignore the complexities of social and institutional constraints, often waste sums that would have been better spent more carefully, and wreak havoc with the existing fabric of society in places they know very little about. In the past, such foundations often provided vital support for public international institutions—the intimate relationship between the Rockefeller Foundation and the League comes to mind.[26] Now, however, because the vast sums at the foundations' disposal outweigh those available to many long-established international agencies, they have started to displace the latter and complicate their activities instead of enhancing them. Thus malaria specialists at the World Health Organization have complained that the Gates Foundation's dominance of malaria research is creating a "cartel" of malaria scientists who validate each other's research and hinder a real debate.[27]

For about a century, governments used tax revenues to fund this kind of research through public bodies; now we have a model in which private wealth takes a leading role in accumulating and organizing expertise. No less obviously inclined to waste, corruption, and arrogance than the older public governmental version, this new model is even more unaccountable and opaque. In 2009, for instance, Bill Gates, Warren Buffett, and David Rockefeller called a meeting of their fellow super-philanthropists—people like George Soros, Oprah Winfrey, and Ted Turner—to discuss what they could do in response to the global financial crisis and the longer-term environmental and health problems facing the world. When the participants gathered at an Upper East Side residence in New York on May 5, the meeting was shrouded in secrecy. It was scarcely surprising—the combined wealth of the people in the room was reckoned to be around $125 billion—and that was after already spending billions in the previous twelve years. Such sums dwarfed the social spending budgets of most member states of the UN down the road. But whereas the UN has a General Assembly and the Economic and Social Council and many other means of disseminating and debating its activities, the Good Club (as journalists dubbed it) has nothing. Did they just have tea? Or did they decide, as some newspaper accounts have it, that it was up to them to tackle the threat of planetary overpopulation—probably the top global fear of wealthy American philanthropists for about a century? We cannot know. But we have learned enough about the history of private wealth to know that alone these do-gooders are inadequate vehicles to supply the global public goods that well-run multilateral international institutions can deal with more systematically and openly.[28]

Some of the big new givers question this. The whole point of philanthropy, according to eBay billionaire Jeff Skoll, is to accelerate "a movement from institutions to individuals."[29] In the implicit pro-business, antipolitical thrust of this comment, it would be hard to find a better encapsulation of the fundamental challenge: domestically and to an even greater extent internationally, many people (and not just dot-com billionaires) in the West have lost faith in the capacity of government. The civil servant is as unpopular as the entrepreneur is idolized. Ignoring their built-in advantages—their long memories, their accountability, their experience in accommodating and mediating real political conflicts within and across societies—opinion across much of the developed world remains suspicious of the institutions of the public sector. Half a century ago, some commentators argued that at the international level a Relationship Society was giving way to an Institution Society, by which they meant that old-fashioned horizontal relations between states—the stuff of nineteenth-century diplomacy—were being replaced by hierarchies of power that were topped off by supranational bodies with an autonomous existence of their own and increasing powers to centralize decision making. The trend has been thrown into reverse, and many formerly powerful governing institutions are dwindling in importance.

Some would say this does not matter. Don't we now inhabit a brave new fast-moving, porous, networked world where large institutions are about as useful as dinosaurs? Networks in contrast sound equalizing and youthful, a way of bringing the corridors of power into contact with the streets. Yet networks exist in many forms, and many of them too are opaque and unrepresentative to any collective body. Networks too are good for some things, and not so good for others, as Marx and Lenin understood. It is very well, as the Internet commentator Clay Shirky does in his book *Here Comes Everybody,* to talk about "organizing without organization" and to praise the efficiency of loosely affiliated groupings, but they are rarely sources of durable political achievement. Anarchist internationalism, as the 1890s showed, bursts like a meteor and then vanishes again.[30]

THAT INTERNATIONAL INSTITUTIONS may not be internally democratic in their workings has been known for some time and does not appear particularly surprising. They are, after all, chiefly executive bureaucracies, and mostly their most powerful members like them that way. International legislatures have never lived up to the hope of nineteenth-century internationalists, and as the fate of the European Parliament and the UN General Assembly demonstrate, they are unlikely to make much impact on the twenty-first.[31]

What does seem novel, in historical terms, is the collapsing importance of the public bodies that give national sovereignty meaning and the way that organs of international government and regulation have come to assail the internal legitimacy, capacity, and cohesion of individual states. They are not actually turning democracies into dictatorships—few people believe in dictatorships anymore—although the turn to Putin in Russia suggests such a drift is possible. But they are certainly hollowing out representative institutions and curtailing their capacity to act. Bodies that were once designed to foster sovereignty are now recast to curtail it. And this is not merely the curtailing of autonomy that is always implicit when states decide to join international organizations and respect their rules; it is the consequence of major changes in those rules themselves. "The pattern of influence and decision-making that rules the world has an increasingly marginal connection with sovereignty," notes Koskenniemi in a recent article.[32]

This multifaceted erosion of sovereignty is a momentous change that has been based upon a radical alteration in attitudes to the state and bureaucracy over the past thirty years.[33] In its various nineteenth-century incarnations, after all, internationalism was preeminently a movement to restore sovereign power to the peoples of the world, and those who governed in their name. Its approach to the nation-state and its institutions was almost entirely positive. The originary moment of 1919 saw the goal of the League of Nations as a world made "safe for democracy," a goal understood—in an imperial idiom—as a society of sovereign polities. After 1945, the United Nations promoted the creed of sovereignty more widely, more adamantly, and more deeply. Nazism's assault on the sovereignty of small nations was repudiated and in Europe democracy was restored; colonialism's denial of sovereign rights around the world was also castigated. The state was rendered sacrosanct, international boundaries were mutually recognized in Asia, Africa, and Europe, and the meaning of democracy itself was broadened to "promote social progress and better standards of life in larger freedom" (in the words of the UN Charter). International institutions enabled states to survive and flourish, and as civil services expanded rapidly, states enabled their citizens.[34]

In the construction of this system of sovereign nations, no power played a more important role than the United States. Washington never had complete control of the process, of course, and there were compromises on all sides. After 1945, welfare states grew faster and economic nationalizations went farther across the globe than American policymakers might have wished, for example, and trade liberalization proceeded more slowly. But these points of disagreement and tension were not decisive. The American Century at its apogee coincided with the heyday of national planning in the Third World and the welfare state in Europe. American foundations funded roads, medical services, libraries, and schools, and American social sciences—from midcentury macroeconomics to modernization theory—provided the legitimation for this expansion of state capacity around the world. Countries gradually became reintegrated in a global trade network, but capital movements remained restricted, and in general people made money from producing and exchanging goods rather than from money itself. As late as 1971, it was assumed that conditionality would not work if demanded by the IMF since client states would permit no interference in their internal affairs.[35]

And then, between the mid-1970s and the early 1980s, all of this changed, as the United States ceased to support a version of liberalism embedded in strong domestic institutions.[36] Confronted with an unforeseen challenge to reshape the rules of international order in a way that gave priority to the needs of the developing world—the Third World's New International Economic Order—the United States reacted by moving against the old midcentury conception of the enabling state on several fronts: international human rights activism saw the state as tyrant and mobilized global civil society against it; the World Bank and the IMF exploited the crisis-prone character of the new financialization of the world to redraw the boundaries of public and private sectors in vulnerable debtor countries. As governance replaced government, welfare nets frayed, and income and wealth inequality rose sharply. Formal structures disintegrated and informal economies—black markets, smuggling, and crime networks—flourished, leaving only the ubiquitous concept of the "failed state" itself as implicit acknowledgment that states really were rather important. In turn, the threat of state failure rationalized invasions and occupations that returned swaths of Africa and parts of the Balkans to rule by international executive. This was in no sense a reversion to the emancipatory perspectives of mid-nineteenth-century internationalists but rather the crafting of a "leaner, meaner state" in one country after another across the world, dissolving society in the name of the individual, using international organizations as the handmaidens and new paradigms—the efficient market hypothesis, the Responsibility to Protect—to provide intellectual rationalization.

If the corrosive impact of this process on the idea of sovereignty itself has not much bothered mainstream American observers, it is partly because it has been moralized and turned into something virtuous, and partly because it has happened less there than anywhere else. The United States remains *the* exceptional power, able more than any other over the past half century to exempt itself from otherwise universally binding international commitments and obligations, its untrammeled sovereignty jealously guarded by Congress. Combining the language of universalism with the status of the exception has allowed American values and influence to spread at relatively little internal cost in terms of policy constraint. And this freedom has actually increased with the shift from a world of formal treaty obligations—a world that had always made Congress unhappy—to one of informal rules and norms, which the United States itself has been well positioned to craft. Only in the fears on the American right of eroding sovereignty and the implausible specter of world government do we get a glimmering of what the stakes may be when the American era finally ends.[37]

Beyond the borders of the United States, on the other hand, it has been far more self-evident that international institutions and norms have developed into means of curtailing sovereignty rather than enhancing it, trends that could not but affect the standing of international bodies themselves and undercut their ability to command continued support. The real-world challenges mount around us in the shape of climate change, financial instability, poverty, crime, and disease. With the WTO's Doha Round paralyzed and the World Bank chastened, the IMF incapable of helping to rectify the global imbalances that threaten the world economy, and no single agency able to coordinate the response to global warming, the institutions of international governance stand in urgent need of renovation. Yet the fundamental nineteenth-century insight that effective internationalism rests on effective nationalism remains pertinent. Voters around the world still see their primary allegiance to their national state rather than to any larger polity, a fact that reflects the continuing role of the state as primary purveyor of public goods but that many international bodies are loath to acknowledge.[38]

Now we are on the verge of a new era, and as Western predominance approaches an end, the prognosticators speculate on what will come next. Some American commentators seem particularly anxious at their country's possible loss of influence. But taking a more detached view and in more formal terms, the mere fact that some states are gaining strength as others lose it says little. And so far as China in particular is concerned, it has much to gain and little of any consequence to lose from participating in a system designed to favor leading nations. Like any great power, it will use these institutions to further its own ends, but like its predecessors it will not always prevail. Thus there is no reason to think that the shift in the global balance need of itself mark the end of the international institutions established in the Anglo-American ascendancy.

Indeed from the perspective of the question of sovereignty, positive as well as negative consequences may emerge from the decline in American and European financial and political clout. As long ago as 1995, the British political economist Susan Strange argued that "the only way to remove the present, hegemonic, do-nothing veto on better global governance is to build, bit by bit, a compelling opposition based on European-Japanese cooperation, but embracing Latin Americans, Asians and Africans." The prospective lineup now looks different but the point remains valid. The rising powers, China above all, have little liking for the IMF, at least in its older incarnation, and attach much greater importance to the idea of preserving sovereignty and some space for domestic political discretion. If their influence grows, the institutions the United States created may be brought back under new direction to the principles that originally animated them. A broader array of voices and perspectives will enrich the rather rigid forms of economic thinking that have predominated since the 1970s.[39]

Getting the institutional architecture right is the subject of endless position papers and reform proposals. But there are two kinds of more fundamental change that will need to take place too.[40] In the current crisis, politicians have essentially acted as underwriters, essential but subordinate to the dictates of communities of financial market makers they hesitate to contradict. More generally, the politicians have become policymakers, who listen in the first place to private interests and their lobbyists and try to adjudicate among them. Time will show whether they are any longer capable of governing. If that fails to happen, the responsibility will not be theirs alone. One of the reasons for the midcentury popularity of the state and sovereignty was that both had proved themselves in extreme circumstances. Twentieth-century total wars were fought by states that mobilized entire societies around shared perils and experiences. By creating models of equity, solidarity, and sacrifice, they transformed public attitudes in ways that endured into peacetime. Without a comparable transformation in our own views about the nature of government, the public good and the role of the state, without our developing a new kind of faith in our own collective capacity to shape the future, there is no real incentive for our politicians to change. They may not be trusted by their electorates—polls show levels of trust plumbing new lows—but they have no reason to care so long as this lack of trust does not translate into mobilization, resistance, and sustained pressure for reform.

To the nineteenth-century internationalists with whom this book began, the future conjured up a new dispensation for mankind, a dispensation they looked forward to with a confidence based upon their control over a universe of facts: hence Bentham's vision of a perfect system of law that depended on the accumulation of all useful knowledge, or Karl Marx's path to a communist future through the history of capitalism's past. To twentieth-century institution builders from Smuts to Roosevelt, from Robert Jackson to Walt Rostow, the future could be planned and tackled with foresight on behalf of entire communities and nations, perhaps even for the world as a whole. Today, when the primacy of the fact is challenged by the Web—a recent article hails the fact's death—the future, more important than ever, has been privatized, monetized, and turned into a source of profit. An entire corporate sector is dedicated to commodifying and modeling it; our financial markets in general take the future as the determinant of present values in a way that simply was not true a century ago.[41] No one now feels the burden of an essential but unknowable future more acutely than the stockbroker and trader. But this money-driven individualistic future has crowded out an older vision of what the public good might look like.

In the ongoing atomization of society, citizens and classes have both vanished as forces for change and given way to a world of individuals, who come together as consumers of goods or information, and who trust the Internet more than they do their political representatives or the experts they watch on television.[42] Governing institutions today have lost sight of the principle of politics rooted in the collective values of a res publica, even as they continue to defend the "civilization of capital." As for the rituals of international life, these are now well established. The world's heads of state flock annually to the United Nations General Assembly. There are discussions of reform and grandiose declarations of global targets, which mostly go unmet. Politicians, journalists, bankers, and businessmen make their pilgrimage to the heavily guarded Alpine precinct of Davos, seeking to confirm through this triumph of corporate sponsorship that a global ruling elite exists and that they belong to it. Our representatives continue to hand over power to experts and self-interested self-regulators in the name of efficient global governance while a skeptical and alienated public looks on. The idea of governing the world is becoming yesterday's dream.[43]

Notes

INTRODUCTION

1 Andrew Preston, "The Politics of Realism and Religion: Christian Responses to Bush's New World Order," *Diplomatic History* 34, no. 1 (January 2010): 95–118.

2 Michael Barkun, *A Culture of Conspiracy: Apocalyptic Visions in Contemporary America* (Berkeley, 2003), 39-78; the theology of anti-internationalism is complex and understudied. On the critical Christian Reconstruction movement, see John Sugg, "A Nation under God," *Mother Jones,* December 2005.

3 Thomas L. Hughes, "The Twilight of Internationalism," *Foreign Policy* 61 (Winter 1985–86): 28-46; Richard Perle, "Thank God for the Death of the UN," *Guardian,* March 20, 2003.

4 See, for example, John Gerard Ruggie, *Constructing the World Polity: Essays on International Institutionalization* (New York: Routledge, 1998); John Ikenberry, *Liberal Leviathan: the Origins, Crisis and Transformation of the American World Order* (Princeton, NJ: Princeton University Press, 2011).

5 "Nuclear Wikileaks: Cables Show Cosy US Relationship with IAEA Chief," Julian Borger's Security Blog, *Guardian,* November 30, 2010, http://www.guardian.co.uk/world/julian-borger-global-security-blog/2010/nov/30/iaea-wikileaks.

PROLOGUE: THE CONCERT OF EUROPE, 1815–1914

1 Carsten Holbraad, *The Concert of Europe: A Study in German and British International Theory, 1815–1914* (London: Longmans, 1970), 17.

2 The standard work on a complex phenomenon is Holbraad, *The Concert of Europe.*

3 Jean Hanoteau, ed., *Memoirs of General de Caulaincourt, Duke of Vincenza, 1812–1813* (London: Cassell, 1935), 418–19.

4 Holbraad, *The Concert of Europe,* 20.

5 Ibid., 126; Anne Orford, *International Authority and the Responsibility to Protect* (Cambridge: Cambridge University Press, 2011).

6 Liliana Obregon, "The Colluding Worlds of the Lawyer, the Scholar and the Policymaker: A View of International Law from Latin America," *Wisconsin International Law Journal* 23, no. 1 (2005), 145–72.

7 *Memoir, Letters, and Remains of Alexis de Tocqueville,* 2 vols. (London: Macmillan, 1861), ii, 202.

CHAPTER 1: UNDER THE SIGN OF THE INTERNATIONAL

1 Cited in Merle Curti, "Francis Lieber and Nationalism," *Huntington Library Quarterly* 4, no. 3 (April 1941): 263–92.

2 Book of Isaiah, esp. chapters 64–66.

3 *Troilus and Cressida,* Act 1, scene 3. My thanks to Fergus Bremner for this reference.

4 Daniele Archibugi, "Methods of International Organization in Perpetual Peace Projects," *Review of International Studies* 18, no. 4 (October 1992): 295–317. The essential reference work in F. H. Hinsley, *Power and the Pursuit of Peace: Theory and Practice in the History of Relations between States* (Cambridge: Cambridge University Press, 1967).

5 Isaac Nakhimovsky, "The 'Ignominious Fall of the European Commonwealth': Gentz, Hauterive, and the Debate of 1800," in *Collegium: Studies across Disciplines in the Humanities and Social Sciences* 10 (Helsinki: Helsinki Collegium for Advanced Studies), 212–28.

6 Edmund Burke, "Letters on a Regicide Peace" [1796]; Novalis. "Christianity or Europe" in F. Beiser, ed., *The Early Political Writings of the German Romantics* (Cambridge: Cambridge University Press, 1996), 59–81.

7 J. T. Burns, "Bentham and the French Revolution," *Transactions of the Royal Historical Society* 16 (1966): 95–114.

8 Albert S. Miles, David L. Dagley, and Christina H. Yau, "Blackstone and His American Legacy," *Australia and New Zealand Journal of Law and Education* 5, no. 2 (2000): 46–59, at 57.

9 Jeremy Bentham, *An Introduction to the Principles of Morals and Legislation* (Oxford: Clarendon Press, 1907), 326 note 1.

10 M. W. Janis, "Jeremy Bentham and the Fashioning of 'International Law,'" *American Journal of International Law* 78, no. 2 (April 1984): 405–18.

11 Abbé de Pradt, *The Congress of Vienna* (Philadelphia, 1816): 32–42, 202–15.

12 *The London Literary Gazette and Journal of Belles Lettres, Arts, Sciences Etc. for the Year 1823* (London, 1823), 361; on monarchical unease, see Johannes Paulmann, "Searching for a 'Royal International': the Mechanics of Monarchical Relations in Nineteenth-Century Europe," in Martin Geyer and Johannes Paulmann, eds., *The Mechanics of Internationalism: Culture, Society and Politics from the 1840s to the First World War* (Oxford: Oxford University Press, 2001), 145–77, at 167.

13 I. F. Clarke, *The Pattern of Expectation, 1644–2001* (London: Jonathan Cape, 1979), chapter 3.

14 Felix Bodin, *Le roman de l'avenir* (Paris, 1834). The book now appears to be rare: an English translation by Brian Stapleford is available: Felix Bodin, *The Novel of the Future* (Encino, CA: Black Coat Press, 2008).

15 Above all, see James Belich, *Replenishing the Earth: The Settler Revolution and the Rise of the Anglo-World, 1783–1939* (Oxford: Oxford University Press, 2009), chapters 6–7.

16 See Duncan Bell, *The Idea of Greater Britain: Empire and the Future of World Order, 1860–1900* (Princeton, NJ: Princeton University Press, 2007), 64: "Before the 1870s, a highly integrated global polity . . . was rarely if ever considered a feasible political option; afterward it became a familiar demand."

17 See chapter 4 below.

18 Bell, *The Idea of Greater Britain,* 90.

19 For these and other examples, see W. H. G. Armytage, *Yesterday's Tomorrows: A Historical Survey of Future Societies* (London: Routledge and Kegan Paul, 1968), 36–39.

20 George Griffith, *The Angel of the Revolution: A Tale of the Coming Terror* (London, 1893), chapter 48, "The Ordering of Europe."

21 Clyde J. Wright, ed., *Protocols of the Meetings of the Learned Elders of Zion* (Whitefish, MT: Kessinger Publishing, 2010), passim.

CHAPTER 2: BROTHERHOOD

1 Samuel Wreford, "Peace" (London, 1851), 34–35.

2 Jerome Reich, "The Slave Trade at the Congress of Vienna: A Study in British Public Opinion," *Journal of Negro History* 53, no. 2 (April 1968): 129–43.

3 Philo Pacificus, *A Solemn Review of the Custom of War, Showing that War Is the Effect of Popular Delusion* (Cambridge, Mass., 1816), 35–36; Eric Sager, "The Social Origins of Victorian Pacifism," *Victorian Studies* 23, no. 2 (Winter 1980): 211–36; Alexander Tyrrell, "Making the Millennium: The Mid-Nineteenth Century Peace Movement," *Historical Journal* 21, no. 1 (March 1978): 75–95.

4 Tyrrell, "Making the Millennium," 86; Douglas Maynard, "Reform and the International Organization Movement," *Proceedings of the American Philosophical Society* 107, no. 3 (June 1963): 220–31.

5 Merle Curti, *The American Peace Crusade, 1815–1860* (Durham, NC: Duke University Press, 1929), esp. 137–38.

6 Gavin Henderson, "The Pacifists of the Fifties," *Journal of Modern History* 9, no. 3 (September 1937): 314–41, at 319.

7 William Wells Brown, *The American Fugitive in Europe* (Boston and New York, 1855), 58–59.

8 Ibid., 219–26.

9 Horace Greeley, *Glances at Europe: In a Series of Letters from Great Britain, France, Italy, Switzerland etc. during the Summer of 1851* (New York, 1851), 280–81.

10 Orlando Figes, *Crimea: The Last Crusade* (London: Allen Lane, 2010).

11 Peel cited in Anthony Howe, "Free Trade and Global Order: The Rise and Fall of a Victorian Vision," in Duncan Bell, ed., *Victorian Visions of Global Order* (Cambridge: Cambridge University Press, 2007), 26.

12 Cited in J. A. Hobson, *Richard Cobden: The International Man* (London: Henry Holt and Co., 1919), 50.

13 Howe, "Free Trade and Global Order," 27.

14 Benjamin Constant, *De l'esprit de conquête et de l'usurpation* (1814) in *Constant: Political Writings* (Cambridge: Cambridge University Press, 1988), 51–168.

15 Howe, "Free Trade and Global Order," 38.

16 Ricardo cited in Peter Cain, "Capitalism, War, and Internationalism in the Thought of Richard Cobden," *British Journal of International Studies* 5 (1979): 229–47, at 231.

17 Maynard, "Reform and the International Organization Movement," 226.

18 Joshua Levitt, *An Essay on the Best Way of Developing Improved Political and Commercial Relations between Great Britain and the United States of America* (London, 1869), 55–59.

19 Lord Hobart, "The 'Mission of Richard Cobden,'" *Macmillan's Magazine* 15 (January 1867): 177–86.

20 Richard Cobden, "The Balance of Power," in F. W. Chesson, ed., *The Political Writings of Richard Cobden* (London: T. Fisher Unwin, 1903), part 2: 3. The original pamphlet was published in 1836.

21 Hobson, *Richard Cobden,* 115; Disraeli and Aberdeen cited in Henderson, "The Pacifists of the Fifties," 326.

22 Giuseppe Mazzini, "On the Superiority of Representative Government" (1832), in S. Recchia and N. Urbinati, eds., *A Cosmopolitanism of Nations: Giuseppe Mazzini's Writings on Democracy, Nation Building, and International Relations* (Princeton, NJ: Princeton University Press, 2009), 43–44.

23 Ibid., 24; on Cobden, D. Nicholls, "Richard Cobden and the International Peace Congress Movement, 1848–1853," *Journal of British Studies* 30, no. 4 (October 1991): 351–76, at 357.

24 Mazzini, "On the Superiority of Representative Government," 28 ("On Nonintervention").

25 Ibid., 29.

26 Salvo Mastellone, *Mazzini and Marx: Thoughts upon Democracy in Europe* (London: Praeger, 2003), 21, 79.

27 Peter Brock, "Polish Democrats and English Radicals, 1832–1862," *Journal of Modern History* 25, no. 2 (June 1953): 139–56; Peter Brock, "Joseph Cowen and the Polish Exiles," *Slavonic and East European Review* 32, no. 78 (December 1953): 52–69; Peter Brock, "The Polish Revolutionary Commune in London," *Slavonic and East European Review* 35, no. 84 (December 1956): 116–28.

28 Mastellone, *Mazzini and Marx,* 85, 111–12; G. Claeys, "Mazzini, Kossuth, and British

Radicalism, 1848–1854," *Journal of British Studies* 28, no. 3 (July 1989): 232; H. Weisser, "Chartist Internationalism, 1845–1848," *Historical Journal* 14, no. 1 (March 1971): 49–66. For the Mazzinian background, see E. Morelli, *L'Inghilterra di Mazzini* (Rome, 1965), 85.

29 "The Great Men of the Exile," Karl Marx and Friedrich Engels, *Collected Works,* vol. 11, Marx and Engels, 1851–1853 (New York, n.d.), 284.

30 [Friedrich Engels], "The Free Trade Congress at Brussels," *Northern Star* 520 (October 9, 1847).

31 Karl Marx, "The Defeat of Cobden, Bright and Gibson," *New-York Daily Tribune,* 4990 (April 17, 1857).

32 Eccarius to Marx, September 26, 1864, *Founding of the First International* (USSR: International Publishers, 1937), 56.

33 "Report of International Meeting in St. Martin's Hall, Sept. 28, 1864," *Founding of the First International,* 2–7.

34 On the Mazzinian tenor of Odger's address, see Henry Collins and Chimen Abramsky, *Karl Marx and the British Labour Movement: Years of the First International* (London: Macmillan, 1965), 35.

35 Marx to Engels, November 4, 1864, *Founding of the First International,* 36–37.

36 Collins and Abramsky, *Karl Marx and the British Labour Movement,* 37.

37 Morelli, *Inghilterra,* 203.

38 Marx to Engels, September 11, 1867, Karl Marx and Friedrich Engels, *Collected Works,* vol. 42, *Marx and Engels, 1864–66* (London, 1987), 424.

39 Collins and Abramsky, *Karl Marx and the British Labour Movement,* 216.

40 E. Morelli, "Mazzini e la Comune," in Morelli, *Mazzini: Quasi una Biografia* (Rome: Edizione dell'Ateneo, 1984), 138.

41 Giuseppe Mazzini, "The International: Addressed to the Working Class," Part 1, *Contemporary Review* 20 (June–November 1872): 155–68; see also F. Fiumara, *Mazzini e l'Internazionale* (Pisa, 1968), 42–43; K. Willis, "The Introduction and Critical Reception of Marxist Thought in Britain, 1850–1900," *Historical Journal* 20, no. 2 (June 1977): 417–59, at 427.

42 C. Duggan, "Giuseppe Mazzini in Britain and Italy," in C. A. Bayly and E. Biagini, eds., *Giuseppe Mazzini and the Globalization of Democratic Nationalism, 1830–1920* (Oxford: Oxford University Press, 2008), 187–211 on his fading influence.

43 Alice de Rosen Jervis, translator, *Mazzini's Letters* (London, Dent and Sons, 1930), 168 ("to a German," February 1861).

44 Lord Acton, "Nationality" (1862), in *The History of Freedom and Other Essays* (London, 1909), 298.

45 J. Rae, *Contemporary Socialism,* 3rd ed. (London, 1901), iv–v.

46 *The Beehive,* August 17, 1867.

CHAPTER 3: THE EMPIRE OF LAW

1 Amos Hershey, "History of International Law since the Peace of Westphalia," *American Journal of International Law* 6, no. 1 (January 1912), 50–51.

2 Hidemi Suganami, *The Domestic Analogy and World Order Proposals* (Cambridge: Cambridge University Press, 1989), 17.

3 The classic work is by Martti Koskenniemi, *The Gentle Civiliser of Nations: The Rise and Fall of International Law* (Cambridge: Cambridge University Press, 2001). On governmental internationalism, see Madeleine Herren, "Governmental Internationalism and the Beginning of a New World Order in the Late Nineteenth Century," in Martin Geyer and Johannes Paulmann, eds., *The Mechanics of Internationalism: Culture, Society and Politics from the 1840s to The First World War* (Oxford: Oxford University Press, 2001), 121–45.

4 "Instructions for the Government of Armies of the United States in the Field," April 24, 1863 (Lieber Code), section 1, part 29; Lieber to Ruggles in Merle Curti, "Francis Lieber on Nationalism," *Huntington Library Quarterly* 4, no. 3 (April 1941): 263–92.

5 Koskenniemi, *The Gentle Civiliser of Nations.*
6 Ibid., chapter 1, also page 61.
7 Ibid., 123.
8 Ibid., 47.
9 E. Benveniste, "Civilisation—contribution à l'histoire du mot," in *Problèmes de linguistique générale* (Paris: Gallimard, 1966); Anthony Pagden, "The 'Defense of Civilization' in Eighteenth-Century Social Theory," *History of the Human Sciences* 1, no. 1 (May 1988): 33–45.
10 John Stuart Mill, "On Civilization" (1836), in John M. Robson, ed., *The Collected Works of John Stuart Mill,* vol. 18 (Toronto: University of Toronto Press, 1977); Koskenniemi, *The Gentle Civiliser of Nations,* 54–55.
11 Gerrit Gong, *The Standard of Civilization in International Law* (Oxford: Oxford University Press, 1984). Also Martti Koskenniemi, "Histories of International Law: Dealing with Eurocentrism," Treaty of Utrecht chair lecture, University of Utrecht, 2011.
12 Japanese diplomat cited in Geoffrey Best, *Humanity in Warfare: The Modern History of the International Law of Armed Conflicts* (London: Weidenfeld and Nicholson, 1980), 141.
13 For this, see Anne Orford, *International Authority and the Responsibility to Protect* (Cambridge: Cambridge University Press, 2011).
14 Andrew Fitzmaurice, "Liberalism and Empire in Nineteenth-Century International Law," *American Historical Review* 117, no. 1 (February 2012): 122–40; G. de Baere and A. Mills, "T. M. C. Asser and Public and Private International Law: The Life and Legacy of a 'Practical Legal Statesman,'" Working Paper 73, Leuven Center for Global Governance Studies, September 2011, 10; on Nys, Koskenniemi, "Histories of International Law," 6.
15 Koskenniemi, *The Gentle Civiliser of Nations,* 67.
16 Dan Morrill, "Tsar Nicholas II and the Call for the First Hague Conference," *Journal of Modern History* 46, no. 2 (June 1974): 296–313.
17 Eyal Benvenisti, *The International Law of Occupation* (Princeton, NJ: Princeton University Press, 2004).
18 Bulow cited in James Sheehan, *Where Have All the Soldiers Gone? The Transformation of Modern Europe* (New York: Houghton Mifflin Harcourt, 2008), 26; Moltke cited in Best, *Humanity in Warfare,* 144.
19 Nehal Bhuta, "The Antinomies of Transformative Occupation," *European Journal of International Law* 16, no. 4 (September 2005): 727.
20 Eldridge Colby, "How to Fight Savage Tribes," *American Journal of International Law* 21:2 (April 1927), 287.
21 W. R. Stead, "Internationalism at Paris and Pekin," *Review of Reviews* 22 (September 1900): 241.
22 Johannes Prenzler, ed., *Die Reden Kaiser Wilhelms II* (*The Speeches of Kaiser Wilhelm II*), 4 vols. (Leipzig, n.d.), 2:209–12. The unofficial version of speech is reprinted in Manfred Görtemaker, *Deutschland im 19. Jahrhundert. Entwicklungslinien* (*Germany in the 19th Century: Paths in Development*) (Opladen: Leske und Budrich, 1996), Schriftenreihe der Bundeszentrale für politische Bildung, vol. 274: 357.
23 Benvenisti, *The International Law of Occupation,* 33–47; for the Habsburgs, see Jonathan Gumz, *The Resurrection and Collapse of Empire in Habsburg Serbia, 1914–1918* (Cambridge: Cambridge University Press, 2009).
24 Cited in Fitzmaurice, "Liberalism and Empire in Nineteenth-Century International Law," 134.
25 Michael J. Devine, *John W. Foster: Politics and Diplomacy in the Imperial Era, 1873–1917* (Athens: Ohio University Press, 1981), 108.
26 Cobden cited in David Nicholls, "Richard Cobden and the International Peace Congress Movement, 1848–1853," *Journal of British Studies* 30, no. 4 (October 1991): 351–76; Lewis Appleton, *Memoirs of Henry Richard, the Apostle of Peace* (London, 1889), 210–12; John Watson

Foster cited in Jack Hammersmith, "John Watson Foster: 'A Pacifist after a Fashion,'" *Indiana Magazine of History* 84, no. 2 (June 1988): 124.

27 H. Evans, *Sir Randal Cremer: His Life and Work* (London, 1909), 51.

28 Ibid.

29 T. Boyle, "The Venezuela Crisis and the Liberal Opposition, 1895–1896," *Journal of Modern History* 50, no. 3 (1978): 1185–1212.

30 Warren F. Kuehl, *Seeking World Order: The United States and International Organization to 1920* (Nashville, TN: Vanderbilt University Press, 1969), 64–65; "Award Ceremony Speech: Presentation Speech by Gunnar Knudsen, Presiding, on December 10, 1906," available online at http://nobelprize.org/nobel_prizes/peace/laureates/1906/press.html.

31 Randal Cremer, "The Progress and Advancement of International Arbitration" (Nobel acceptance speech), January 15, 1905, available online at http://nobelprize.org/nobel_prizes/peace/laureates/1903/cremer-lecture.html.

32 On Bryan, see Merle Eugene Curti, *Bryan and World Peace,* Smith College Studies in History XVI: 3–4 (Northampton, MA: April–July 1931).

33 "Who Began It," *The Arbitrator* 186 (August 1887): 3; Ibid., 5 ("A Political Atheist"—re Lord Salisbury).

34 J. Westlake, "International arbitration," *International Journal of Ethics* 7, no. 1 (October 1896): 1–20. For similar views expressed by German lawyers, see Suganami, *The Domestic Analogy and World Order Proposals,* 70–75.

35 Kuehl, *Seeking World Order,* chapter 4; Benjamin Coates, "Transatlantic Advocates: American International Law and U.S. Foreign Relations, 1898–1914" (DPhil dissertation, Columbia University, September 2010), chapter 2, quotations at 80, 108.

36 Charles Brower et al., "Rereading Root," *Proceedings of the American Society of International Law* 100 (March 29–April 1, 2006): 203–16.

CHAPTER 4: SCIENCE THE UNIFIER

1 Arthur Schuster, "International Science," *Nature* 74 (1906), cited in Peter Alter, "The Royal Society and the International Association of Academies, 1897–1919," *Notes and Records of the Royal Society of London* 34, no. 2 (March 1980): 241–64.

2 Newmarch cited in Theodore M. Porter, *The Rise of Statistical Thinking, 1820-1900* (Princeton, NJ: Princeton University Press, 1986), 59.

3 See his 1814 *The Reorganisation of European Society,* cited in F. H. Hinsley, *Power and the Pursuit of Peace: Theory and Practice in the History of Relations between States* (Cambridge: Cambridge University Press, 1967), 102.

4 Cited in ibid., 106.

5 See John Tresch, *The Romantic Machine: Utopian Science and Technology after Napoleon* (Chicago: University of Chicago Press, 2012), and especially Tresch, "The Machine Awakens: The Science and Politics of the Fantastic Automaton," *French Historical Studies* 34, no. 1 (Winter 2011): 88–123.

6 Georg Iggers, ed., *The Doctrine of Saint-Simon: An Exposition* (New York: Schocken, 1972), 58–63; see also D. Guillo, "Biology-Inspired Sociology of the Nineteenth Century: A Science of 'Social Organization,'" *Revue française de sociologie* 43 (2002): 123–55.

7 *Doctrines of Saint-Simon,* 71.

8 Arthur John Booth, *Saint-Simon and Sain-Simonism: A Chapter in the History of Socialism in France* (London, 1871); Christos Baloglou, "The Diffusion of the Ideas of Saint-Simon in the Hellenic State and Their Reception Thereby (1825–1837)," *Economic History Yearbook* 1 (2006): 159–77.

9 J. B. Bury, *The Idea of Progress: An Inquiry into Its Origin and Growth* (London: Macmillan, 1932), 300–301.

10 H. Shoen, "Prince Albert and the Application of Statistics to Problems of Government," *Osiris* 5 (1938): 276–318.

11 Robert P. Crease, *World in the Balance: The Historic Quest for an Absolute System of Measurement* (New York: Norton, 2011), 128.
12 Daniel R. Headrick, *The Invisible Weapon: Telecommunications and International Politics, 1851–1945* (New York: Oxford University Press, 1991), 116–37.
13 B. Guinot, "History of the Bureau Internationale de l'Heure," *Polar Motion: Historical and Scientific Problems,* ASP Conference Series 208 (2000): 175–77.
14 John Faries, *The Rise of Internationalism* (New York: W. D. Gray, 1915), 16 (published version of the 1913 dissertation). The Otlet comment in "The Union of World Associations: A World Center" (1914) was published in W. Boyd Rayward, ed., *International Organization and the Dissemination of Knowledge: Selected Essays of Paul Otlet* (Amsterdam: Elsevier, 1990), 112–29; data from Michael Wallace and J. David Singer, "Intergovernmental Organization in the Global System, 1815–1914: A Quantitative Description," *International Organization* 24, no. 2 (Spring 1970), 239–87.
15 Patrick Zylberman, "Making Food Safety an Issue: Internationalized Food Politics and French Public Health from the 1870s to the Present," *Medical History* 48 (January 2004): 1–28; S. Bates, "One World in Penology," *Journal of Criminal Law and Criminology* 38, no. 6 (March–April 1948): 565–75; L. Luzzatti, "The International Institute of Agriculture," *North American Review* (May 1906): 651–59.
16 C. Tapia and J. Taieb, "Conférences et Congrès internationaux de 1815 à 1913," *Relations internationales* 5 (1976): 11–35, at 17.
17 My thanks to Boyd Rayward, doyen of Otlet scholars, for his generous assistance.
18 Figures in Peter Alter, "The Royal Society and the International Association of Academies, 1897–1919," *Notes and Records of the Royal Society of London* 34, no. 2 (March 1980): 241–64; Tapia and Taieb, "Conférences et Congrès internationaux de 1815 à 1913."
19 Carola Hein, *The Capital of Europe: Architecture and Urban Planning for the European Union* (London: Praeger, 2004), chapter 2.
20 See "Notes for M. Durand, Prefect of Police" (December 21, 1915) and "The Organization of the Society of Nations" (1916) in Rayward, *International Organization and the Dissemination of Knowledge,* 130–47.
21 "The Belgian Appeal to the World" (1931), in ibid., 211–12.
22 Crease, *World in the Balance,* 128–36, 156–62.
23 E. Minelli, "World Health Organization: The Mandate of a Specialized Agency of the United Nations," at http://www.gfmer.ch/TMCAM/WHO_Minelli/Index.htm.
24 Ronald Doel, Dieter Hoffmann, and Nikolai Krementsov, "National States and International Science: A Comparative History of International Science Congresses in Hitler's Germany, Stalin's Russia, and Cold War United States," *Osiris* 20 (2005): 49–76.
25 Donald J. Harlow, "History in Fine," http://donh.best.vwh.net/Esperanto/EBook/chap07.html.
26 Lancelot Hogben and Frederick Bodmer, *The Loom of Language* (London, 1944), chapter 12; Arika Okrent, *In the Land of Invented Languages* (New York: Random House, 2010), 107–9.
27 My thanks for her patience in discussing this with me to my colleague Deborah Coen, whose book on this subject is in preparation. For meteorology, see Paul Edwards, *A Vast Machine: Computer Models, Climate Data, and the Politics of Global Warming* (Cambridge, MA: MIT Press, 2010).

CHAPTER 5: THE LEAGUE OF NATIONS

1 Lippmann cited in Ronald Steel, *Walter Lippmann and the American Century* (New York: Transaction Publishers, 1980), 96.
2 George Burton Adams, *The British Empire and a League of Peace: Suggesting the Purpose and Form of an Alliance of the English-Speaking Peoples* (New York: G. P. Putnam's Sons, 1919), 14.
3 Madeleine Herren, "Governmental Internationalism and the Beginning of a New World Order in the Late Nineteenth Century," in Martin H. Geyer and Johannes Paulmann, eds.,

The Mechanics of Internationalism: Culture, Society, and Politics from the 1840s to the First World War (Oxford: Oxford University Press, 2001), 121–45.

4 Stephen Wertheim, "The Wilsonian Chimera: Why Debating Wilson's Vision Hasn't Saved American Foreign Relations," *White House Studies* 10, no. 4 (2011): 343–59; slogans from Thomas Knock, *To End All Wars: Woodrow Wilson and the Quest for a New World Order* (Princeton, NJ: Princeton University Press, 1992), 194–95.

5 Herren, "Governmental Internationalism," 138.

6 Benjamin Coates, "Transatlantic Advocates: American International Law and U.S. Foreign Relations, 1898–1914" (DPhil dissertation, Columbia University, September 2010); John P. Campbell, "Taft, Roosevelt, and the Arbitration Treaties of 1911," *Journal of American History* 53, no. 2 (September 1966): 279–98; Stephen Wertheim, "The League That Wasn't: American Designs for a Legalist-Sanctionist League of Nations and the Intellectual Origins of International Organization," *Diplomatic History* 35, no. 5 (November 2011): 797–836.

7 Wertheim, "The League That Wasn't," 809–10.

8 Stephen Wertheim, "The League of Nations: A Retreat from International Law?" *Journal of Global History* 7, no. 2 (2012).

9 Some good remarks can be found in Knock, *To End All Wars,* 4–5.

10 Lloyd Ambrosius, *Woodrow Wilson and the American Diplomatic Tradition: The Treaty Fight in Perspective* (Cambridge: Cambridge University Press, 1987), 46.

11 Joseph Byrne Lockey, *Essays in Pan-Americanism* (Berkeley: University of California Press, 1939), 16–17, 74–75.

12 Mark T. Gilderhus, *Pan American Visions: Woodrow Wilson in the Western Hemisphere, 1913–1921* (Tucson: University of Arizona Press, 1986), 54; Ambrosius, *Woodrow Wilson and the American Diplomatic Tradition,* 16.

13 Peter Raffo, "The Anglo-American Preliminary Negotiations for a League of Nations," *Journal of Contemporary History* 9, no. 4 (October 1974): 153–76.

14 Gilderhus, *Pan American Visions,* 93.

15 Woodrow Wilson, Message to Congress, April 2, 1917, Woodrow Wilson, *War Messages,* 65th Cong., 1st Sess. Senate Doc. No. 5, Serial No. 7264 (Washington, D.C., 1917), 3–8.

16 Milan Babik, "George Heron and the Eschatological Foundations of Woodrow Wilson's Foreign Policy, 1917–1919," *Diplomatic History* 35, no. 5 (November 2011): 837–57; on Wilson's theological influences, see esp. Mark Benbow, *Leading Them to the Promised Land: Woodrow Wilson, Covenant Theology, and the Mexican Revolution, 1913–1915* (Kent, OH: Kent State University Press, 2010).

17 My thanks to Thomas Meaney for the point about the open character of the Brest-Litovsk negotiations.

18 The speeches can be found in James Brown Scott, *Official Statements of War Aims and Peace Proposals: December 1916 to November 1918* (Washington, D.C.: Carnegie Endowment for International Peace, 1921).

19 Ibid., 381.

20 Ambrosius, *Woodrow Wilson and the American Diplomatic Tradition,* 53.

21 Janet Manson, "Leonard Woolf as an Architect of the League of Nations," *South Carolina Review* (2007): 1–13.

22 George Egerton, Great Britain and the Creation of the League of Nations (Chapel Hill: University of North Carolina Press, 1978), 421.

23 Raffo, "The Anglo-American Preliminary Negotiations for a League of Nations," 154; Egerton, *Great Britain and the Creation of the League of Nations,* passim.

24 Cited in Wertheim, "The League of Nations," 5.

25 On Smuts and Commonwealth, see my *No Enchanted Palace: The End of Empire and the Ideological Origins of the United Nations* (Princeton, NJ: Princeton University Press, 2009).

26 J. C. Smuts, *The League of Nations: A Practical Suggestion* (London: Hodder and Stoughton, 1918), vi.

27 Ibid., vii.

28 Stephen Wertheim, "The League That Wasn't: American Designs for a Legalist-Sanctionist League of Nations and the Intellectual Origins of International Organization, 1914–1920," *Diplomatic History* 35, no. 5 (November 2011): 797–836, at 801; Wertheim, "The League of Nations," 2.

29 Stefan Matthias Hell, "Siam and the League of Nations: Modernization, Sovereignty, and Multilateral Diplomacy, 1920–1940" (PhD dissertation, University of Leiden, 2007), 29.

30 Warren Kuehl, *Seeking World Order: The United States and International Organization to 1920* (Nashville, TN: Vanderbilt University Press, 1969), 334.

31 Wendy Wolff, ed., *The Senate, 1789–1989, vol. 3, Classic Speeches, 1830–1993* (Washington, D.C.: U.S. Government Printing Office, 1994), 569–76.

32 Warrden Kuehl and Lynne Dunn, *Keeping the Covenant: American Internationalists and the League of Nations, 1920–1939* (Kent, OH: Kent State University Press, 1997), chapters 1, 8.

33 Raymond Fosdick, *The League and the United Nations after Fifty Years: The Six Secretaries-General* (Newtown, CT: n.p., 1972), 26.

34 Zara Steiner cited in Susan Pedersen, "Back to the League of Nations," *American Historical Review* 112, no. 4 (October 2007): 1091–1117.

35 Pedersen, "Back to the League of Nations."

36 Budget data in Fosdick, *The League and the United Nations after Fifty Years,* 11.

37 Raymond Fosdick, *Letters on the League of Nations* (Princeton: Princeton University Press, 1966), 20.

38 See Pierre Renouvin, *Les formes du gouvernement de guerre* (Paris, 1925), and Yann Decorzant, "Internationalism in the Economic and Financial Organization of the League of Nations," in Daniel Laqua, ed., *Internationalism Reconfigured: Transnational Ideas and Movements between the World Wars* (London: I. B. Tauris, 2011), 115–34.

39 Raymond Fosdick, *Chronicle of a Generation: An Autobiography* (New York: Harper, 1958), 188–89; Fosdick, "The League of Nations Is Alive," *Atlantic Monthly,* June 1920.

40 George Slocombe, *A Mirror to Geneva: Its Growth, Grandeur and Decay* (New York: Henry Holt, 1938), 52, 63.

41 Ibid., 62.

42 Fosdick, *Letters on the League of Nations,* 22–23.

43 Zimmern cited in Katharina Rietzler, "Experts for Peace: Structures and Motivations of Philanthropic Internationalism in the Interwar Years," in Laqua, ed., *Internationalism Reconfigured,* 50.

44 Sunil Amrith, *Decolonising International Health: India and Southeast Asia, 1930-1965* (Basingstoke: Palgrave, 2006), chapter 1.

45 Vincent Lagendijk, *Electrifying Europe: The Power of Europe in the Construction of Electricity Networks* (Amsterdam: Aksant, 2008), 93–95.

46 Cited in Murray Newton Rothbard, *A History of Money and Banking in the United States* (Auburn, AL: Ludwig von Mises Institute, 2002), 443.

47 The key text is Robert Boyce, *British Capitalism at the Crossroads, 1919–1932* (Cambridge: Cambridge University Press, 1987).

48 Jo-Anne Pemberton, "New Worlds for Old: The League of Nations in the Age of Electricity," *Review of International Studies* 28, no. 2 (April 2002): 311–36.

49 Frank Beyersdorf, "'Credit or Chaos?': The Austrian Stabilisation Program of 1923 and the League of Nations," in Laqua, ed., *Internationalism Reconfigured,* 151.

50 Pedersen, "Back to the League of Nations"; Marta Balinska, *For the Good of Humanity: Ludwik Rajchman, Medical Statesman* (Budapest: Central European University Press, 1998); Wertheim, "The League of Nations," 20.

CHAPTER 6: THE BATTLE OF IDEOLOGIES

1 Carl Schmitt, "The *Grossraum* Order of International Law with a Ban on Intervention for Spatially Foreign Powers: A Contribution to the Concept of *Reich* in International Law (1939–1941)," in Carl Schmitt, *Writings on War,* translated and edited by Timothy Nunan (Cambridge: Cambridge University Press, 2011), 75–125.

2 "Remarks about Mazzini," January 5, 1919, in Arthur S. Link et al., eds., *The Papers of Woodrow Wilson* (Princeton, NJ: Princeton University Press, 1966–93), vol. 53: 614–15.
3 Sir John Hope Simpson, *The Refugee Problem* (Oxford: Oxford University Press, 1939), 10.
4 Louise W. Holborn, "The League of Nations and the Refugee Problem," *Annals of the American Academy of Political and Social Science,* vol. 203 (May 1939), 124.
5 I. S. K. Soboleff, *Nansen Passport: Round the World on a Motorcycle* (London: G. Bell & Sons, 1936). My thanks to Joyce Chaplin for this reference.
6 Mark Levene, *War, Jews, and the New Europe: The Diplomacy of Lucien Wolf, 1914–1919* (Oxford: Oxford University Press, 1992), 98; Agnes Headlam-Morley, ed., *A Memoir of the Peace Conference, 1919* (London: Methuen, 1972), 27.
7 Erez Manela, *The Wilsonian Moment: Self-Determination and the International Origins of Anticolonial Nationalism* (New York: Oxford University Press, 2007).
8 Clarence Contee, "Du Bois, the NAACP, and the Pan-African Congress of 1919," *Journal of Negro History* 57, no. 1 (January 1972), 13–28; Jay Winter, *Dreams of Peace and Freedom: Utopian Moments in the Twentieth Century* (New Haven, CT: Yale University Press, 2008), 64–66.
9 Noriko Kawamura, "Wilsonian Idealism and Japanese Claims at the Paris Peace Conference," *Pacific Historical Review* 66, no. 4 (November 1997): 503–26, at 506.
10 Naoko Shimazu, *Japan, Race, and Equality: The Racial Equality Proposal of 1919* (London: Taylor and Francis, 2002).
11 Winter, *Dreams of Peace and Freedom,* 67–71.
12 See Robert Vitalis, "Birth of a Discipline," in David Long and Brian Schmidt, eds., *Imperialism and Internationalism in the Discipline of International Relations* (Albany: SUNY Press, 2005), 159–81.
13 J. E. T. Philipps, "The Tide of Color: I—Pan-African and Anti-White," *Journal of the Royal African Society* 21, no. 82 (January 1922), 129–35; on Philipps, see John Tosh, "Colonial Chiefs in a Stateless Society: A Case-Study from Northern Uganda," *Journal of African History* 14, no. 3 (1973): 473–90.
14 David Long, "Paternalism and the Internationalization of Imperialism," in Long and Schmidt, eds., *Imperialism and Internationalism in the Discipline of International Relations,* 71–95.
15 Cited in ibid., 82–83.
16 Ernest B. Haas, "The Reconciliation ofConflicting Colonial Policy Aims: Acceptance of the League of Nations Mandate System," *International Organization* 6, no. 4 (November 1952): 522–24; Timothy Mitchell, *Carbon Democracy: Political Power in the Age of Oil* (London: Verso, 2011), 73–75.
17 Timothy Paris, "British Middle East Policy-Making after the First World War: The Lawrentian and Wilsonian Schools," *Historical Journal* 41, no. 3 (September 1998), 773–93; see also Mitchell, *Carbon Democracy,* 88–90.
18 Haas, "The Reconciliation of Conflicting Colonial Policy Aims," 528.
19 Ibid., 525, 530; W. Roger Louis, "The United States and the African Peace Settlement of 1919: The Pilgrimage of George Louis Beer," *Journal of African History* 4, no. 3 (1963): 413–33.
20 Roger Louis, "The United States and the African Peace Settlement of 1919," 421.
21 Jawaharlal Nehru, *Glimpses of World History* (New York, 1942), 638.
22 Quincy Wright, "The Bombardment of Damascus," *American Journal of International Law* 20, no. 2 (April 1926): 263–280.
23 R. M. Douglas, "Did Britain Use Chemical Weapons in Mandatory Iraq?" *Journal of Modern History* 81, no. 4 (December 2009): 859–87; Priya Satia, "The Defense of Inhumanity: Air Control in Iraq and the British Idea of Arabia," *American Historical Review* 111, no. 1 (February 2006).
24 Cf. Jan Triska and Howard Koch, "Asian-African Coalition and International Organization: Third Force or Collective Impotence?" *Review of Politics* 21, no. 2 (April 1959): 417–55, at 420.

25 *International Press Correspondence* (Vienna) 7, no. 16 (February 25, 1927): 331, cited in Jan Triska and Howard Koch, "Asian-African Coalition and International Organization: Third Force or Collective Impotence?"; John Hargreaves, "The Comintern and Anti-Colonialism: New Research Opportunities," *African Affairs* 92, no. 367 (April 1993): 255–61; Jonathan Derrick, *Africa's "Agitators": Militant Anti-Colonialism in Africa and the West, 1918–1939* (New York: Columbia University Press, 2008), 172–82.

26 Priya Chacko, "The Internationalist Nationalist: Pursuing an Ethical Modernity with Jawaharlal Nehru," in Robbie Shilliam, ed., *International Relations and Non-Western Thought: Imperialism, Colonialism, and Investigations of Global Modernity* (London: Routledge, 2011), 178–97.

27 Arthur Ransome, *Six Weeks in Russia* (1919).

28 Lenin, "The Third International and its Place in History" (April 15, 1919), *Collected Works* (Moscow, 1972), vol. 29: 305–13. For background, Branko Lazitch and Milorad Drachkovitch, *Lenin and the Comintern,* vol. 1 (Stanford: Hoover Institution Press, 1972).

29 Stephen White, "Colonial Revolution and the Communist International, 1919–1924," *Science and Society* 40, no. 2 (Summer 1976): 173–93; John Callaghan, "Colonies, Racism, the CPGB and the Comintern in the Inter-War Years," *Science and Society* 61, no. 4 (Winter 1997–98), 513–25.

30 Masao Nishikawa, *Socialists and International Actions for Peace, 1914–1923* (Berlin, 2007), chapters 4–8.

31 John Riddell, ed., *Founding of the Communist International: Proceedings and Documents of the First Congress, March 1919* (London, 1987), 216.

32 Charles Prince, "The Soviet Union and International Organizations," *American Journal of International Law* 36, no. 3 (July 1942): 428; Jane Degras, ed., *The Communist International, 1919–1943: Documents* (London: Oxford University Press, 1956–65), vol. 2: 1–2.

33 Degras, *The Communist International,* vol. 2: 19, 34–35.

34 Ibid., 2: 195.

35 Ibid., 2: 300.

36 White, "Colonial Revolution and the Communist International."

37 Sean McMeekin, *The Red Millionaire: A Political Biography of Willi Münzenberg, Moscow's Secret Propaganda Tsar in the West* (New Haven, CT: Yale University Press, 2003), 196–201.

38 See E. H. Carr, *Twilight of the Comintern, 1930–1935* (New York: Pantheon, 1982).

39 "Interview between Stalin and Roy Howard," J. V. Stalin, *Collected Works,* vol. 14 (1934–40) (1978), 137.

40 "'Marxism versus Liberalism': An Interview with H. G. Wells," July 23, 1934, ibid., 21–45, and commentary in Silvio Pons, "L'Urss, il Comintern e la remilitarizzazione della Renania," *Studi Storici* 32, no. 1 (January–March 1991), 169–220.

41 John Herz, "The National Socialist Doctrine of International Law and the Problems of International Organization," *Political Science Quarterly* 54, no. 4 (December 1939): 536–54, at 551.

42 Cited in Herz, "The National Socialist Doctrine of International Law and the Problems of International Organization"; V. Gott, "The National Socialist Theory of International Law," *American Journal of International Law* 32, no. 4 (October 1938): 704–18.

43 Marcel Hoden, "Europe without the League," *Foreign Affairs* 18, no. 1 (October 1939): 13–28.

44 Francis O. Wilcox, "The Monroe Doctrine and World War II," *American Political Science Review* 36, no. 3 (June 1942): 433–53.

45 Charles Kruszewski, "Hegemony and International Law," *American Political Science Review* 35, no. 6 (December 1941): 1127–44.

46 Jessamyn Reich Abel, "Warring Internationalisms: Multilateral Thinking in Japan, 1933–1964" (DPhil dissertation, Columbia University, 2004), 135–41.

47 C. R. Badger, "A Study in Italian Nationalism: Giuseppe Mazzini," *Australian Quarterly* 8, no. 31 (September 1936), 70–80.

48 On the intellectuals in the SS, see my *Hitler's Empire: Nazi Rule in Occupied Europe* (New

York: Allen Lane/Penguin, 2008); on Transylvania, see Holly Case, *Between States: The Transylvanian Question and the European Idea during World War II* (Stanford, CA: Stanford University Press, 2009).

49 Wolfgang Friedmann, *What's Wrong with International Law?* (London: Watts, 1941); F. N. Keen, "Review: What's Wrong with International Law?" *Modern Law Review* 5, no. 2 (November 1941): 152–56; Q. Wright, "International Law and the Totalitarian States," *American Political Science Review* 35, no. 4 (August 1941): 738–43.

CHAPTER 7: "THE LEAGUE IS DEAD. LONG LIVE THE UNITED NATIONS."

1 Cited in Harold Josephson, *James T. Shotwell and the Rise of Internationalism in America* (Cranbury, NJ: Associated University Presses, 1975), 258.

2 On Avenol, see James Barros, *Betrayal from Within: Joseph Avenol, Secretary-General of the League of Nations, 1933–1940* (New Haven: Yale University Press, 1969); on the ICPC, see Cyrille Fijnaut, "The International Criminal Police Commission and the Fight against Communism, 1923–1945," in Mark Mazower, ed., *The Policing of Politics in the Twentieth Century: Historical Perspectives* (Oxford, UK: Berghahn Books, 1997), 107–29.

3 Kathryn Lavelle, "Exit, Voice, and Loyalty in International Organizations: U.S. Involvement in the League of Nations," *Review of International Organizations* 2 (2007): 371–93.

4 Documents in Peter Beck, ed., *British Documents on Foreign Affairs,* (University Publications of America, 1992), II: J (League of Nations Series), vol. 8, docs. 73–85. On Sweetser, see Warren Kuehl and Lynne Dunn, *Keeping the Covenant: American Internationalists and the League of Nations, 1920–1939* (Kent, OH: Kent State University Press, 1997), 5; the best account of the transfer is Lavelle, "Exit, Voice, and Loyalty in International Organizations."

5 R. M. Douglas, *The Labour Party, Nationalism, and Internationalism, 1939–1951* (London: Routledge, 2004), 108.

6 Henry Butterfield Ryan, *The Vision of Anglo-America* (Cambridge: Cambridge University Press, 1987), 16–19; Douglas, *The Labour Party, Nationalism, and Internationalism,* 108–11.

7 E. J. Hughes, "Winston Churchill and the Formation of the United Nations Organization," *Journal of Contemporary History* 9 (October 1974): 181.

8 Ibid., 182.

9 Ibid., 187.

10 UK delegation to Eden, November 8, 1941, in Beck, ed., *British Documents,* doc. 95.

11 Ward, *Closest Companion,* cited in Dan Plesch, *America, Hitler, and the UN: How the Allies Won World War II and Forged a Peace* (London: I. B. Tauris, 2011), 32.

12 See the general argument in D. Plesch, "How the United Nations Beat Hitler and Prepared the Peace," *Global Society* 22, no. 1 (January 2008): 137–58, and Plesch, *America, Hitler, and the UN;* also Michael Howard, "The United Nations: From War-Fighting to Peace Planning," in E. R. May and A. E. Laiou, eds., *The Dumbarton Oaks Conversations and the United Nations, 1944–1994, Part 1, Foundations* (Cambridge, MA: Harvard University Press, 1998).

13 Plesch, "How the United Nations Beat Hitler and Prepared the Peace," 145–48.

14 These comments are based on P. A. Reynolds and E. J. Hughes, ed., *The Historian as Diplomat: Charles Kingsley Webster and the United Nations, 1939–1946* (London: Martin Robertson, 1976), 26–27.

15 Gilbert Murray, *From the League of Nations to the U.N.* (London: Oxford University Press, 1948).

16 Douglas, *The Labour Party, Nationalism, and Internationalism,* 115; Plesch, "How the United Nations Beat Hitler and Prepared the Peace," 121.

17 Plesch, "How the United Nations Beat Hitler and Prepared the Peace," 85.

18 Gilbert Murray, "A Conversation with Bryce," in his *From the League of Nations to the U.N.,* 129–30.

19 Butterfield Ryan, *The Vision of Anglo-America,* 100.

20 Ibid., 127.
21 Michael Ellman, "Churchill on Stalin: A Note," *Europe-Asia Studies* 58, no. 6 (September 2006): 965–71.
22 Robert A. Divine, *Second Chance: The Triumph of Internationalism in America during World War II* (New York: Atheneum, 1967), 246–47.
23 Divine, *Second Chance,* 250–52; Reynolds and Hughes, eds., *The Historian as Diplomat,* 69.
24 Frank Costigliola, *Roosevelt's Lost Alliances: How Personal Politics Helped Start the Cold War* (Princeton, NJ: Princeton University Press, 2012), 338.
25 Ibid., 350.
26 Raymond Fosdick, *The League and the United Nations after Fifty Years: The Six Secretaries-General* (Newtown, CT: n.p., 1972), 74; Arthur Sweetser, "From the League to the United Nations," *Annals of the American Academy of Political and Social Science* 246 (July 1946): 1–8.
27 Peter Bernholz, "Are International Organizations Like the Bank for International Settlements Unable to Die?" *Review of International Organizations* 4, no. 4 (2009): 361–81.
28 Chapter 9 tackles this question in more detail.

CHAPTER 8: COLD WAR REALITIES, 1945–49

1 Grayson Kirk, "In Search of the National Interest," *World Politics* 5, no. 1 (October 1952): 110–15.
2 Charles Seymour, "Woodrow Wilson in Perspective," *Foreign Affairs* 34, no. 2 (January 1956): 175–86.
3 Stettinius to Truman, June 26, 1945, *Foreign Relations of the United States,* 1948, I:206.
4 For the military staff planning, see Interview with Donald Blaisdell, October 29, 1973, in http://www.trumanlibrary.org; for the World Health Organization, see Interview with Henry Van Zile Hyde, July 16, 1975, http://www.trumanlibrary.org.
5 Brian Urquhart, *A Life in Peace and War* (New York: Norton, 1991), 95–96.
6 Massigli quoted in P. A. Reynolds and E. J. Hughes, ed., *The Historian as Diplomat: Charles Kingsley Webster and the United Nations, 1939–1946* (London: Martin Robertson, 1976), 77.
7 Ibid., 81.
8 See Andrew Cordier interview, "Recollections of Dag Hammerskjöld and the United Nations," 1964, Columbia University, Oral History Research Office, Butler Library; Evan Luard, *A History of the United Nations,* vol. 1, The Years of Western Domination, 1945–1955 (New York: St. Martin's Press, 1982), 79–85.
9 Raymond Fosdick, *The League and the United Nations after Fifty Years: The Six Secretaries-General* (Newtown, CT: n.p., 1972), 85–86.
10 Luard, *A History of the United Nations,* 347–50.
11 Acheson in Thomas Schoenbaum, *Waging War and Peace: Dean Rusk in the Truman, Kennedy, and Johnson Years* (New York: Simon & Schuster, 1988), 149; the more rounded portrait is in John Lamberton Harper, *American Visions of Europe: Franklin D. Roosevelt, George F. Kennan, and Dean Acheson* (Cambridge: Cambridge University Press, 1996), 266–71.
12 Kennan to Marshall, February 24, 1948, *Foreign Relations of the United States,* 1948, I:529.
13 Harper, *American Visions of Europe.*
14 Elizabeth Edwards Spalding, *The First Cold Warrior: Harry Truman, Containment and the Remaking of Liberal Internationalism* (Lexington: University Press of Kentucky, 2006), 53–59.
15 Robert Jackson, "Interview," March 27, 1978, Columbia University, Oral History Research Office, Butler Library, 275; Clayton memo of May 27, 1947, *Foreign Relations of the United States, 1947,* III:230–32.
16 On language added at the last minute: Interview with George Elsey, page 358, http://www.trumanlibrary.org; on public opinion, E. Timothy Smith, *Opposition beyond the Water's Edge: Liberal Internationalists, Pacifists, and Containment, 1945–1953* (Westport, CT: Greenwood Press 1999), 56.
17 For example, Juliusz Katz-Suchy, "One World through the United Nations," *American Academy of Political and Social Science* 258 (July 1948): 90–100; Walter Lippmann, *The Cold War: A Study in U.S. Foreign Policy* (Cambridge, MA: Harvard University Press, 1947).

18 Interview with Charles Kindleberger, http://www.trumanlibrary.org.

19 Lawrence Kaplan, *The United States and NATO: the Formative Years* (Lexington: University Press of Kentucky, 1984); Smith, *Opposition beyond the Water's Edge,* 84–87.

20 Joseph Preston Baratta, *The Politics of World Federation* (Westport, CT: Praeger, 2004), ii, 369–71.

21 Robert Heinlein, "Solution Unsatisfactory," in his *Expanded Universe* (Riverdale, NY: Baen, 2003), 74–116, at 101.

22 Baratta, *The Politics of World Federation,* 304–5. My thanks to Ira Katznelson for his help with this subject.

23 Robert Hutchins et al., *Preliminary Draft of a World Constitution* (Chicago: University of Chicago Press, 1948); Baratta, *The Politics of World Federation,* 324–27.

24 Baratta, *The Politics of World Federation,* chapter 17.

25 Kennan to Marshall, February 24, 1948, *Foreign Relations of the United States,* 1948, I:526–27.

26 Edward Meade Earle, "H. G. Wells, British Patriot in Search of a World State," *World Politics* 2, no. 2 (January 1950), 181–208; on Earle, see David Ekbladh, "Present at the Creation: Edward Meade Earle and the Depression-Era Origins of Security Studies," *International Security* 36, no. 3 (Winter 2011–12): 107–41.

27 Reinhold Niebuhr, *The Children of Light and the Children of Darkness* (New York: Charles Scribner's Sons, 1944), 158–65.

28 Stephanie Steinle, "'Plus ça change, plus c'est la même chose': Georg Schwarzenberger's *Power Politics,*" *Journal of the History of International Law* 5 (2003): 387–402; on international relations, see Nicolas Guilhot, ed., *The Invention of International Relations Theory: Realism, the Rockefeller Foundation, and the 1954 Conference on Theory* (New York: Columbia University Press, 2011); but cf. Robert Vitalis, "Birth of a Discipline," in David Long and Brian Schmidt, eds., *Imperialism and Internationalism in the Discipline of International Relations* (Albany: SUNY Press, 2005), for a reminder that the subject went back further in the United States into the race science of the early 1900s.

29 Peter Stirk, "John H. Herz: Realism and the Fragility of the International Order," *Review of International Studies* 31 (2005): 285–306; Herz, "Idealist Internationalism and the Security Dilemma," *World Politics* 2, no. 2 (January 1950): 157–80.

30 Guilhot, *The Invention of International Relations Theory.*

31 Not enough has been written about Rusk. The best source at present is Schoenbaum, *Waging War and Peace,* cited in note 11 above.

CHAPTER 9: THE SECOND WORLD, AND THE THIRD

1 Hans Kohn, "The United Nations and National Self-Determination," *Review of Politics* 20, no. 4 (October 1958): 526–45.

2 Cited in Christopher Thorne, *The Issue of War: States, Societies, and the Far Eastern Conflict of 1941–45* (London: Oxford University Press, 1985), 47.

3 Zhdanov cited in Giuliano Procacci, ed., *The Cominform: Minutes of the Three Conferences, 1947/1948/1949* (Milan: Feltrinelli Editore, 1994), 249, 443 note 135.

4 Rupert Emerson and Inis Claude, "The Soviet Union and the United Nations: An Essay in Interpretation," *International Organization* 6, no. 1 (February 1952): 1–26.

5 Alexander Dallin, *The Soviet View of the United Nations* (Cambridge, MA: MIT Press, 1959), 23–24.

6 Philip Mosely, "The Soviet Union and the United Nations," *International Organization* 19, no. 3 (Summer 1965): 666–77; *New York Times,* February 17, 1951; Emerson and Inis Claude, "The Soviet Union and the United Nations."

7 Leonid Garbanskij, "International Conferences after Stalin," in Silvio Pons and Robert Service, eds., *Dictionary of Twentieth Century Communism* (Princeton, NJ: Princeton University Press, 2010); Zbigniew Brzezinski, *The Soviet Bloc: Unity and Conflict* (Cambridge, MA: Harvard University Press, 1967).

8 Morgenthau cited in Dallin, *The Soviet View of the United Nations,* 39.
9 More on this later in this chapter.
10 Henri Grimal, *Decolonization: The British, Dutch, and Belgian Empires, 1919–1963* (London: Routledge and Kegan Paul, 1978), 116. On Nehru see Manu Bhagavan, *The Peacemakers: India and the Quest for One World* (New Delhi: HarperCollins India, 2012).
11 Grimal, *Decolonization,* 125.
12 Ibid., 150.
13 Ibid., 161.
14 Lorna Lloyd, "'A Family Quarrel': The Development of the Dispute over Indians in South Africa," *Historical Journal* 34, no.3 (September 1991): 719.
15 Shabtai Rosenne, "The International Court and the United Nations: Reflections on the Period, 1946–1954," *International Organization* 9, no. 2 (May 1955): 244–56; Heidi Hubbard, "Separation of Powers within the United Nations: A Revised Role for the International Court," *Stanford Law Review* 38, no. 1 (November 1985): 165–94; cf. George Finch, "International Law in the United Nations Organization," *Proceedings of the American Society of International Law at its Annual Meeting* 39 (April 13–14, 1945): 28–44; Alan Brinkley, *The Publisher: Henry Luce and His American Century* (New York: Knopf, 2010), 382.
16 "United Nations," November 14, 1949, in Anna Kasten Nelson, ed., *The State Department Policy Planning Staff Papers 1949* (New York: Garland, 1983), 187–98.
17 Matthew Jones, "A 'Segregated Asia': Race, the Bandung Conference, and Pan-Asian Fears in American Thought and Policy, 1954–55," *Diplomatic History* 29, no. 5 (November 2005): 841–68.
18 Ian Hall, "The Revolt against the West: Decolonization and Its Repercussions in British International Thought, 1945–1975," *International History Review* 33, no. 1 (2011): 43–64; Samuel Moyn, *The Last Utopia* (Cambridge, MA: Harvard University Press, 2010), 96.
19 Cited in Roland Burke, *Decolonization and the Evolution of International Human Rights* (Philadelphia: University of Pennsylvania Press, 2010), 17; Jason Parker, "Cold War II: The Eisenhower Administration, the Bandung Conference, and the Reperiodisation of the Postwar Era," *Diplomatic History* 30, no. 5 (November 2006), 867–92.
20 Andrew Johns and Kathryn Statler, eds., *The Eisenhower Administration, the Third World, and the Globalization of the Cold War* (New York: Rowman & Littlefield, 2006).
21 Parker, "Cold War II," 886–87; Jones, "A 'Segregated Asia,'" 864.
22 Grimal, *Decolonization,* 175–77.
23 Hall, "The Revolt against the West," 50
24 My thanks to John Kelly on this point.
25 Cited in Vernon Van Dyke, "Self-Determination and Minority Rights," *International Studies Quarterly* 13, no. 3 (September 1969): 223–53.
26 Elliot Goodman, "The Cry of National Liberation: Recent Soviet Attitudes toward National Self-Determination," *International Organization* 14, no. 1 (Winter 1960): 92–106; 1962 survey of African students in Paris cited in David Engerman, "The Second World's Third World," *Kritika: Explorations in Russian and Eurasian History* 12, no. 1 (Winter 2011): 183–211.
27 Roland Burke, *Decolonization and the Evolution of International Human Rights* (Philadelphia: University of Pennsylvania Press, 2010), 55–57.
28 de Gaulle cited in David L. Bosco, *Five to Rule Them All: The UN Security Council and the Making of the Modern World* (New York: Oxford University Press, 2009), 82.
29 Dean Rusk, "The Broadening Base of Cooperation," *American Journal of Economics and Sociology* 19, no. 1 (October 1959): 64.
30 Dean Rusk, "Working with Developing Nations," *American Journal of Economics and Sociology* 22, no. 2 (April 1963): 329–30.
31 Dean Rusk, "The Impact of Independence," *World Affairs* 128, no. 1 (April–June 1965): 10–13.

32 Dean Rusk, "The Bases of United States Foreign Policy," *Proceedings of the Academy of Political Science* 27, no. 2 (January 1962), 98–110; Dean Rusk, "The Toilsome Path to Peace," *Western Political Quarterly* 17, no. 3 (September 1964), 5–11.

33 Engerman, "The Second World's Third World," 208.

34 A realistic appraisal of Moscow's internationalism is Alvin Z. Rubinstein, *Moscow's Third World Strategy* (Princeton, NJ: Princeton University Press, 1988); see also A. Korbonski and F. Fukuyama, ed., *The Soviet Union and the Third World: The Last Three Decades* (Ithaca, NY: Cornell University Press, 1987).

35 The broad argument is brilliantly presented in Anne Orford, *International Authority and the Responsibility to Protect* (Cambridge: Cambridge University Press, 2010); on the role of Andrew Cordier in the Congo, see Madeleine Kalb, *The Congo Cables: The Cold War in Africa—from Eisenhower to Kennedy* (New York: Macmillan, 1982).

36 Manley Hudson, "Membership in the League of Nations," *American Journal of International Relations* 18, no. 3 (July 1924): 436–58; Maurice Mendelson, "Diminutive States in the United Nations," *Comparative Law Quarterly* 21, no. 4 (October 1972): 609–30; Jeff King and A. J. Hobbins, "Hammerskjöld and Human Rights: The Deflation of the UN Human Rights Program, 1953–1961," *Journal of the History of International Law* 5 (2003): 337–86; Richard Jackson, *The Non-Aligned, the UN, and the Superpowers* (New York: Praeger, 1983), 146–47.

37 Vernon Van Dyke, "Self-Determination and Minority Rights," *International Studies Quarterly* 13, no. 3 (September 1969): 234.

38 Elmer Plischke, "Self-Determination: Reflections on a Legacy," *World Affairs* 140, no. 1 (Summer 1977): 41–57.

39 Vijay Prashad, *The Darker Nations: A People's History of the Third World* (New York: New Press, 2007), 102.

40 Bosco, *Five to Rule Them All,* 117; Jackson, *The Non-Aligned, the UN, and the Superpowers,* 160–61, 211–13.

41 Steven Holloway and Rodney Tomlinson, "The New World Order and the General Assembly: Bloc Realignment at the UN in the Post–Cold War World," *Canadian Journal of Sociology* 28, no. 2 (June 1995): 227–54.

CHAPTER 10: DEVELOPMENT AS WORLD-MAKING, 1949–73

1 The background is described in "Oral History Interview with Joseph Coppock" (1974), Harry Truman Library, at http://www.trumanlibrary.org/oralhist/coppockj.htm#102.

2 S. Yakobson, "Soviet Concepts of Point Four," *Annals of the American Academy of Political and Social Sciences* 268 (March 1950): 129–39.

3 Matthew Connelly, *Fatal Misconception: The Struggle to Control the World's Population* (Cambridge, MA: Harvard University Press, 2008), chapter 4.

4 David Ekbladh, *The Great American Mission: Modernization and the Construction of an American World Order* (Princeton, NJ: Princeton University Press, 2010), 95.

5 Ibid., 96.

6 "Oral History Interview with Joseph D. Coppock," Harry S. Truman Library and Museum, http://www.trumanlibrary.org/oralhist/coppockj.htm.

7 Data from U.S. Department of Commerce, *Statistical Abstract of the United States, 1954* (Washington, D.C.: U.S. Government Printing Office, 1954), 899–900, 974.

8 Soviet data in Alexander Dallin, *The Soviet View of the United Nations* (Cambridge, MA: MIT Press, 1959), 65.

9 Cited in Ekbladh, *Great American Mission,* 100.

10 Ibid., 46–47.

11 Paul Rosenstein-Rodan, "Problems of Industrialization of Eastern and Southeastern Europe," *Economic Journal* 53 (1943): 202–11, at 210–11; Paul Rosenstein-Rodan, "The

International Development of Economically Backward Areas," *International Affairs* 20, no. 2 (April 1944): 157–65.

12 Joseph Morgan Hodge, *Triumph of the Expert: Agrarian Doctrines of Development and the Legacies of British Colonialism* (Athens, OH: Ohio University Press, 2007).

13 Nick Cullather, *The Hungry World* (Cambridge, MA: Harvard University Press, 2010), 58.

14 On geographers, see Neil Smith, *American Empire: Roosevelt's Geographer and the Prelude to Globalization* (Berkeley: University of California Press, 2003).

15 Recollections of Jackson in "Oral Interview with Henry Van Zile Hyde," July 16, 1975, in http://www.trumanlibrary.org/oralhist/hydehvz1.htm; "Oral Interview with Sir Robert Jackson," Butler Library, Oral History Collection, Columbia University.

16 James Gibson, *Jacko, Where Are You Now? A Life of Robert Jackson* (Richmond, UK: Parsons Publishing, 2006).

17 Amy Staples, *The Birth of Development: How the World Bank, Food and Agricultural Organization, and World Health Organization Changed the World, 1945–1965* (Kent, OH: Kent State University Press, 2006), 84–96.

18 Nancy Stepan, *Eradication: Ridding the World of Diseases Forever* (Ithaca, NY: Cornell University Press, 2011), chapter 4; Staples, *The Birth of Development*, chapters 8–10.

19 James Ferguson, *Anti-Politics Machine: "Development," Depoliticization, and Bureaucratic Power in Lesotho* (Minneapolis: University of Minnesota Press, 1994); Inderjeet Parmar, *Foundations of the American Century: The Ford, Carnegie, and Rockefeller Foundations in the Rise of American Power* (New York: Columbia University Press, 2012), 156.

20 Connelly, *Fatal Misconception*, passim.

21 Michele Alacevich, *The Political Economy of the World Bank: The Early Years* (Stanford, CA: Stanford University Press, 2009).

22 Staples, *The Birth of Development*, 38–39.

23 Devesh Kapur, John Prior Lewis, and Richard Charles Webb, *The World Bank: Its First Half-Century* (Washington, D.C.: Brookings Institution, 1997), 11–12.

24 H. W. Arndt, *Economic Development: The History of an Idea* (Chicago: University of Chicago Press, 1987); data from Klaus Huefner, http://www.globalpolicy.org/un-finance.html.

25 Odd Arne Westad, *The Global Cold War* (Cambridge: Cambridge University Press, 2007), 67.

26 Ibid., 68.

27 Nick Cullather, *The Hungry World: America's Cold War Battle against Poverty in Asia* (Cambridge, MA: Harvard University Press, 2010), 112. See also David Milne, *America's Rasputin: Walt Rostow and the Vietnam War* (New York: Hill & Wang, 2008), and Nils Gilman, *Mandarins of the Future: Modernization Theory in Cold War America* (Baltimore: Johns Hopkins University Press, 2003).

28 Gilman, *Mandarins of the Future;* Milne, *America's Rasputin.*

29 Gerald Meier and Dudley Seers, eds., *Pioneers in Development* (Oxford: Oxford University Press, 1984), 3–27, esp. 8; Michael Latham, *The Right Kind of Revolution: Modernization, Development, and U.S. Foreign Policy from the Cold War to the Present* (Ithaca, NY: Cornell University Press, 2011), 42.

30 David Ekbladh, *The Great American Mission: Modernization and the Construction of an American World Order* (Princeton, NJ: Princeton University Press, 2010), 191.

31 Thomas Field, "Ideology as Strategy: Military-Led Modernization and the Origins of the Alliance for Progress in Bolivia," *Diplomatic History* 36, no. 1 (January 2012): 147–77; Bradley Simpson, *Economists with Guns: Authoritarian Development and U.S.-Indonesian Relations* (Stanford, CA: Stanford University Press, 2008).

32 Cullather, *The Hungry World,* passim.

33 E. Philip Morgan, "Social Analysis, Project Development and Advocacy in U.S. Foreign Assistance," *Public Administration and Development* 3 (1983): 61–71.

34 Gibson, *Jacko, Where Are You Now?,* chapter 12.

35 Cited in Alan R. Raucher, *Paul G. Hoffman: Architect of Foreign Aid* (Lexington: University of Kentucky Press, 1985), 147.

36 Kissinger to Nixon, undated, *Foreign Relations of the United States,* 1969–1972, V:448–49.

37 The best account of the writing of the Jackson report and its impact is in Margaret Joan Anstee, *Never Learn to Type: A Woman at the United Nations* (London: John Wiley & Sons, 2003), chapter 13; see also Rosemary Galli, "The United Nations Development Program, 'Development,' and 'Multinational Corporations,'" *Latin American Perspectives* 3, no. 4 (Autumn 1976): 65–85.

38 "Poor vs Rich: a New Global Conflict," *Time* 106, no. 25 (December 22, 1975): 42.

39 Arndt, *Economic Development,* 81–82.

40 Craig Murphy, *United Nations Development Program: A Better Way?* (Cambridge: Cambridge University Press, 2006), 60–66; Che Guevara, "On Development," speech of March 25, 1964, to UNCTAD.

41 Edgar J. Dosman, *The Life and Times of Raul Prebisch, 1901–1986* (Montreal: Queens University School of Policy, 2008), 390–95.

42 Giuliano Garavini, *After Empires: European Integration and the North-South Divide* (Oxford: Oxford University Press, forthcoming), 58.

43 Bush to Nixon, June 27, 1972, *Foreign Relations of the United States,* 1969–1972, V:63–65.

44 Judith Stein, *Pivotal Decade: How the United States Traded Factories for Finance in the Seventies* (New Haven, CT: Yale University Press, 2010), 91.

CHAPTER 11: THE UNITED STATES IN OPPOSITION

1 Stephen Krasner, *Structural Conflict: The Third World against Global Liberalism* (Berkeley: University of California Press, 1985), 299.

2 Pendleton Herring, "Woodrow Wilson—Then and Now," *Political Science* 7, no. 3 (Summer 1974): 256–59.

3 On Moynihan, see Godfrey Hodgson, *The Gentleman from New York: Daniel Patrick Moynihan* (New York: Houghton Mifflin Harcourt, 2000), and more analytically, Justin Vaisse, *Neoconservatism: The Biography of a Movement* (Cambridge, MA: Harvard University Press, 2010), 122–25.

4 Daniel P. Moynihan, "Was Woodrow Wilson Right? Morality and American Foreign Policy," *Commentary* 57 (May 1974): 25–31.

5 Henry Kissinger, "Domestic Structure and Foreign Policy," *Daedalus* 95, no. 2 (Spring 1966): 503–29.

6 On Kennan, "Interview with George Kennan," *Foreign Policy* 7 (Summer 1972): 5–21.

7 Daniel P. Moynihan, "The United States in Opposition," *Commentary* 59 (March 1975): 31–43.

8 William F. Buckley Jr., *United Nations Journal: A Delegate's Odyssey* (New York: Putnam, 1974); Shirley Hazzard, *Defeat of an Ideal: A Study of the Self-Destruction of the UN* (New York: Little, Brown, 1973).

9 Anon., "Moynihanism at the United Nations," *Third World Quarterly* 2, no. 3 (July 1980): 500–521.

10 A brilliant treatment—and the Podhoretz quote—is in Daniel Jonathan Sargent, "From Internationalism to Globalism: The United States and the Transformation of International Politics in the 1970s" (DPhil thesis, Department of History, Harvard University, February 2008), quotation on 465.

11 Giuliano Garavini, *After Empires: European Integration and the North-South Divide* (Oxford: Oxford University Press, forthcoming), 231; Krasner, *Structural Conflict,* 26–27.

12 *Le Soir,* September 27, 1973, cited in Garavini, *After Empires,* 278.

13 Stephen Gill, *American Hegemony and the Trilateral Commission* (Cambridge: Cambridge University Press, 1990), 136–37.

14 Stein, *Pivotal Decade: How the United States Traded Factories for Finance in the Seventies* (New Haven, CT: Yale University Press, 2010), 158; Gill, *American Hegemony and the Trilateral Commission,* 145.
15 Stein, *Pivotal Decade,* 92.
16 Stevenson to Johnson, November 1964, *Foreign Relations of the United States,* 1964–1968, XXXIII:669; Waldheim to Bush, *Foreign Relations of the United States,* 1969–1972, V:63–65; R. N. Gardner, *The United States and the United Nations: Can We Do Better?* (undated pamphlet [but 1972], American Assembly, Columbia University), 8–9.
17 Richard Melanson, "Human Rights and the American Withdrawal from the ILO," *Universal Human Rights* 1, no. 1 (January–March 1979): 43–61.
18 Cited in Robert Rothstein, *Global Bargaining: UNCTAD and the Quest for a New International Economic Order* (Princeton, NJ: Princeton University Press, 1979), 178–79.
19 Ibid., 260–65.
20 Paul Volcker, "The Political Economy of the Dollar" (The Fred Hirsch Lecture), *Federal Reserve Bank of New York Quarterly Review* (Winter 1978–79): 1–12.
21 Alasdair Roberts, *The Logic of Discipline: Global Capitalism and the Architecture of Government* (Oxford: Oxford University Press, 2010).
22 Garavini, *After Empires,* 378.
23 Roland Burke, *Decolonization and the Evolution of International Human Rights* (Philadelphia: University of Pennsylvania Press, 2010), 17–19.
24 Ibid., 25.
25 A good discussion is in Roger Normand and Sarah Zaidi, *Human Rights at the United Nations: The Political History of Universal Justice* (Bloomington: Indiana University Press, 2008), 222 et seq.
26 Frantz Fanon, *The Wretched of the Earth* (New York: Penguin, 2001 ed.), 36, 74.
27 A. Dirk Moses, "The United Nations, Humanitarianism and Human rights: War Crimes/Genocide Trials for Pakistani Soldiers in Bangladesh, 1971–1974," in Stefan Ludwig Hoffmann, ed., *Human Rights in the Twentieth Century* (Cambridge: Cambridge University Press, 2011), 258–83.
28 Samuel Huntington, *Political Order in Changing Societies* (New Haven, CT: Yale University Press, 1968).
29 Burke, *Decolonization and the Evolution of International Human Rights,* 8.
30 Samuel Moyn, *The Last Utopia* (Cambridge, MA: Harvard University Press, 2010), 138–39.
31 Ibid., 155.
32 Tony Smith, *America's Mission: The United States and the Worldwide Struggle for Democracy in the Twentieth Century* (Princeton, NJ: Princeton University Press, 1955), 245–47.
33 Steve Charnovitz, "Two Centuries of Participation: NGOs and International Governance," *Michigan Journal of International Law* 18, no. 183 (Winter 1997): 183–286.
34 Howard B. Tolley, *The International Commission of Jurists: Global Advocates for Human Rights* (Philadelphia: University of Pennsylvania Press, 1994), 25–27.
35 Peter Benenson, "The Forgotten Prisoners," *Observer,* May 28, 1961.
36 Tom Buchanan, "'The Truth Will Set You Free': The Making of Amnesty International," *Journal of Contemporary History* 37, no. 4 (2002): 575–97, at 593.
37 Helena Cook, "Amnesty International at the United Nations," in Peter Willetts, ed., *"The Conscience of the World": The Influence of Non-Governmental Organisations in the United Nations System* (London: Brookings Institution Press, 1996), 147–81.
38 Sarah Snyder, *Human Rights Activism and the End of the Cold War: A Transnational History of the Helsinki Network* (Cambridge: Cambridge University Press, 2011), 10–11.
39 William Korey, *Taking On the World's Repressive Regimes: The Ford Foundation's Human Rights Policies and Practices* (New York: Palgrave Macmillan, 2007), 100–110.
40 Ibid., 111–12.
41 Ibid., chapter 5; Nicolas Guilhot, *The Democracy Makers: Human Rights and the Politics of*

Global Order (New York: Columbia University Press, 2005), 74–75; Vaisse, *Neoconservatism*, 138–39, 190–91.

42 Guilhot, *The Democracy Makers*, 84–88; on the NED's nongovernmental character, see National Endowment for Democracy, *2012 Strategy Document*, 9 (a "wholly non-governmental organization").

43 Moisés Naím, "Democracy's Dangerous Impostors," *Washington Post*, April 21, 2007; Freedom House, "Our Leadership," http://www.freedomhouse.org/content/our-leadership.

44 Thomas Hughes, "The Twilight of Internationalism," *Foreign Policy* 61 (1985–86): 25–48.

45 Lawrence Samuel, *Future: A Recent History* (Austin: University of Texas Press, 2009), 123.

46 Deborah Barrett and David John Frank, "Population Control for National Development: From World Discourse to National Policies," in John Boli and George M. Thomas, eds., *Constructing World Culture: International Non-Governmental Organizations since 1875* (Stanford, CA: Stanford University Press, 1999), 198–222.

47 J. Brooks Flippen, *Conservative Conservationist: Russell E. Train and the Emergence of American Environmentalism* (Baton Rouge: LSU Press, 2006), 8–10.

48 J. Brooks Flippen, *Nixon and the Environment* (Albuquerque: University of New Mexico Press, 2000).

49 Tony Brenton, *The Greening of Machiavelli: The Evolution of International Environmental Politics* (London: Royal Institute of International Affairs, 1994), 38.

50 Allen Springer, "United States Environmental Policy and International Law: Stockholm Principle 21 Revisited," in John E. Carroll, ed., *International Environmental Diplomacy: The Management and Resolution of Transfrontier Environmental Problems* (Cambridge: Cambridge University Press, 1988), 455–67.

51 George Kennan, "To Prevent a World Wasteland," *Foreign Affairs* 48, no. 3 (April 1970): 401–13; Maria Ivanova, "Moving Forward, Looking Back: Learning from UNEF's History," in Ken Conca and Geoffrey D. Dabelko, eds., *Green Planet Blues: Four Decades of Global Environmental Politics* (Boulder, CO: Westview Press, 2010), 143–61.

52 Gareth Porter, Janet Welsh Brown, and Pamela S. Chasek, *Global Environmental Politics* (Boulder, CO: Westview Press, 2000), 161–63.

53 Fred Turner, *From Counterculture to Cyberculture: Stewart Brand, the Whole Earth Network, and the Rise of Digital Utopianism* (Chicago: University of Chicago Press, 2006); Andrew G. Kirk, *Counterculture Green: The Whole Earth Catalog and American Environmentalism* (Lawrence: University Press of Kansas, 2007).

54 On Brand and Kahn, see Kirk, *Counterculture Green*, 167–68.

55 Paul Aligica, "Julian Simon and the 'Limits to Growth': Neo-Malthusianism," *Electronic Journal of Sustainable Development* 1, no. 3 (2009), 73–84; Samuel, *Future*, 146.

56 Springer, "United States Environmental Policy," 53, 64.

57 Norichika Kanie, "Governance with Multilateral Environmental Agreements: A Healthy or Ill-Equipped Fragmentation?" in Conca and Dabelko, eds., *Green Planet Blues*, 126–43.

CHAPTER 12: THE REAL NEW INTERNATIONAL ECONOMIC ORDER

1 *Sunday Times*, May 21, 1978, cited in Andrew Glyn, *Capitalism Unleashed: Finance, Globalization, and Welfare* (Oxford: Oxford University Press, 2006), 1.

2 Louis W. Pauly, *Who Elected the Bankers? Surveillance and Control in the World Economy* (Ithaca, NY: Cornell University Press, 1997), chapters 5–6.

3 Funkhouser to Hart, September 10, 1953, in United States Congress, Senate Committee on Foreign Relations: Hearings, *Multinational Corporations and United States Foreign Policy* (Washington, D.C.: U.S. Government Printing Office, 1975), 135–39.

4 Cited in Steven Ludlam, "The Gnomes of Washington: Four Myths of the 1976 IMF Crisis," *Political Studies* 50 (1992): 713–27.

5 On the crisis, see Kevin Hickson, *The IMF Crisis of 1976 and British Politics* (London: I. B. Tauris, 2005).

6 Two essential guides are Greta Krippner, *Capitalizing on Crisis: The Political Origins of the Rise of Finance* (Cambridge, MA: Harvard University Press, 2011), and Rawi Abdelal, *Capital Rules: The Construction of Global Finance* (Cambridge, MA: Harvard University Press, 2007).
7 Figures from Jeffry A. Frieden, *Global Capitalism: Its Fall and Rise in the Twentieth Century* (New York: Norton, 2006), 343; on Wriston, see Jeff Madrick, *Age of Greed: The Triumph of Finance and the Decline of America, 1970 to the Present* (New York: Vintage, 2011), 101–3.
8 Kevin Hickson, *The IMF Crisis of 1976 and British Politics* (London: I. B. Tauris, 2005), passim; Harold James, *International Monetary Cooperation since Bretton Woods* (New York: Oxford University Press, 1996), 280.
9 For the background, Andrew Glyn, *Capitalism Unleashed: Finance, Globalization, and Welfare* (Oxford: Oxford University Press, 2006), is indispensable.
10 Pauly, *Who Elected the Bankers?* 104–5.
11 Hickson, *The IMF Crisis of 1976*, 132–36.
12 James Boughton, "Jacques Polak and the Evolution of the International Monetary System," *IMF Economic Review* 59, no. 2 (June 2011): 379–99; Randall Stone, "The Scope of IMF Conditionality," *International Organization* 62, no. 4 (Fall 2008): 589–620.
13 Paul Volcker, "The Political Economy of the Dollar" (The Fred Hirsch Lecture), *Federal Reserve Bank of New York Quarterly Review* (Winter 1978–79), 1–12; Eric Helleiner, *States and the Reemergence of Global Finance: From Bretton Woods to the 1990s* (Ithaca, NY: Cornell University Press, 1994), chapter 6.
14 Data from Nouriel Roubini and Stephen Mihm, *Crisis Economics: A Crash Course in the Future of Finance* (New York: Penguin Press, 2010), 83; see Louis Hyman, *Debtor Nation: A History of America in Red Ink* (Princeton, NJ: Princeton University Press, 2011), chapter 7.
15 Glyn, *Capitalism Unleashed*, 66.
16 Helleiner, *States and the Reemergence of Global Finance*, chapter 6.
17 The standard study is Eichengreen and Bordo, "Crises Then and Now," cited in Ha-Joon Chang, *Bad Samaritans: The Myth of Free Trade and the Secret History of Capitalism* (New York: Bloomsbury Press, 2008), 87; see too Martin Wolf, *Fixing Global Finance* (Baltimore: John Hopkins University Press, 2008), 31.
18 Pauly, *Who Elected the Bankers?* 118–19; Helleiner, *States and the Reemergence of Global Finance*, 176.
19 There is a good discussion of congressional attitudes to the Brady plan in Kathryn Lavelle, *Legislating International Organizations: The U.S. Congress, the IMF, and the World Bank* (Oxford: Oxford University Press, 2011), 118–19, 133–34.
20 Cited in ibid., 119.
21 Abdelal, *Capital Rules*, 14, 157–61; Liam Clegg, "Global Governance behind Closed Doors: The IMF Boardroom, the Enhanced Structural Adjustment Facility, and the Intersection of Material Power and Norm Stabilization in Global Politics," *Reviews in International Organization* (2011): 1–24.
22 Chang, *Bad Samaritans*, 27; on economics, see Marion Fourcade, *Economists and Societies: Discipline and Profession in the United States, Britain and France, 1890s to 1990s* (Princeton, NJ: Princeton University Press, 2009); and for the intellectual shifts, a summary in Daniel Rodgers, *Age of Fracture* (Cambridge, MA: Harvard University Press, 2011), chapter 2 and page 249.
23 Glyn, *Capitalism Unleashed*, 37.
24 Greg Grandin, *Empire's Workshop: Latin America, the United States and the Rise of the New Imperialism* (New York: Metropolitan Books, 2006), 185–90.
25 Hilary Appel, "Voucher Privatization in Russia: Structural Consequences and Mass Response in the Second Period of Reform," *Europe-Asia Studies* 49, no. 8 (December 1997): 1433–49; Rodgers, *Age of Fracture*, 248–49; E. Wayne Merry cited in Yves Smith, *ECONned: How Unenlightened Self-Interest Undermined Democracy and Corrupted Capitalism* (New York: Palgrave Macmillan, 2010), 121.

26 IMF Historical Data, various.

27 Helleiner, *States and the Reemergence of Global Finance,* 177.

28 Walter B. Wriston, George P. Shultz, and William E. Simon, "Who Needs the IMF?" *Wall Street Journal,* February 3, 1998.

29 Abdelal, *Capital Rules,* chapter 7.

30 Lavelle, *Legislating International Organization,* 119; Joshua Cooper Ramo, "The Three Musketeers," *Time,* February 15, 1999.

31 "Statement at the First Plenary Session of the International Meeting on Cooperation and Development in Cancun, Mexico," October 22, 1981; figures on the secular decline in U.S. foreign aid in George Soros, *On Globalization* (New York: PublicAffairs, 2002), 18; data on trade/GDP from Alfred Eckes and Thomas Zeiler, *Globalization and the American Century* (Cambridge: Cambridge University Press, 2003), 268.

32 See Paul Collier, *The Bottom Billion* (Oxford: Oxford University Press, 2007); Ruggiero comments at "UNCTAD and WTO: A Common Goal in a Global Economy," August 10, 1996, at http://www.unctad.org/templates/webflyer.asp?docid=3607&intItemID=2298&lang=1.

33 Richard Peet, *Unholy Trinity: The IMF, World Bank, and WTO* (London: Zed Books, 2009). See, for much more, Paul Blustein, *Misadventures of the Most Favored Nations: Clashing Egos, Inflated Ambitions, and the Great Shambles of the World Trade System* (New York: PublicAffairs, 2009).

34 William Jefferson Clinton, State of the Union address, January 27, 2000.

35 Nayan Chanda, *Bound Together: How Preachers, Adventurers, and Warriors Shaped Civilization* (New Haven, CT: Yale University Press, 2007), 245–71.

36 See Justin Fox, *The Myth of the Rational Market: A History of Risk, Reward, and Delusion on Wall Street* (New York: HarperBusiness, 2009), and Yanis Varoufakis, *The Global Minotaur: America, the True Origins of the Financial Crisis, and the Future of the World Economy* (New York: Zed Books, 2011).

37 Fox, The *Myth of the Rational Market,* xii.

38 Erskine Childers, "The United Nations and Global Institutions: Discourse and Reality," *Global Governance* 3, no. 3 (September-December 1997): 269–76.

39 See the wonderful critique, in Chang, *Bad Samaritans,* 21; on Friedman, Belén Fernández, *The Imperial Messenger: Thomas Friedman at Work* (London: Verso, 2011).

40 On al-Qaeda and globalization, see Faisal Devji, *Landscapes of the Jihad: Militancy, Morality, Modernity* (Ithaca, NY: Cornell University Press, 2005).

41 John Williamson, "Did the Washington Consensus Fail?" (speech at CSIS, Washington, D.C., November 6, 2002), Institute for International Economics: 169.

42 Martin Wolf, *Fixing Global Finance* (Baltimore: Johns Hopkins University Press, 2008). See also IMF economist Raghuram Rajan, "Has Financial Development Made the World Riskier?" (2005), Proceedings of the Jackson Hole Conference organized by the Kansas City Federal Reserve.

43 Nicolas Guilhot, *The Democracy Makers: Human Rights and the Politics of Global Order* (New York: Columbia University Press, 2005), 198.

44 Figures in Paul Blustein, *The Chastening: Inside the Crisis That Rocked the Global Financial System and Humbled the IMF* (New York: PublicAffairs, 2003 ed.), 159.

45 Joseph Stiglitz, *Globalization and Its Discontents* (New York: Norton, 2002); Sebastian Mallaby, *The World's Banker: A Story of Failed States, Financial Crises, and the Wealth and Poverty of Nations* (New York: Penguin, 2004).

46 Guilhot, *The Democracy Makers,* 212.

47 See the work of Bob Tricker, *Corporate Governance: Principles, Policies, and Practices* (New York: Oxford University Press, 2009), for the cuddly version and the articles of Michael Jensen of the Harvard Business School for the often avowedly antidemocratic neoliberal version. See, for instance, his 1978 "Can the Corporation Survive?" and "Corporate

Governance and Economic Democracy: An Attack on Freedom," in C. J. Huizenga, ed., *Proceedings of Corporate Governance: A Definitive Exploration of the Issues* (UCLA Extension, 1983). A serious intellectual history of the term remains to be written. For some valuable comments, see Guilhot, *The Democracy Makers,* 211–13.

48 For instance, nothing is said about corporate governance in Thomas Weiss, "What Happened to the Idea of World Government?" *International Studies Quarterly* 53 (2009): 253–71; see also Thomas G. Weiss and Ramesh Thakur, *Global Governance and the UN: An Unfinished Journey* (Bloomington: Indiana University Press, 2010).

49 Lawrence Finkelstein, "What Is Global Governance?" *Global Governance* 1 (1995): 367–72; Ved Nanda, "The 'Good Governance' Concept Revisited," *Annals of the American Academy of Political and Social Science* 603 (January 2006): 269–83; more fundamentally, Martin Shapiro, "Administrative Law Unbounded: Reflections on Government and Governance," *Indiana Journal of Global Legal Studies* 8, no. 2 (Spring 2001): 369–77.

50 John Gerard Ruggie, "The United Nations and Globalization: Patterns and Limits of Institutional Adaptation," *Global Governance* 9, no. 3 (July–September 2003), 301–21.

51 Olav Stokke, *The United Nations and Development: From Aid to Cooperation (*Bloomington: Indiana University Press, 2009), 369; Mark Malloch Brown, *The Unfinished Global Revolution: The Pursuit of a New International Politics* (New York: Penguin Press, 2011).

52 Mark Duffield, *Development, Security, and Unending War: Governing the World of People* (Cambridge, UK: Polity, 2007).

53 Sebastian Mallaby, "The Reluctant Imperialist," *Foreign Affairs* 81, no. 2 (March–April 2002): 2–7.

54 G. John Ikenberry and Anne-Marie Slaughter, *Forging World of Liberty under Law: U.S. National Security in the 21st Century* (Final Report of the Princeton Project on National Security) (Princeton, NJ: Princeton University Press, 2006), passim.

55 Martyn Davies, "How China Delivers Development Assistance to Africa," University of Stellenbosch, 2008; Carol Lancaster, "The Chinese Aid System," Center for Global Development, 2007; Kevin Gallagher, "Forget the Received Wisdom: Chinese Finance in Latin America is a Win-Win," *Guardian,* March 16, 2012.

56 From a vast literature, see Thomas A. Kelley, "Exporting Western Law to the Developing World: The Case of Niger," *Global Jurist* 7, no. 3 (2007): 1–38. See too Serge Michel and Michel Beuret, *China Safari: On the Trail of Beijing's Expansion in Africa* (New York: Nation Books, 2009), 106–9; Yves Dezalay and Bryant Garth, *Asian Legal Revivals: Lawyers in the Shadow of Empire* (Chicago: University of Chicago Press, 2010). My thanks to Thomas Kelley for discussing this issue with me.

57 The ideological character of the American hostility to the state is discussed in Peter Evans, "The Eclipse of the State? Reflections on Stateness in an Era of Globalization," *World Politics* 50, no. 1 (October 1997): 62–87; see also his superb "In Search of the 21st Century Developmental State," Center for Global Political Economy, Sussex Working Papers, 2008; cf. Ian Bremmer, *The End of the Free Market: Who Wins the War between States and Corporations?* (New York: Penguin, 2010).

CHAPTER 13: HUMANITY'S LAW

1 Cited by Anne Orford, *International Authority and the Responsibility to Protect* (Cambridge: Cambridge University Press, 2011), 132.

2 Kofi Annan, "Two Concepts of Sovereignty," *Economist* 352 (September 18, 1999), 49–50.

3 On the idea that the contemporary global predicament involves reconciling these two principles of order, see Edward Keene, *Beyond the Anarchical Society: Grotius, Colonialism, and Order in World Politics* (Cambridge: Cambridge University Press, 2002), chapter 5.

4 On constitutional missions, see Vijayashri Sripati, "UN Constitutional Assistance Projects in Comprehensive Peace Missions: An Inventory, 1989–2011," *International*

Peacekeeping 19, no. 1 (March 2012): 93–113; on the overall shift, Michael Doyle and Nicholas Sambanis, *United Nations Peacekeeping Operations* (Princeton, NJ: Princeton University Press, 2006).

5 Orford, *International Authority and the Responsibility to Protect.*

6 Figures from Doyle and Sambanis, *Making War and Building Peace,* 6.

7 On the term see Serge Sur, "Sur les États défaillants," *Commentaire* 112 (Winter 2005); Paul Williams, "State Failure in Africa: Causes, Consequences, and Responses," at www.europaworld.com. More analytically, Tanisha Fazal, *State Death: The Politics and Geography of Conquest, Occupation, and Annexation* (Princeton, NJ: Princeton University Press, 2008).

8 Orford, *International Authority and the Responsibility to Protect,* 91; Doyle and Sambanis, *Making War and Building Peace,* 1.

9 James Traub, *The Best Intentions: Kofi Annan and the UN in an Era of American World Power* (New York: Farrar, Straus and Giroux 2006), 91–93; David Hannay, *New World Disorder* (London: I. B. Tauris, 2008), 109.

10 A typically trenchant analysis is in Hannay, *New World Disorder.*

11 Stephen Wertheim, "A Solution from Hell: The United States and the Rise of Humanitarian Interventionism," *Journal of Genocide Research* 12, no. 3–4 (2010): 149–72.

12 Traub, *The Best Intentions,* 62–66.

13 Tony Blair, *A Journey: My Political Life* (New York: Knopf, 2010); Mark Malloch Brown, *The Unfinished Global Revolution: The Pursuit of a New International Politics* (New York: Penguin Press, 2011), 70.

14 "Transcript: Albright Interview on NBC-TV February 19," February 19, 1998, at http://www.fas.org/news/iraq/1998/02/19/98021907_tpo.html.

15 See the discussion in John F. Murphy, *The United States and the Rule of Law in International Affairs* (Cambridge: Cambridge University Press, 2004), 166–67; David Bosco, *Five to Rule Them All: The UN Security Council and the Making of the Modern World* (New York: Oxford University Press, 2009), 210.

16 Justin Vaisse, *Neoconservatism: The Biography of a Movement* (Cambridge, MA: Harvard University Press, 2010), 141.

17 Orford, *International Authority and the Responsibility to Protect.*

18 Tony Karon, "Bush Plays It Clintonesque in Kosovo," *Time,* July 24, 2001.

19 Robert Cooper, *The Postmodern State and the World Order* (London: Demos, 2000); "The 2005 Failed States Index," *Foreign Policy,* available at http://www.foreignpolicy.com/articles/2005/07/01/the_failed_states_index_2005.

20 Serena Sharma, "Toward a Global Responsibility to Protect: Setbacks on the Path to Implementation," *Global Governance* 16 (2010): 121–38.

21 Samantha Power, "The Human-Rights Vacuum," *Time,* October 11, 2007.

22 Lise Morje Howard, "Sources of Change in United States–United Nations Relations," *Global Governance* 16 (2010): 485–503; Lee Feinstein and Anne-Marie Slaughter, "A Duty to Prevent," *Foreign Affairs,* January–February 2004.

23 *Forging a World of Liberty under Law: The Princeton Project on National Security* (2006), available at http://www.princeton.edu/~ppns/report/FinalReport.pdf, passim; also Inderjeet Parmar, *Foundations of the American Century: the Ford, Carnegie, and Rockefeller Foundations in the Rise of American Power* (New York: Columbia University Press, 2012), 242–47.

24 Orford, *International Authority and the Responsibility to Protect,* 106.

25 David Schmitz, *Brent Scowcroft: Internationalism and Post-Vietnam War American Foreign Policy* (Lanham, MD: Rowman & Littlefield, 2011), 105.

26 Murphy, *The United States and the Rule of Law in International Affairs,* 317 et seq.

27 See David Scheffer, *All the Missing Souls: A Personal History of the War Crimes Tribunals* (Princeton, NJ: Princeton University Press, 2012).

28 Ruti G. Teitel, *Humanity's Law* (New York: Oxford University Press, 2011), 87.

29 Security Council Resolution 1593, in http://www.un.org/News/Press/docs/2005/sc8351.doc.htm.

30 Phil Clark, ed., *Debating International Justice in Africa* (Oxford: Oxford University Press, 2010).

31 See Michael Ignatieff, *American Exceptionalism and Human Rights* (Princeton, NJ: Princeton University Press, 2005).

32 Nick Turse, "America's Secret Empire of Drone Bases," *Nation,* October 17, 2011.

33 "Report of the Special Rapporteur on Extrajudicial, Summary, or Arbitrary executions, Philip Alston," May 28, 2010, UN General Assembly, Human Rights Council; cf. Nick Turse, "The Life and Death of American Drones," *Nation,* December 20, 2011.

34 Gary Marchant et al., "International Governance of Autonomous Military Robots," *Columbia Science and Technology Law Review* 12 (2011): 272–315; also P. W. Singer, *Wired for War: The Robotics Revolution and Conflict in the Twenty-First Century* (New York: Penguin Press, 2009); Anne-Marie Slaughter, "How to End the Butchery in Syria," *New York Times,* February 23, 2012.

35 See the more optimistic conclusions of Teitel, *Humanity's Law;* for an example of the right to self-defense, see Singer, *Wired for War,* 407.

CHAPTER 14: WHAT REMAINS: THE CRISIS IN EUROPE AND AFTER

1 Alexis de Tocqueville, *Democracy in America* (New York: Penguin, 2003), 804 ("What Sort of Despotism Democratic Nations Have to Fear").

2 Martin Shapiro, "'Deliberative,' 'Independent' Technocracy vs. Democratic Politics: Will the Globe Echo the EU?" *Law and Contemporary Problems* 68, no. 3–4 (Summer–Autumn 2005): 341–56, at 354.

3 For background, see Bertrand Vayssiere, "Le manifeste de Ventotene (1941): Acte de naissance du fédéralisme européen," *Guerres mondiales et conflits contemporains* 217, no. 1 (2005): 69–76; Charles Delzell, "The European Federalist Movement in Italy: First Phase, 1918–1947," *Journal of Modern History* 32, no. 3 (September 1960): 241–50.

4 See Rawi Abdelal, *Capital Rules: The Construction of Global Finance* (Cambridge, MA: Harvard University Press, 2007).

5 The key text is J. H. H. Weiler, *The Constitution of Europe: "Do the New Clothes Have an Emperor?" and Other Essays on European Integration* (Cambridge: Cambridge University Press, 1999).

6 Martin Heipertz and Amy Verdun, *Ruling Europe: The Politics of the Stability and Growth Pact* (Cambridge: Cambridge University Press, 2010).

7 Michelle Everson, "Is the European Court of Justice a Legal or Political Institution Now?" *Guardian,* August 10, 2010; Eric Stein, "Lawyers, Judges, and the Making of a Transnational Constitution," *American Journal of International Law* 75, no. 1 (January 1981): 1–27; Max Haller, *European Integration as an Elite Process: The Failure of a Dream?* (New York: Routledge, 2008), 104–7.

8 Weiler, *The Constitution of Europe,* 98; Joshua Louis Miller, "A New 'Democratic Life' for the European Union? Administrative Lawmaking, Democratic Legitimacy, and the Lisbon Treaty," *Contemporary Politics* 17, no. 3 (2011): 321–34; Martin Shapiro, "Administrative Law Unbounded: Reflections on Government and Governance," *Indiana Journal of Global Legal Studies* 8, no. 2 (Spring, 2001): 369–77.

9 David Levi-Faur and Jacint Jordana, "The Rise of Regulatory Capitalism: The Global Diffusion of a New Order," *Annals of the American Academy of Political and Social Science* 598, no. 1 (March 2005).

10 On the ISDA see Stephen Gill, ed., *Global Crises and the Crisis of Global Leadership* (Cambridge: Cambridge University Press, 2012), 65–66.

11 Tony Porter, "Why International Institutions Matter in the Global Credit Crisis," *Global*

Governance 15 (2009): 1–4, and the brilliant ethnography by Alexandra Ouroussoff, *Wall Street at War: The Secret Struggle for the Global Economy* (London: Polity, 2010).

12 "German President Lashes out at 'Monster' Market and Its Bankers," *Financial Times,* May 15, 2008.

13 On credit default swaps, see Glenn Morgan, "Legitimacy in Financial Markets: Credit Default Swaps in the Current Crisis," *Socio-Economic Review* 8 (2010): 17–45; Financial Services Authority, "Final Notice to Barclays Bank plc," June 27, 2012, at www.fsa.gov.uk.

14 William Cline, *Financial Globalization, Economic Growth and the Crisis of 2007–09* (Washington, D.C.: Peterson Institute for International Economics, 2010); IMF, "Fiscal Implications of Global Economic and Financial Crisis," IMF Occasional Paper 269 (Washington, D.C., 2009), 2–4.

15 Morgan, "Legitimacy in Financial Markets."

16 Eric Stein, "International Integration and Democracy: No Love at First Sight," *American Journal of International Law* 95, no. 3 (July 2001): 489–534; on the "human economy," see Keith Hart, "The Human Economy in a Revolutionary Moment: Political Aspects of the Economic Crisis," at http://thememorybank.co.uk.

17 Tony Judt, *Postwar: A History of Europe since 1945* (New York: Penguin Press, 2005); Jeremy Rifkin, *The European Dream: How Europe's Vision of the Future Is Quietly Eclipsing the American Dream* (New York: Tarcher, 2004); Steven Hill, *Europe's Promise: Why the European Way Is the Best Hope in an Insecure Age* (Berkeley: University of California Press, 2010).

18 Anne-Marie Slaughter, *A New World Order* (Princeton, NJ: Princeton University Press, 2004).

19 Anne-Marie Slaughter, "A New UN for a New Century," *Fordham Law Review* 74, no. 6 (2006): 2961–70.

20 Martti Koskenniemi, "Miserable Comforters: International Relations as New Natural Law," Sir Kenneth Bailey lecture, Melbourne, 2006; see Alexander Somek, "The Concept of 'Law' in Global Administrative Law: A Reply to Benedict Kingsbury," *European Journal of International Law* 20, no. 4 (2020): 985–95.

21 Daniel Drezner, *All Politics Is Global: Explaining International Regulatory Regimes* (Princeton, NJ: Princeton University Press, 2007).

22 For a review, see Magdalena Bexell, Jonas Tallberg, and Anders Uhlin, "Democracy in Global Governance: The Promises and Pitfalls of Transnational Actors," *Global Governance* 16 (2010): 81–101; on the rule of law, see Gerhard Casper, "Rule of Law? Whose Law?" CDDRL Working Papers, Stanford University, August 13, 2004, 10.

23 John Keane, *Global Civil Society?* (Cambridge: Cambridge University Press, 2003).

24 Jan Aart Scholte, ed., *Building Global Democracy? Civil Society and Accountable Global Governance* (Cambridge: Cambridge University Press, 2011); Denielc Archibugi, *The Global Commonwealth of Citizens: Toward a Cosmopolitan Democracy* (Princeton, NJ: Princeton University Press, 2008), 82; Clifford Bob, *The Marketing of Rebellion: Insurgents, Media, and International Activism* (Cambridge: Cambridge University Press, 2005).

25 Joel Fleishman, *The Foundation: A Great American Secret* (2007), esp. 346–48; Michael Edwards, *Small Change: Why Business Won't Save the World* (2010).

26 See Inderjeet Parmar, *Foundations of the American Century: The Ford, Carnegie and Rockefeller Foundations in the Rise of American Power* (New York, 2012).

27 Anne-Emmanuelle Birn, "Gates's Greatest Challenge: Transcending Technology as Public Health Ideology," *Lancet* 366 (August 6, 2005): 514–19; Editorial, "What Has the Gates Foundation Done for Global Health?" *Lancet* 373 (May 9, 2009), 1577; Devi Sridhar and Rajnaei Batniji, "Misfinancing Global Health: A Case for Transparency in Disbursements and Decision Making," *Lancet* 372 (September 27, 2008): 1185–91. For background, see Nancy Stepan, *Eradication: Ridding the World of Diseases Forever?* (Ithaca, NY: Cornell University Press, 2011).

28 Paul Harris, "They're Called the Good Club and They Want to Save the World," *Observer,*

May 30, 2009; John Harlow, "Billionaire Club in Bid to Curb Overpopulation," *Sunday Times,* May 24, 2009; on the need for multilateral institutions, see Sebastian Mallaby, "The Quiet Revolutionary Who Saved the World Bank," *Financial Times,* February 17, 2012.

29 Tom Watson, "Globalizing Philanthropy: Jeff Skoll's Changing World," *Huffington Post,* April 4, 2007.

30 See Clay Shirky, *Here Comes Everybody: The Power of Organizing without Organizations* (New York: Penguin Press, 2008).

31 See the analysis of Robert Dahl, "Can International Organizations Be Democratic? A Skeptic's View," in Ian Shapiro and Casiano Hacking-Cordon, eds., *Democracy's Edges* (Cambridge: Cambridge University Press, 1999), 19–37.

32 Martti Koskenniemi, "What Use for Sovereignty Today?" *Asian Journal of International Law* 1 (2011): 61–70.

33 Hart, "Formal Bureaucracy and the Emergent Forms of the Iinformal Economy," at thememorybank.co.uk.

34 For the broad argument, see Mark Mazower, *Dark Continent: Europe's Twentieth Century* (New York: Knopf, 1998).

35 On the basic argument that one cannot have democracy, national sovereignty, and globalization, see Dani Rodrik, *The Globalization Paradox* (New York: Norton, 2011); on noninterference in 1971, Tim Allen and David Styan, "A Right to Interfere? Bernard Kouchner and the New Humanitarianism," *Journal of International Development* 12 (2000): 825–42.

36 For this argument, see the brilliant Peter Evans, "The Eclipse of the State? Reflections on Stateness in an Era of Globalization," *World Politics* 50 (October 1997): 62-87; on embedded liberalism, see John Gerard Ruggie, "International Regimes, Transactions, and Change: Embedded Liberalism in the Postwar Economic Order," *International Organization* 36, no. 2 (1982): 379–415.

37 On the varieties and complexities of exceptionalism, see especially Harold Hongju Koh, "America's Jekyll-and-Hyde Exceptionalism," in Michael Ignatieff, ed., *American Exceptionalism and Human Rights* (Princeton, NJ: Princeton University Press, 2005), 111–45.

38 Gill, *Global Crises and the Crisis of Global Leadership;* on allegiance to the nation-state, see Dani Rodrik, "The Nation-State Reborn," Project Syndicate, February 13, 2012, http://www.project-syndicate.org/commentary/the-nation-state-reborn.

39 Strange cited in Evans, "The Eclipse of the Nation-State?" 84; also Raghuram G. Rajan, *Fault Lines: How Hidden Fractures Still Threaten the World Economy* (Princeton, NJ: Princeton University Press, 2010), chapter 10.

40 Daron Acemoglu and Simon Johnson, "Captured Europe," Project Syndicate, March 20, 2012. http://www.project-syndicate.org/commentary/captured-europe.

41 Rex Huppke, "Facts, 360 B.C.–A.D. 2012," *Chicago Tribune,* April 19, 2012; on the transformation of economic theory's attitudes to the future, see Perry Mehrling, "The Evolution of Macro-Economics," in David Colander, ed., *Beyond Micro-Foundations: Post-Walrasian Economics* (Cambridge: Cambridge University Press, 1996), 71–87.

42 Jean-Marie Guéhenno, *The End of the Nation-State* (Minneapolis: University of Minnesota Press, 2000), chapter 2.

43 Perry Anderson uses the phrase "the civilization of capital" in his "Internationalism: A Breviary," *New Left Review* 14 (March–April 2002): 5–25; a similar reading of contemporary democracy is Steven Bilakovics, *Democracy without Politics* (Cambridge, MA: Harvard University Press, 2012).

Index

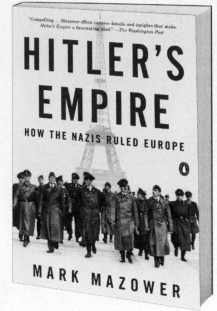